Black Rose ALICE

1

Story & Art by
Setona Mizushiro

CONTENTS

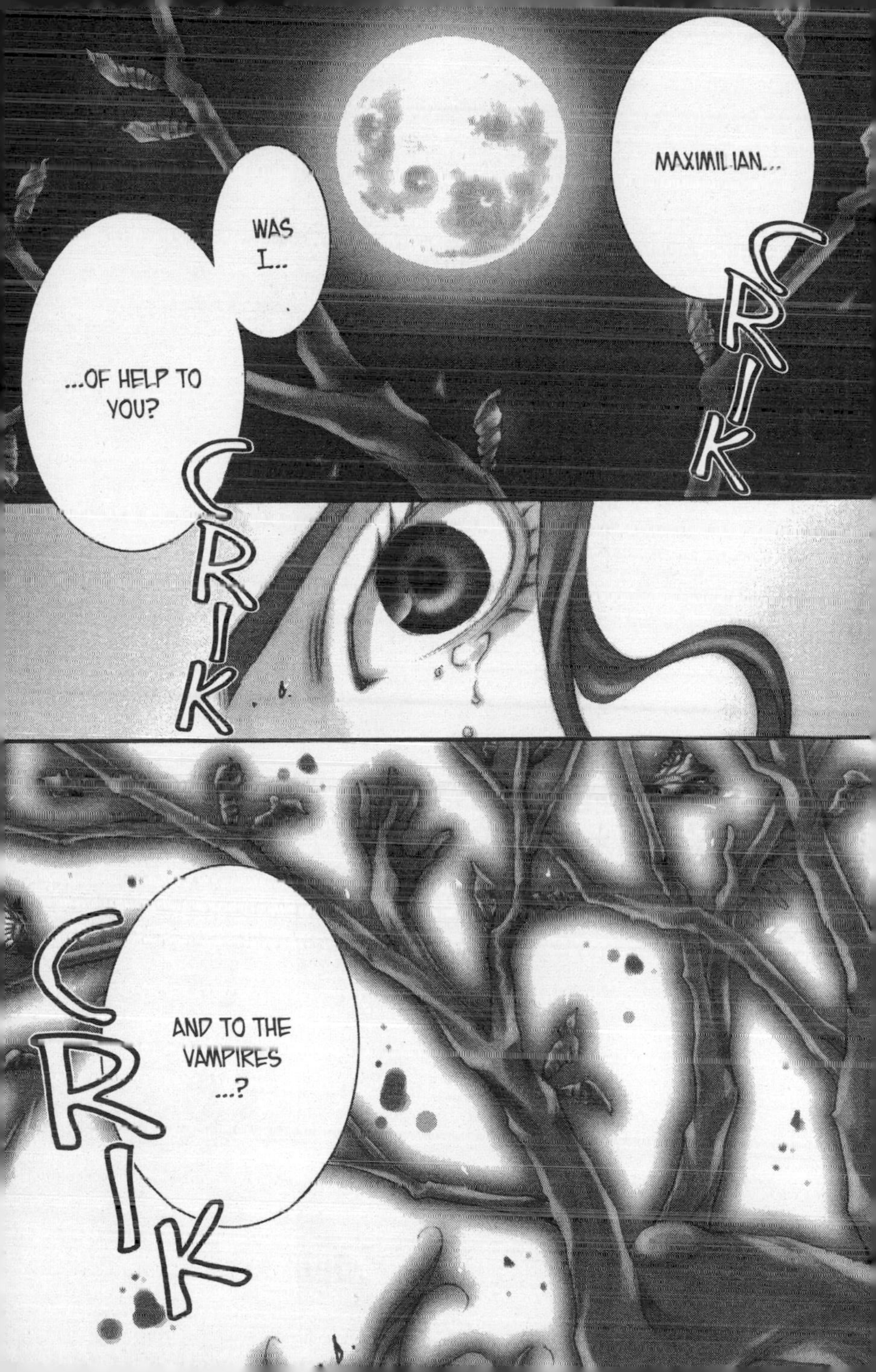
MAXIMILIAN...
CRIK
WAS I...
...OF HELP TO YOU?
CRIK
CRIK
AND TO THE VAMPIRES ...?

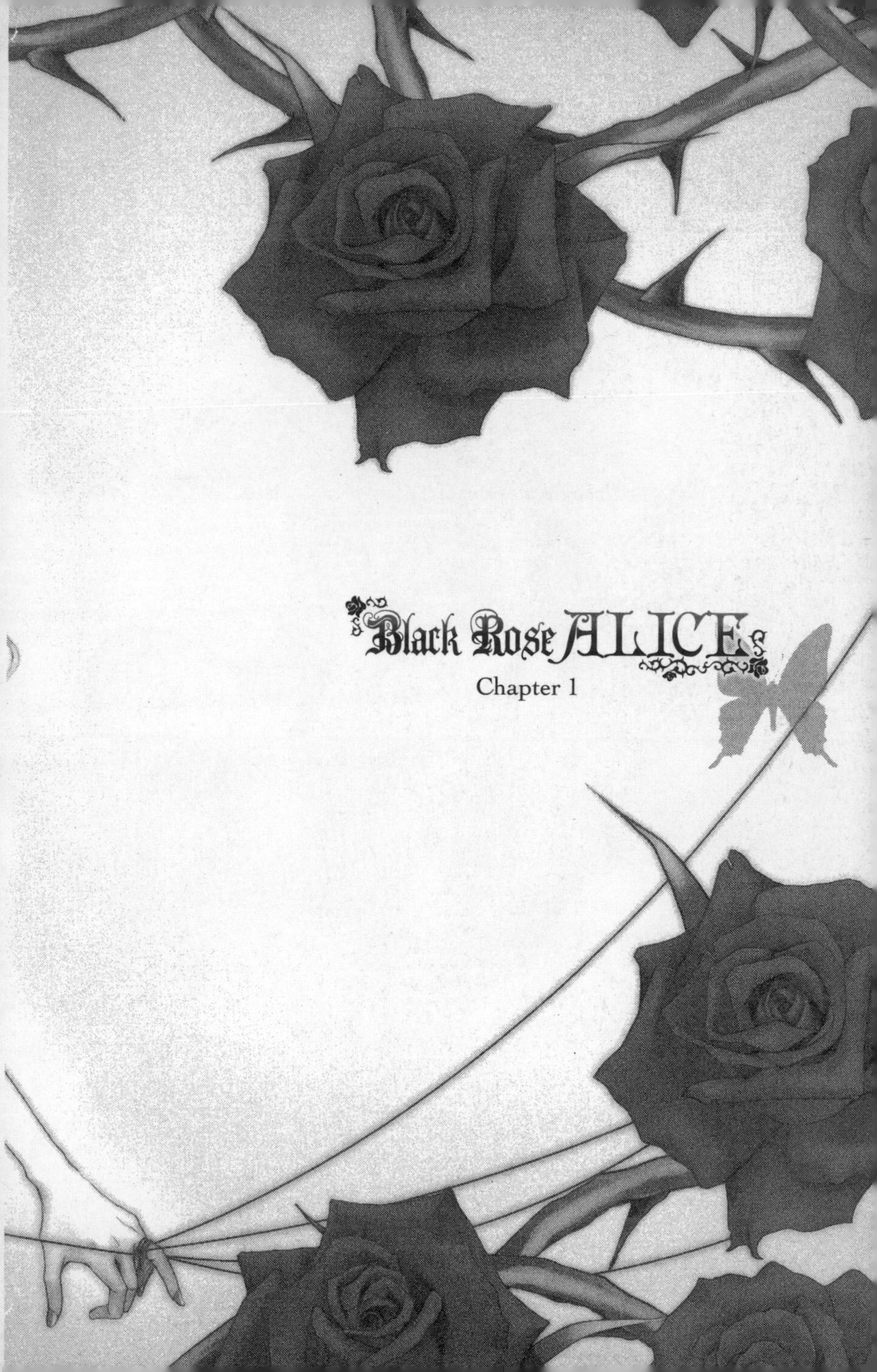

Black Rose ALICE

Chapter 1

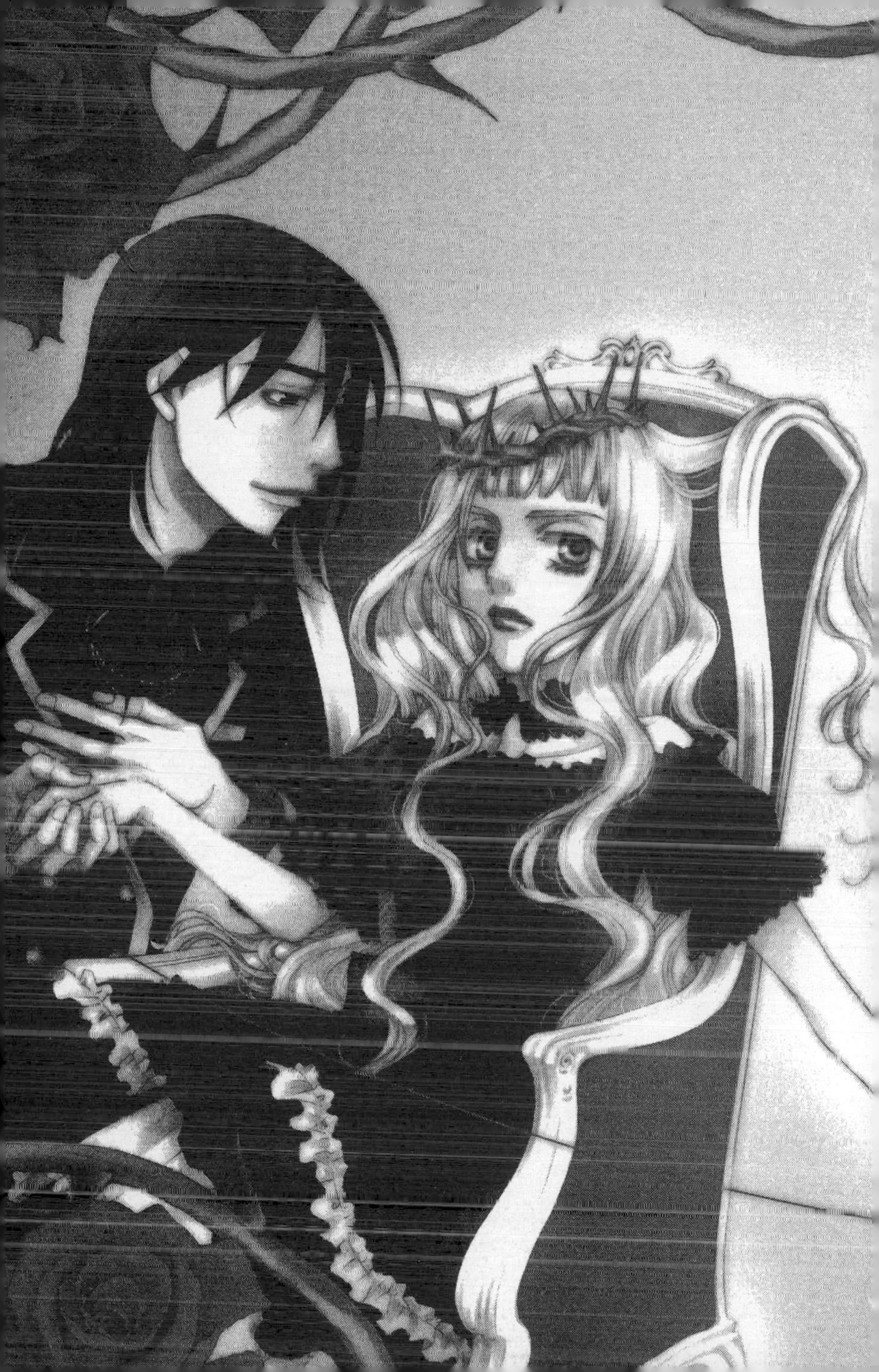

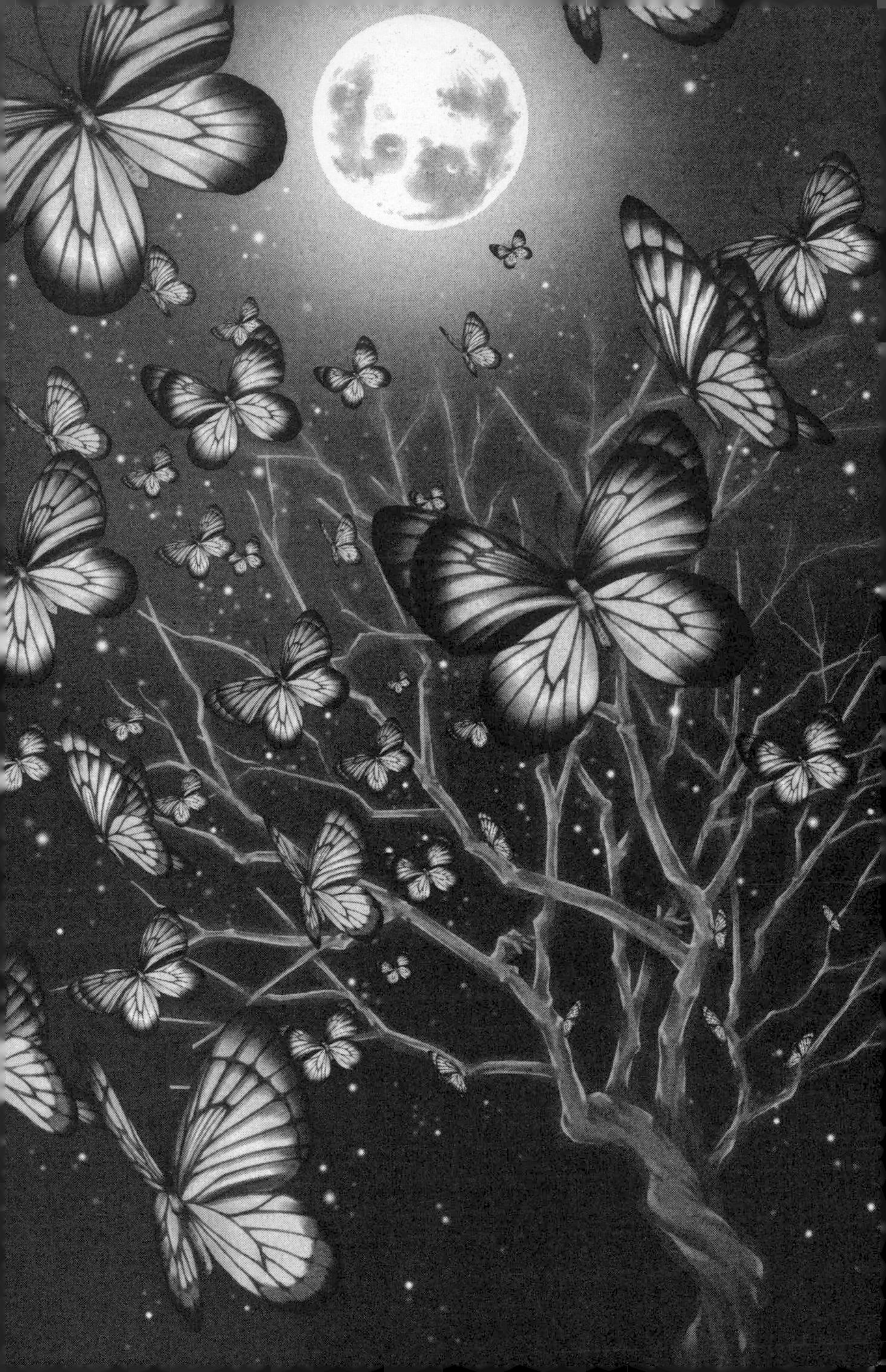

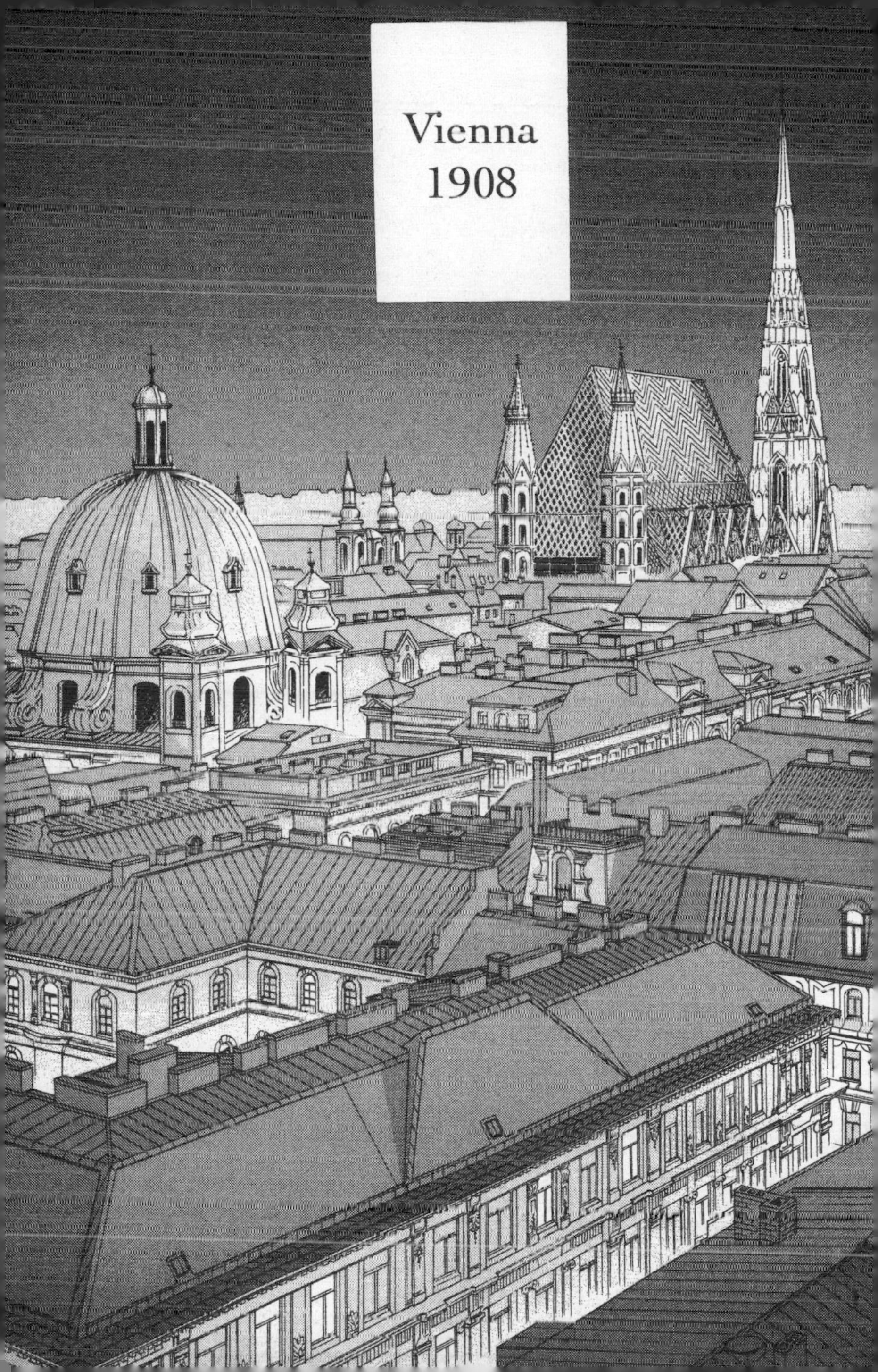
Vienna
1908

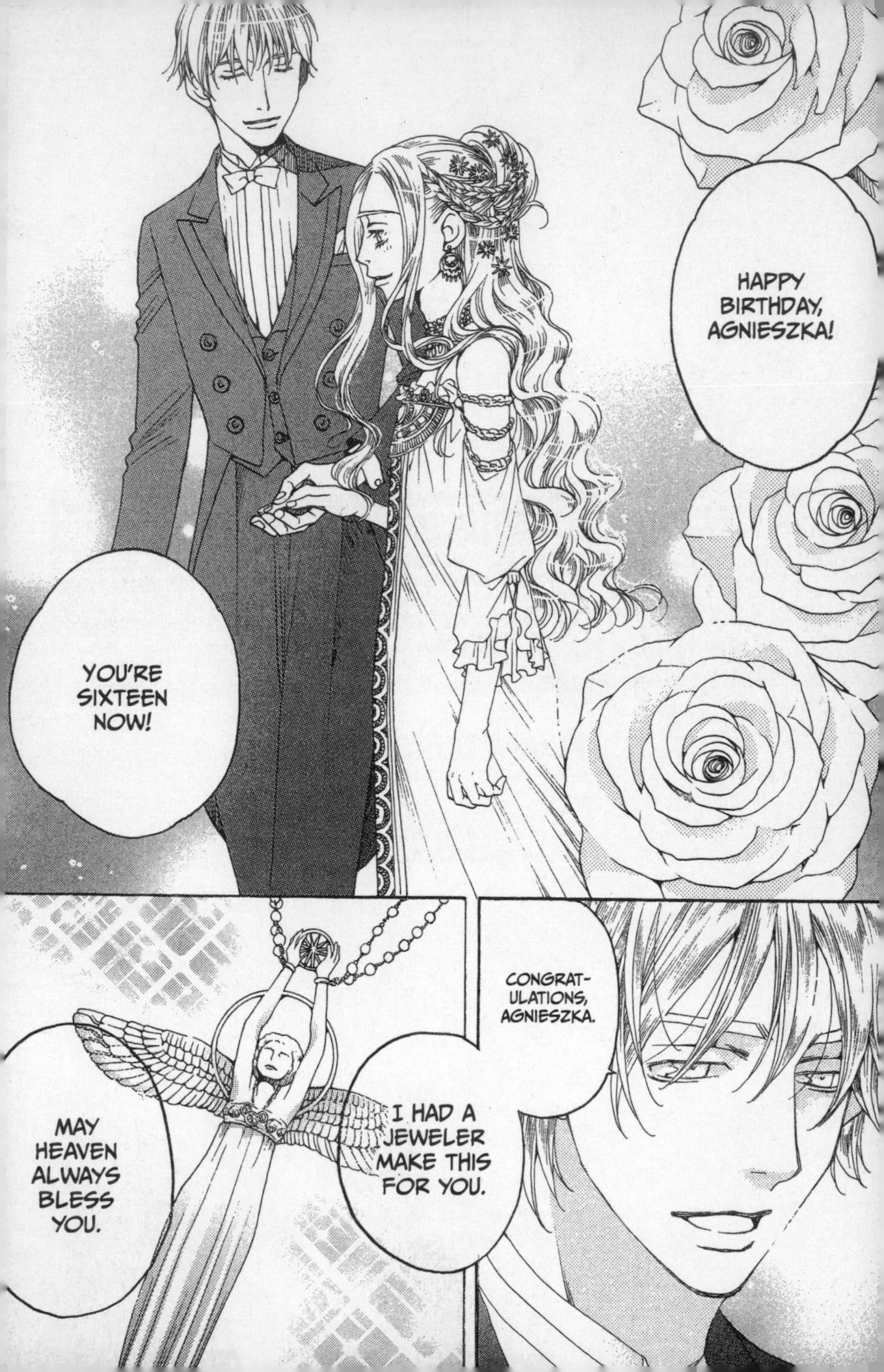
HAPPY BIRTHDAY, AGNIESZKA!
YOU'RE SIXTEEN NOW!
CONGRAT-ULATIONS, AGNIESZKA.
I HAD A JEWELER MAKE THIS FOR YOU.
MAY HEAVEN ALWAYS BLESS YOU.

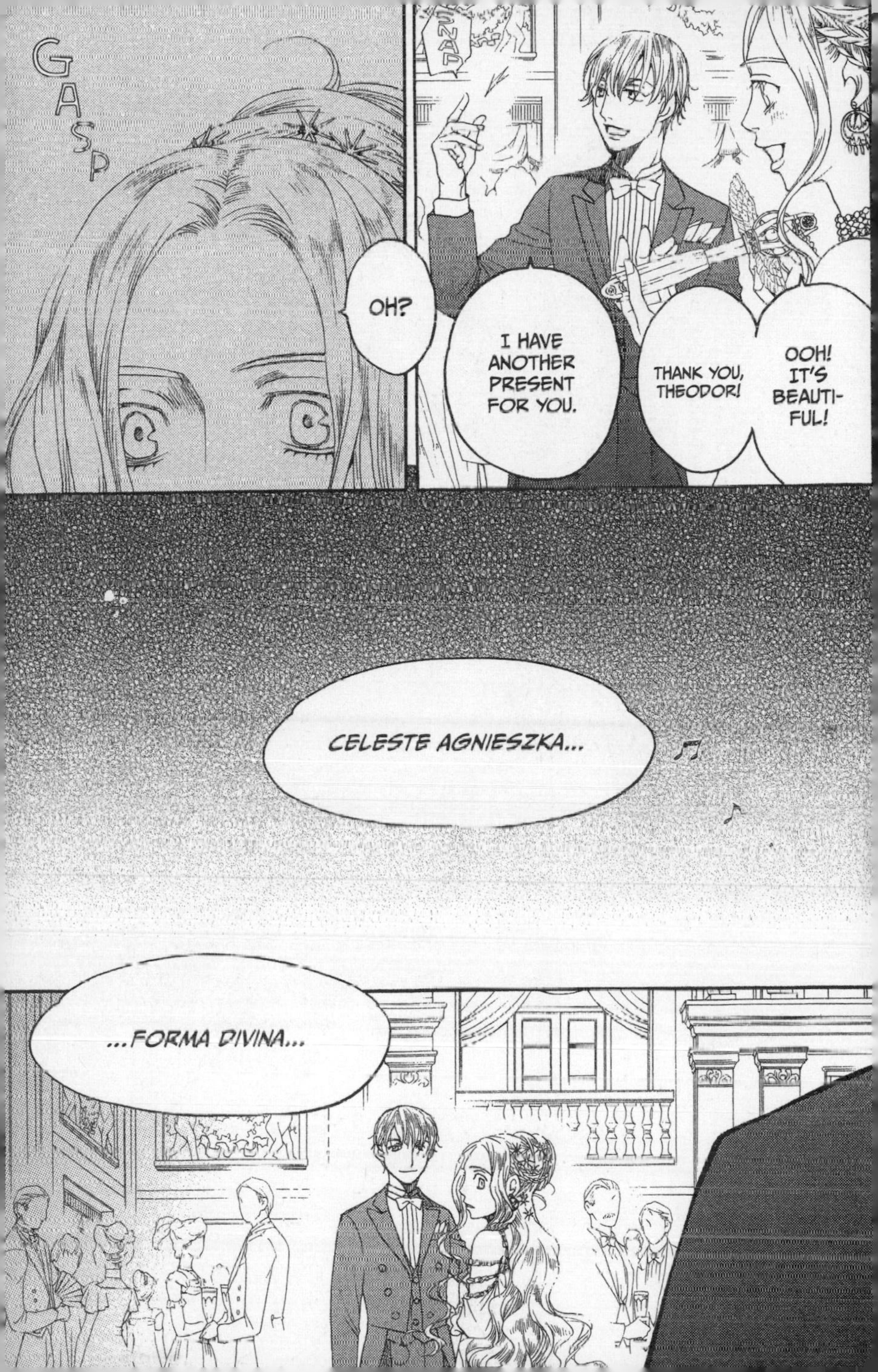
SNAP
OOH! IT'S BEAUTI-FUL!
THANK YOU, THEODOR!
I HAVE ANOTHER PRESENT FOR YOU.
OH?
GASP
CELESTE AGNIESZKA...
...FORMA DIVINA...

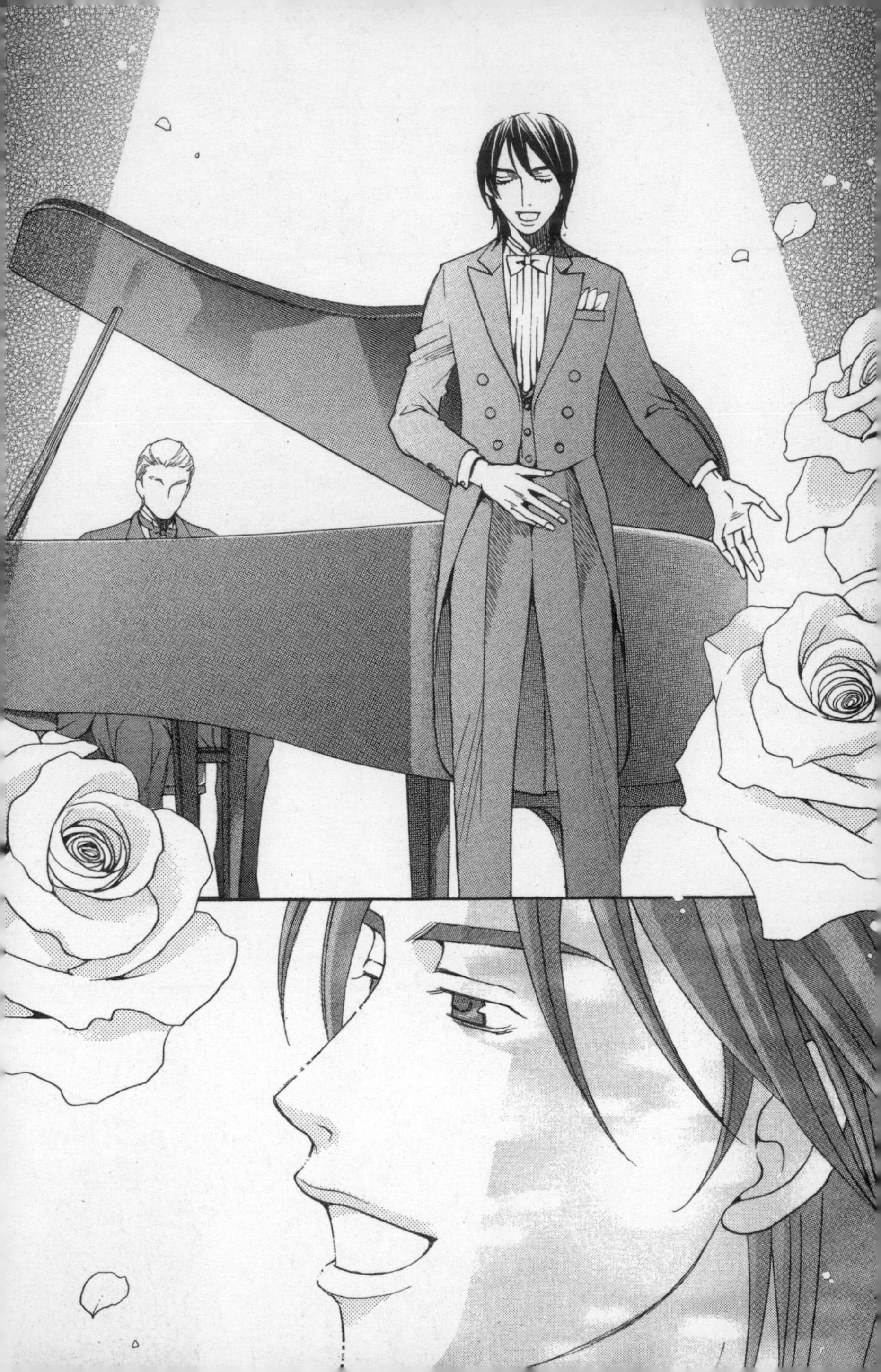

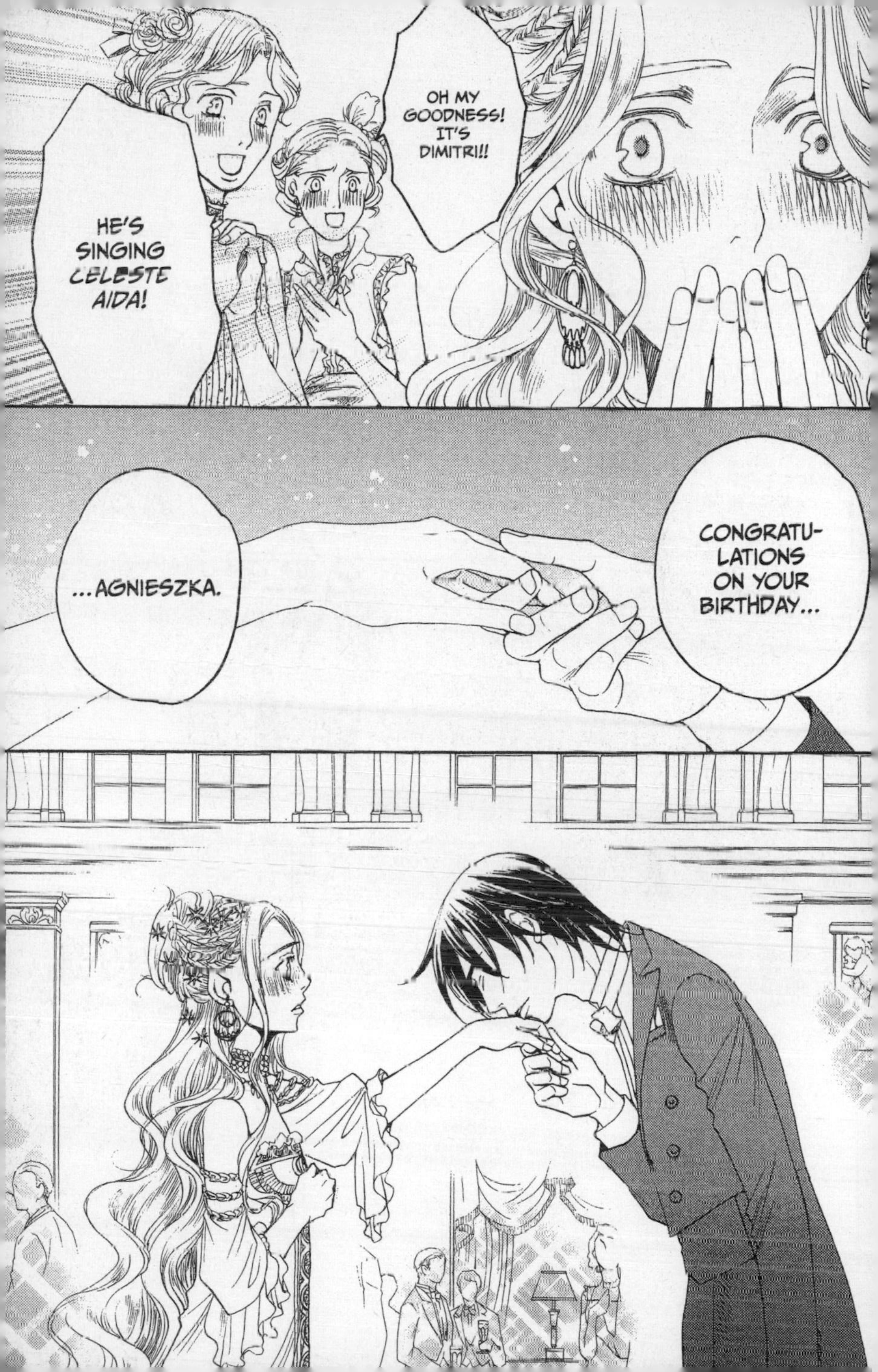
OH MY GOODNESS! IT'S DIMITRI!!
HE'S SINGING CELESTE AIDA!
CONGRATULATIONS ON YOUR BIRTHDAY...
...AGNIESZKA.

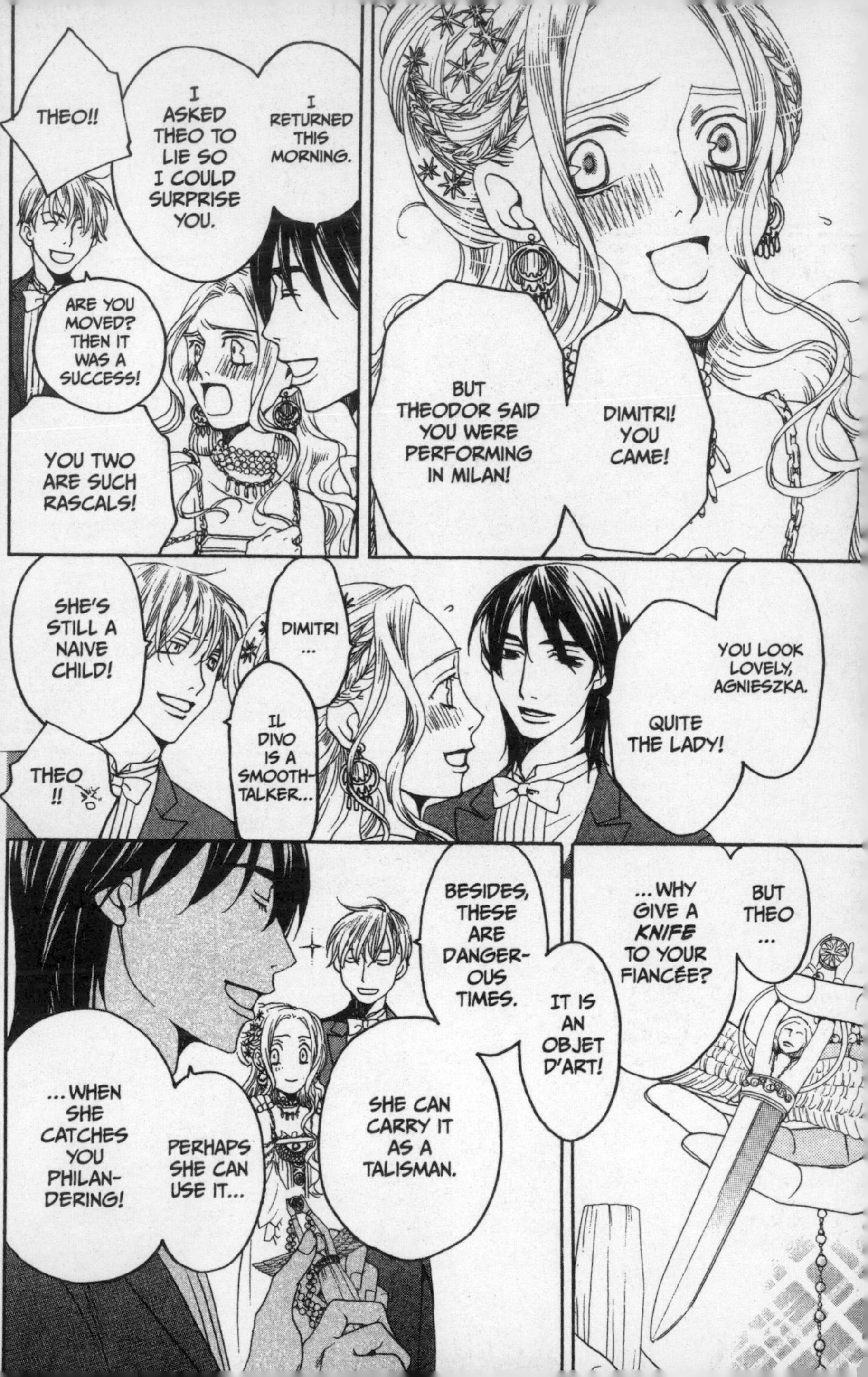
DIMITRI! YOU CAME!
BUT THEODOR SAID YOU WERE PERFORMING IN MILAN!
I RETURNED THIS MORNING.
I ASKED THEO TO LIE SO I COULD SURPRISE YOU.
THEO!!
ARE YOU MOVED? THEN IT WAS A SUCCESS!
YOU TWO ARE SUCH RASCALS!
YOU LOOK LOVELY, AGNIESZKA.
QUITE THE LADY!
DIMITRI...
IL DIVO IS A SMOOTH-TALKER...
SHE'S STILL A NAIVE CHILD!
THEO !!
BUT THEO...
...WHY GIVE A KNIFE TO YOUR FIANCÉE?
IT IS AN OBJET D'ART!
SHE CAN CARRY IT AS A TALISMAN.
BESIDES, THESE ARE DANGEROUS TIMES.
PERHAPS SHE CAN USE IT...
...WHEN SHE CATCHES YOU PHILANDERING!

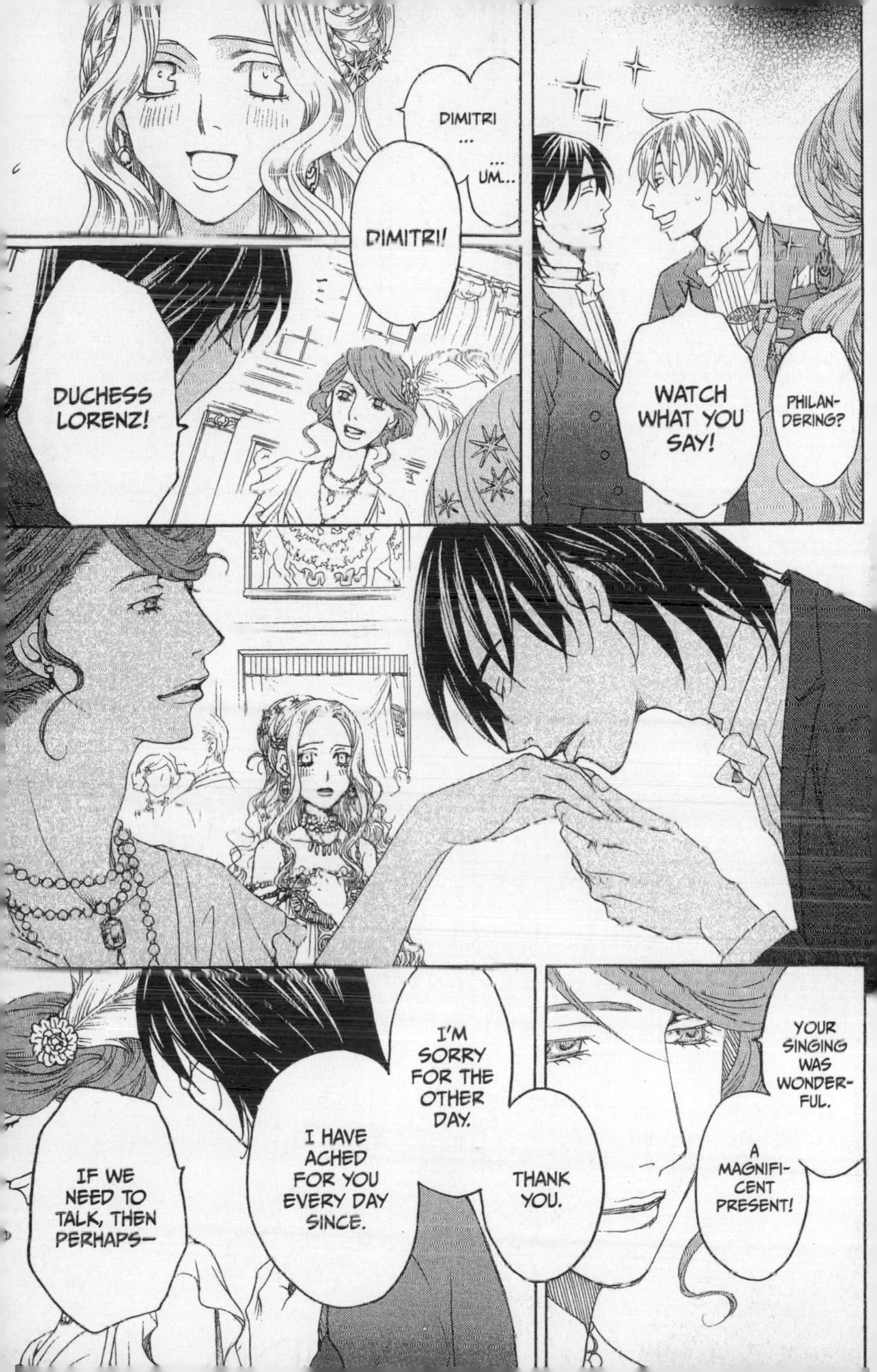
PHILANDERING?
WATCH WHAT YOU SAY!
DIMITRI ...
... UM...
DIMITRI!
DUCHESS LORENZ!
YOUR SINGING WAS WONDERFUL.
A MAGNIFICENT PRESENT!
THANK YOU.
I'M SORRY FOR THE OTHER DAY.
I HAVE ACHED FOR YOU EVERY DAY SINCE.
IF WE NEED TO TALK, THEN PERHAPS—

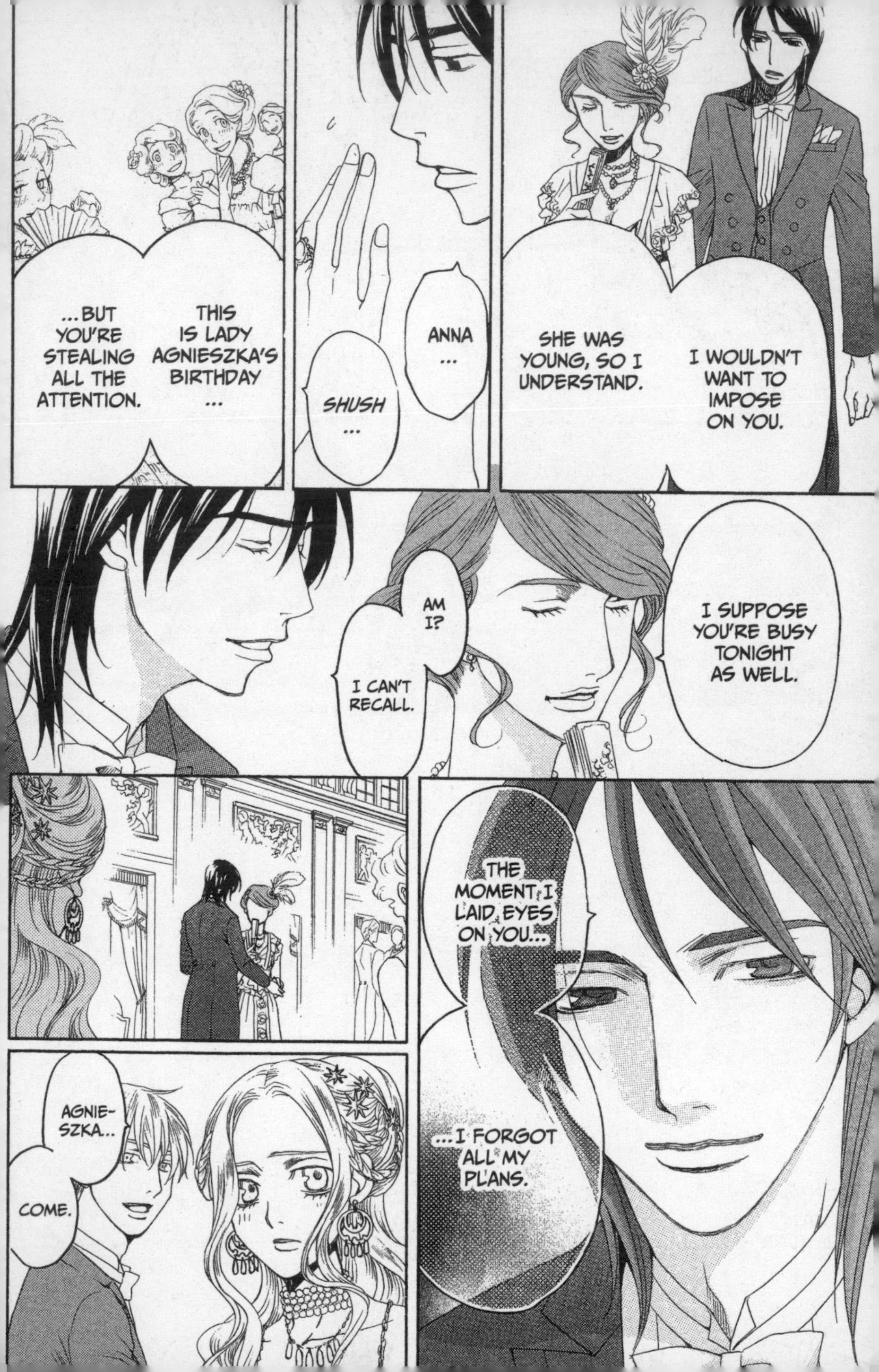
I WOULDN'T WANT TO IMPOSE ON YOU.
SHE WAS YOUNG, SO I UNDERSTAND.
ANNA ...
SHUSH ...
THIS IS LADY AGNIESZKA'S BIRTHDAY ...
...BUT YOU'RE STEALING ALL THE ATTENTION.
I SUPPOSE YOU'RE BUSY TONIGHT AS WELL.
AM I?
I CAN'T RECALL.
THE MOMENT I LAID EYES ON YOU...
...I FORGOT ALL MY PLANS.
AGNIE-SZKA...
COME.

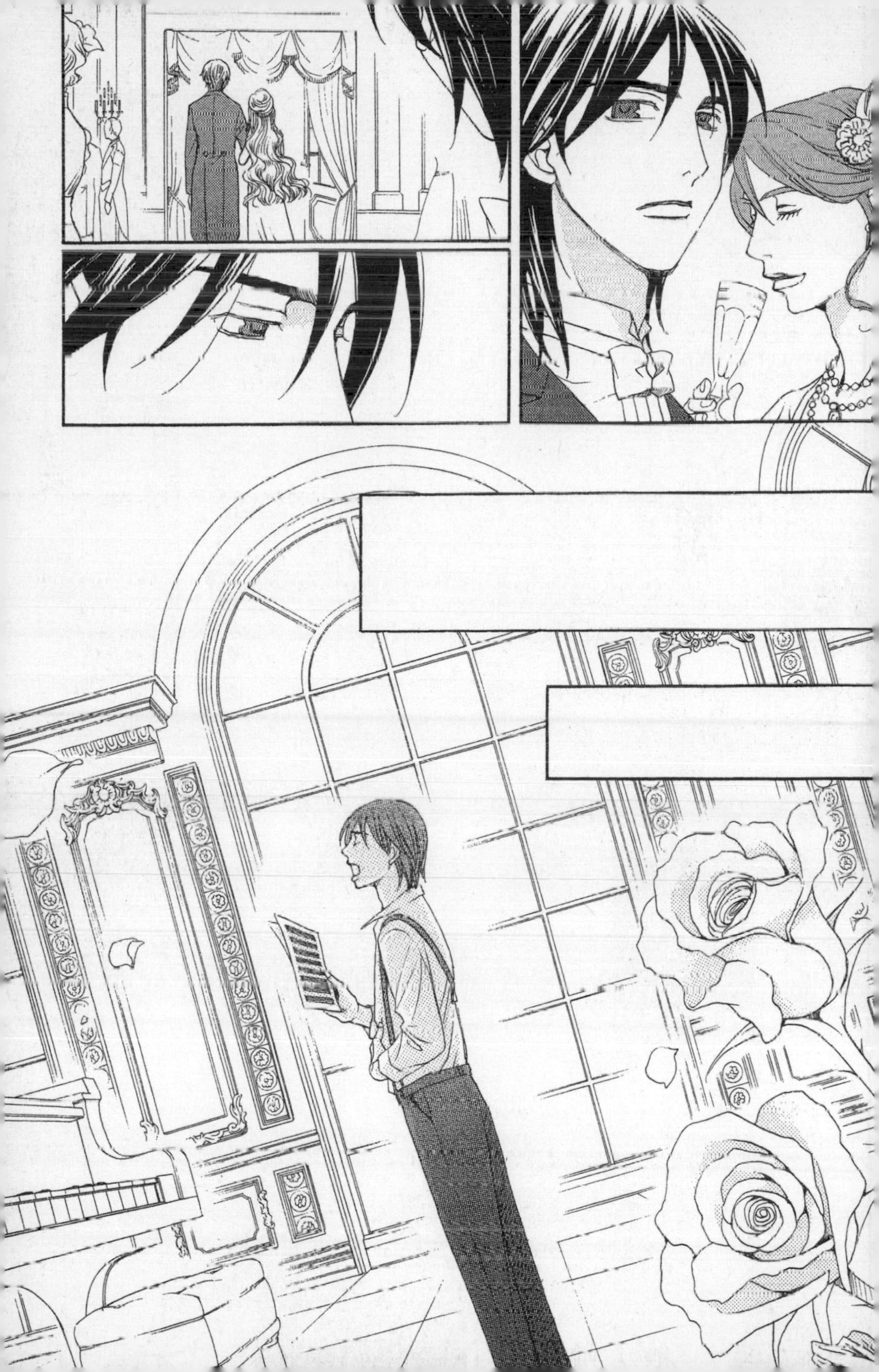

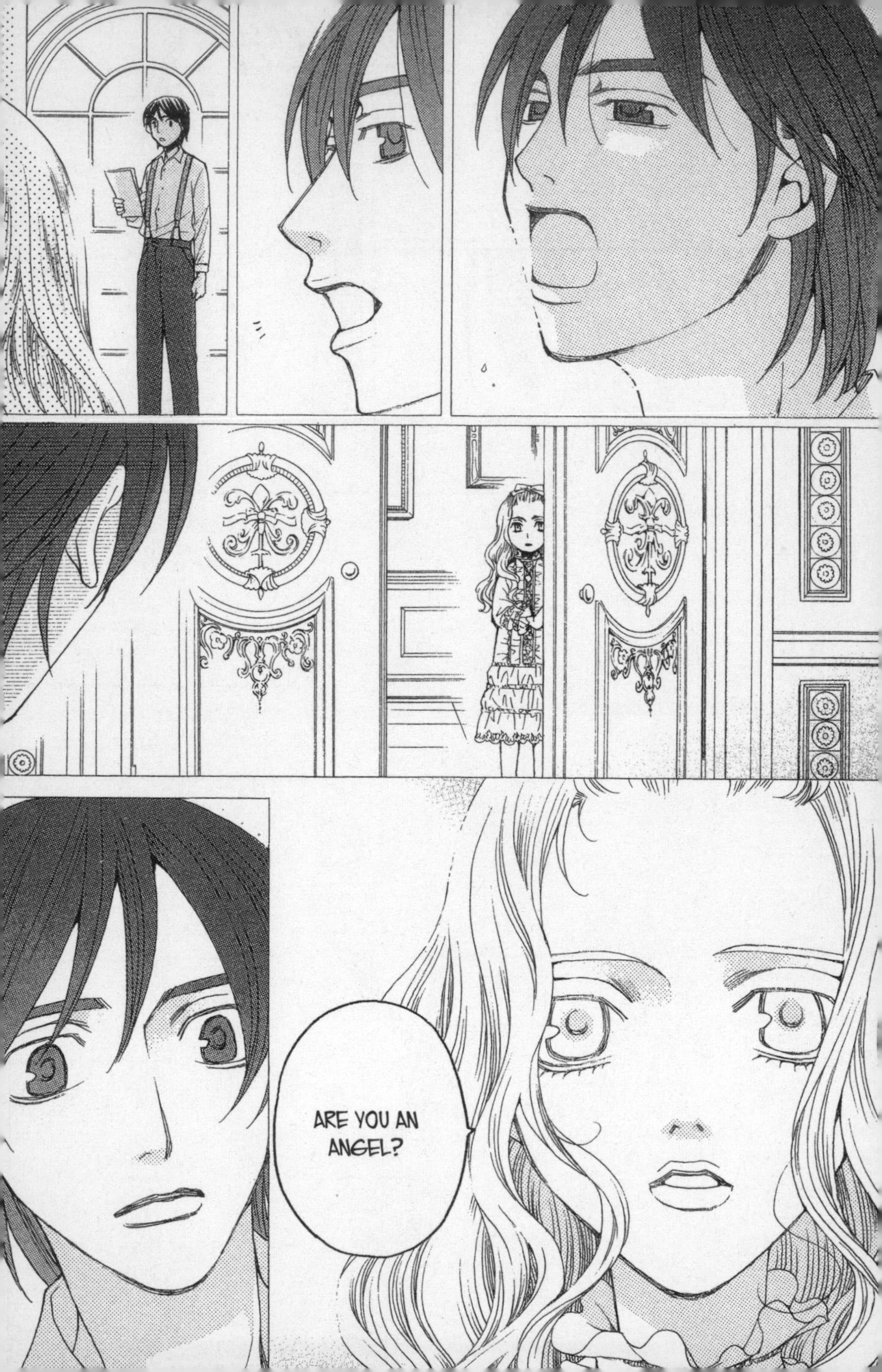
ARE YOU AN ANGEL?

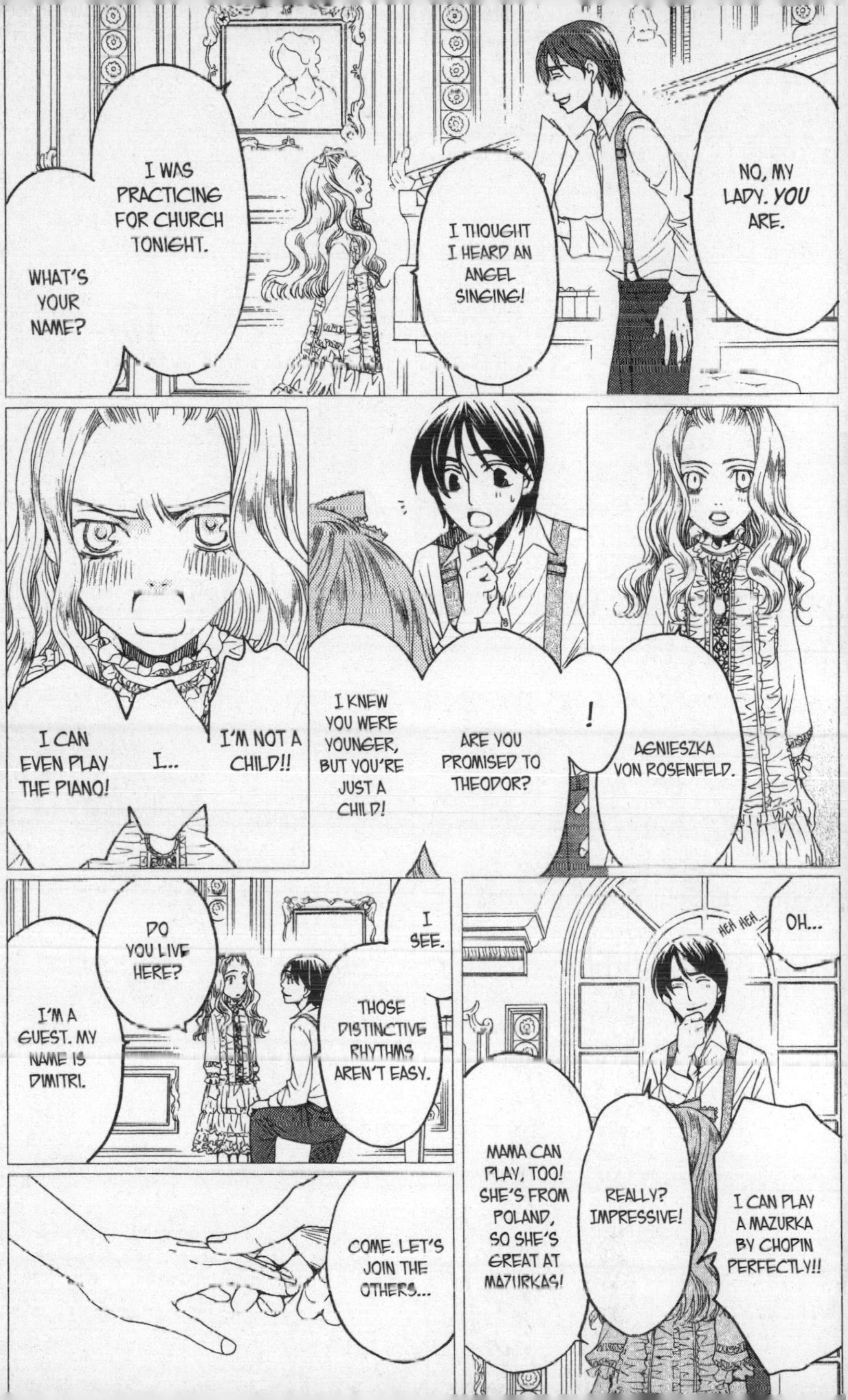
NO, MY LADY. *YOU* ARE.
I THOUGHT I HEARD AN ANGEL SINGING!
I WAS PRACTICING FOR CHURCH TONIGHT.
WHAT'S YOUR NAME?
AGNIESZKA VON ROSENFELD.
!
ARE YOU PROMISED TO THEODOR?
I KNEW YOU WERE YOUNGER, BUT YOU'RE JUST A CHILD!
I'M NOT A CHILD!!
I...
I CAN EVEN PLAY THE PIANO!
HEH HEH...
OH...
I CAN PLAY A MAZURKA BY CHOPIN PERFECTLY!!
REALLY? IMPRESSIVE!
MAMA CAN PLAY, TOO! SHE'S FROM POLAND, SO SHE'S GREAT AT MAZURKAS!
I SEE.
THOSE DISTINCTIVE RHYTHMS AREN'T EASY.
DO YOU LIVE HERE?
I'M A GUEST. MY NAME IS DIMITRI.
COME. LET'S JOIN THE OTHERS...

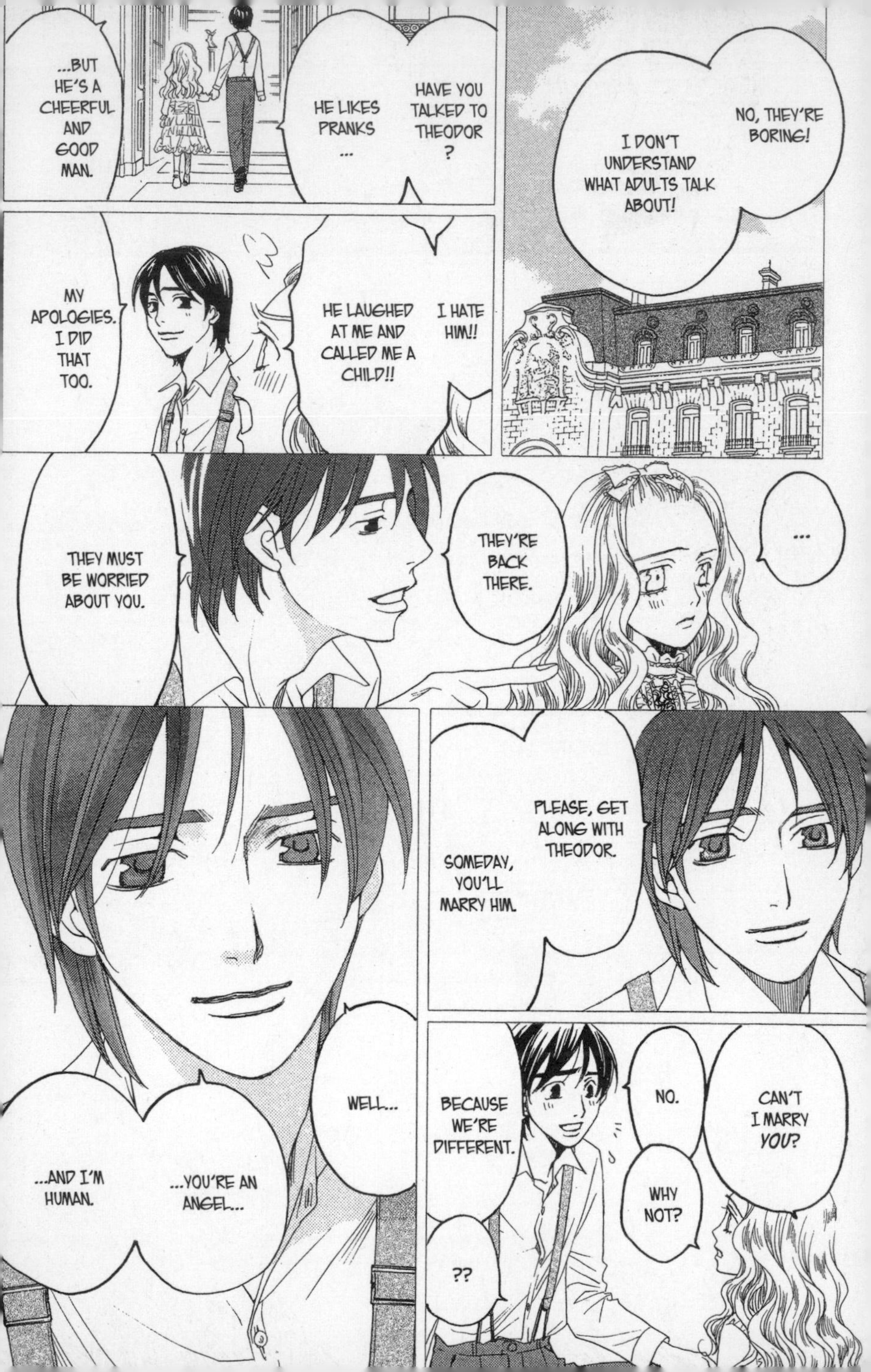
NO, THEY'RE BORING!
I DON'T UNDERSTAND WHAT ADULTS TALK ABOUT!
HAVE YOU TALKED TO THEODOR?
HE LIKES PRANKS...
...BUT HE'S A CHEERFUL AND GOOD MAN.
I HATE HIM!!
HE LAUGHED AT ME AND CALLED ME A CHILD!!
MY APOLOGIES. I DID THAT TOO.
...
THEY'RE BACK THERE.
THEY MUST BE WORRIED ABOUT YOU.
PLEASE, GET ALONG WITH THEODOR.
SOMEDAY, YOU'LL MARRY HIM.
CAN'T I MARRY *YOU*?
NO.
WHY NOT?
??
BECAUSE WE'RE DIFFERENT.
WELL...
...YOU'RE AN ANGEL...
...AND I'M HUMAN.

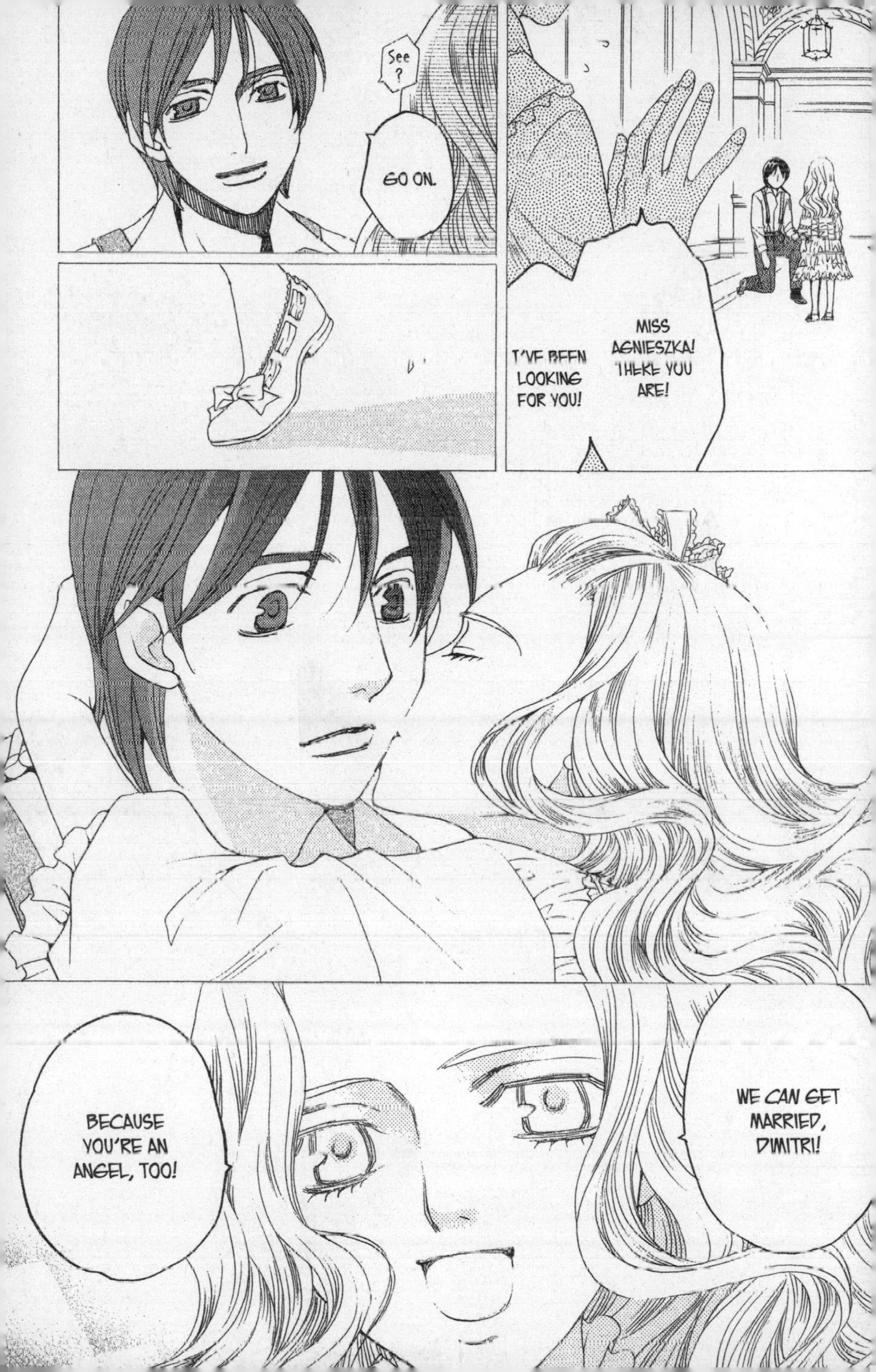

MISS AGNIESZKA! THERE YOU ARE!
I'VE BEEN LOOKING FOR YOU!
See?
GO ON.
WE CAN GET MARRIED, DIMITRI!
BECAUSE YOU'RE AN ANGEL, TOO!

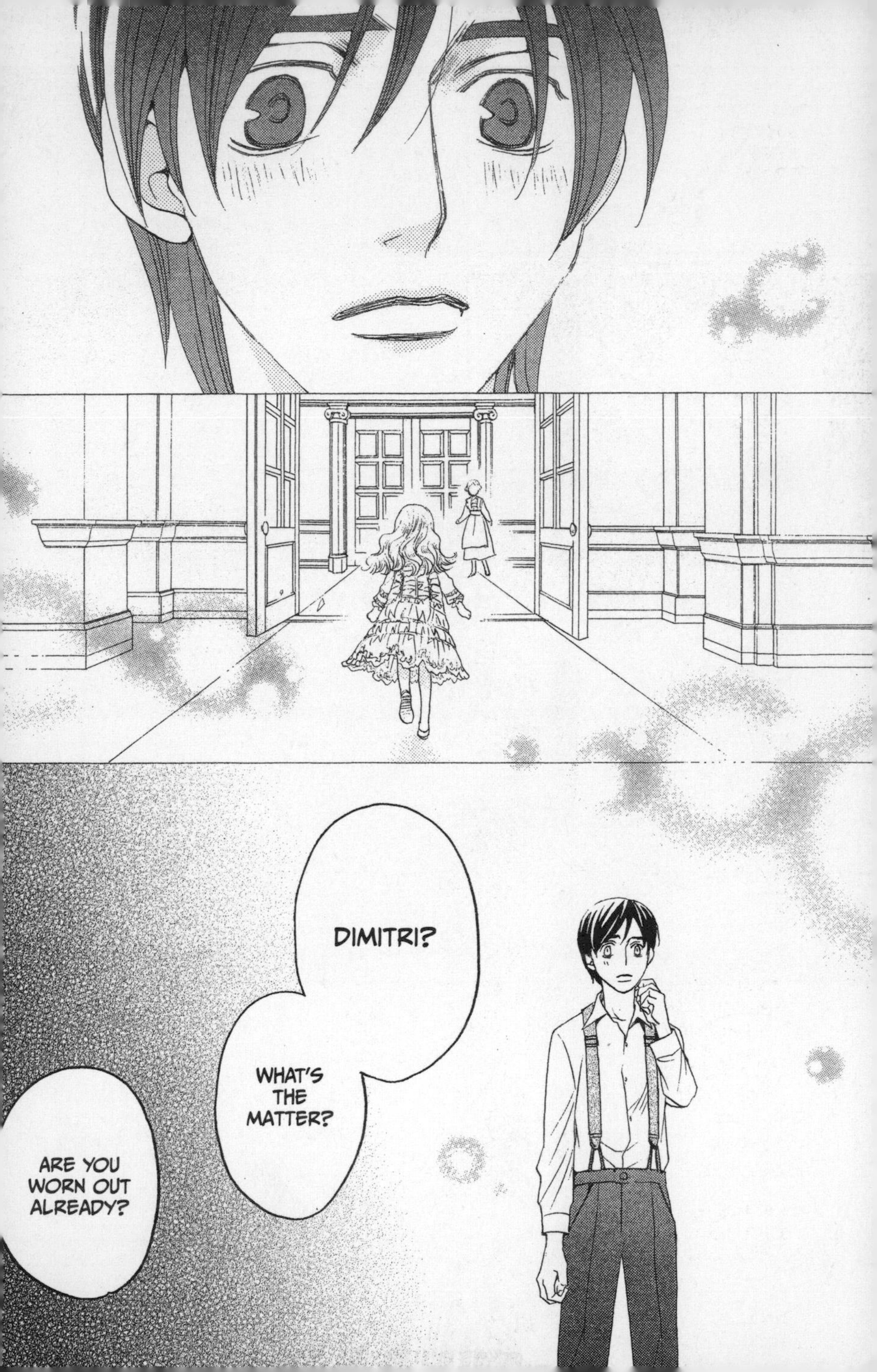
DIMITRI?
WHAT'S THE MATTER?
ARE YOU WORN OUT ALREADY?

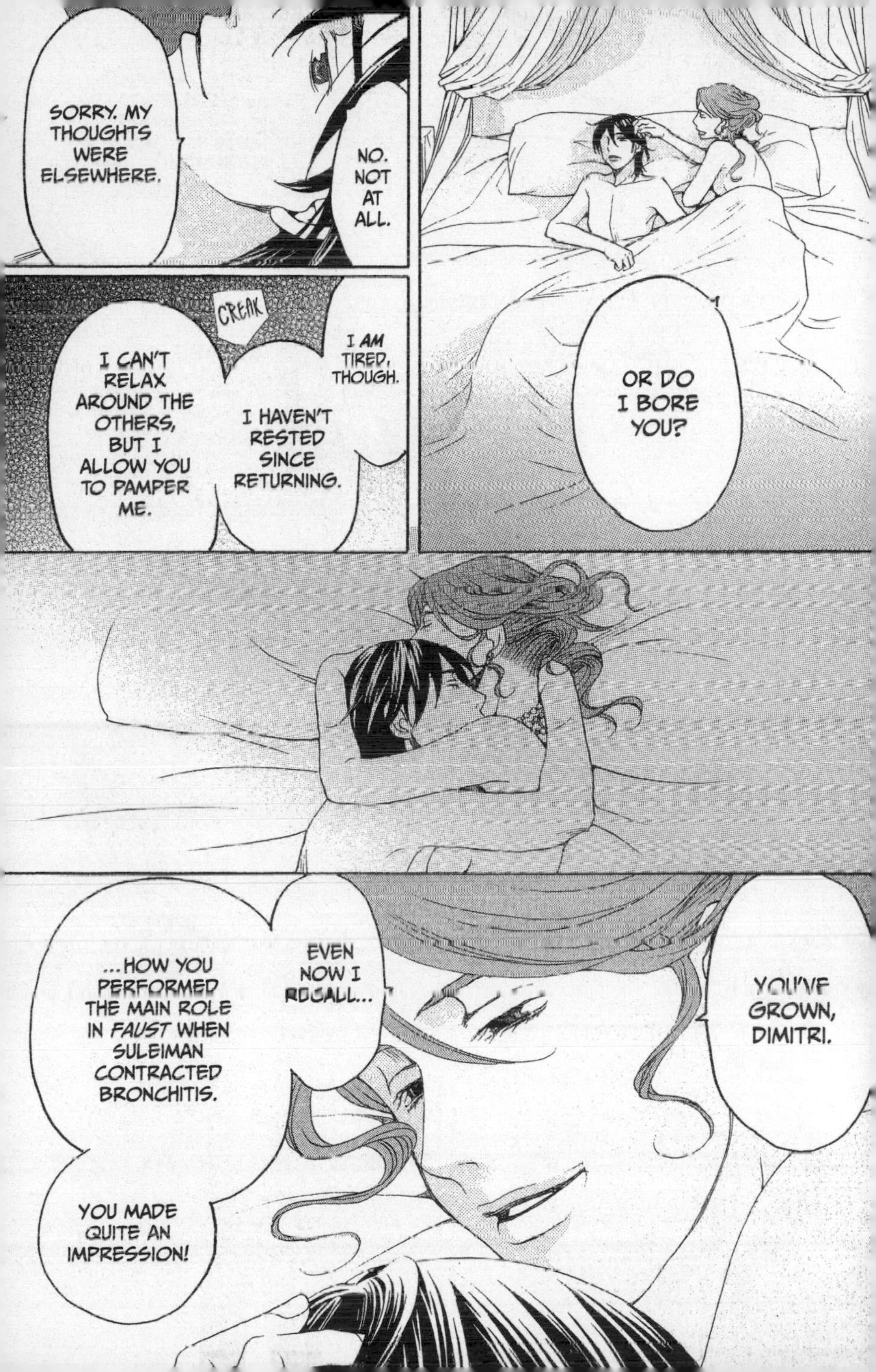
OR DO I BORE YOU?
NO. NOT AT ALL.
SORRY. MY THOUGHTS WERE ELSEWHERE.
I *AM* TIRED, THOUGH.
I HAVEN'T RESTED SINCE RETURNING.
CREAK
I CAN'T RELAX AROUND THE OTHERS, BUT I ALLOW YOU TO PAMPER ME.
YOU'VE GROWN, DIMITRI.
EVEN NOW I RECALL...
...HOW YOU PERFORMED THE MAIN ROLE IN *FAUST* WHEN SULEIMAN CONTRACTED BRONCHITIS.
YOU MADE QUITE AN IMPRESSION!

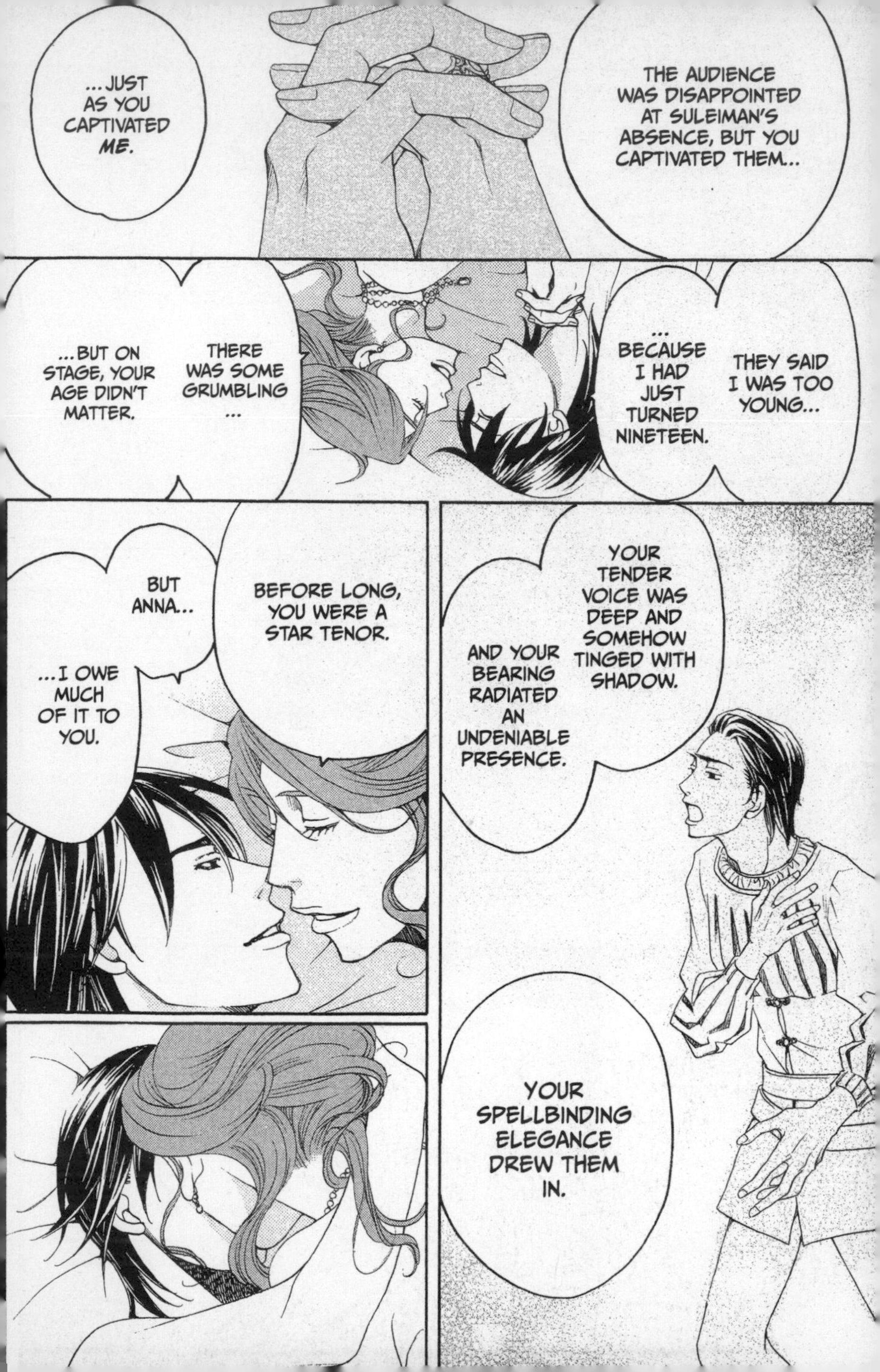
THE AUDIENCE WAS DISAPPOINTED AT SULEIMAN'S ABSENCE, BUT YOU CAPTIVATED THEM...
...JUST AS YOU CAPTIVATED *ME.*
THEY SAID I WAS TOO YOUNG...
...BECAUSE I HAD JUST TURNED NINETEEN.
THERE WAS SOME GRUMBLING...
...BUT ON STAGE, YOUR AGE DIDN'T MATTER.
YOUR TENDER VOICE WAS DEEP AND SOMEHOW TINGED WITH SHADOW.
AND YOUR BEARING RADIATED AN UNDENIABLE PRESENCE.
YOUR SPELLBINDING ELEGANCE DREW THEM IN.
BEFORE LONG, YOU WERE A STAR TENOR.
BUT ANNA...
...I OWE MUCH OF IT TO YOU.

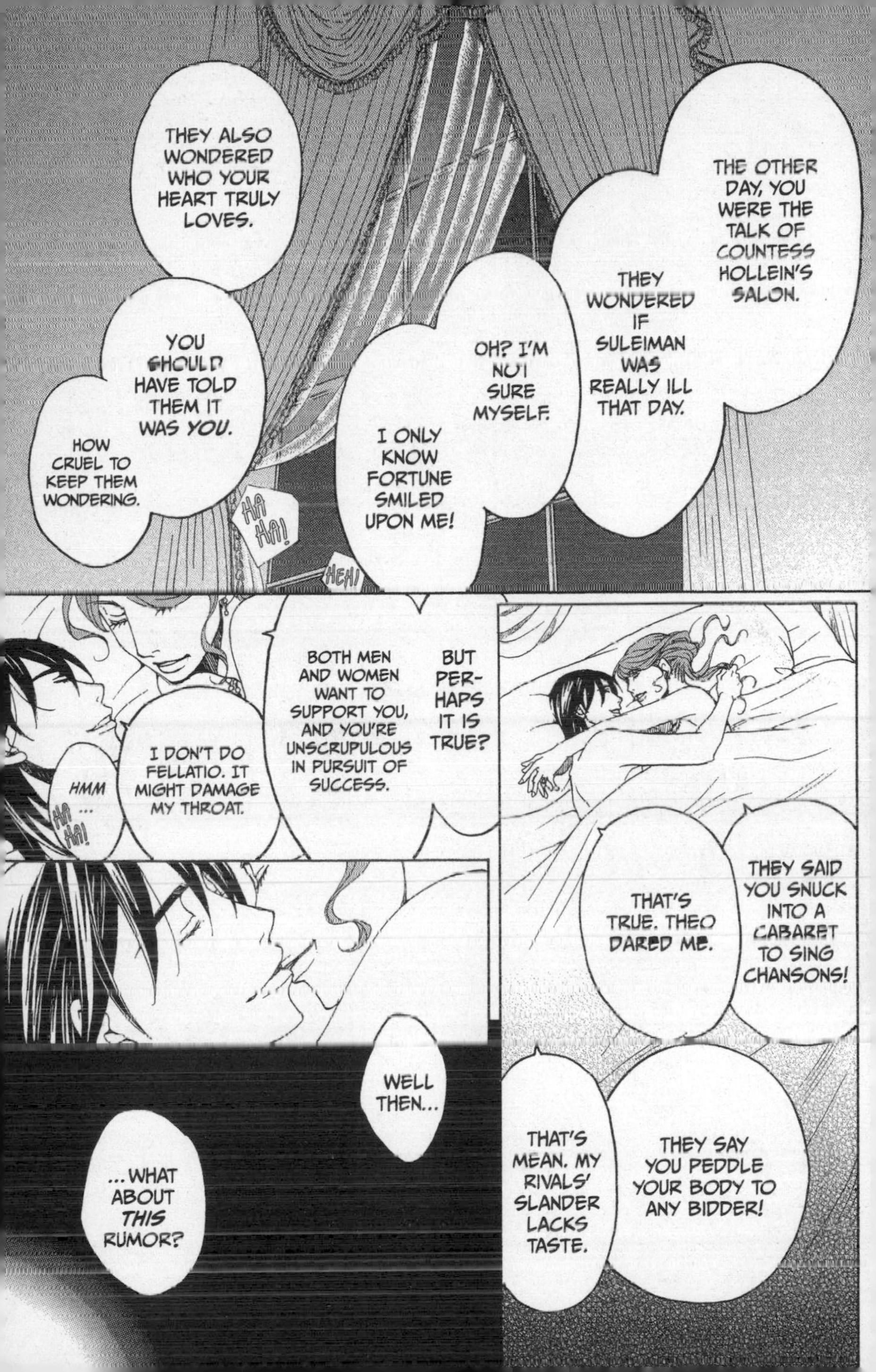
THE OTHER DAY, YOU WERE THE TALK OF COUNTESS HOLLEIN'S SALON.
THEY WONDERED IF SULEIMAN WAS REALLY ILL THAT DAY.
OH? I'M NOT SURE MYSELF.
I ONLY KNOW FORTUNE SMILED UPON ME!
HEH!
THEY ALSO WONDERED WHO YOUR HEART TRULY LOVES.
YOU SHOULD HAVE TOLD THEM IT WAS *YOU*.
HOW CRUEL TO KEEP THEM WONDERING.
HA HA!
THEY SAID YOU SNUCK INTO A CABARET TO SING CHANSONS!
THAT'S TRUE. THEO DARED ME.
THEY SAY YOU PEDDLE YOUR BODY TO ANY BIDDER!
THAT'S MEAN. MY RIVALS' SLANDER LACKS TASTE.
BUT PER-HAPS IT IS TRUE?
BOTH MEN AND WOMEN WANT TO SUPPORT YOU, AND YOU'RE UNSCRUPULOUS IN PURSUIT OF SUCCESS.
I DON'T DO FELLATIO. IT MIGHT DAMAGE MY THROAT.
HMM ...
HA HA!
WELL THEN...
...WHAT ABOUT *THIS* RUMOR?

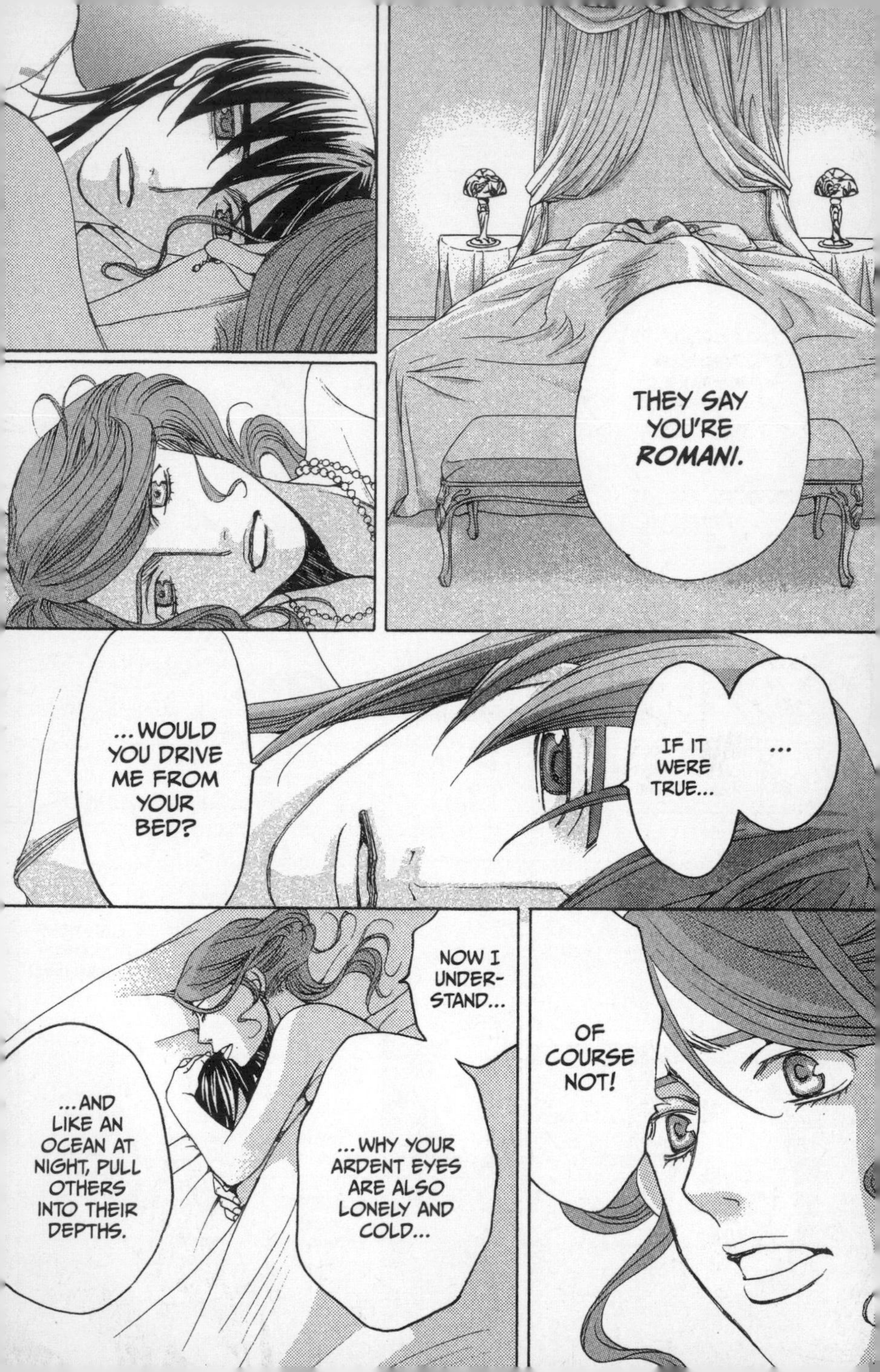
THEY SAY YOU'RE *ROMANI*.
...
IF IT WERE TRUE...
...WOULD YOU DRIVE ME FROM YOUR BED?
OF COURSE NOT!
NOW I UNDER-STAND...
...WHY YOUR ARDENT EYES ARE ALSO LONELY AND COLD...
...AND LIKE AN OCEAN AT NIGHT, PULL OTHERS INTO THEIR DEPTHS.

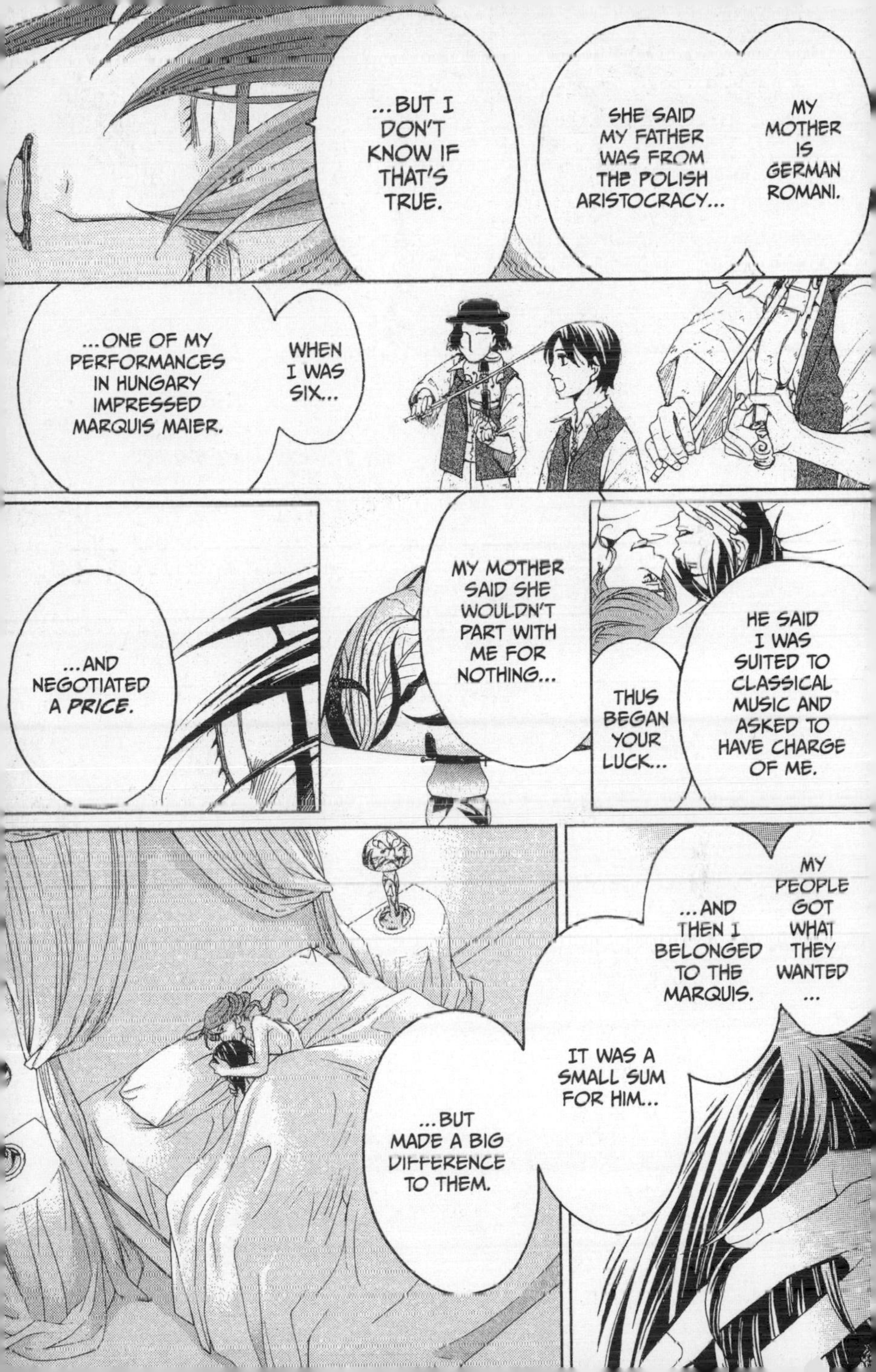
MY MOTHER IS GERMAN ROMANI.
SHE SAID MY FATHER WAS FROM THE POLISH ARISTOCRACY...
...BUT I DON'T KNOW IF THAT'S TRUE.
WHEN I WAS SIX...
...ONE OF MY PERFORMANCES IN HUNGARY IMPRESSED MARQUIS MAIER.
HE SAID I WAS SUITED TO CLASSICAL MUSIC AND ASKED TO HAVE CHARGE OF ME.
THUS BEGAN YOUR LUCK...
MY MOTHER SAID SHE WOULDN'T PART WITH ME FOR NOTHING...
...AND NEGOTIATED A *PRICE*.
MY PEOPLE GOT WHAT THEY WANTED...
...AND THEN I BELONGED TO THE MARQUIS.
IT WAS A SMALL SUM FOR HIM...
...BUT MADE A BIG DIFFERENCE TO THEM.

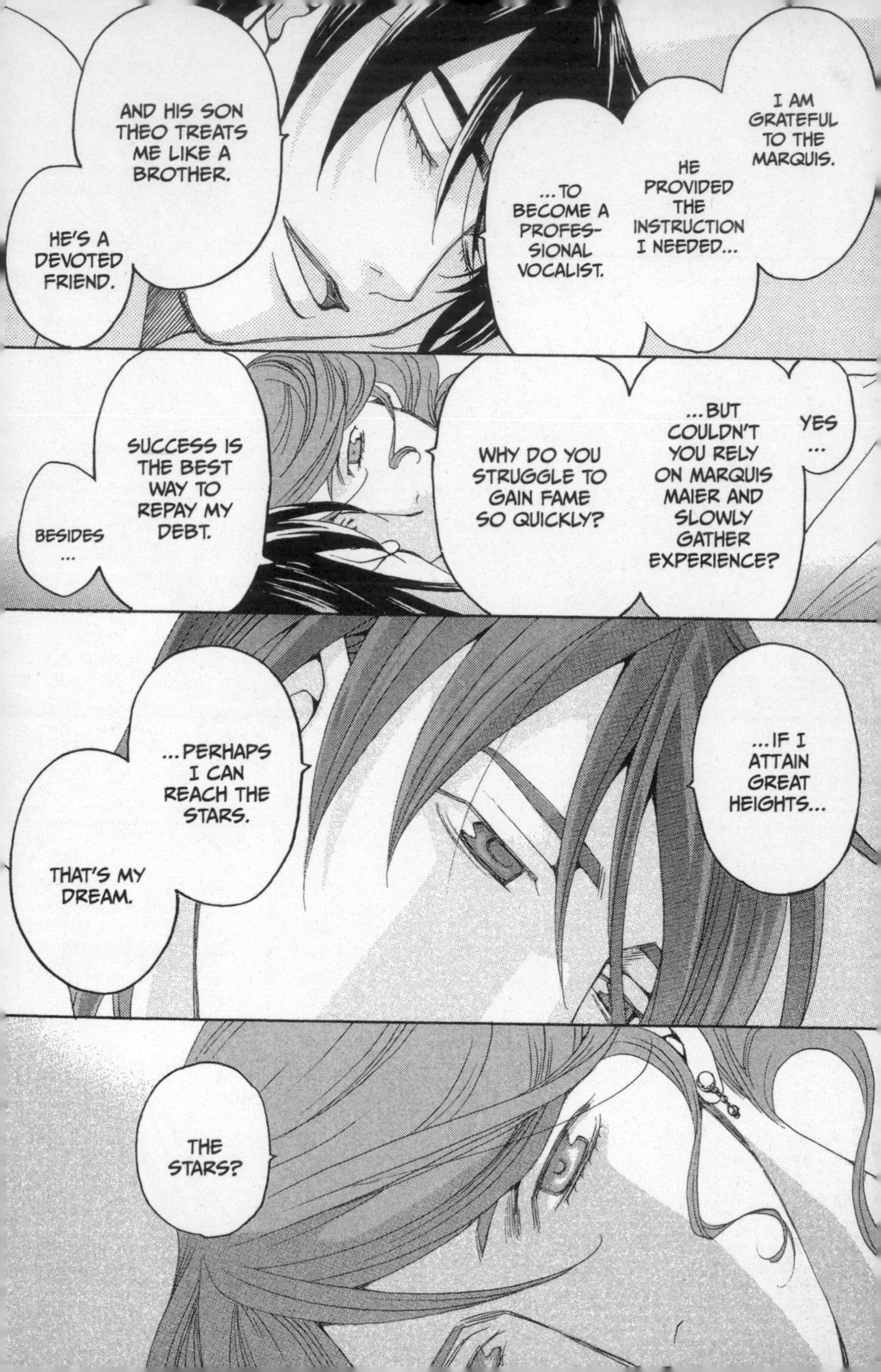
I AM GRATEFUL TO THE MARQUIS.
HE PROVIDED THE INSTRUCTION I NEEDED...
...TO BECOME A PROFESSIONAL VOCALIST.
AND HIS SON THEO TREATS ME LIKE A BROTHER.
HE'S A DEVOTED FRIEND.
YES ...
...BUT COULDN'T YOU RELY ON MARQUIS MAIER AND SLOWLY GATHER EXPERIENCE?
WHY DO YOU STRUGGLE TO GAIN FAME SO QUICKLY?
SUCCESS IS THE BEST WAY TO REPAY MY DEBT.
BESIDES ...
...IF I ATTAIN GREAT HEIGHTS...
...PERHAPS I CAN REACH THE STARS.
THAT'S MY DREAM.
THE STARS?

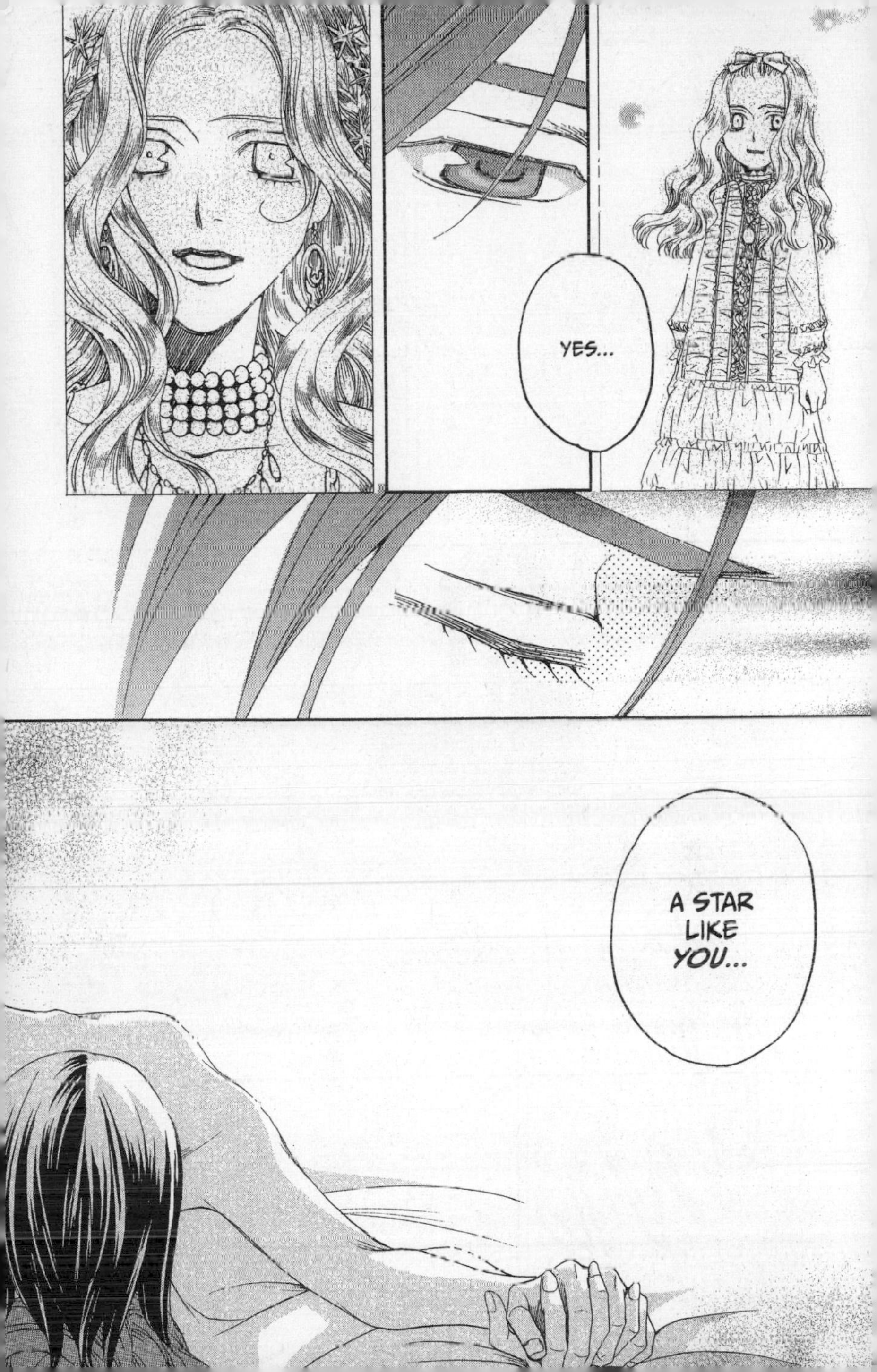
YES...
A STAR LIKE YOU...

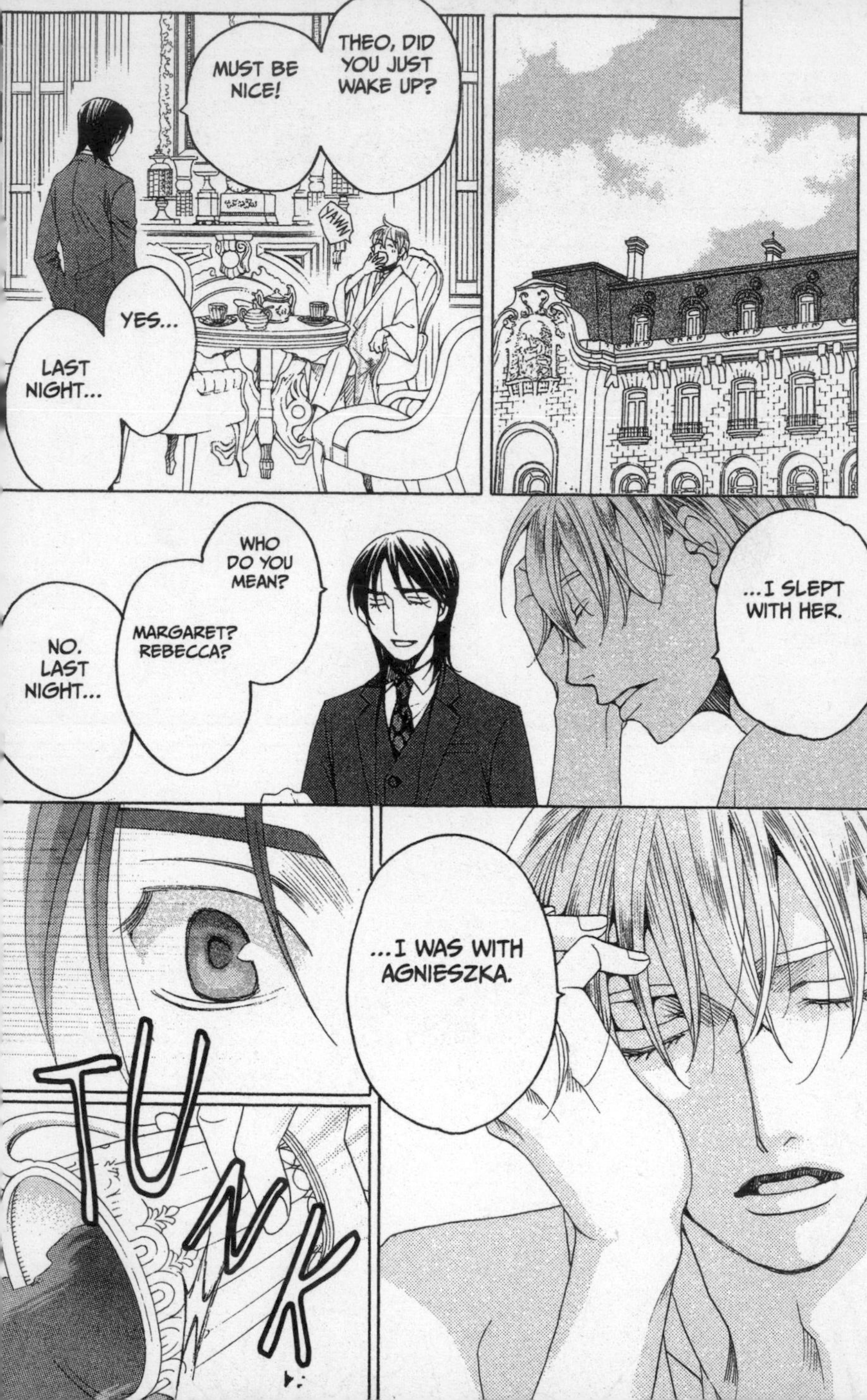
THEO, DID YOU JUST WAKE UP?
MUST BE NICE!
YAWN
YES...
LAST NIGHT...
...I SLEPT WITH HER.
WHO DO YOU MEAN?
MARGARET? REBECCA?
NO. LAST NIGHT...
...I WAS WITH AGNIESZKA.
TUNK

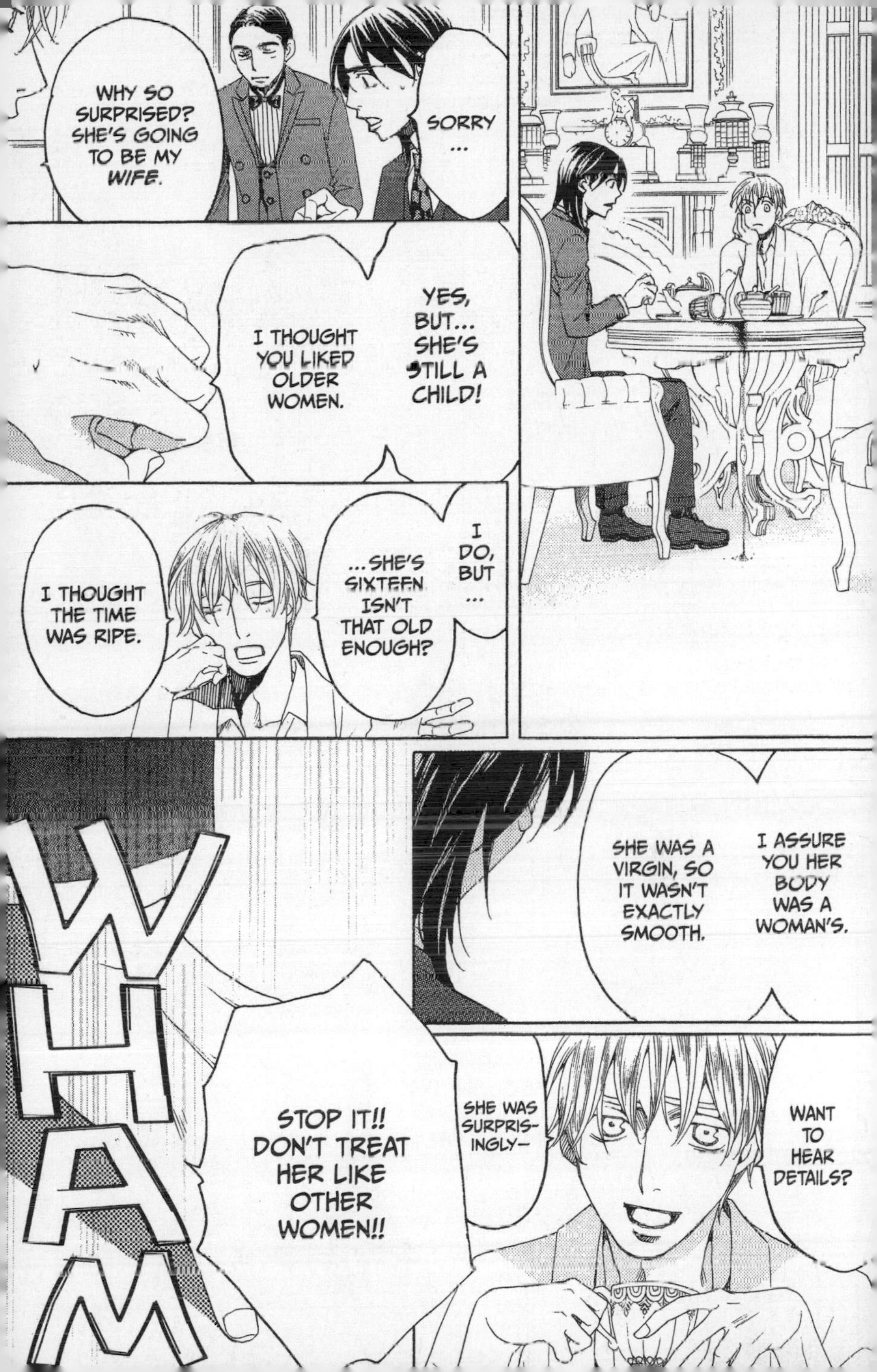
SORRY ...
WHY SO SURPRISED? SHE'S GOING TO BE MY WIFE.
YES, BUT... SHE'S STILL A CHILD!
I THOUGHT YOU LIKED OLDER WOMEN.
I DO, BUT ...
...SHE'S SIXTEEN. ISN'T THAT OLD ENOUGH?
I THOUGHT THE TIME WAS RIPE.
I ASSURE YOU HER BODY WAS A WOMAN'S.
SHE WAS A VIRGIN, SO IT WASN'T EXACTLY SMOOTH.
WANT TO HEAR DETAILS?
SHE WAS SURPRIS-INGLY—
STOP IT!! DON'T TREAT HER LIKE OTHER WOMEN!!
WHAM

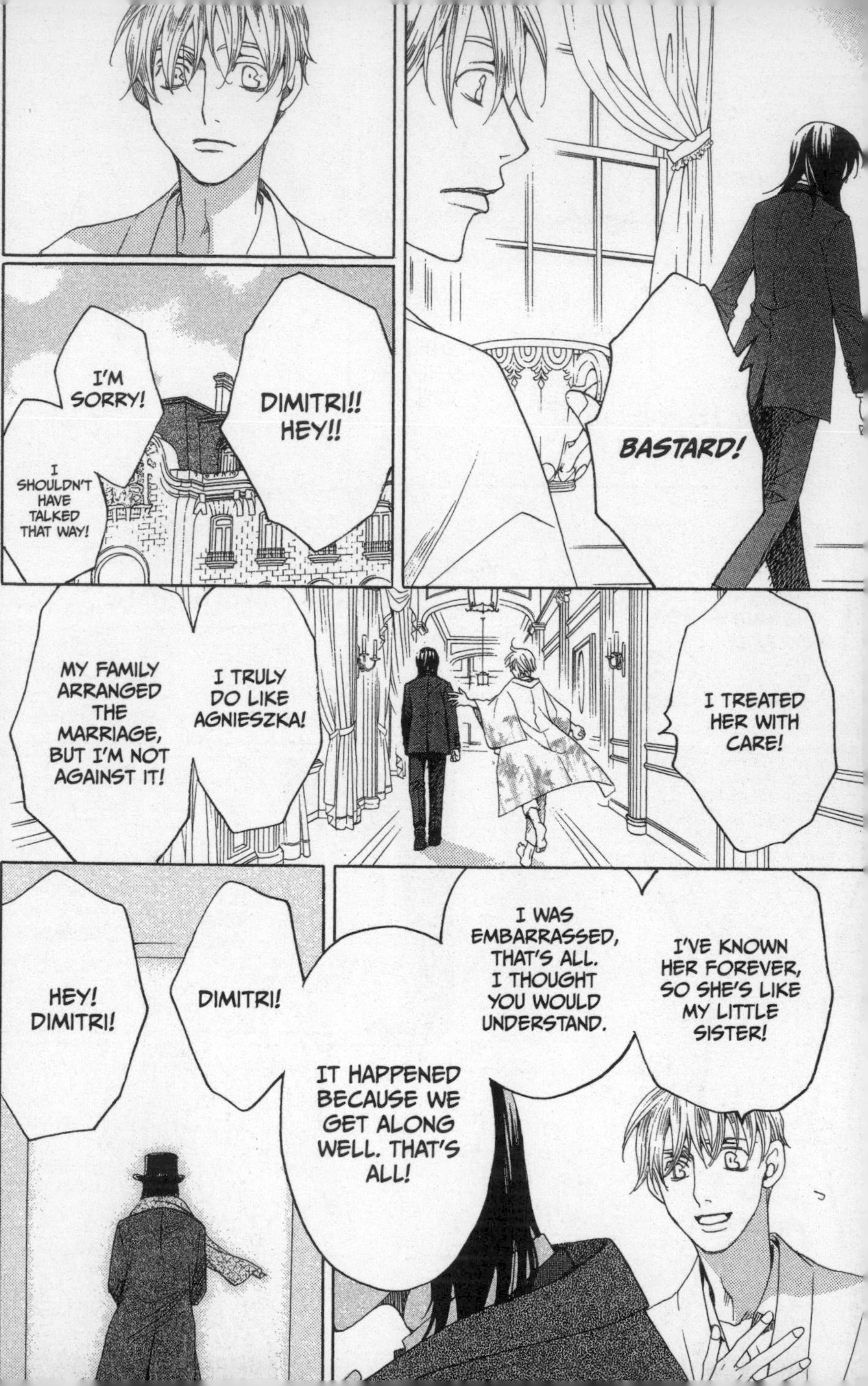
BASTARD!
DIMITRI!! HEY!!
I'M SORRY!
I SHOULDN'T HAVE TALKED THAT WAY!
I TREATED HER WITH CARE!
I TRULY DO LIKE AGNIESZKA!
MY FAMILY ARRANGED THE MARRIAGE, BUT I'M NOT AGAINST IT!
I'VE KNOWN HER FOREVER, SO SHE'S LIKE MY LITTLE SISTER!
I WAS EMBARRASSED, THAT'S ALL. I THOUGHT YOU WOULD UNDERSTAND.
IT HAPPENED BECAUSE WE GET ALONG WELL. THAT'S ALL!
DIMITRI!
HEY! DIMITRI!

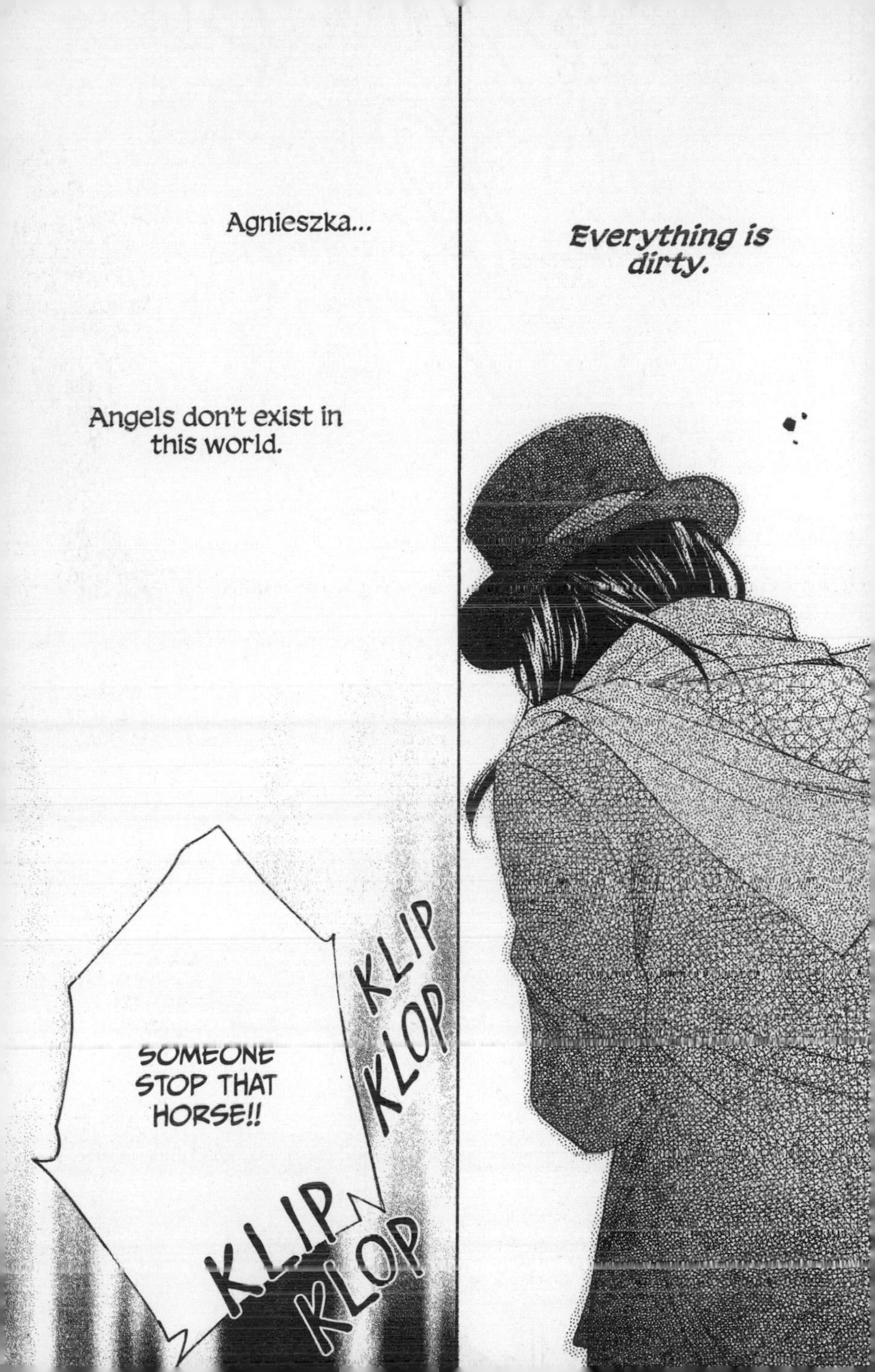
Everything is dirty.
Agnieszka...
Angels don't exist in this world.
KLIP KLOP
SOMEONE STOP THAT HORSE!!
KLIP KLOP

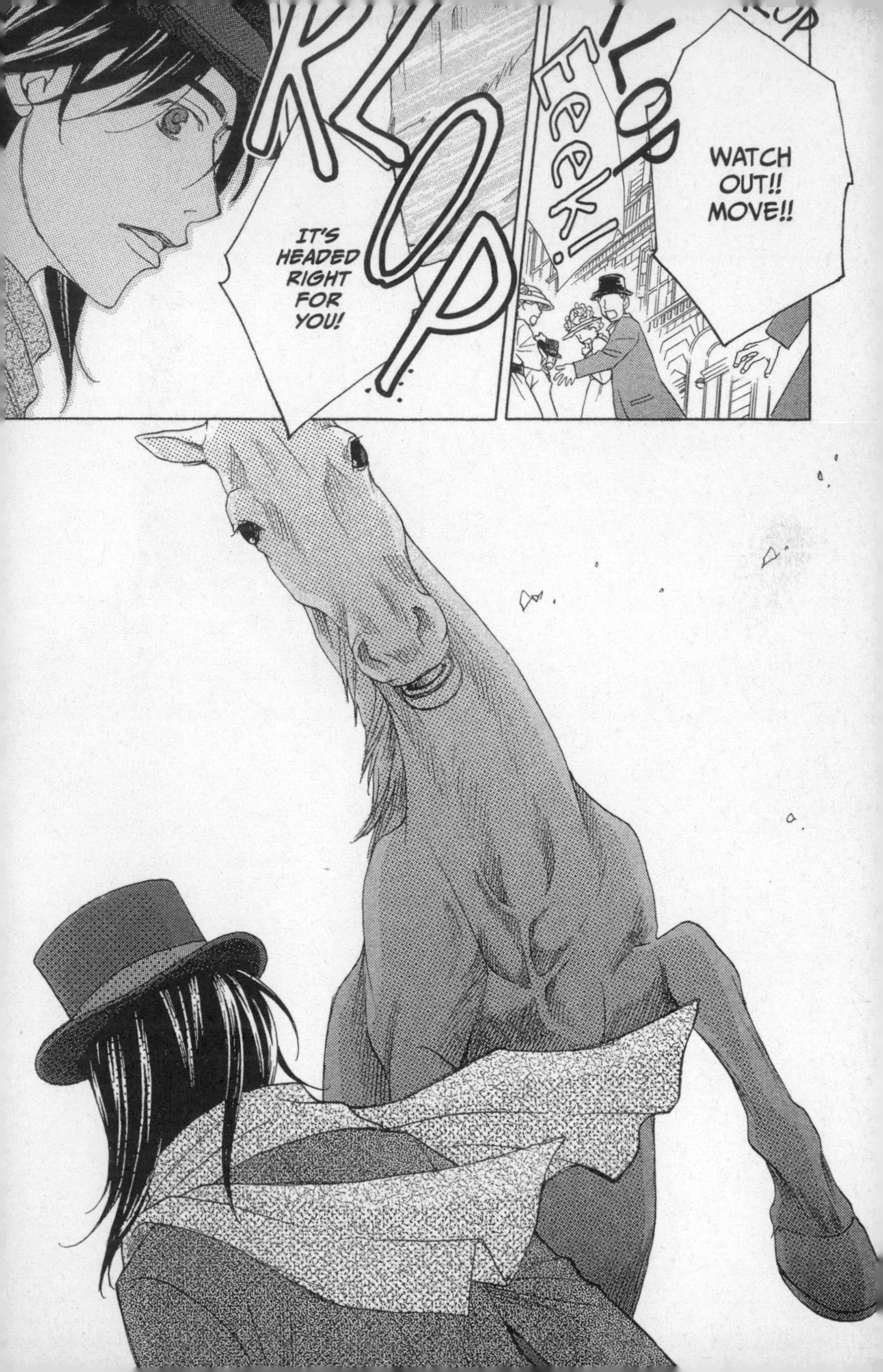
LOP
WATCH OUT!! MOVE!!
LOP
Eeek!
IT'S HEADED RIGHT FOR YOU!
KLOP

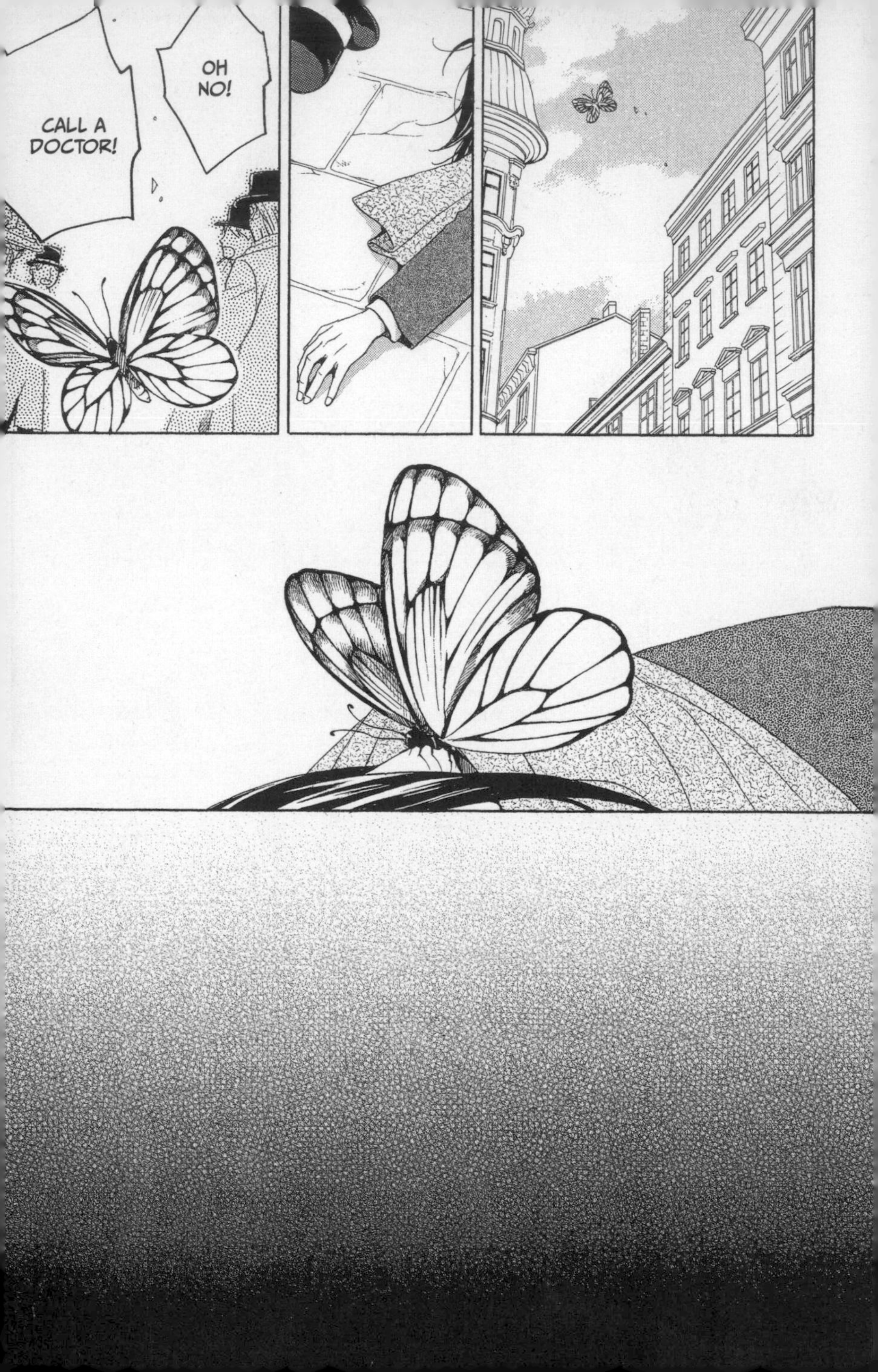
OH NO!
CALL A DOCTOR!

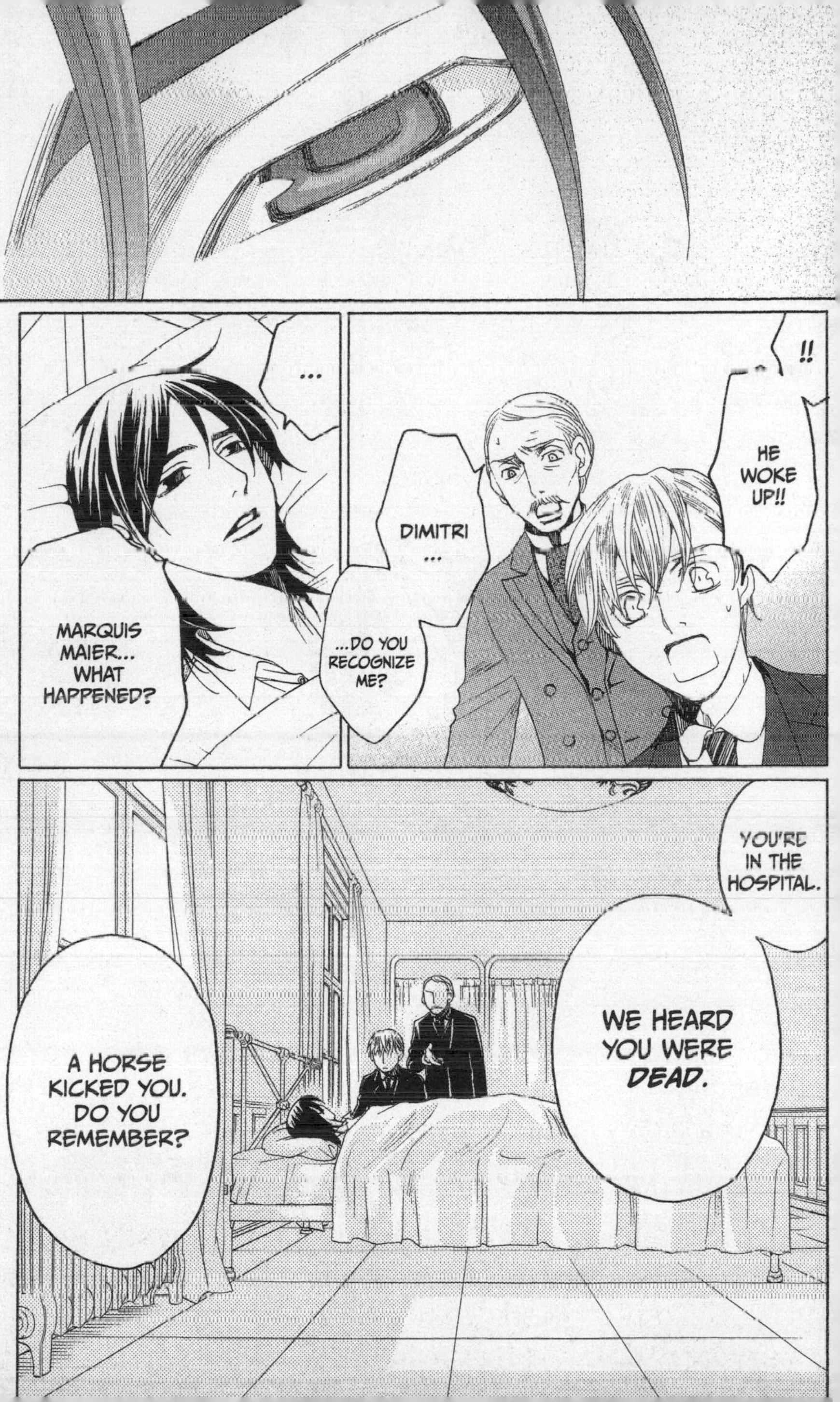
!!
HE WOKE UP!!
DIMITRI ...
...DO YOU RECOGNIZE ME?
...
MARQUIS MAIER... WHAT HAPPENED?
YOU'RE IN THE HOSPITAL.
WE HEARD YOU WERE *DEAD.*
A HORSE KICKED YOU. DO YOU REMEMBER?

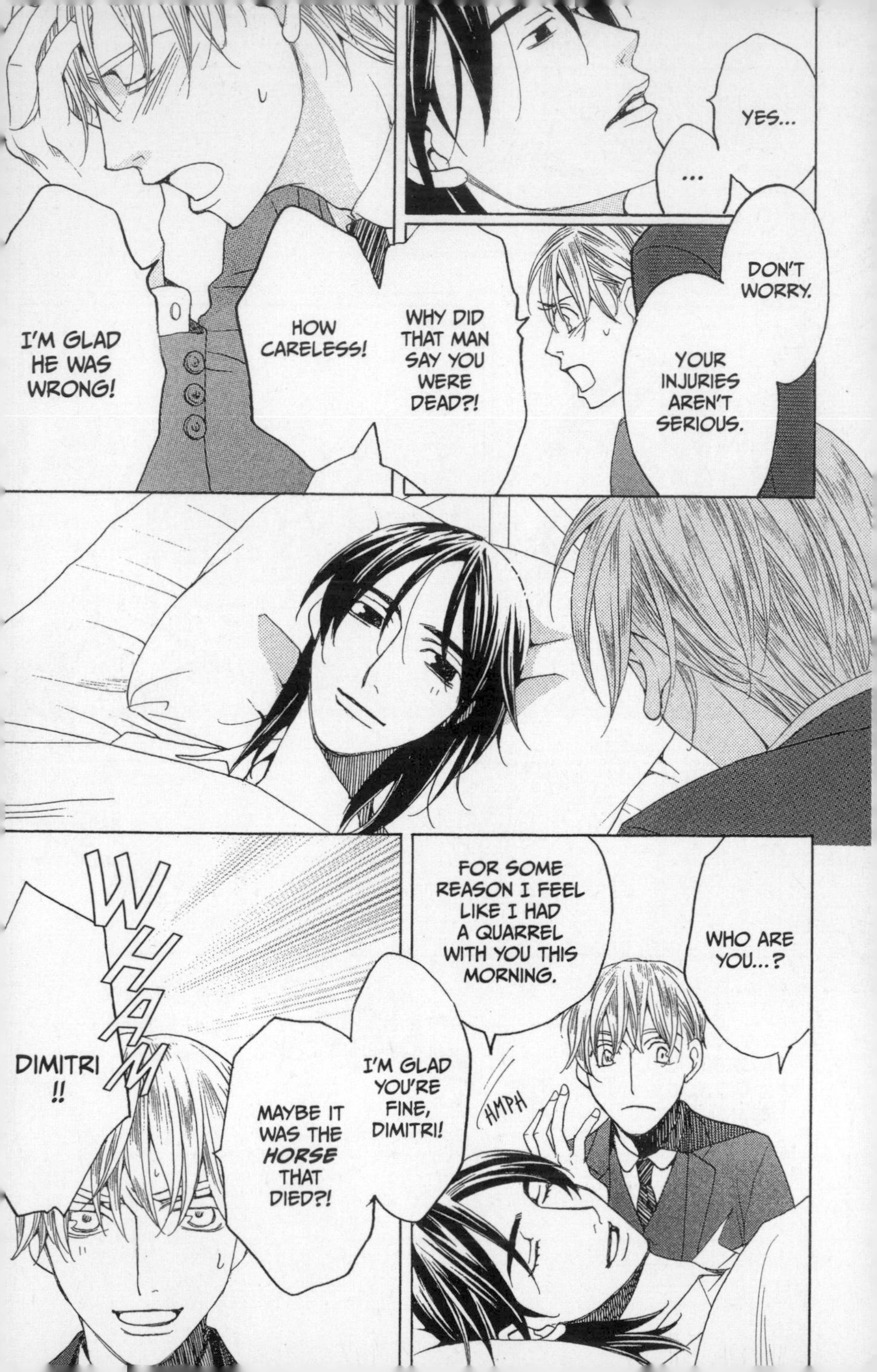
YES...
...
DON'T WORRY.
YOUR INJURIES AREN'T SERIOUS.
WHY DID THAT MAN SAY YOU WERE DEAD?!
HOW CARELESS!
I'M GLAD HE WAS WRONG!
WHO ARE YOU...?
FOR SOME REASON I FEEL LIKE I HAD A QUARREL WITH YOU THIS MORNING.
HMPH
I'M GLAD YOU'RE FINE, DIMITRI!
MAYBE IT WAS THE *HORSE* THAT DIED?!
WHAM
DIMITRI !!

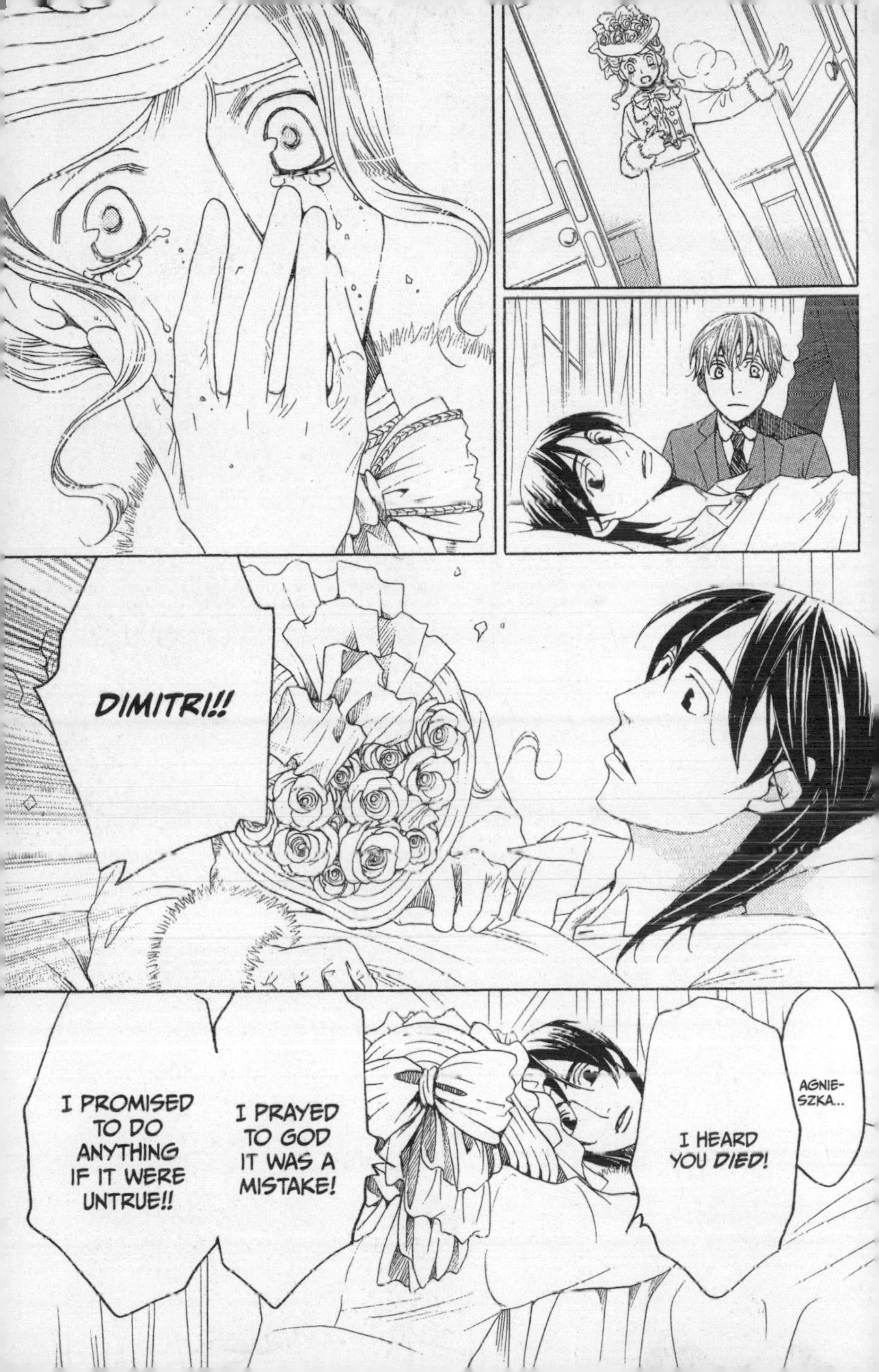
DIMITRI!!
AGNIE-SZKA...
I HEARD YOU DIED!
I PRAYED TO GOD IT WAS A MISTAKE!
I PROMISED TO DO ANYTHING IF IT WERE UNTRUE!!

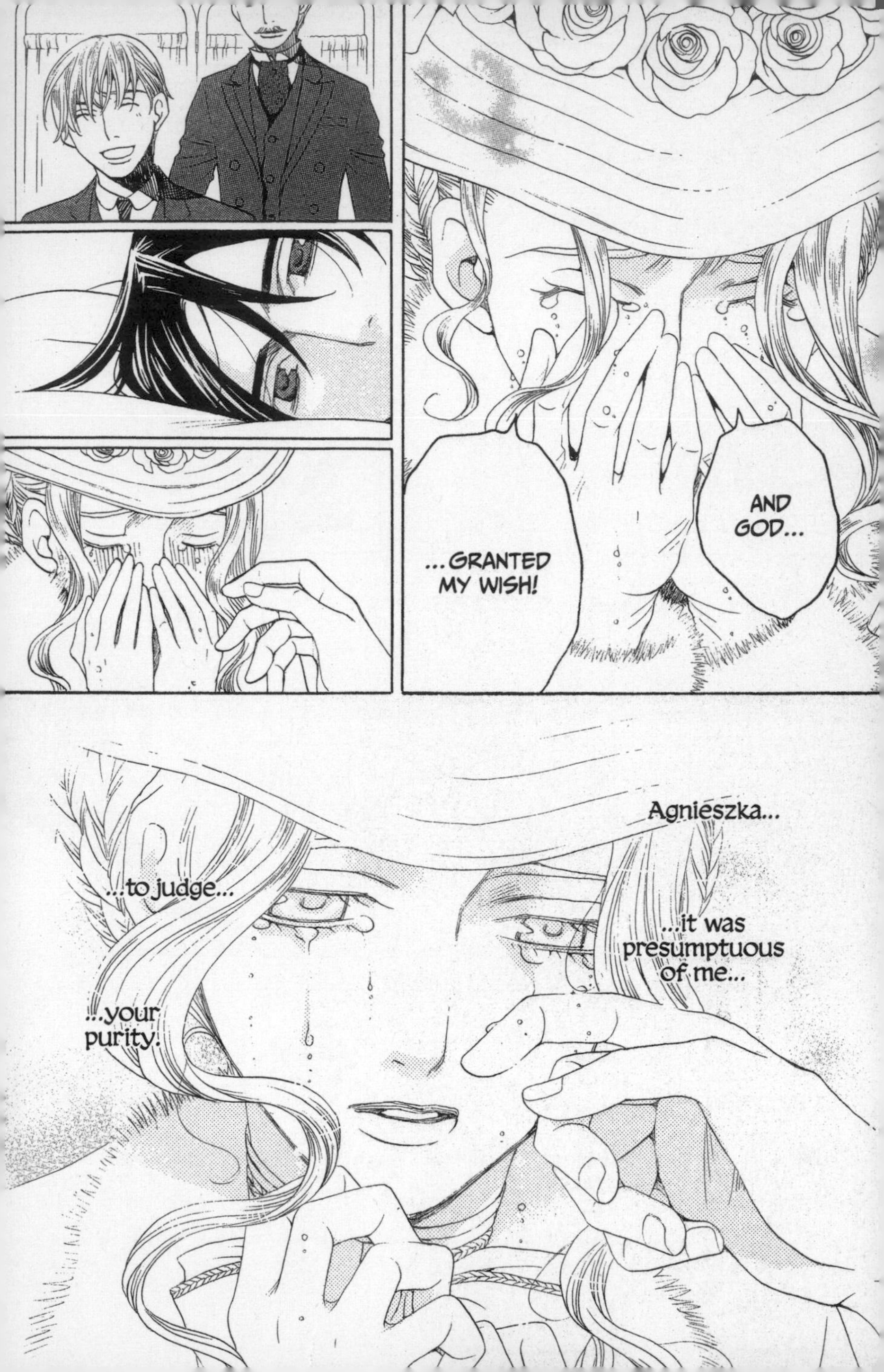
AND GOD...
...GRANTED MY WISH!
Agnieszka...
...it was presumptuous of me...
...to judge...
...your purity.

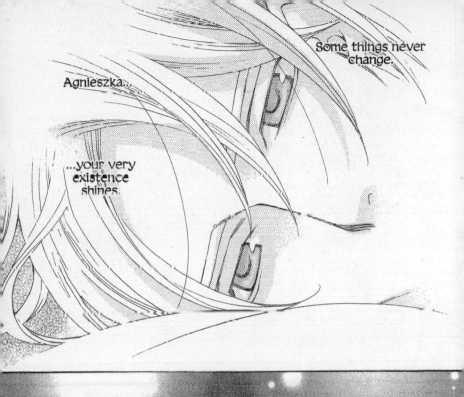

Some things never change.

Agnieszka...

...your very existence shines.

I love you.

That alone is true.

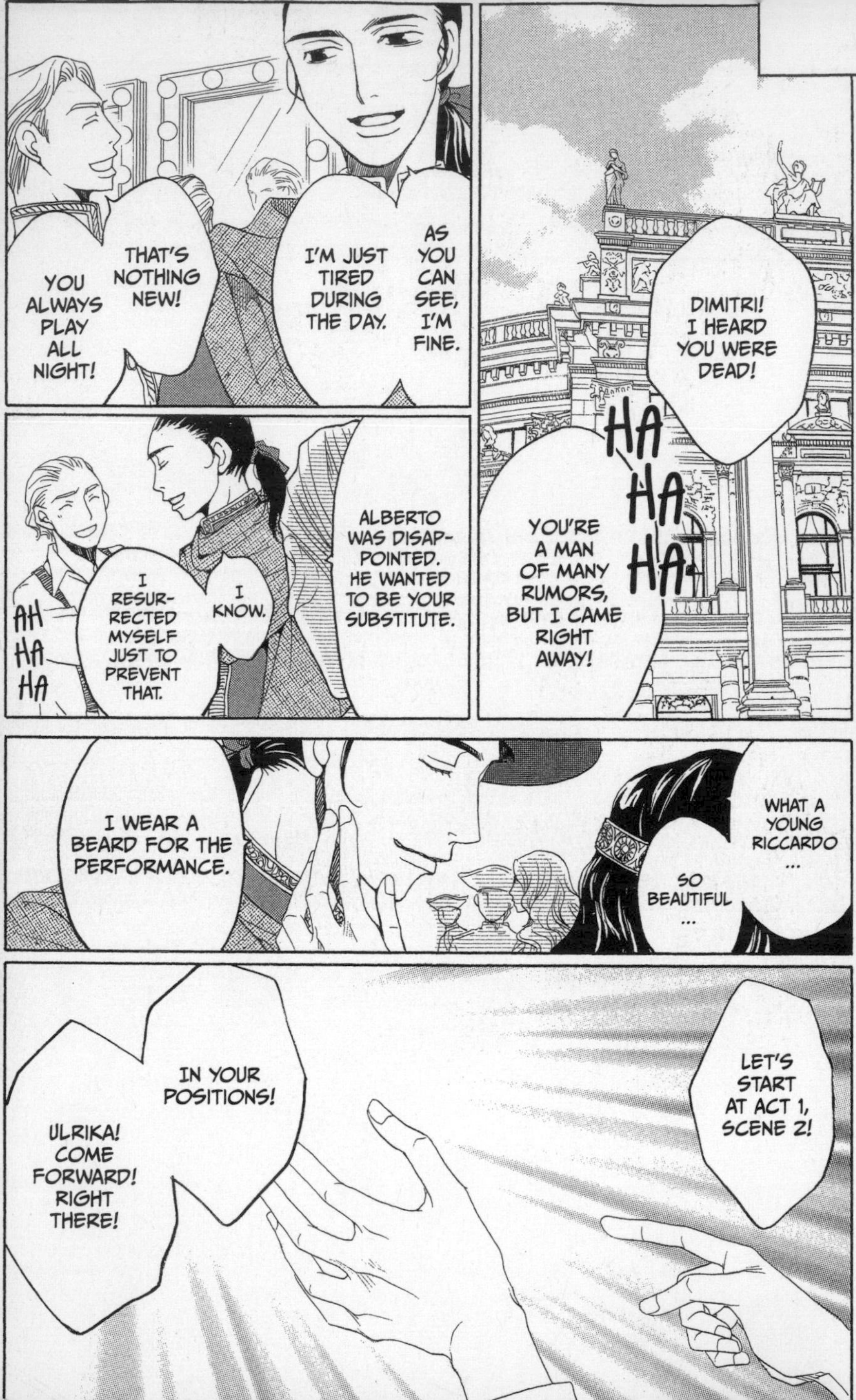
DIMITRI! I HEARD YOU WERE DEAD!
HA HA HA
YOU'RE A MAN OF MANY RUMORS, BUT I CAME RIGHT AWAY!
AS YOU CAN SEE, I'M FINE.
I'M JUST TIRED DURING THE DAY.
THAT'S NOTHING NEW!
YOU ALWAYS PLAY ALL NIGHT!
ALBERTO WAS DISAPPOINTED. HE WANTED TO BE YOUR SUBSTITUTE.
I KNOW.
I RESURRECTED MYSELF JUST TO PREVENT THAT.
AH HA HA
WHAT A YOUNG RICCARDO ...
SO BEAUTIFUL ...
I WEAR A BEARD FOR THE PERFORMANCE.
LET'S START AT ACT 1, SCENE 2!
IN YOUR POSITIONS!
ULRIKA! COME FORWARD! RIGHT THERE!

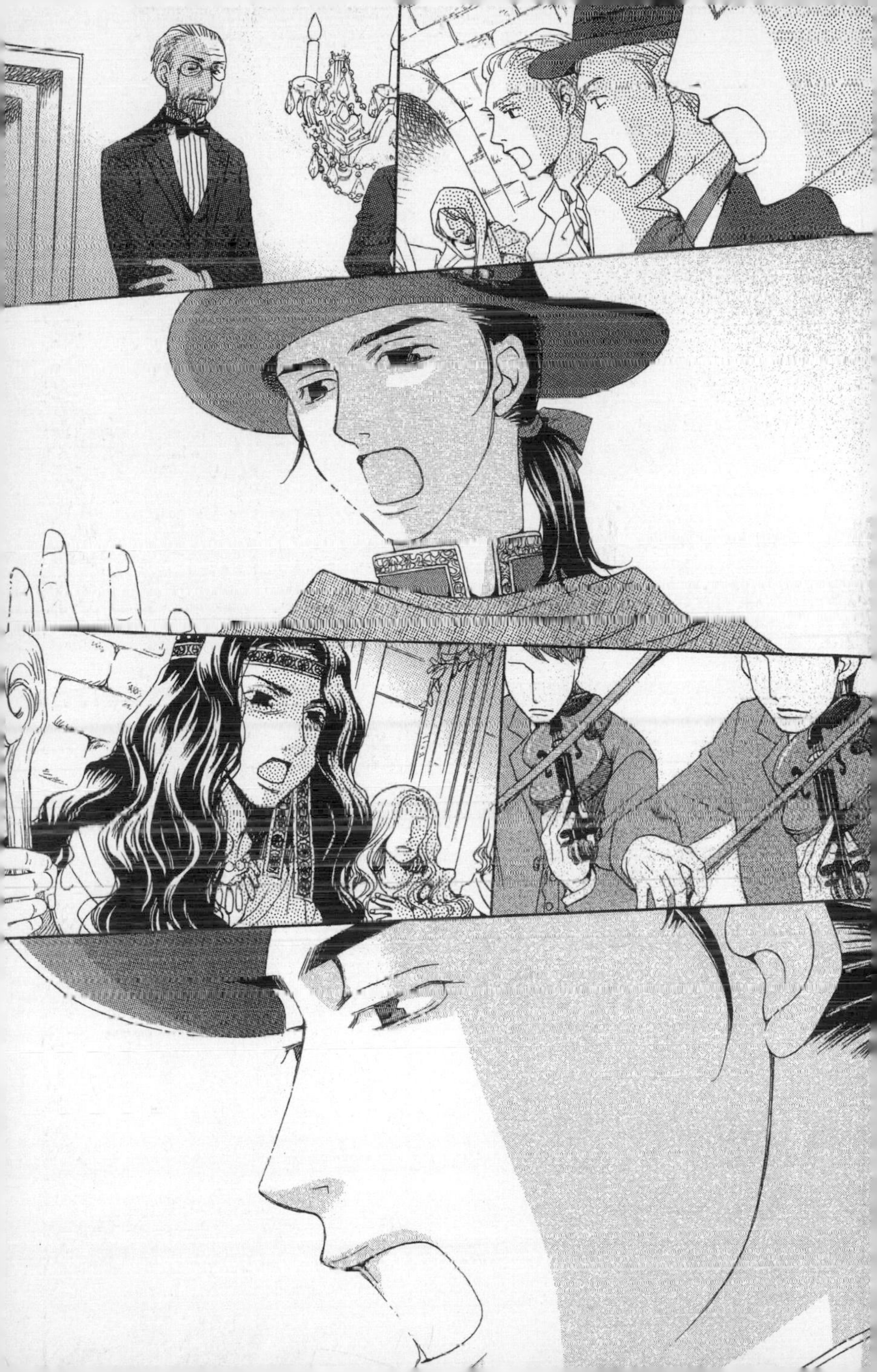

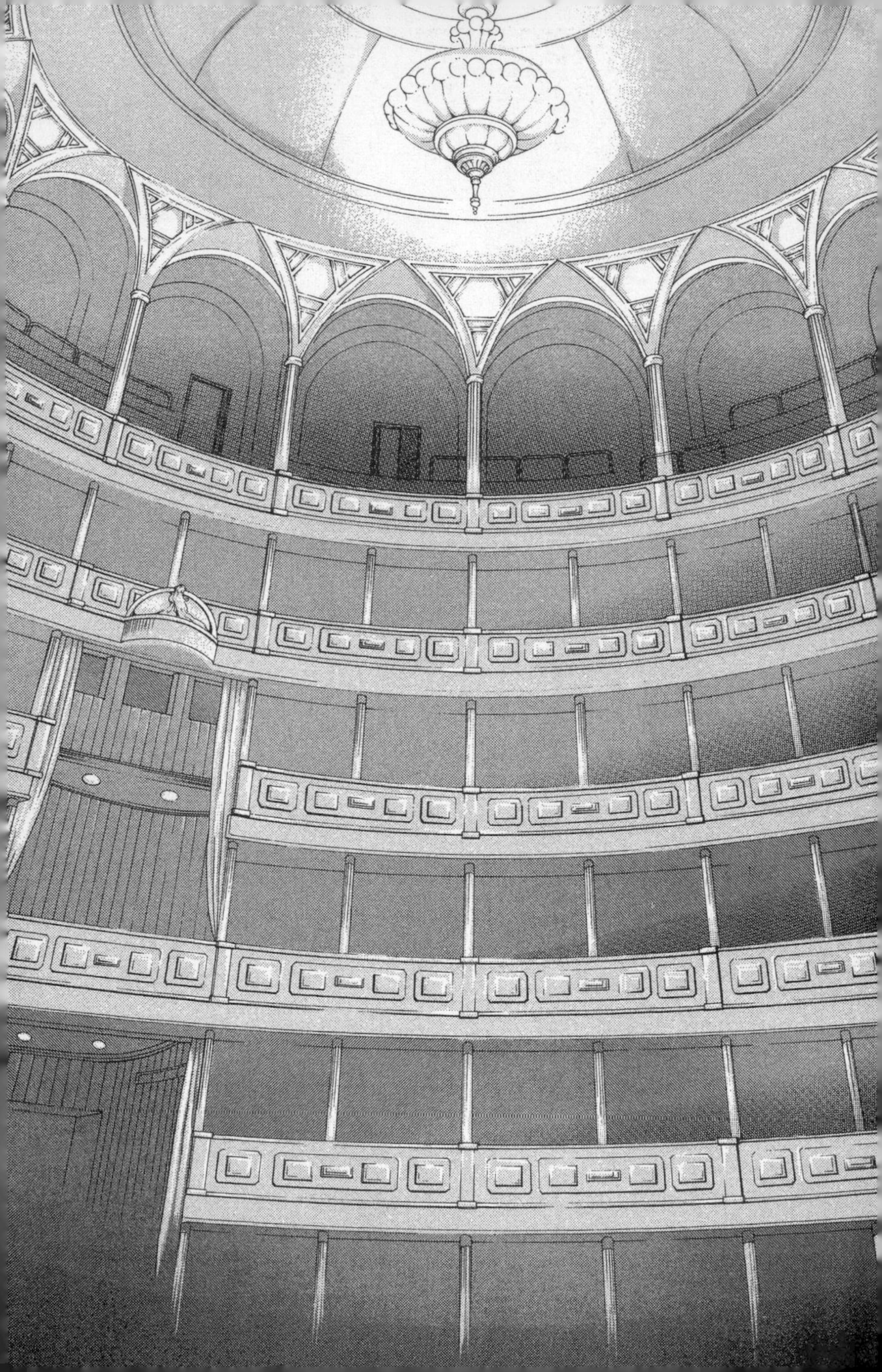

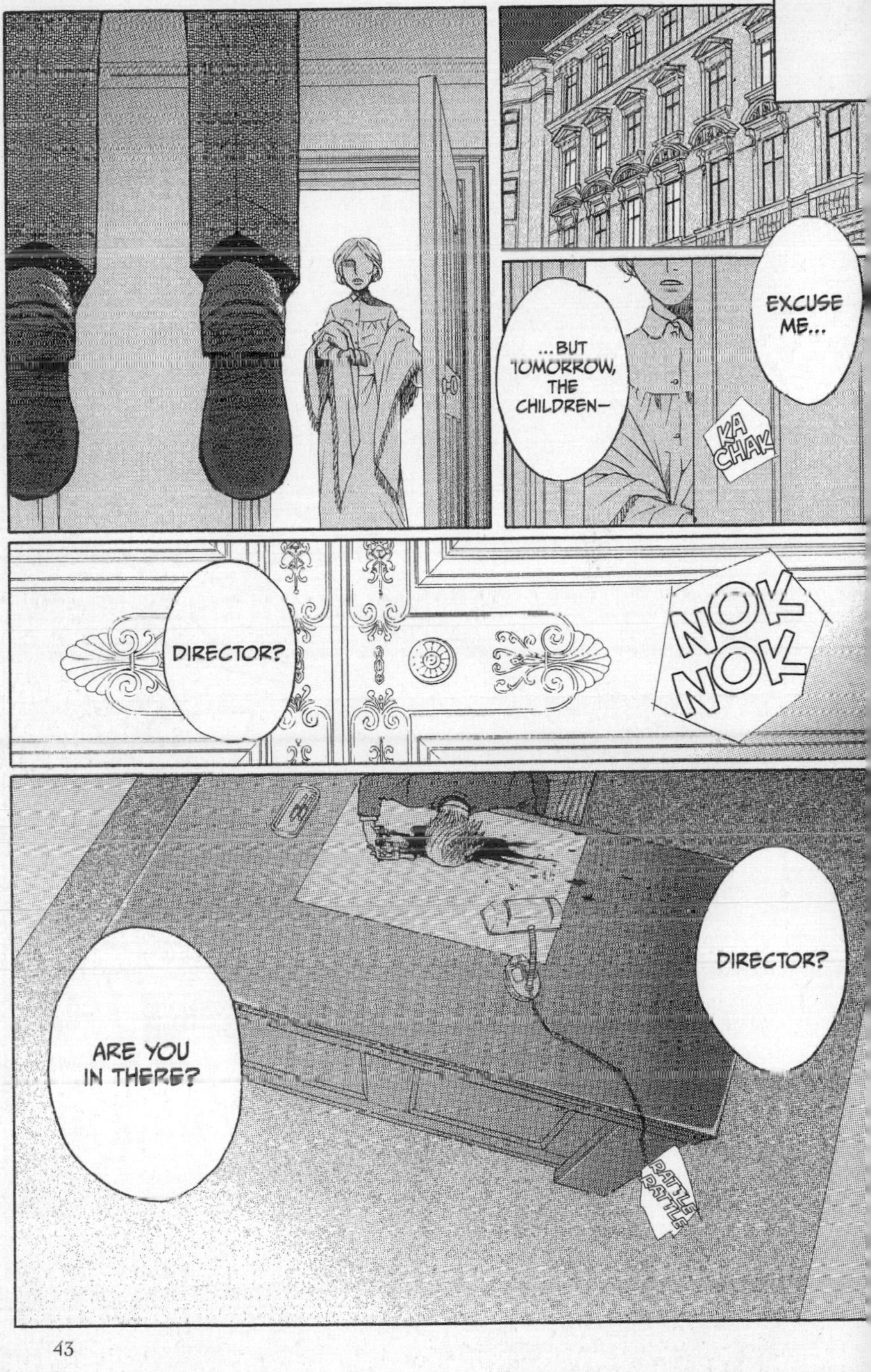
EXCUSE ME...
KA CHAK
...BUT TOMORROW, THE CHILDREN—
NOK NOK
DIRECTOR?
DIRECTOR?
RATTLE RATTLE
ARE YOU IN THERE?

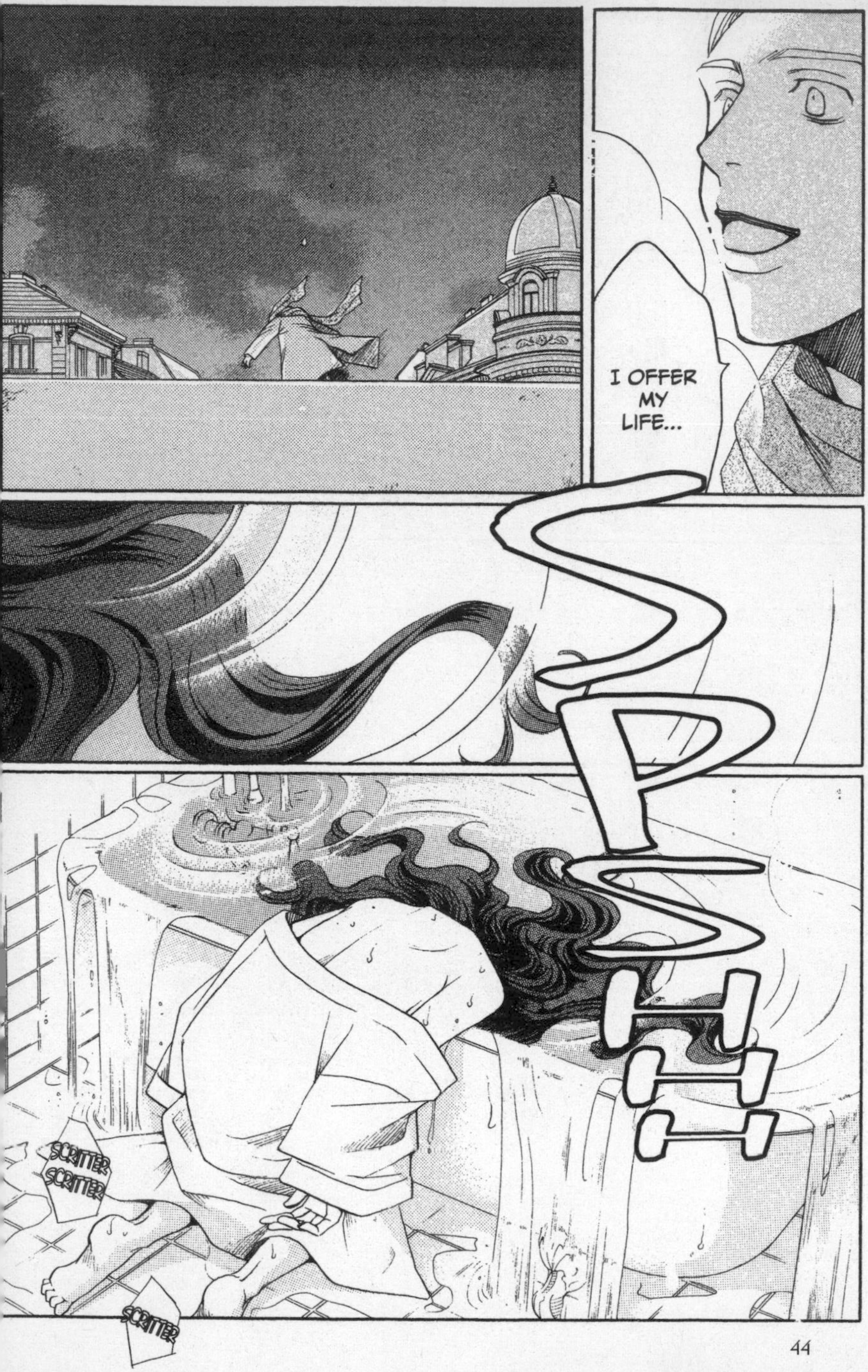
I OFFER MY LIFE...
SPSHHH
SCRITTER SCRITTER
SCRITTER

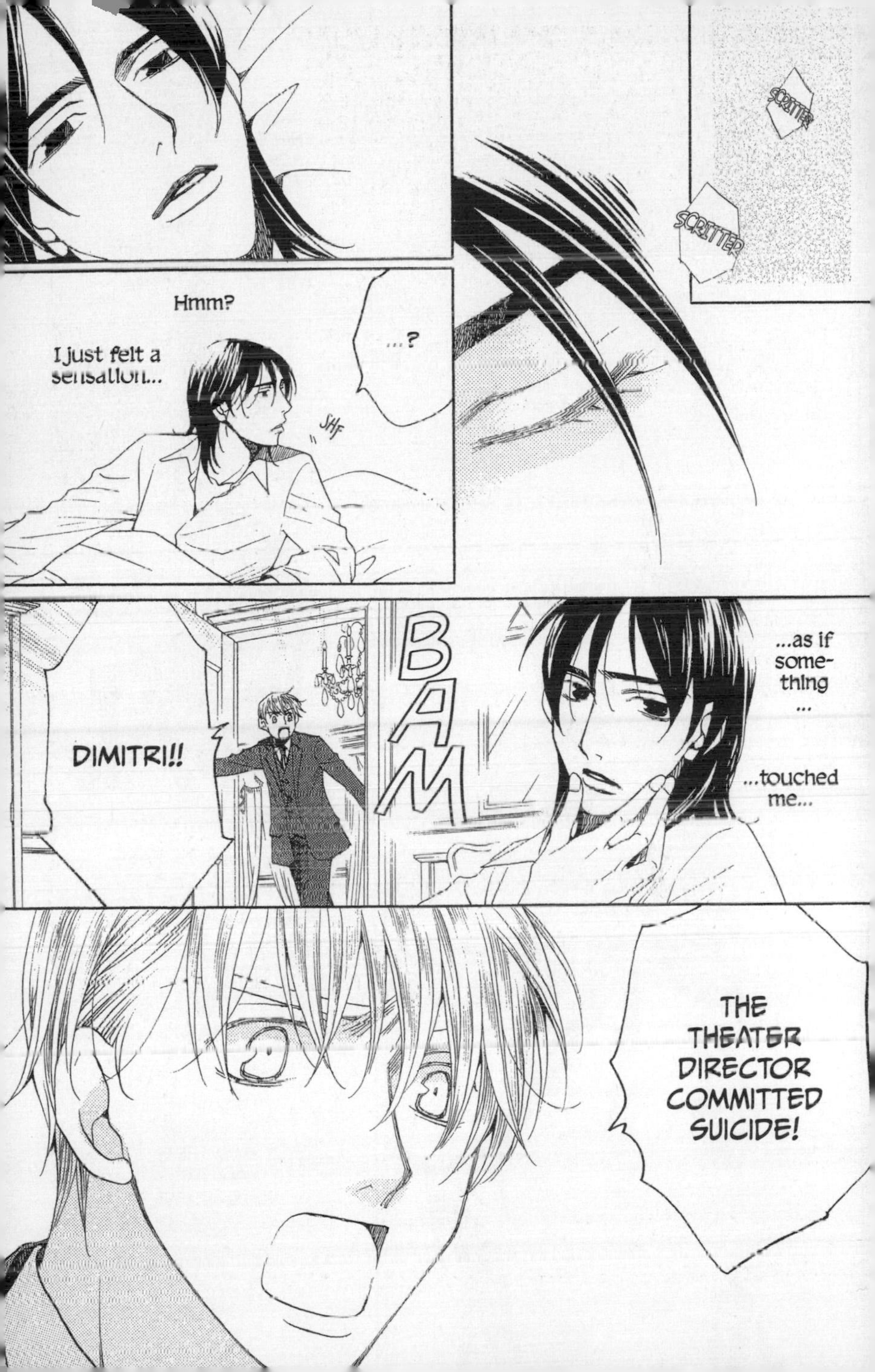
SCRITTER
SCRITTER
...?
Hmm?
I just felt a sensation...
SHF
...as if something ...
...touched me...
BAM
DIMITRI!!
THE THEATER DIRECTOR COMMITTED SUICIDE!

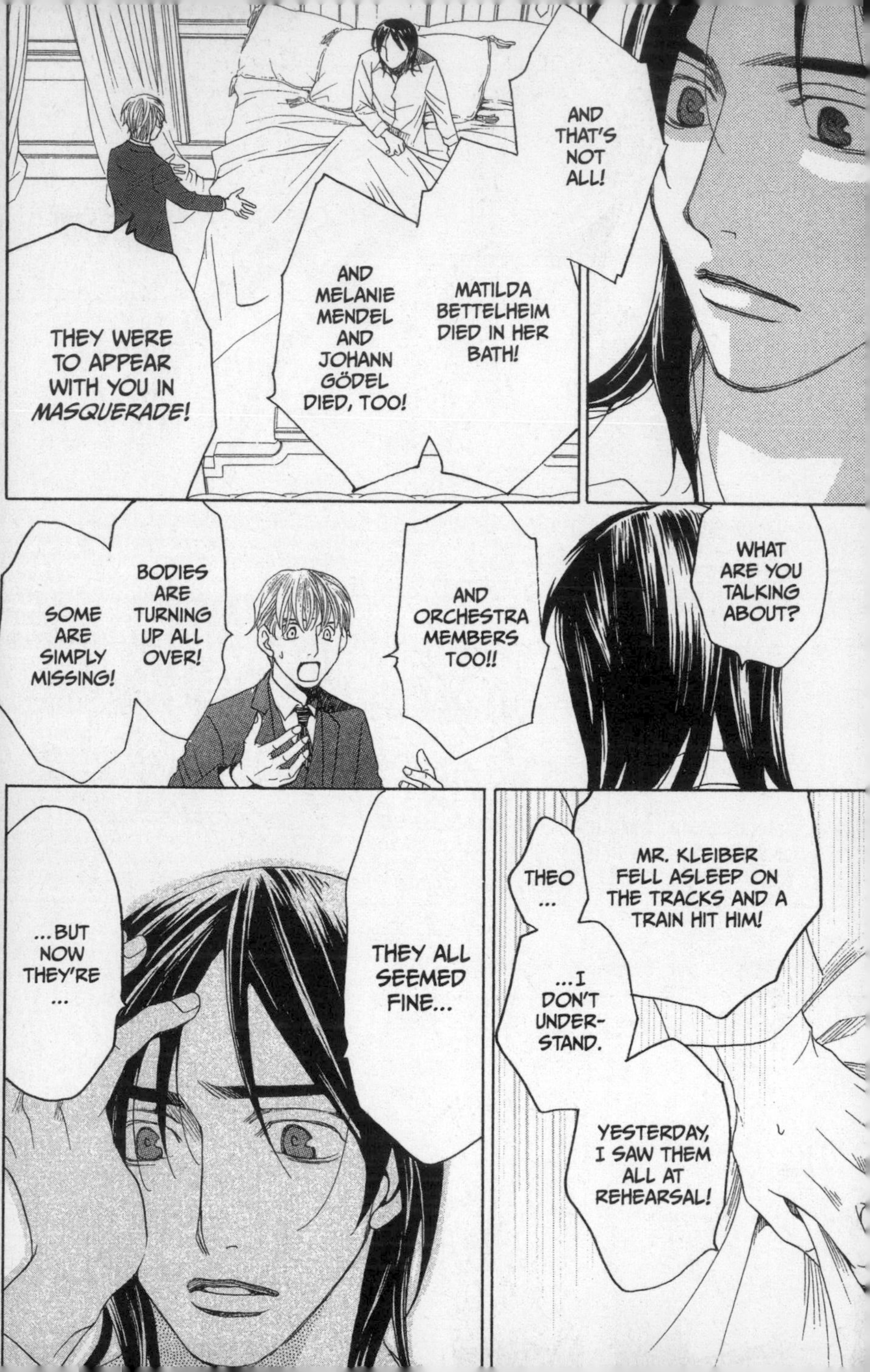
AND THAT'S NOT ALL!
MATILDA BETTELHEIM DIED IN HER BATH!
AND MELANIE MENDEL AND JOHANN GÖDEL DIED, TOO!
THEY WERE TO APPEAR WITH YOU IN *MASQUERADE*!
WHAT ARE YOU TALKING ABOUT?
AND ORCHESTRA MEMBERS TOO!!
BODIES ARE TURNING UP ALL OVER!
SOME ARE SIMPLY MISSING!
MR. KLEIBER FELL ASLEEP ON THE TRACKS AND A TRAIN HIT HIM!
THEO ...
...I DON'T UNDER-STAND.
YESTERDAY, I SAW THEM ALL AT REHEARSAL!
THEY ALL SEEMED FINE...
...BUT NOW THEY'RE ...

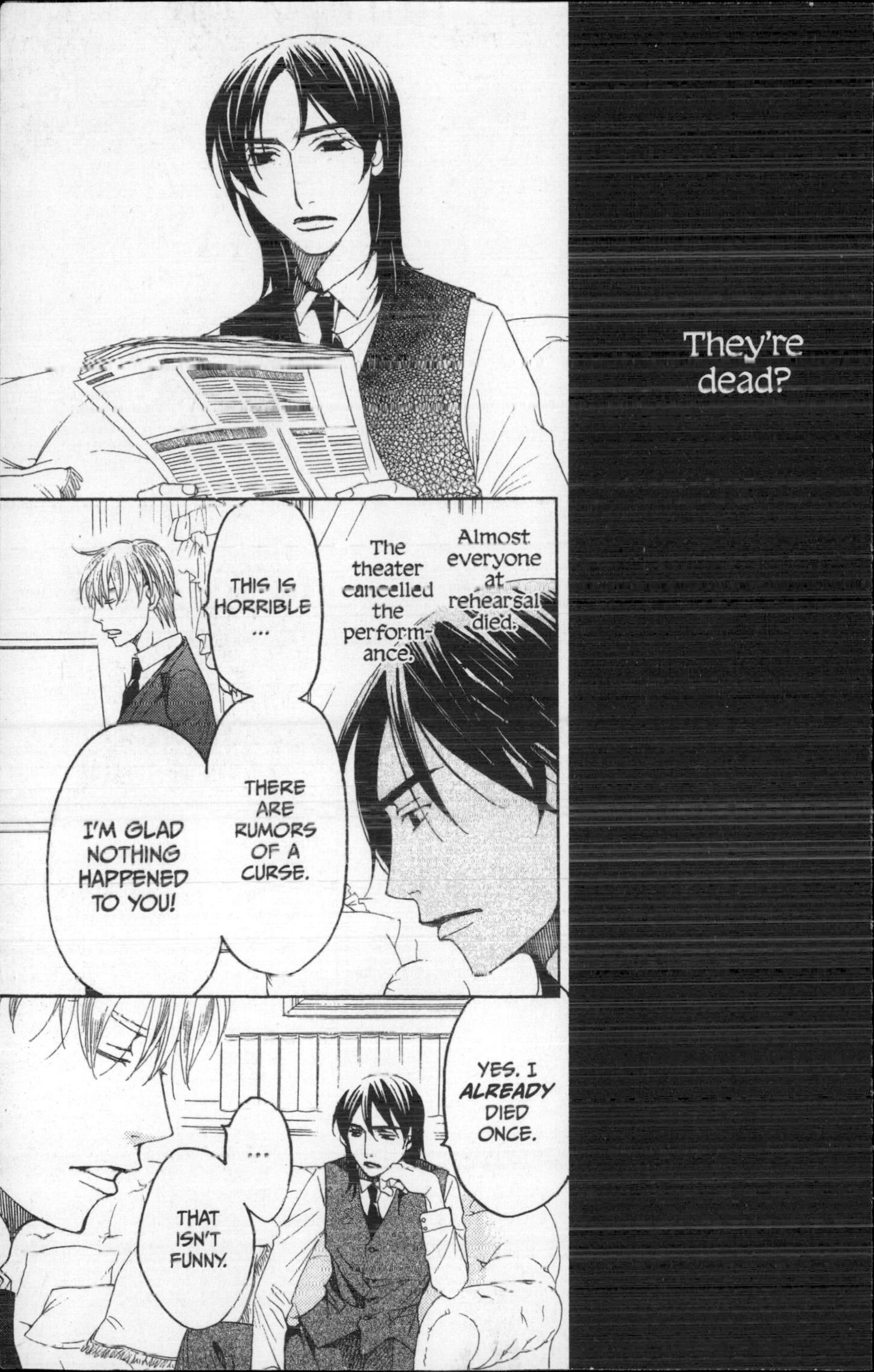
They're dead?
Almost everyone at rehearsal died.
The theater cancelled the performance.
THIS IS HORRIBLE ...
THERE ARE RUMORS OF A CURSE.
I'M GLAD NOTHING HAPPENED TO YOU!
YES. I *ALREADY* DIED ONCE.
...
THAT ISN'T FUNNY.

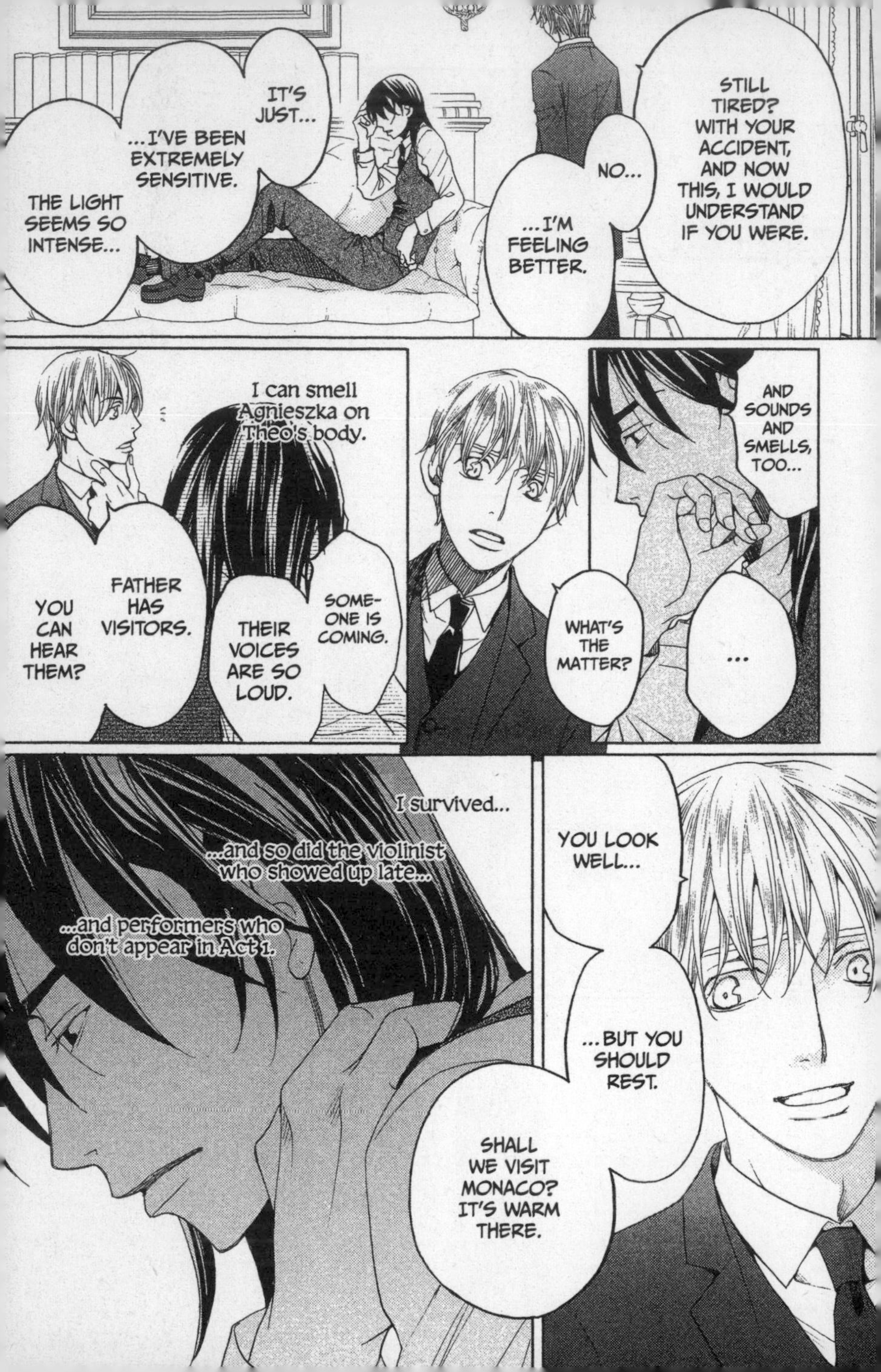
STILL TIRED? WITH YOUR ACCIDENT, AND NOW THIS, I WOULD UNDERSTAND IF YOU WERE.
NO...
...I'M FEELING BETTER.
IT'S JUST...
...I'VE BEEN EXTREMELY SENSITIVE.
THE LIGHT SEEMS SO INTENSE...
AND SOUNDS AND SMELLS, TOO...
...
WHAT'S THE MATTER?
I can smell Agnieszka on Theo's body.
SOME-ONE IS COMING.
THEIR VOICES ARE SO LOUD.
FATHER HAS VISITORS.
YOU CAN HEAR THEM?
YOU LOOK WELL...
...BUT YOU SHOULD REST.
SHALL WE VISIT MONACO? IT'S WARM THERE.
I survived...
...and so did the violinist who showed up late...
...and performers who don't appear in Act 1.

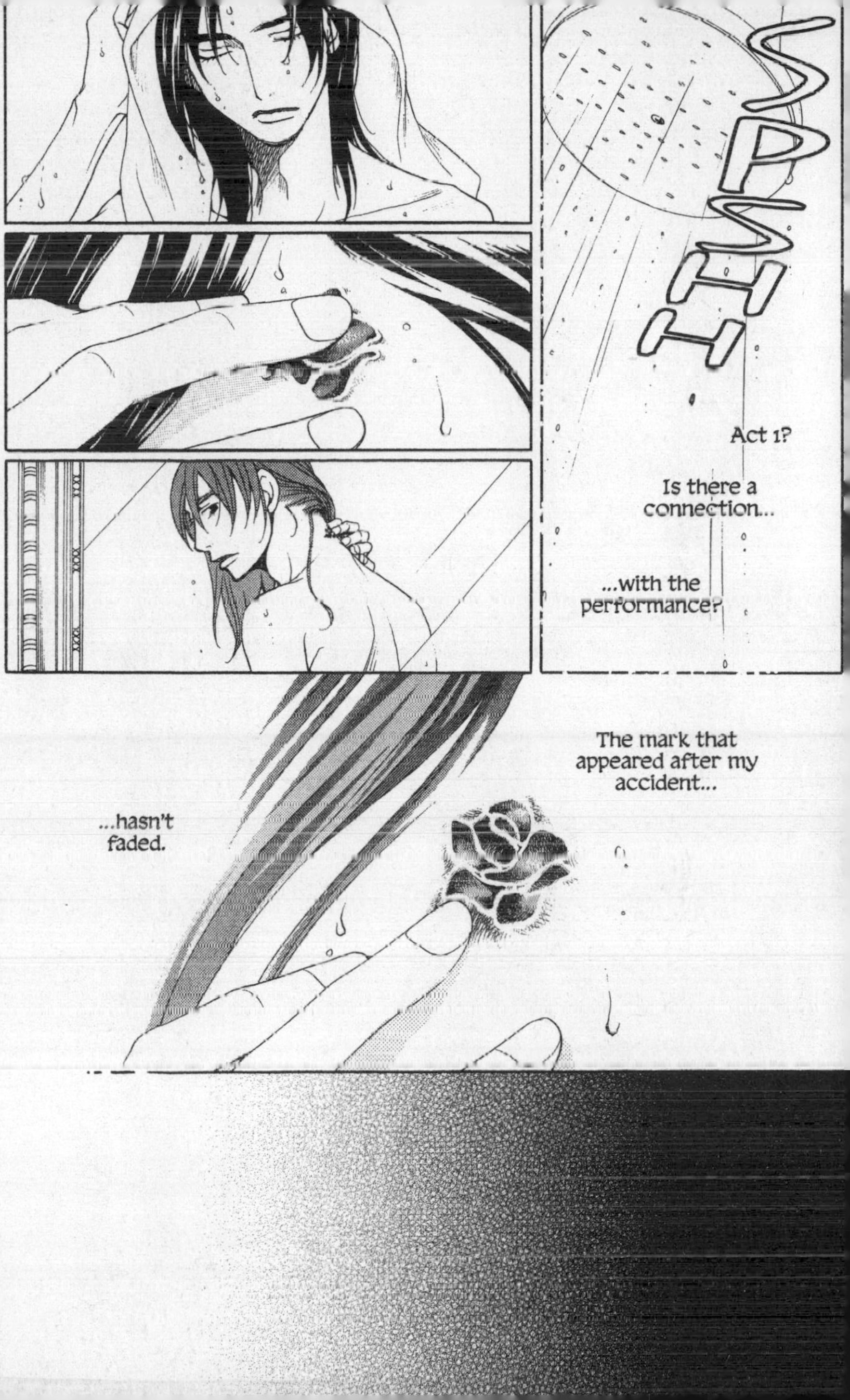
SPSSHH
Act 1?
Is there a connection...
...with the performance?
The mark that appeared after my accident...
...hasn't faded.

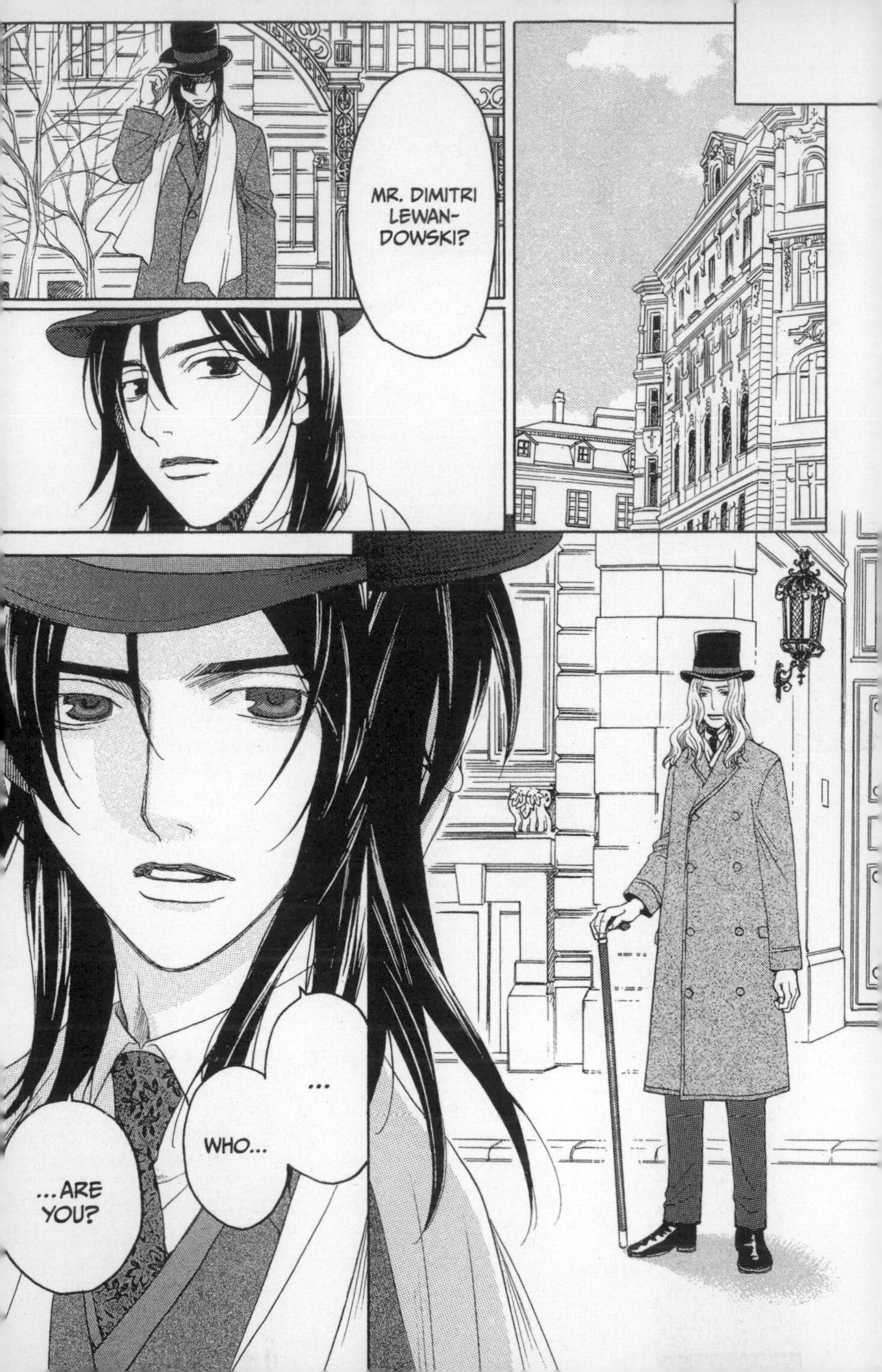
MR. DIMITRI LEWAN-DOWSKI?
...
WHO...
...ARE YOU?

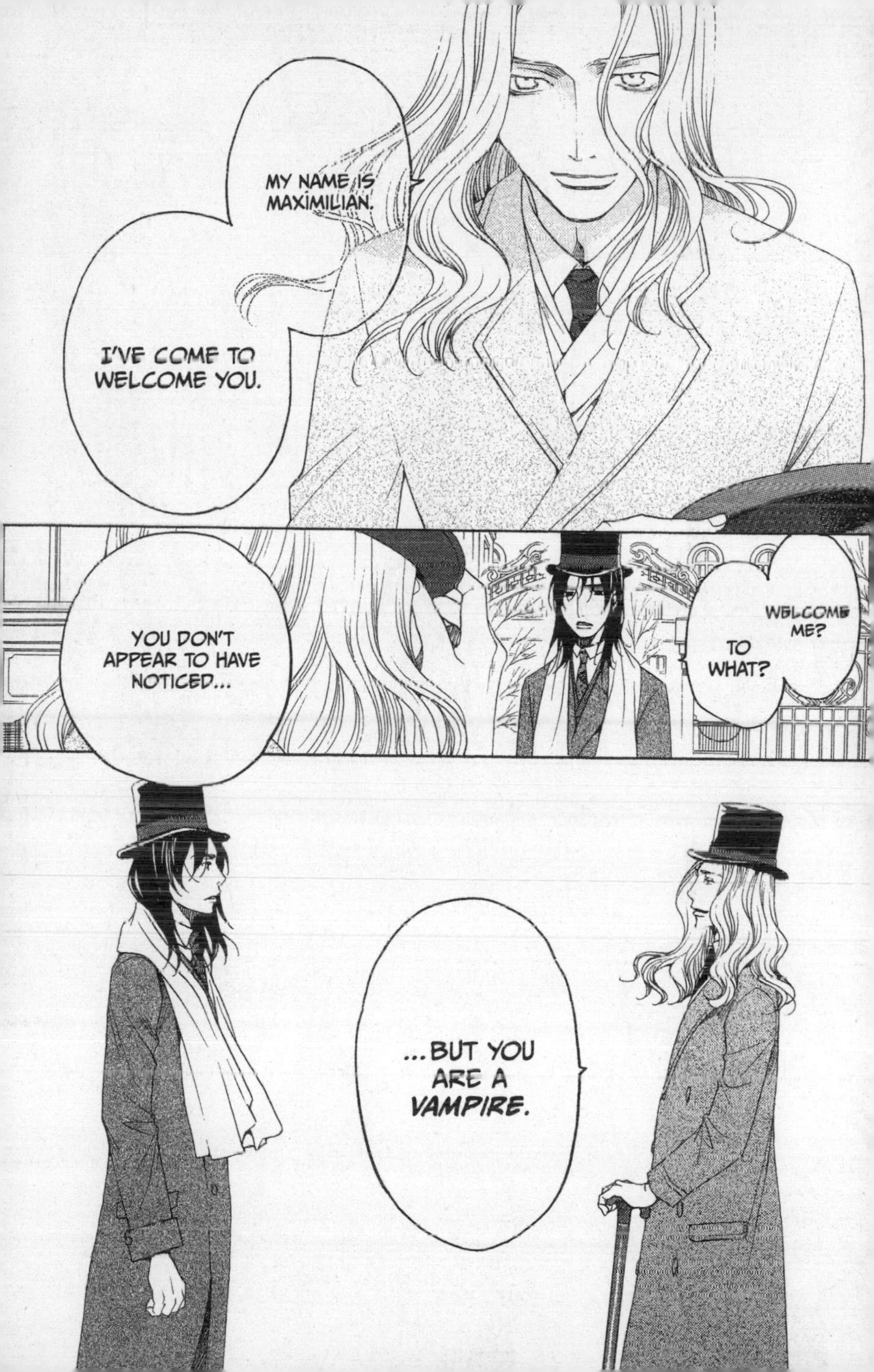
MY NAME IS MAXIMILIAN.
I'VE COME TO WELCOME YOU.
WELCOME ME? TO WHAT?
YOU DON'T APPEAR TO HAVE NOTICED...
...BUT YOU ARE A *VAMPIRE*.

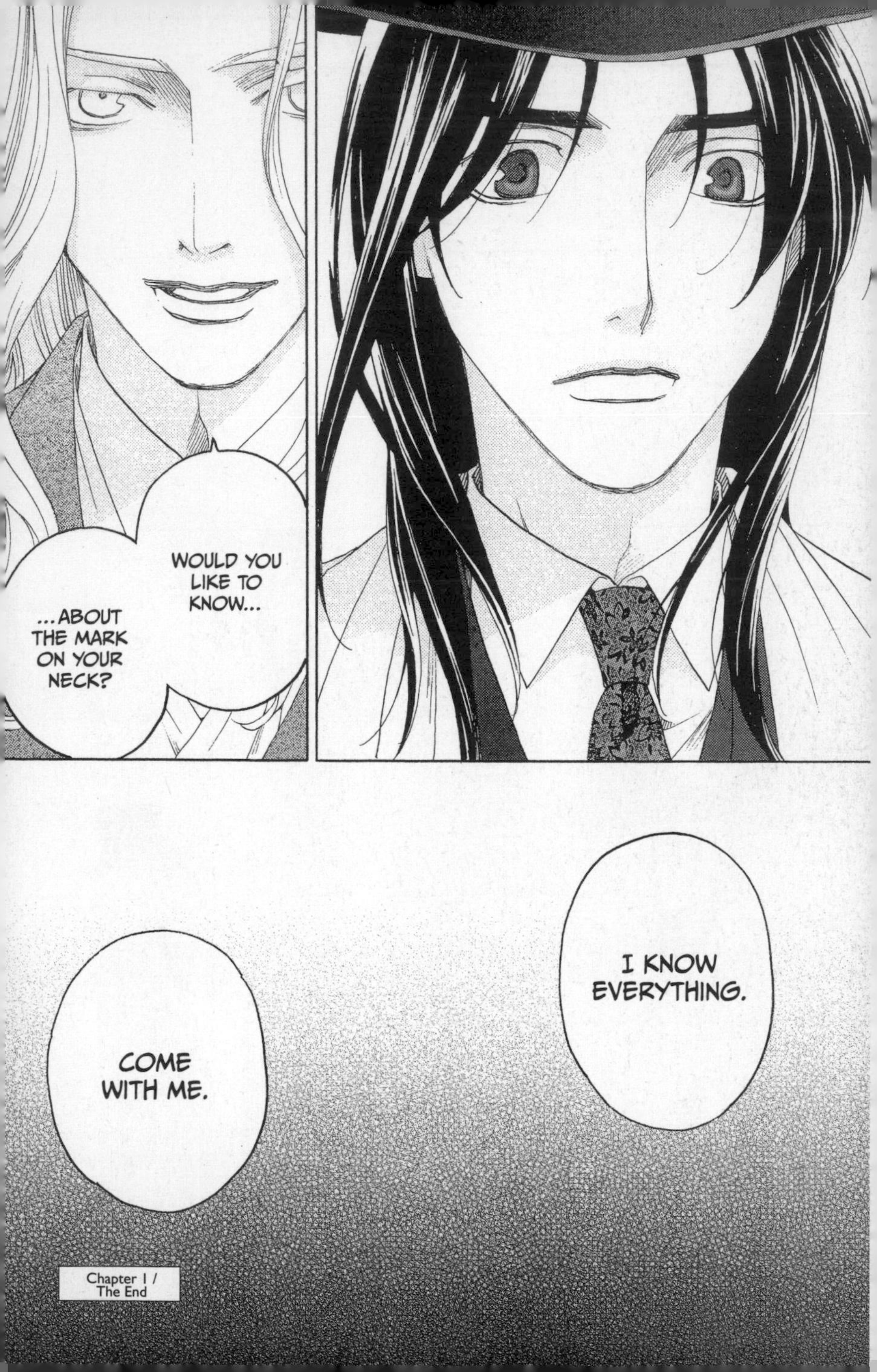
WOULD YOU LIKE TO KNOW...
...ABOUT THE MARK ON YOUR NECK?
I KNOW EVERYTHING.
COME WITH ME.
Chapter 1 / The End

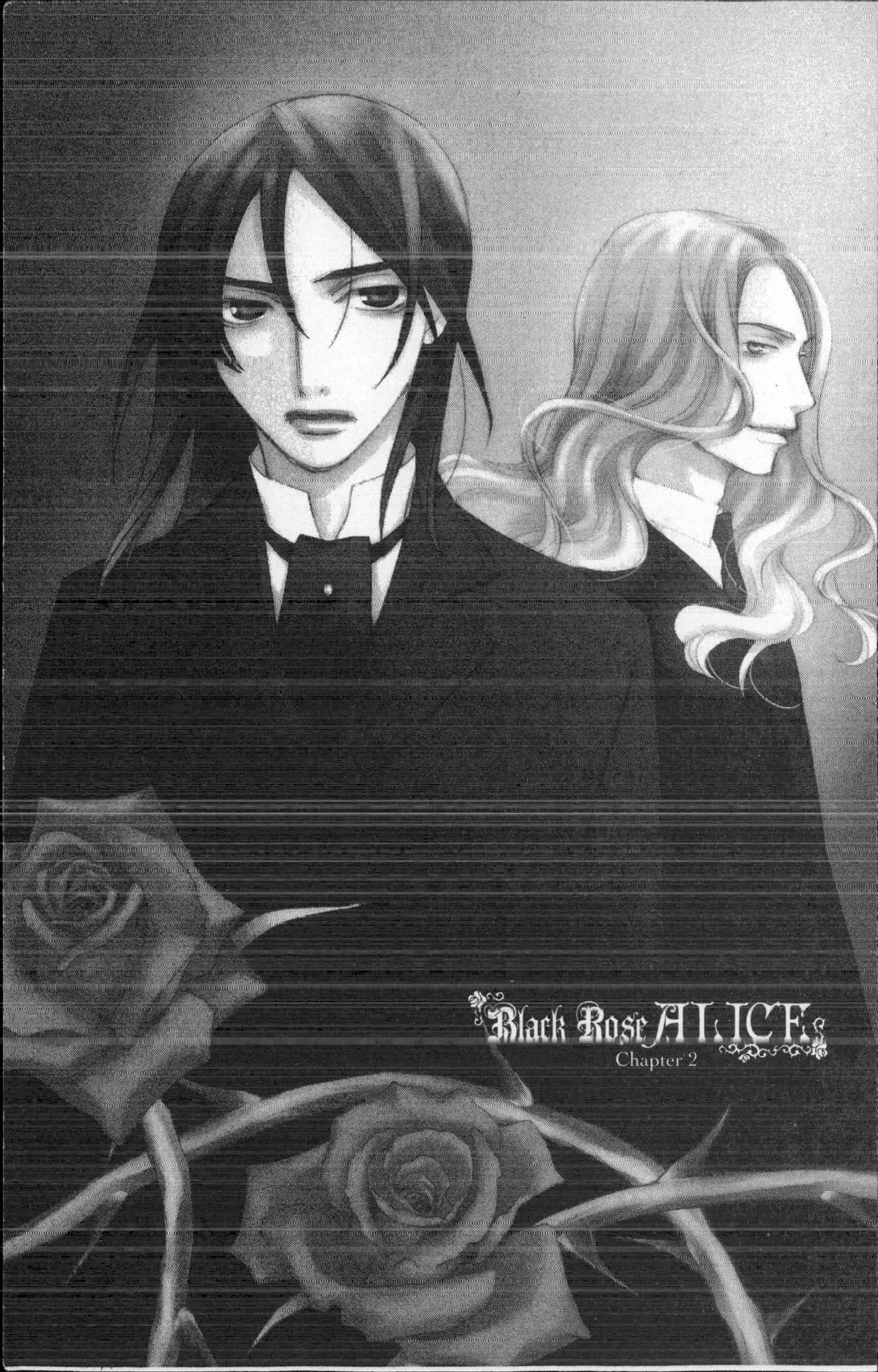
Black Rose ALICE
Chapter 2

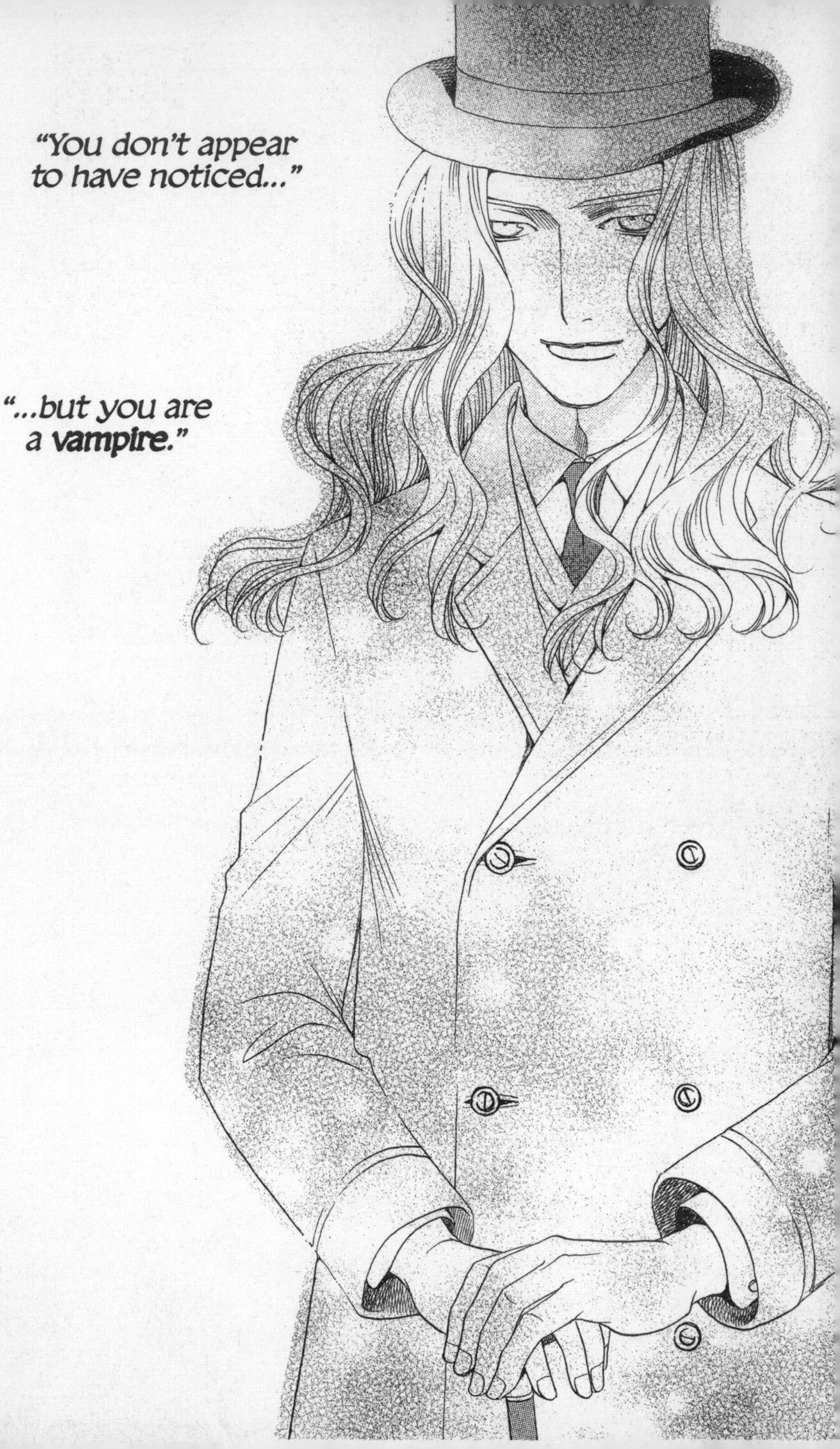
"You don't appear to have noticed..."
"...but you are a **vampire.**"

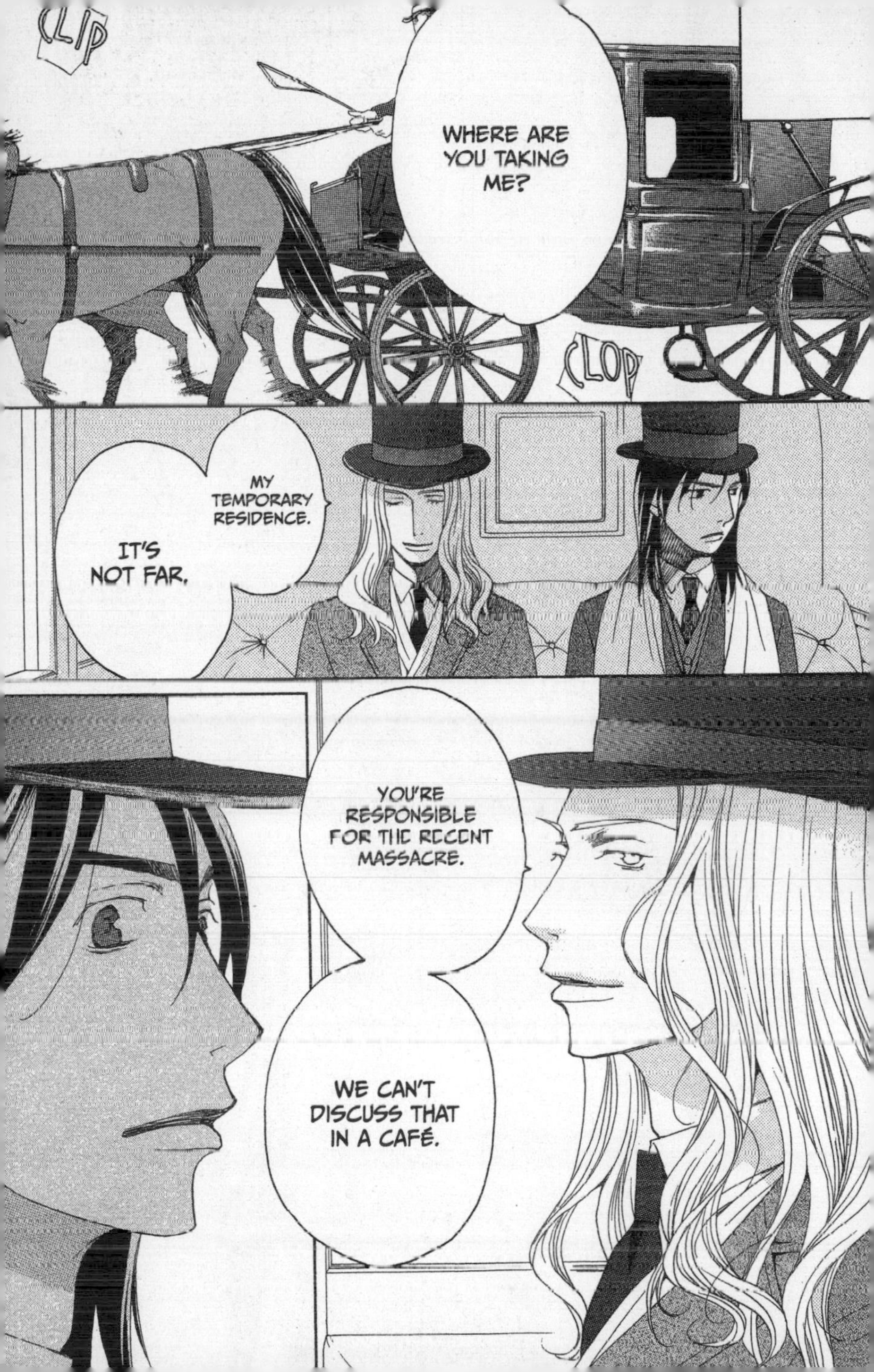
WHERE ARE YOU TAKING ME?
CLIP
CLOP
MY TEMPORARY RESIDENCE.
IT'S NOT FAR.
YOU'RE RESPONSIBLE FOR THE RECENT MASSACRE.
WE CAN'T DISCUSS THAT IN A CAFÉ.

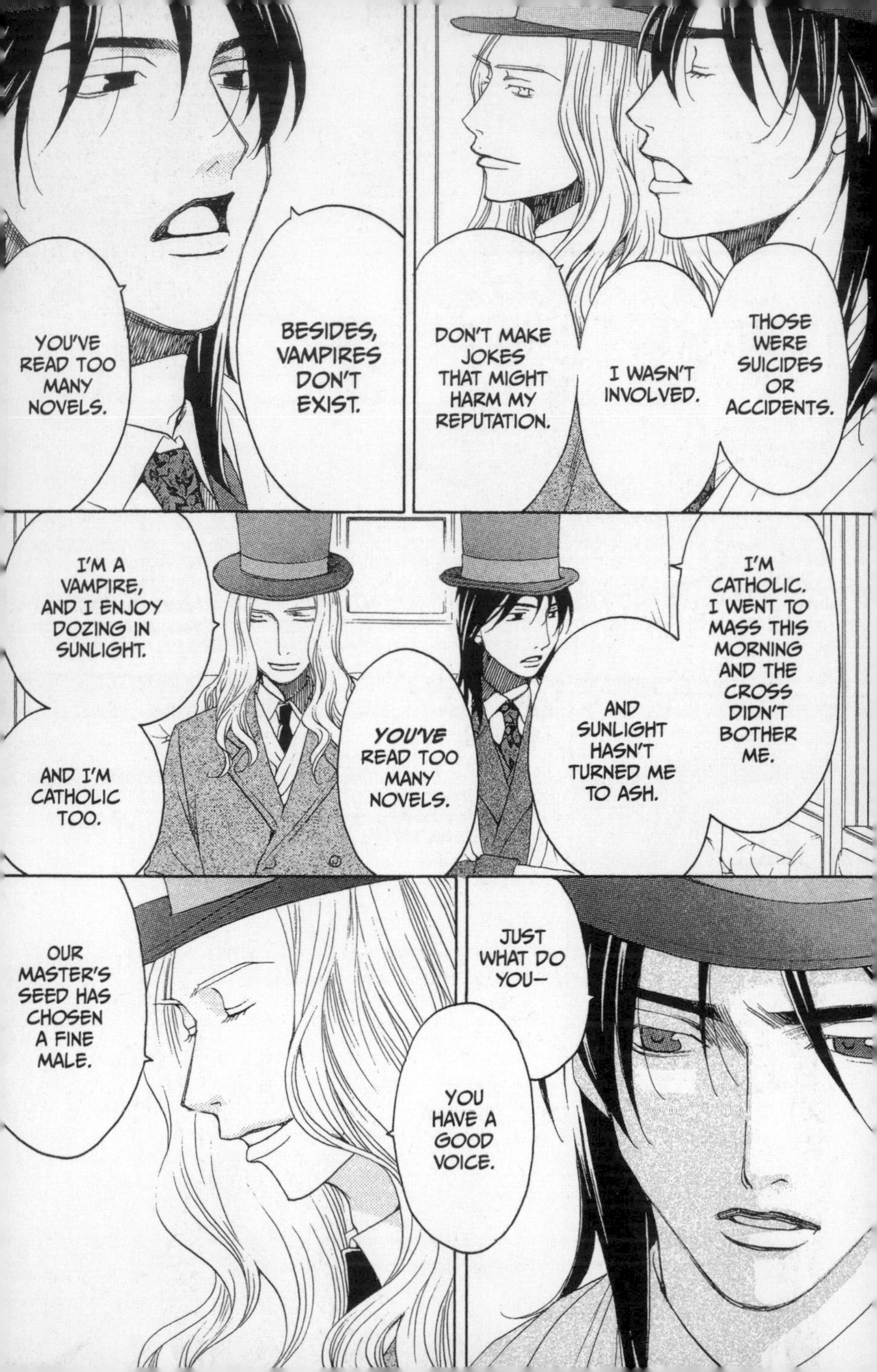
THOSE WERE SUICIDES OR ACCIDENTS.
I WASN'T INVOLVED.
DON'T MAKE JOKES THAT MIGHT HARM MY REPUTATION.
BESIDES, VAMPIRES DON'T EXIST.
YOU'VE READ TOO MANY NOVELS.
I'M CATHOLIC. I WENT TO MASS THIS MORNING AND THE CROSS DIDN'T BOTHER ME.
AND SUNLIGHT HASN'T TURNED ME TO ASH.
YOU'VE READ TOO MANY NOVELS.
I'M A VAMPIRE, AND I ENJOY DOZING IN SUNLIGHT.
AND I'M CATHOLIC TOO.
JUST WHAT DO YOU—
YOU HAVE A GOOD VOICE.
OUR MASTER'S SEED HAS CHOSEN A FINE MALE.

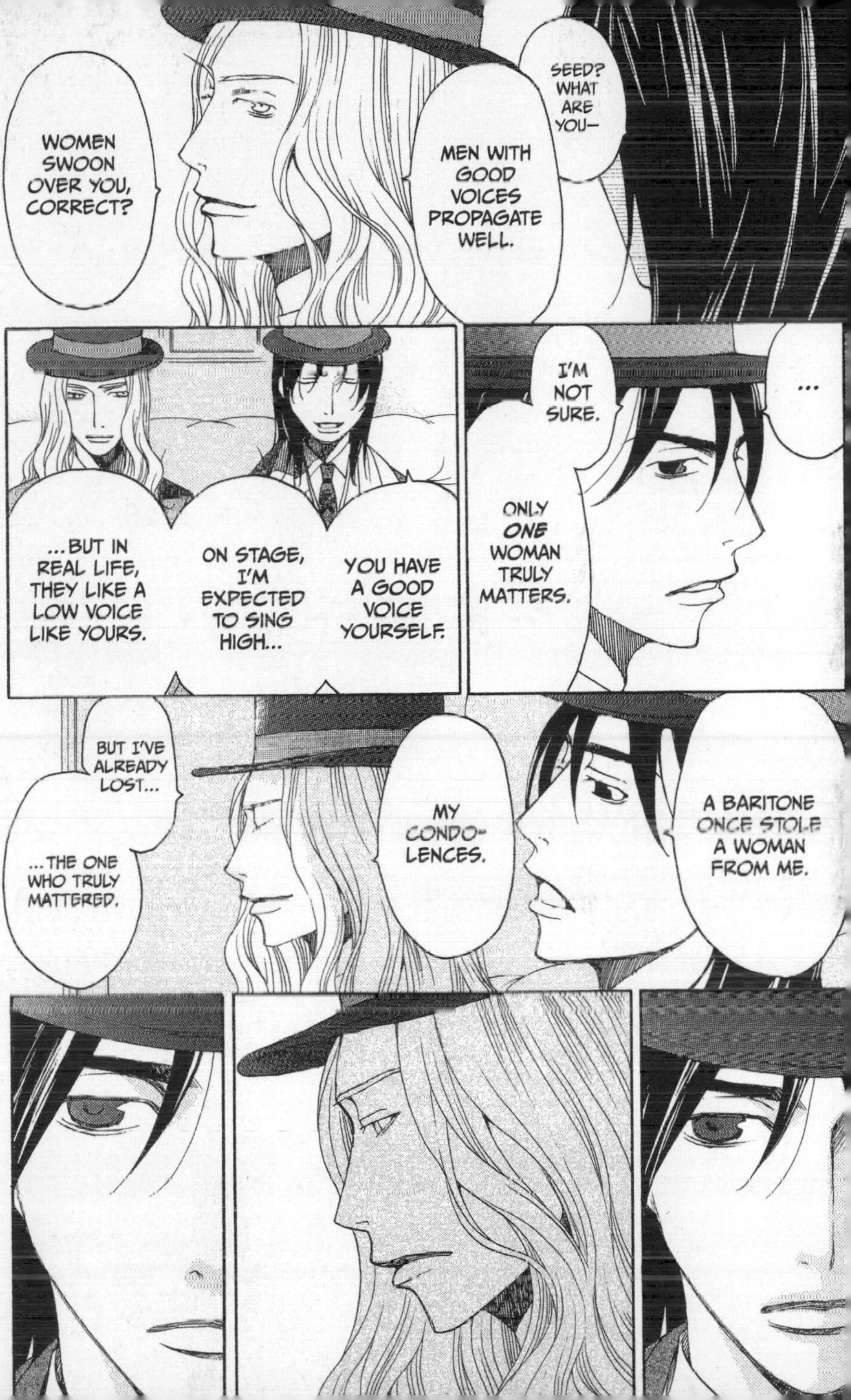
SEED? WHAT ARE YOU—
MEN WITH GOOD VOICES PROPAGATE WELL.
WOMEN SWOON OVER YOU, CORRECT?
...
I'M NOT SURE.
ONLY *ONE* WOMAN TRULY MATTERS.
YOU HAVE A GOOD VOICE YOURSELF.
ON STAGE, I'M EXPECTED TO SING HIGH...
...BUT IN REAL LIFE, THEY LIKE A LOW VOICE LIKE YOURS.
A BARITONE ONCE STOLE A WOMAN FROM ME.
MY CONDO-LENCES.
BUT I'VE ALREADY LOST...
...THE ONE WHO TRULY MATTERED.

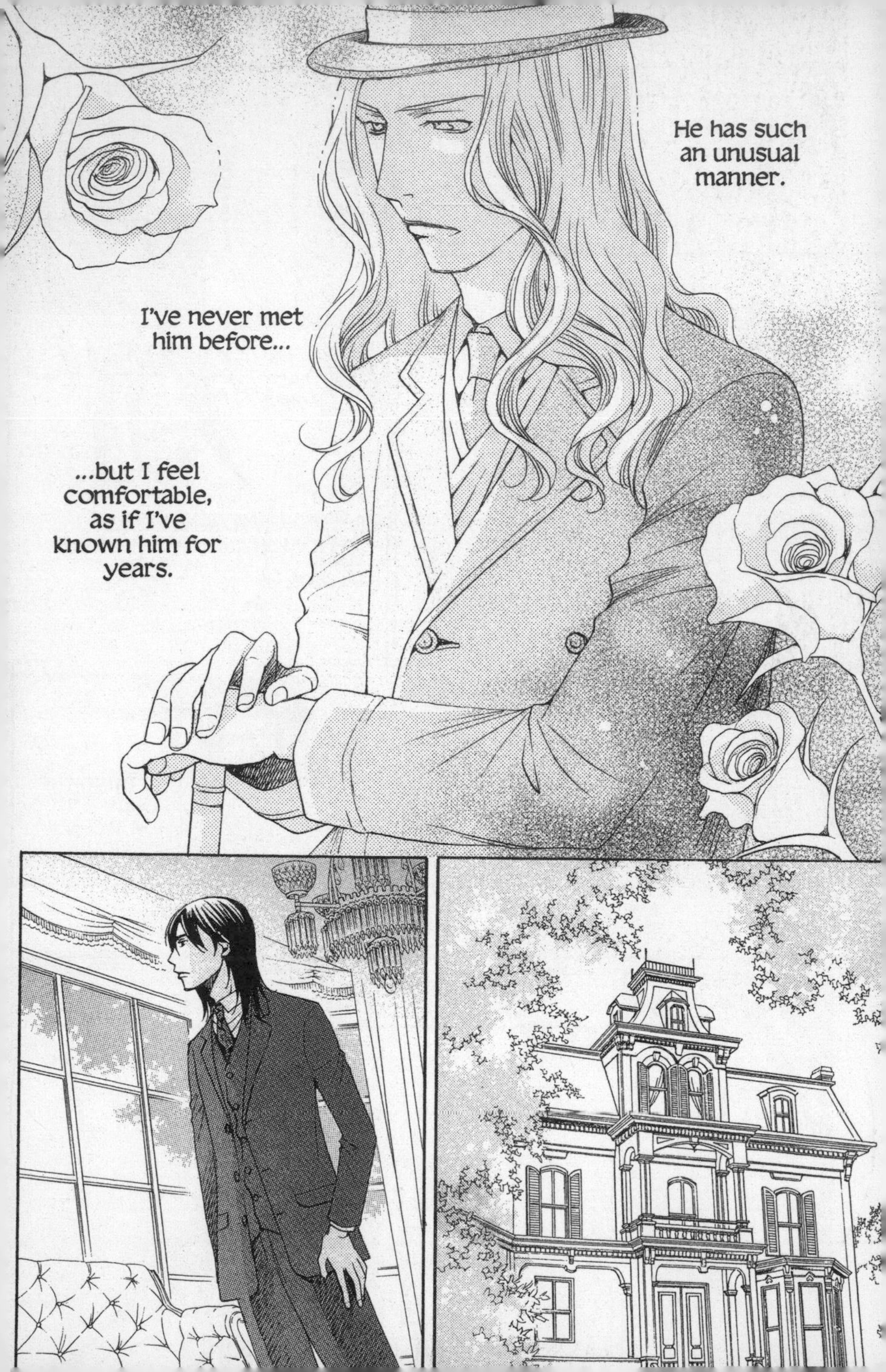
He has such an unusual manner.
I've never met him before...
...but I feel comfortable, as if I've known him for years.

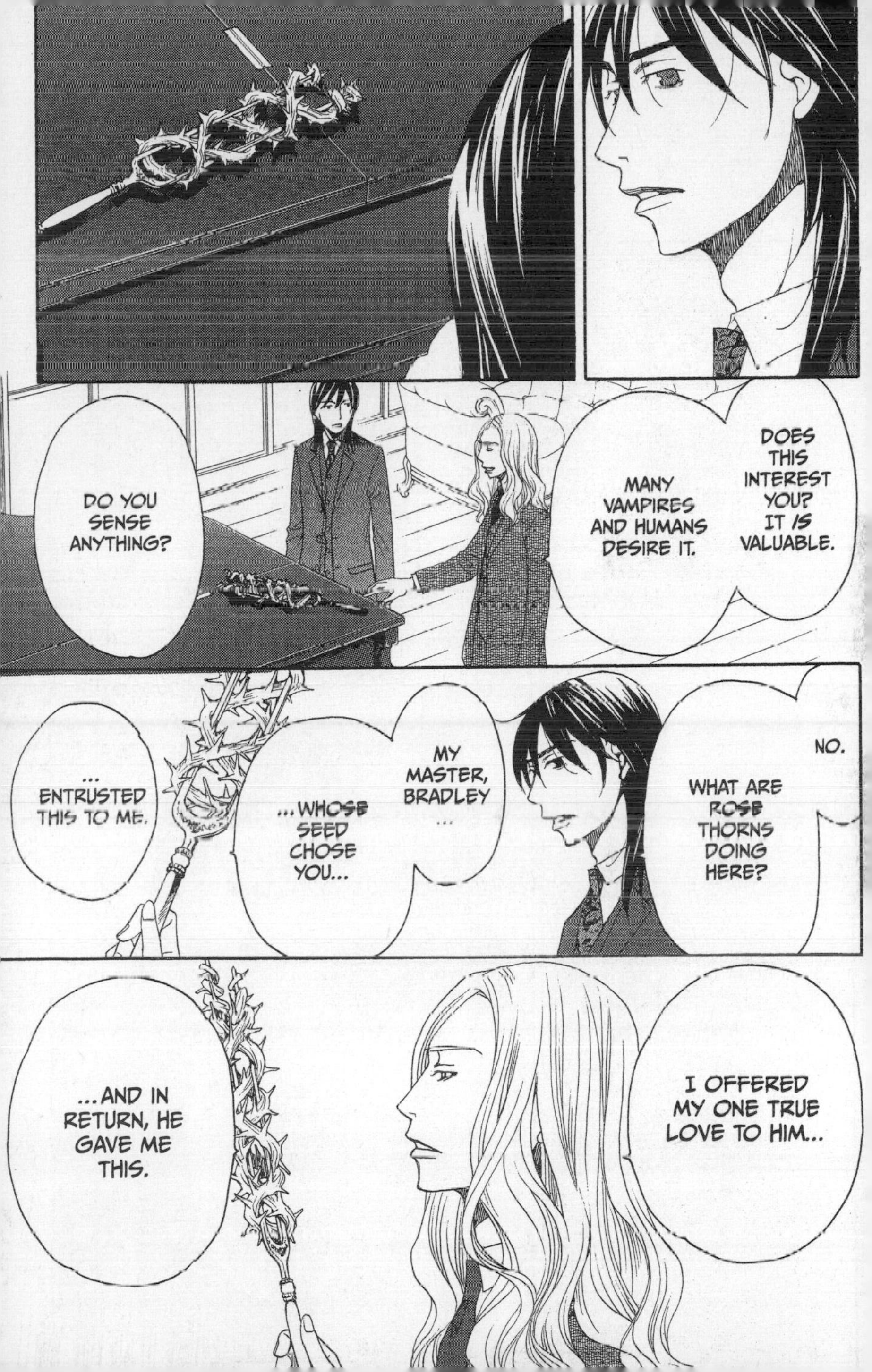
DOES THIS INTEREST YOU? IT *IS* VALUABLE.
MANY VAMPIRES AND HUMANS DESIRE IT.
DO YOU SENSE ANYTHING?
NO.
WHAT ARE ROSE THORNS DOING HERE?
MY MASTER, BRADLEY ...
...WHOSE SEED CHOSE YOU...
... ENTRUSTED THIS TO ME.
I OFFERED MY ONE TRUE LOVE TO HIM...
...AND IN RETURN, HE GAVE ME THIS.

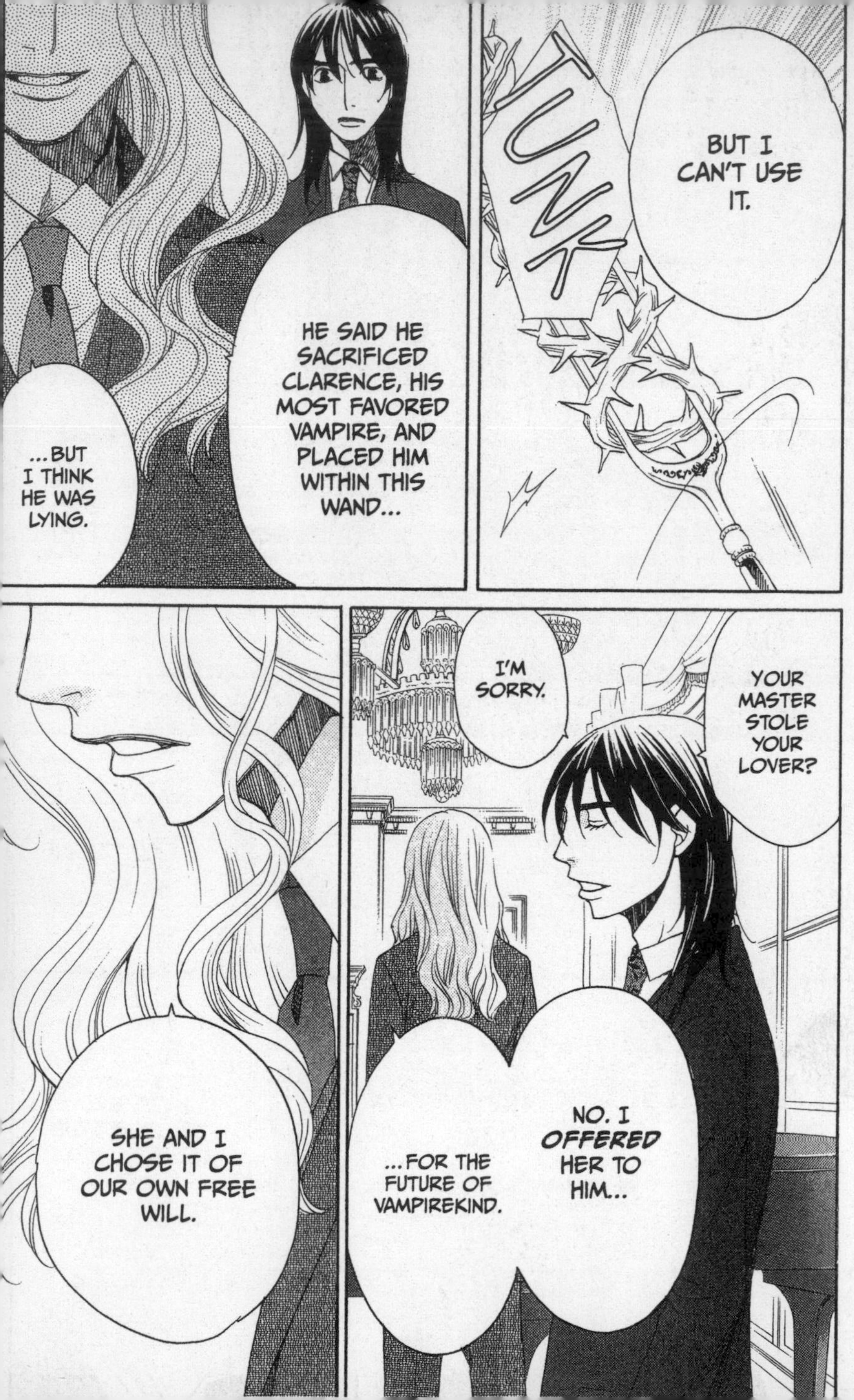
BUT I CAN'T USE IT.
TUNK
HE SAID HE SACRIFICED CLARENCE, HIS MOST FAVORED VAMPIRE, AND PLACED HIM WITHIN THIS WAND...
...BUT I THINK HE WAS LYING.
YOUR MASTER STOLE YOUR LOVER?
I'M SORRY.
NO. I *OFFERED* HER TO HIM...
...FOR THE FUTURE OF VAMPIREKIND.
SHE AND I CHOSE IT OF OUR OWN FREE WILL.

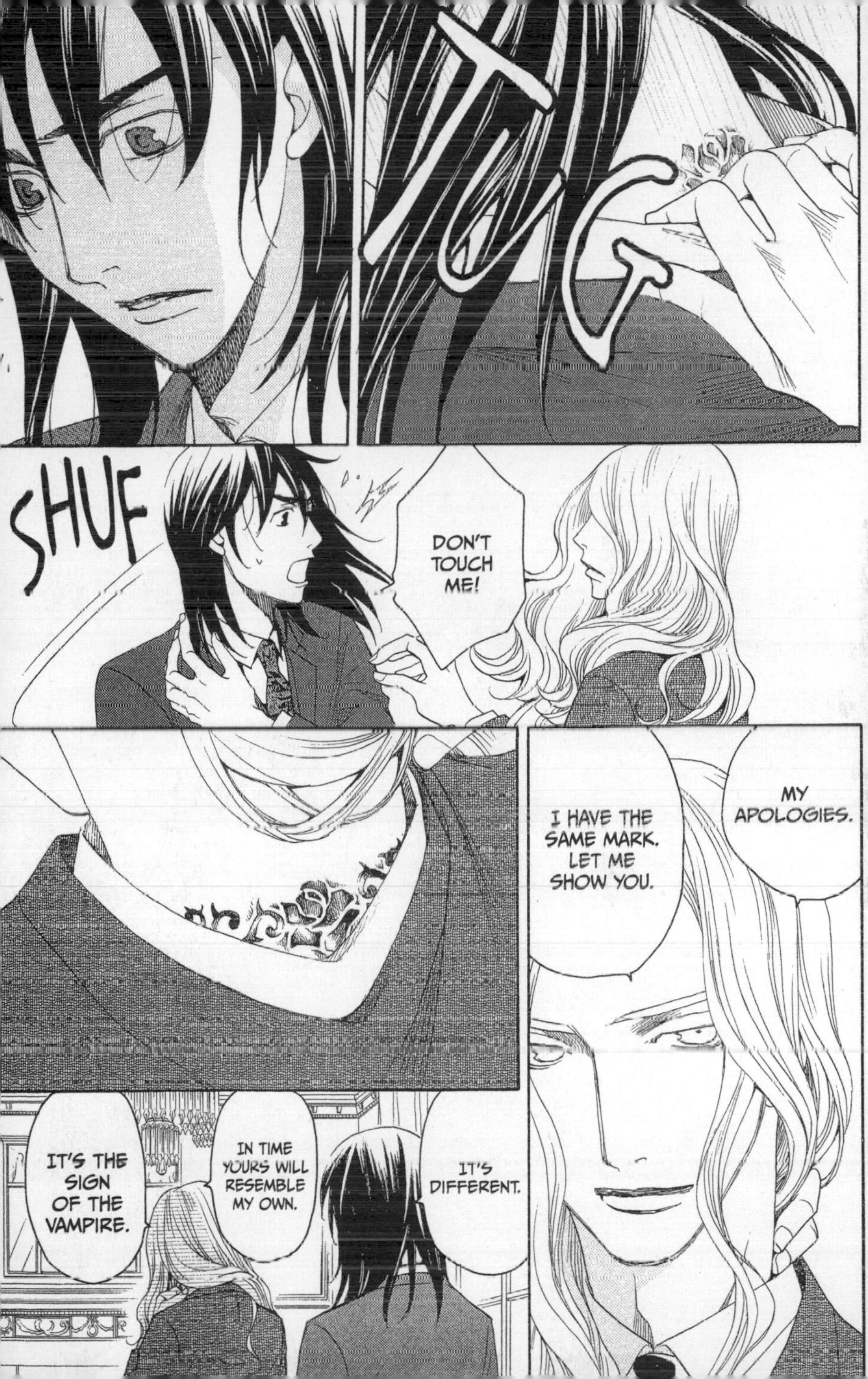
TUG
DON'T TOUCH ME!
SHUF
MY APOLOGIES.
I HAVE THE SAME MARK. LET ME SHOW YOU.
IT'S DIFFERENT.
IN TIME YOURS WILL RESEMBLE MY OWN.
IT'S THE SIGN OF THE VAMPIRE.

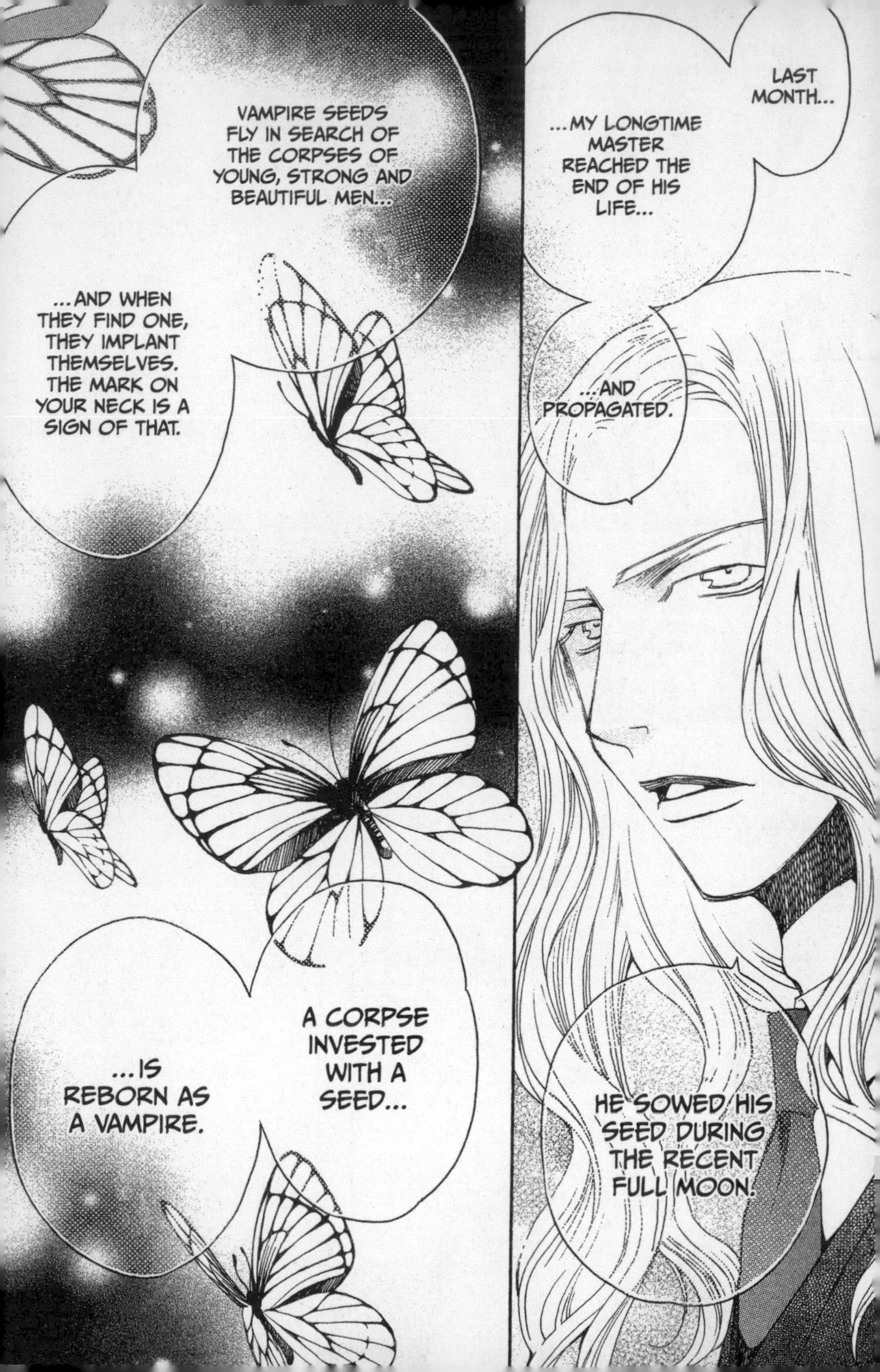
LAST MONTH...
...MY LONGTIME MASTER REACHED THE END OF HIS LIFE...
...AND PROPAGATED.
HE SOWED HIS SEED DURING THE RECENT FULL MOON.
VAMPIRE SEEDS FLY IN SEARCH OF THE CORPSES OF YOUNG, STRONG AND BEAUTIFUL MEN...
...AND WHEN THEY FIND ONE, THEY IMPLANT THEMSELVES. THE MARK ON YOUR NECK IS A SIGN OF THAT.
A CORPSE INVESTED WITH A SEED...
...IS REBORN AS A VAMPIRE.

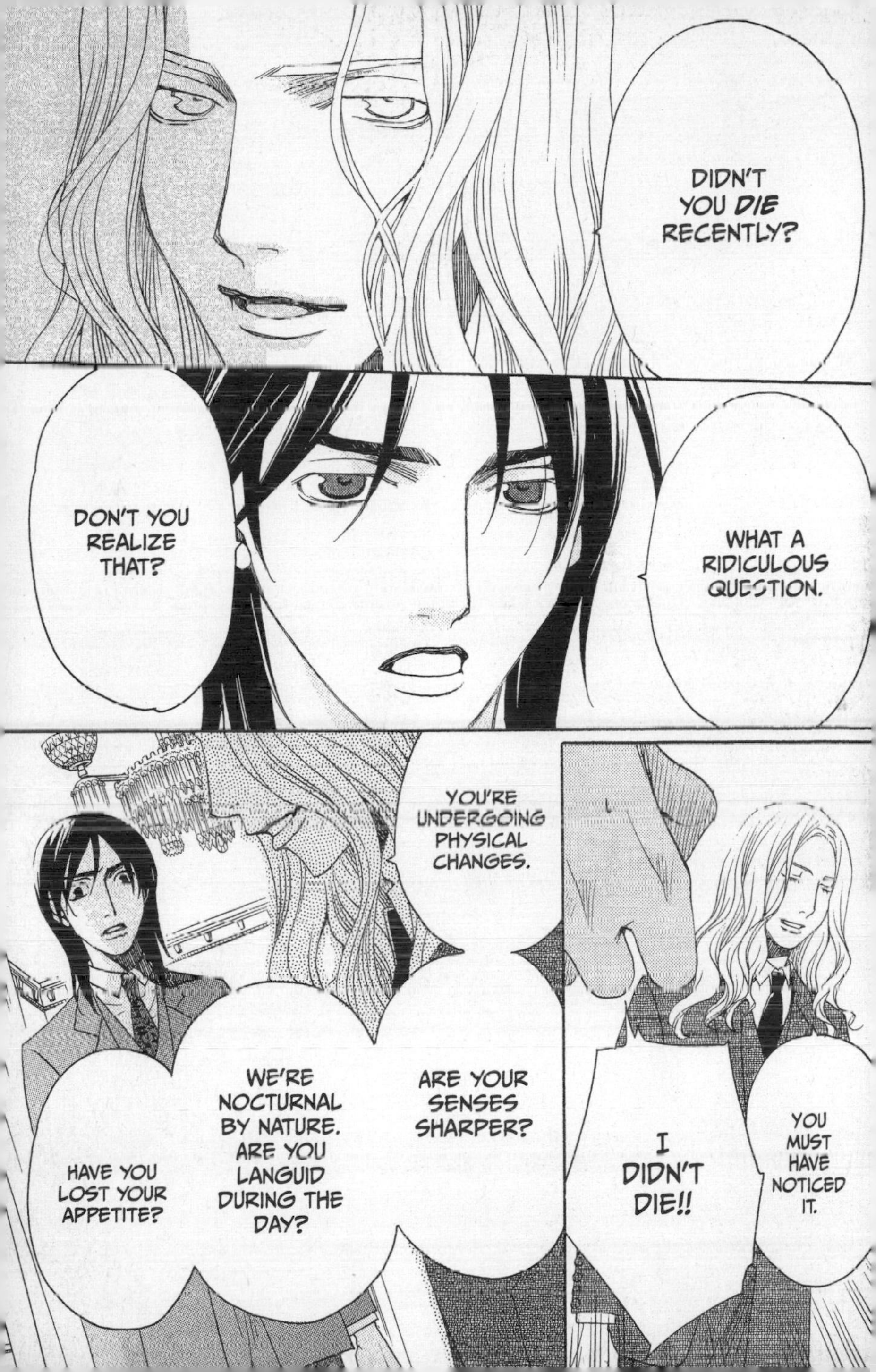
DIDN'T YOU *DIE* RECENTLY?
WHAT A RIDICULOUS QUESTION.
DON'T YOU REALIZE THAT?
YOU MUST HAVE NOTICED IT.
I DIDN'T DIE!!
YOU'RE UNDERGOING PHYSICAL CHANGES.
ARE YOUR SENSES SHARPER?
WE'RE NOCTURNAL BY NATURE. ARE YOU LANGUID DURING THE DAY?
HAVE YOU LOST YOUR APPETITE?

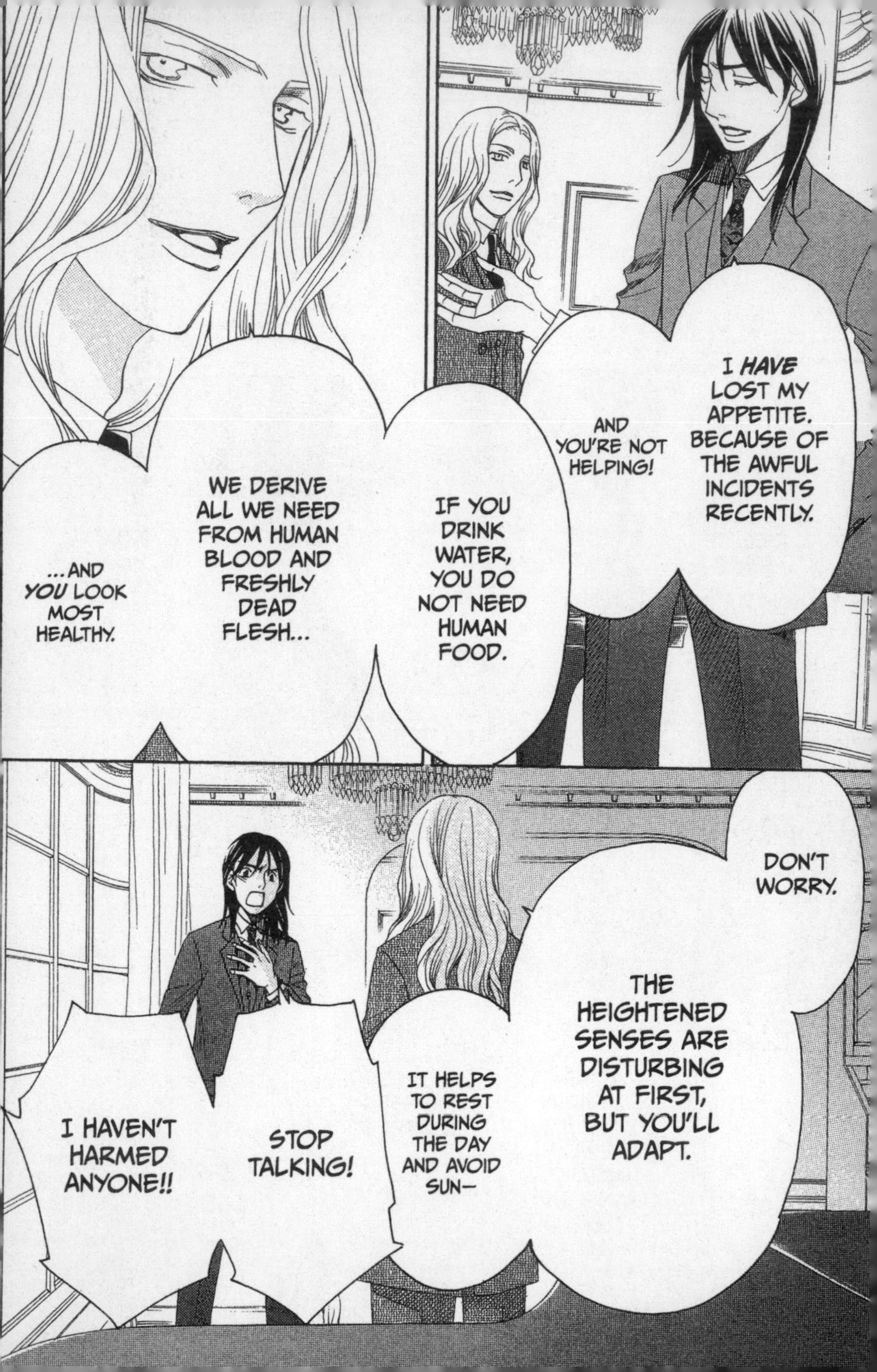
I *HAVE* LOST MY APPETITE. BECAUSE OF THE AWFUL INCIDENTS RECENTLY.
AND YOU'RE NOT HELPING!
IF YOU DRINK WATER, YOU DO NOT NEED HUMAN FOOD.
WE DERIVE ALL WE NEED FROM HUMAN BLOOD AND FRESHLY DEAD FLESH...
...AND *YOU* LOOK MOST HEALTHY.
DON'T WORRY.
THE HEIGHTENED SENSES ARE DISTURBING AT FIRST, BUT YOU'LL ADAPT.
IT HELPS TO REST DURING THE DAY AND AVOID SUN—
STOP TALKING!
I HAVEN'T HARMED ANYONE!!

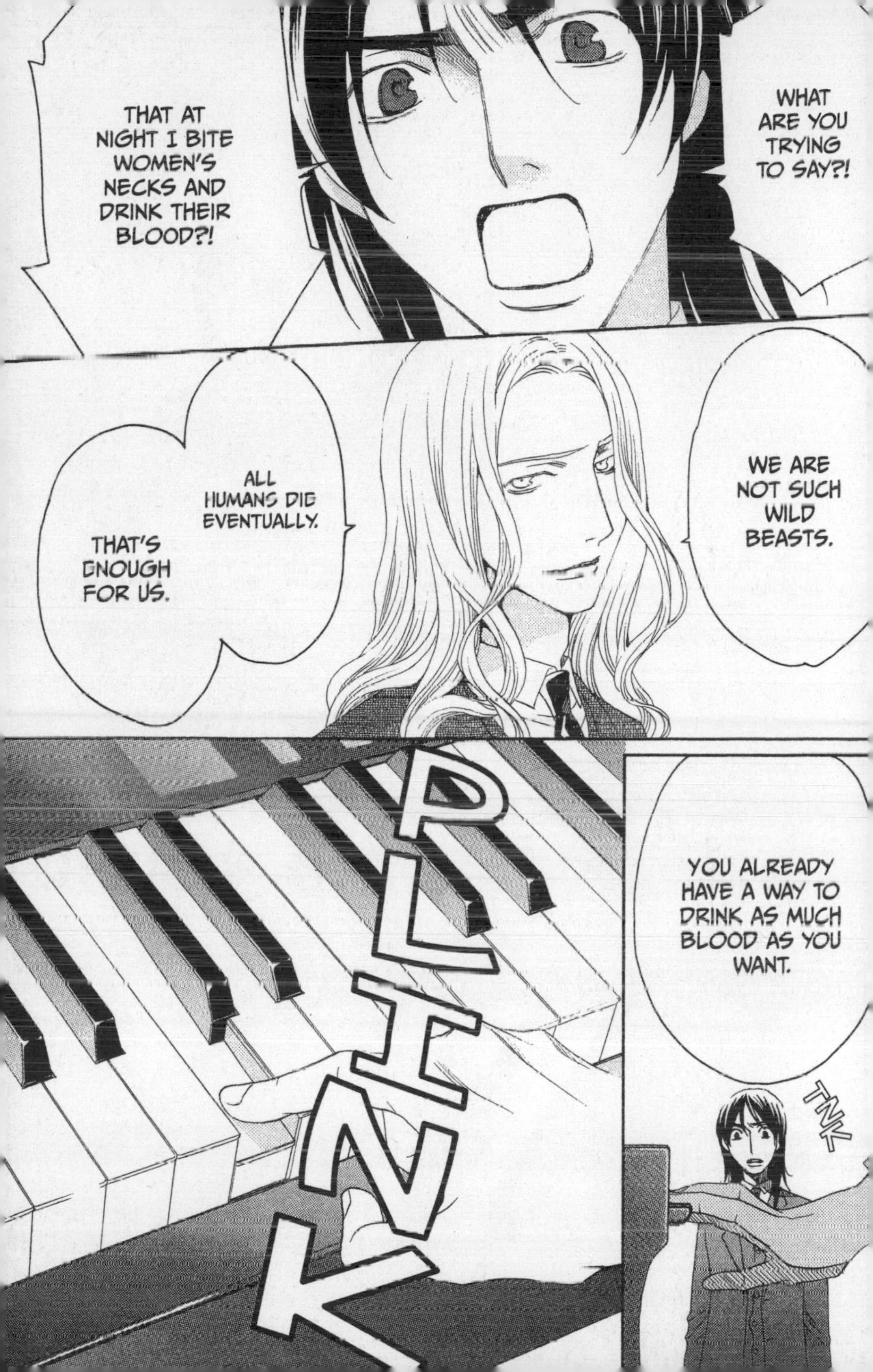
WHAT ARE YOU TRYING TO SAY?!
THAT AT NIGHT I BITE WOMEN'S NECKS AND DRINK THEIR BLOOD?!
WE ARE NOT SUCH WILD BEASTS.
ALL HUMANS DIE EVENTUALLY.
THAT'S ENOUGH FOR US.
YOU ALREADY HAVE A WAY TO DRINK AS MUCH BLOOD AS YOU WANT.
TNK
PLINK

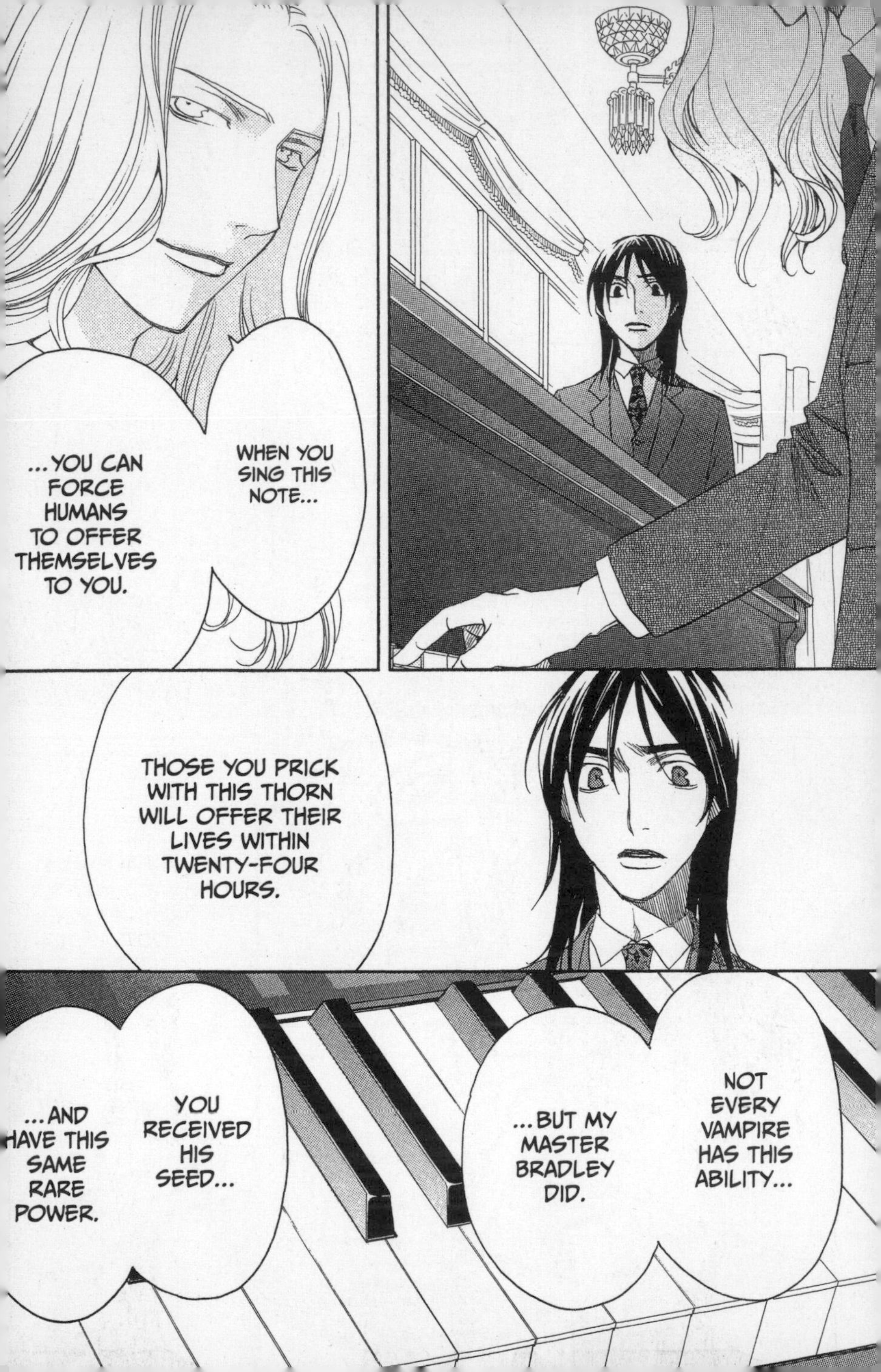
WHEN YOU SING THIS NOTE...
...YOU CAN FORCE HUMANS TO OFFER THEMSELVES TO YOU.
THOSE YOU PRICK WITH THIS THORN WILL OFFER THEIR LIVES WITHIN TWENTY-FOUR HOURS.
NOT EVERY VAMPIRE HAS THIS ABILITY...
...BUT MY MASTER BRADLEY DID.
YOU RECEIVED HIS SEED...
...AND HAVE THIS SAME RARE POWER.

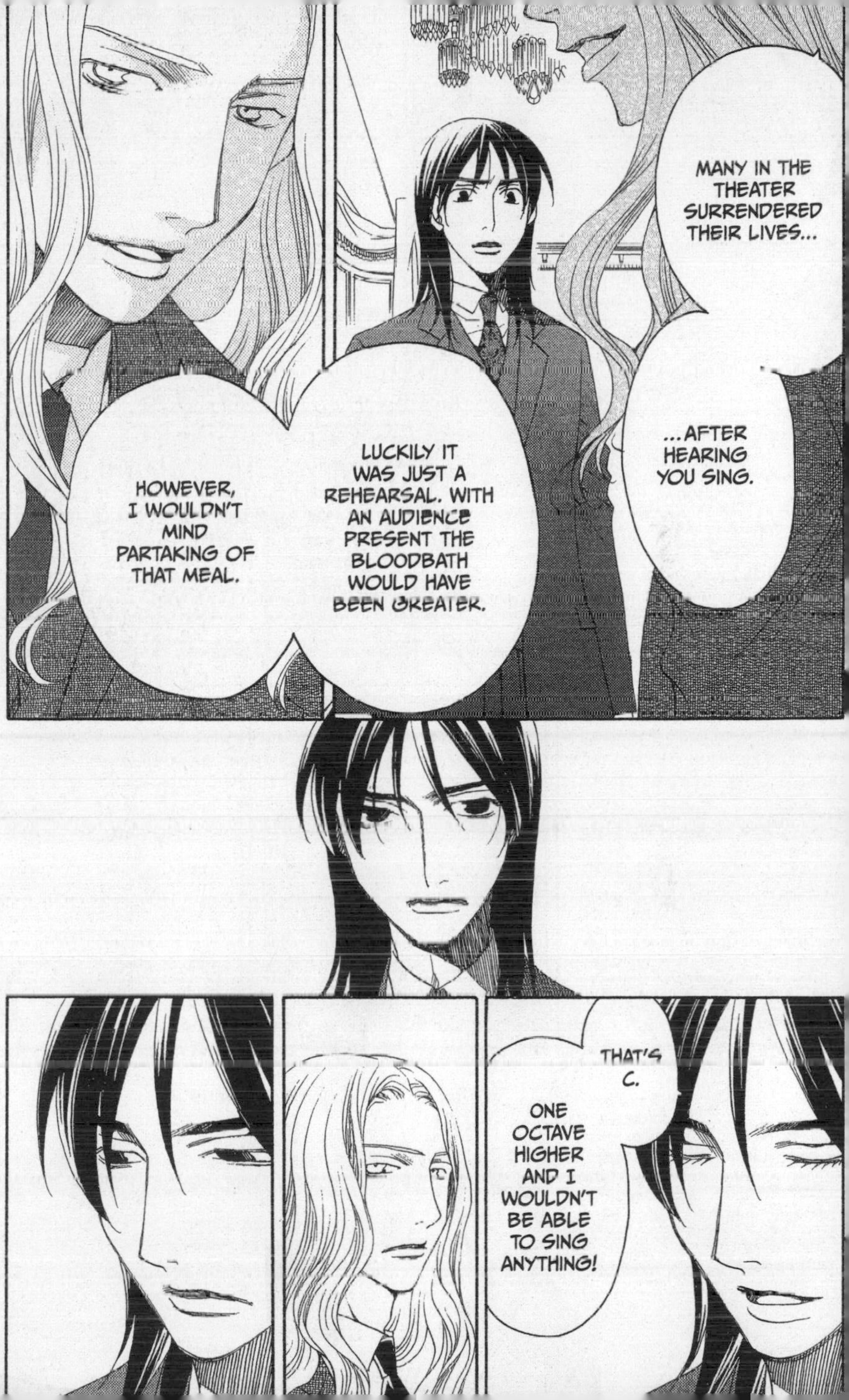
MANY IN THE THEATER SURRENDERED THEIR LIVES...
...AFTER HEARING YOU SING.
LUCKILY IT WAS JUST A REHEARSAL. WITH AN AUDIENCE PRESENT THE BLOODBATH WOULD HAVE BEEN GREATER.
HOWEVER, I WOULDN'T MIND PARTAKING OF THAT MEAL.
THAT'S C.
ONE OCTAVE HIGHER AND I WOULDN'T BE ABLE TO SING ANYTHING!

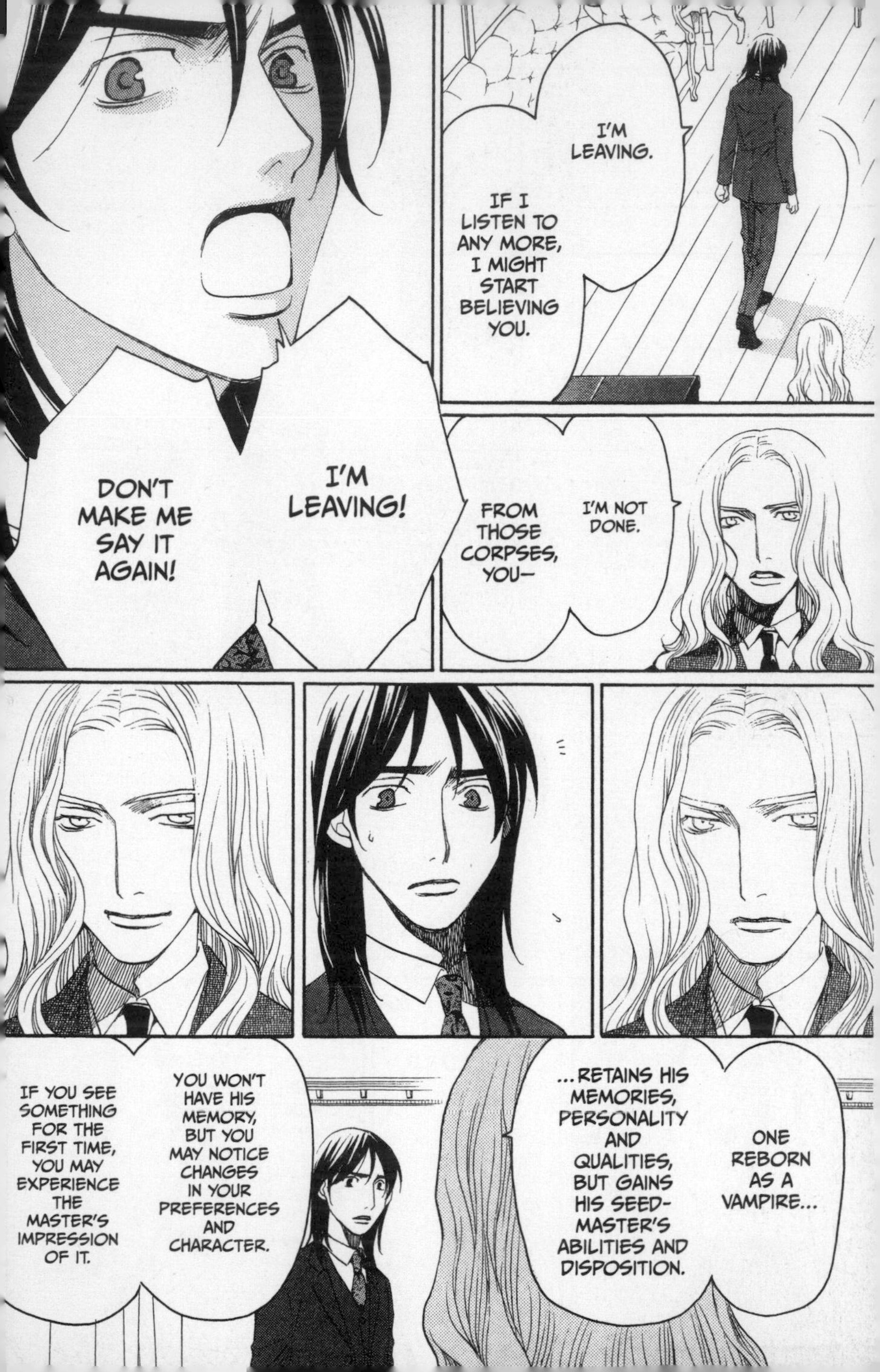
I'M LEAVING.
IF I LISTEN TO ANY MORE, I MIGHT START BELIEVING YOU.
I'M NOT DONE.
FROM THOSE CORPSES, YOU—
I'M LEAVING!
DON'T MAKE ME SAY IT AGAIN!
ONE REBORN AS A VAMPIRE...
...RETAINS HIS MEMORIES, PERSONALITY AND QUALITIES, BUT GAINS HIS SEED-MASTER'S ABILITIES AND DISPOSITION.
YOU WON'T HAVE HIS MEMORY, BUT YOU MAY NOTICE CHANGES IN YOUR PREFERENCES AND CHARACTER.
IF YOU SEE SOMETHING FOR THE FIRST TIME, YOU MAY EXPERIENCE THE MASTER'S IMPRESSION OF IT.

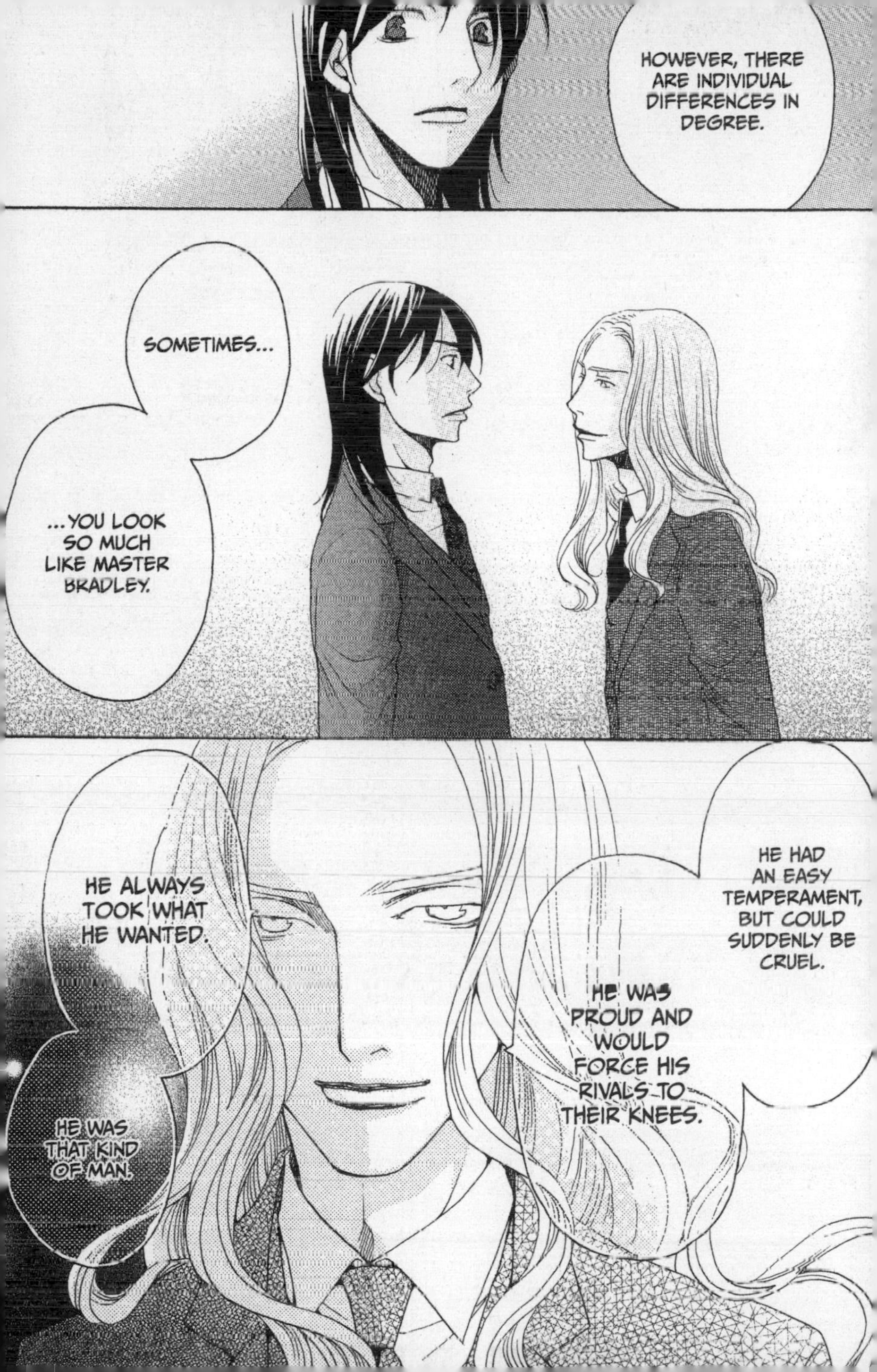
HOWEVER, THERE ARE INDIVIDUAL DIFFERENCES IN DEGREE.
SOMETIMES...
...YOU LOOK SO MUCH LIKE MASTER BRADLEY.
HE HAD AN EASY TEMPERAMENT, BUT COULD SUDDENLY BE CRUEL.
HE WAS PROUD AND WOULD FORCE HIS RIVALS TO THEIR KNEES.
HE ALWAYS TOOK WHAT HE WANTED.
HE WAS THAT KIND OF MAN.

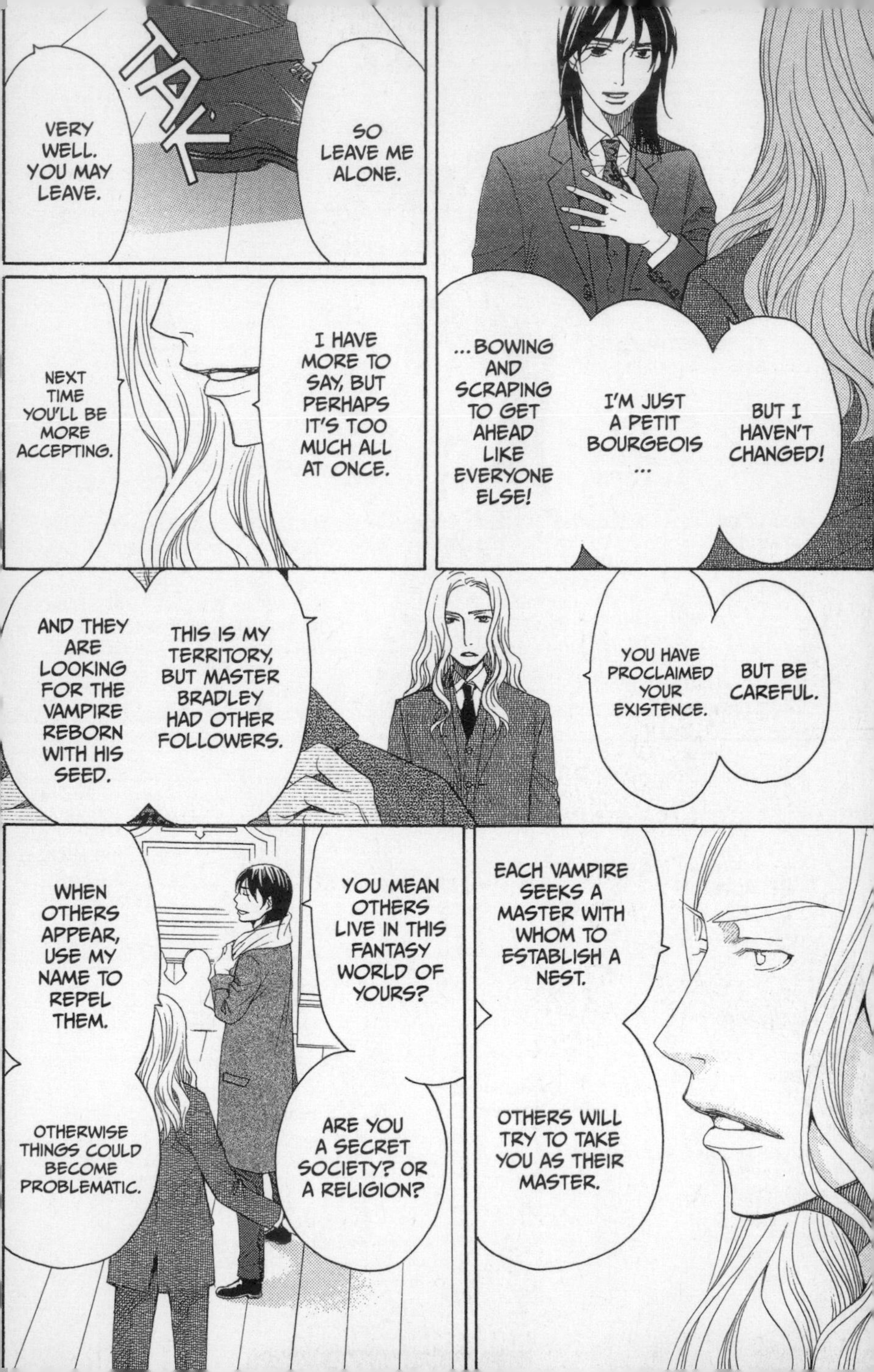

BUT I HAVEN'T CHANGED!
I'M JUST A PETIT BOURGEOIS ...
...BOWING AND SCRAPING TO GET AHEAD LIKE EVERYONE ELSE!
SO LEAVE ME ALONE.
TAK
VERY WELL. YOU MAY LEAVE.
I HAVE MORE TO SAY, BUT PERHAPS IT'S TOO MUCH ALL AT ONCE.
NEXT TIME YOU'LL BE MORE ACCEPTING.
BUT BE CAREFUL.
YOU HAVE PROCLAIMED YOUR EXISTENCE.
THIS IS MY TERRITORY, BUT MASTER BRADLEY HAD OTHER FOLLOWERS.
AND THEY ARE LOOKING FOR THE VAMPIRE REBORN WITH HIS SEED.
EACH VAMPIRE SEEKS A MASTER WITH WHOM TO ESTABLISH A NEST.
OTHERS WILL TRY TO TAKE YOU AS THEIR MASTER.
YOU MEAN OTHERS LIVE IN THIS FANTASY WORLD OF YOURS?
ARE YOU A SECRET SOCIETY? OR A RELIGION?
WHEN OTHERS APPEAR, USE MY NAME TO REPEL THEM.
OTHERWISE THINGS COULD BECOME PROBLEMATIC.

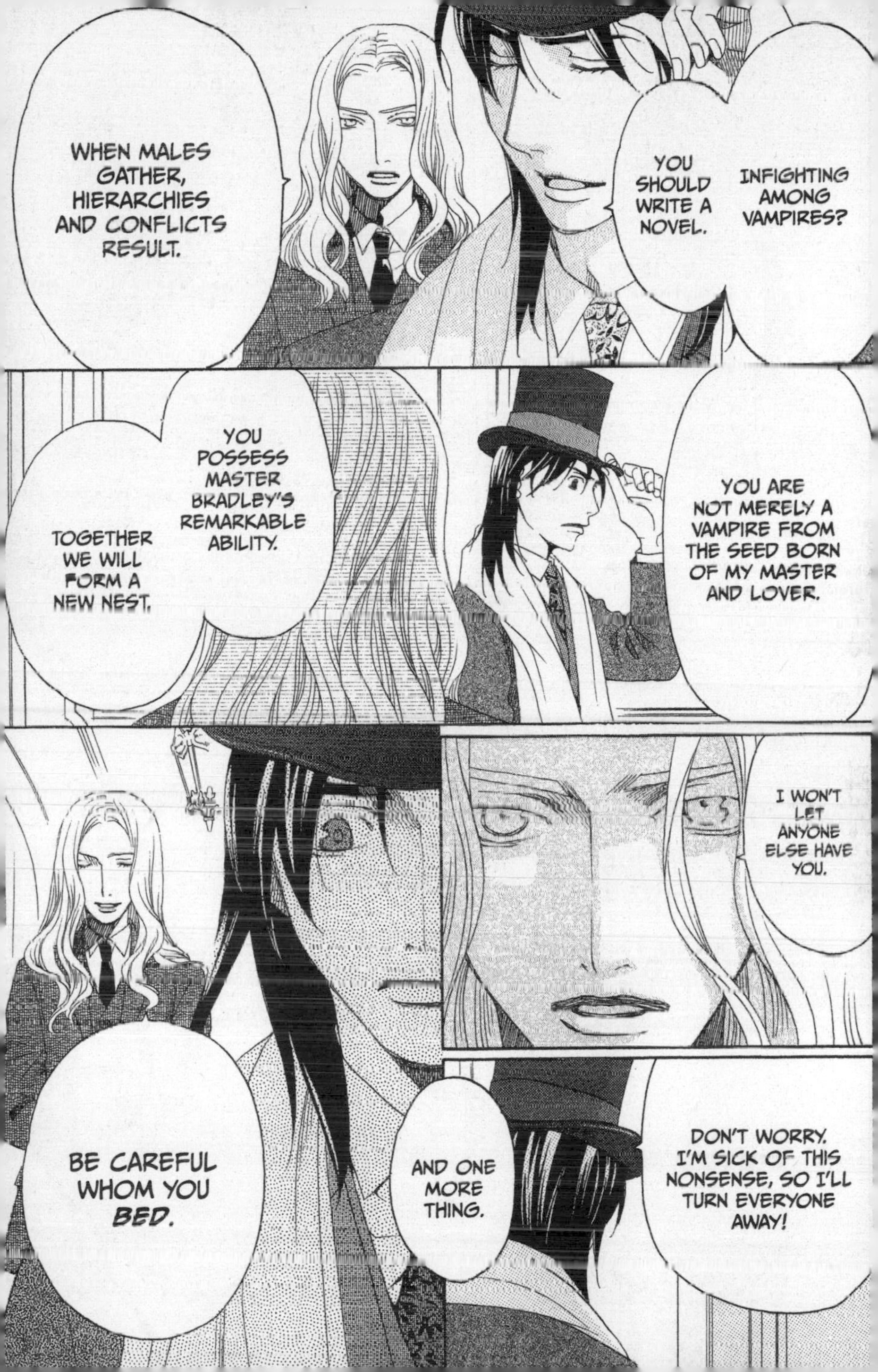
INFIGHTING AMONG VAMPIRES?
YOU SHOULD WRITE A NOVEL.
WHEN MALES GATHER, HIERARCHIES AND CONFLICTS RESULT.
YOU ARE NOT MERELY A VAMPIRE FROM THE SEED BORN OF MY MASTER AND LOVER.
YOU POSSESS MASTER BRADLEY'S REMARKABLE ABILITY.
TOGETHER WE WILL FORM A NEW NEST.
I WON'T LET ANYONE ELSE HAVE YOU.
DON'T WORRY. I'M SICK OF THIS NONSENSE, SO I'LL TURN EVERYONE AWAY!
AND ONE MORE THING.
BE CAREFUL WHOM YOU *BED*.

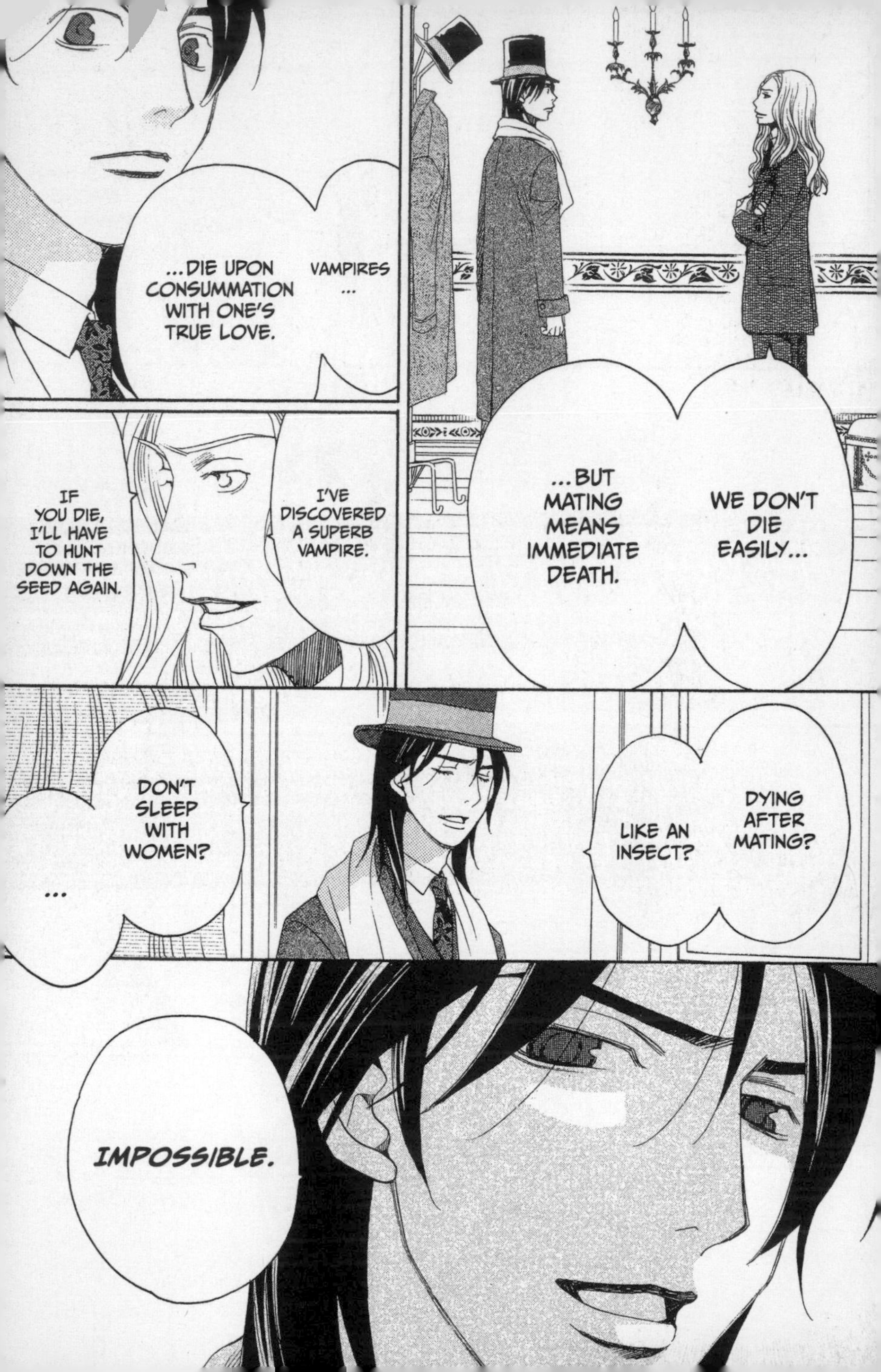
WE DON'T DIE EASILY...
...BUT MATING MEANS IMMEDIATE DEATH.
VAMPIRES...
...DIE UPON CONSUMMATION WITH ONE'S TRUE LOVE.
I'VE DISCOVERED A SUPERB VAMPIRE.
IF YOU DIE, I'LL HAVE TO HUNT DOWN THE SEED AGAIN.
DYING AFTER MATING?
LIKE AN INSECT?
DON'T SLEEP WITH WOMEN?
...
IMPOSSIBLE.

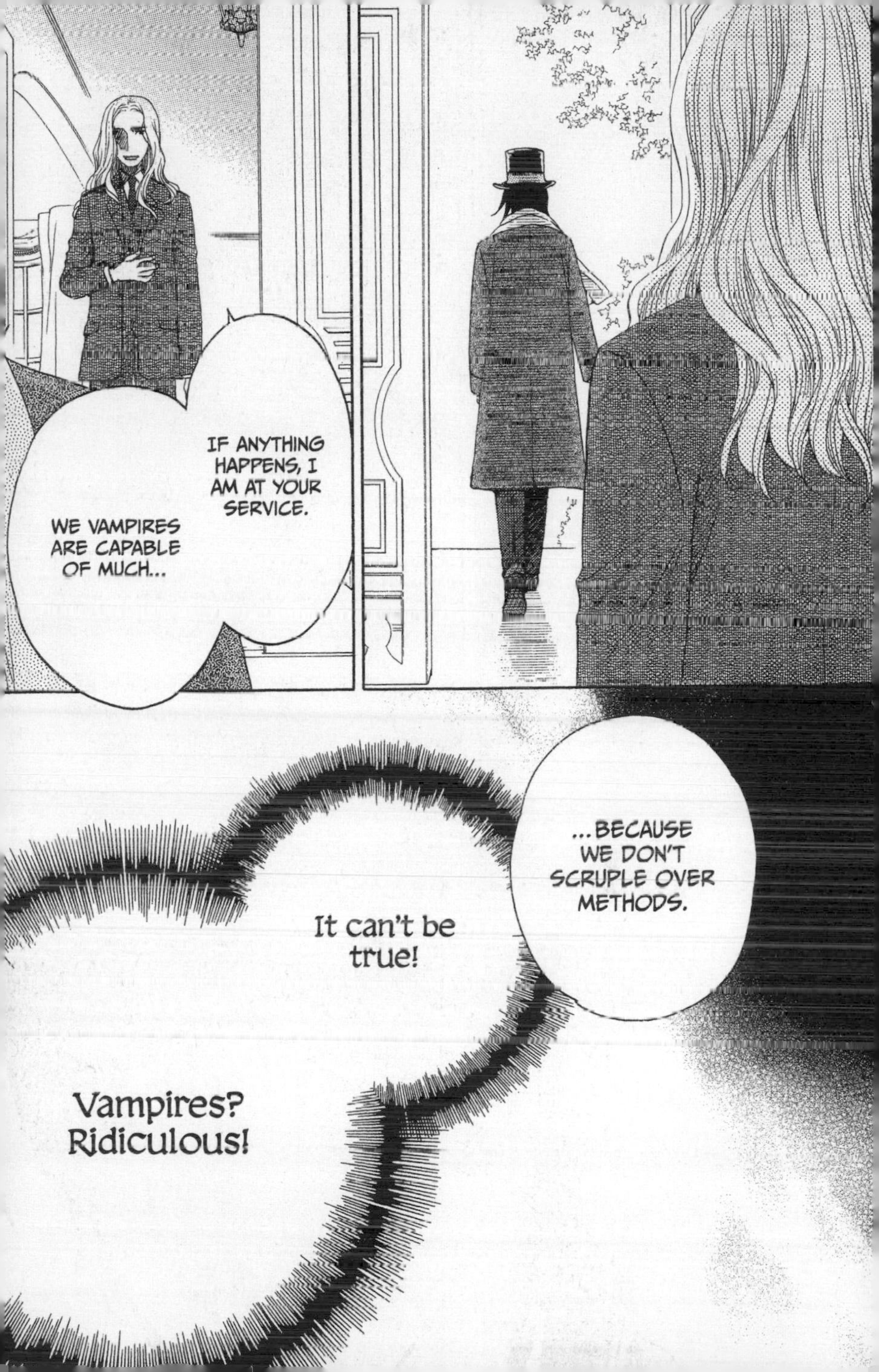
IF ANYTHING HAPPENS, I AM AT YOUR SERVICE.
WE VAMPIRES ARE CAPABLE OF MUCH...
...BECAUSE WE DON'T SCRUPLE OVER METHODS.
It can't be true!
Vampires? Ridiculous!

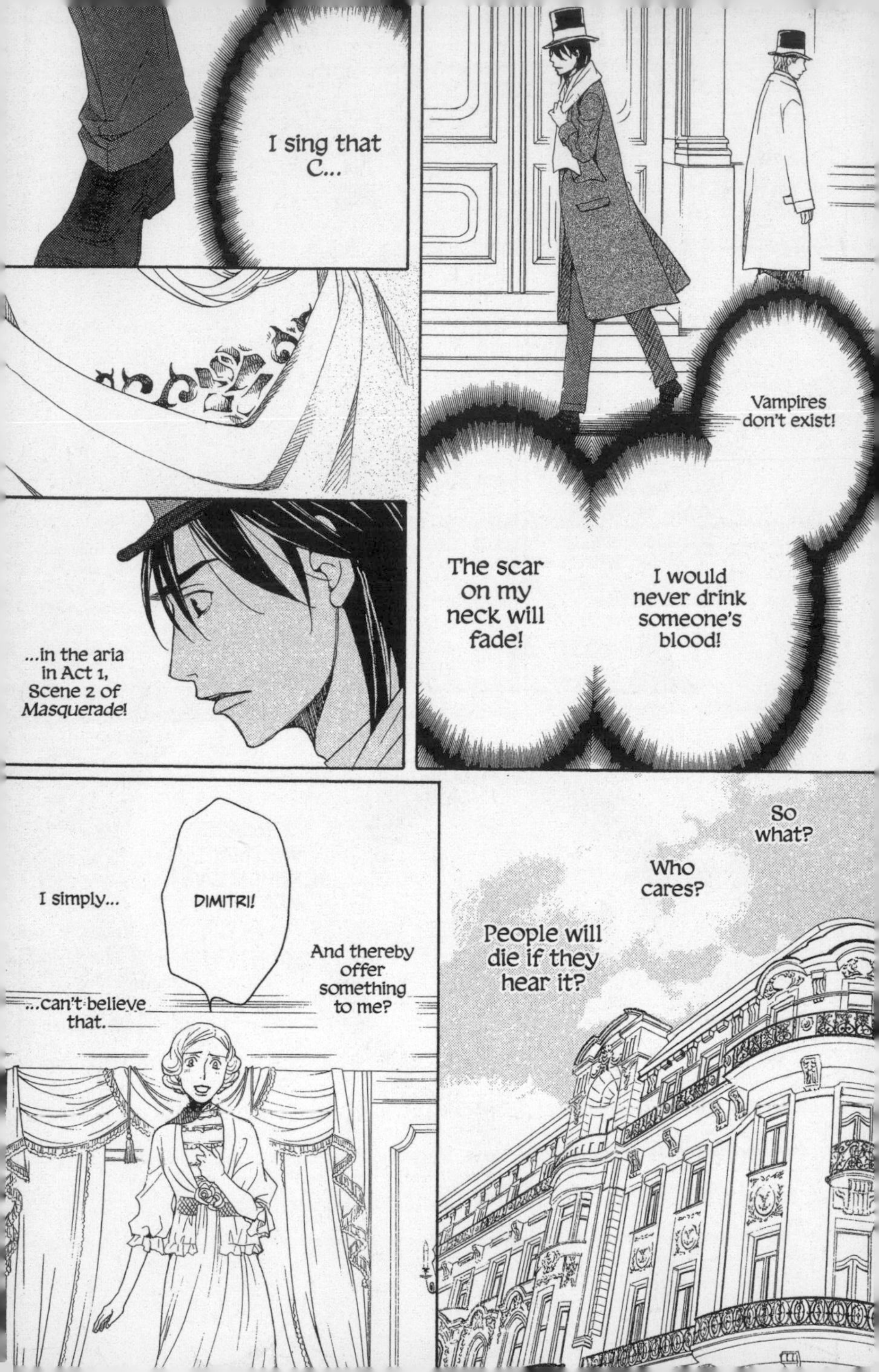

Vampires don't exist!
I would never drink someone's blood!
The scar on my neck will fade!
I sing that C...
...in the aria in Act 1, Scene 2 of Masquerade!
So what?
Who cares?
People will die if they hear it?
DIMITRI!
And thereby offer something to me?
I simply...
...can't believe that.

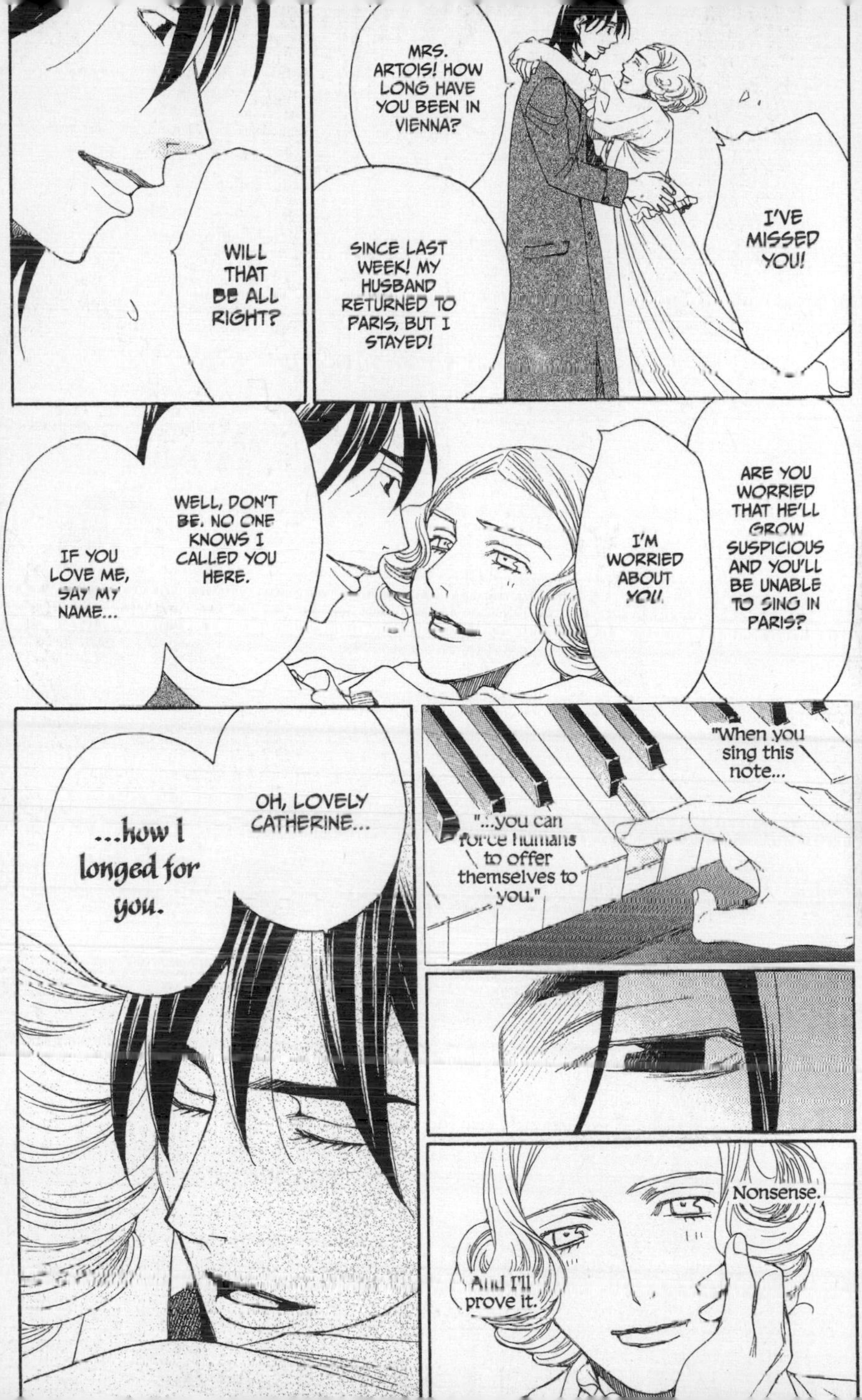
I'VE MISSED YOU!
MRS. ARTOIS! HOW LONG HAVE YOU BEEN IN VIENNA?
SINCE LAST WEEK! MY HUSBAND RETURNED TO PARIS, BUT I STAYED!
WILL THAT BE ALL RIGHT?
ARE YOU WORRIED THAT HE'LL GROW SUSPICIOUS AND YOU'LL BE UNABLE TO SING IN PARIS?
I'M WORRIED ABOUT YOU.
WELL, DON'T BE. NO ONE KNOWS I CALLED YOU HERE.
IF YOU LOVE ME, SAY MY NAME...
"When you sing this note...
"...you can force humans to offer themselves to you."
Nonsense.
And I'll prove it.
OH, LOVELY CATHERINE...
...how I longed for you.

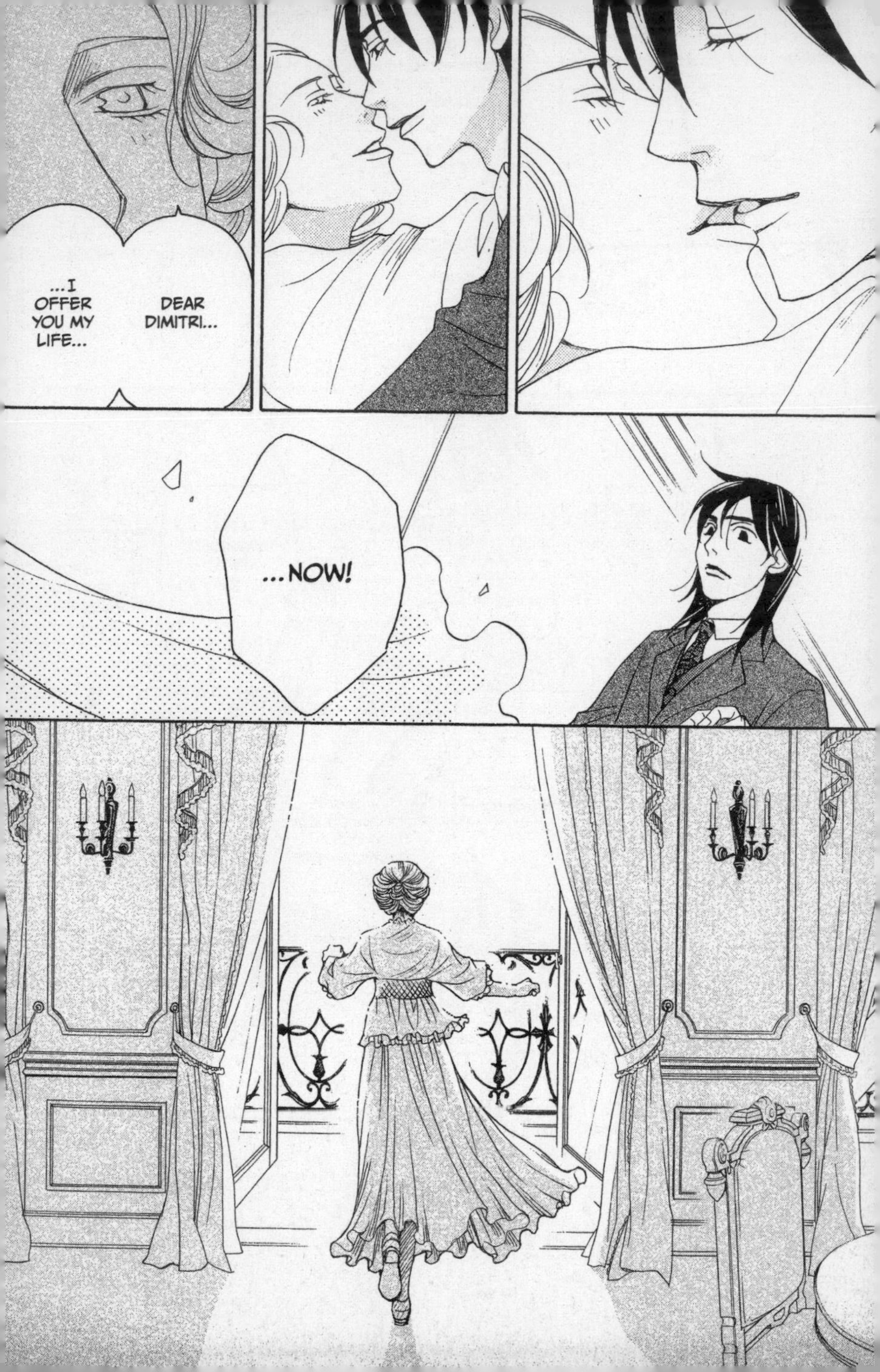
DEAR DIMITRI...
...I OFFER YOU MY LIFE...
...NOW!

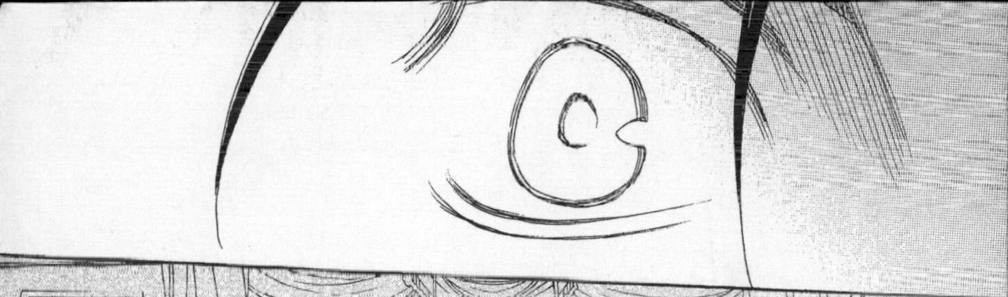
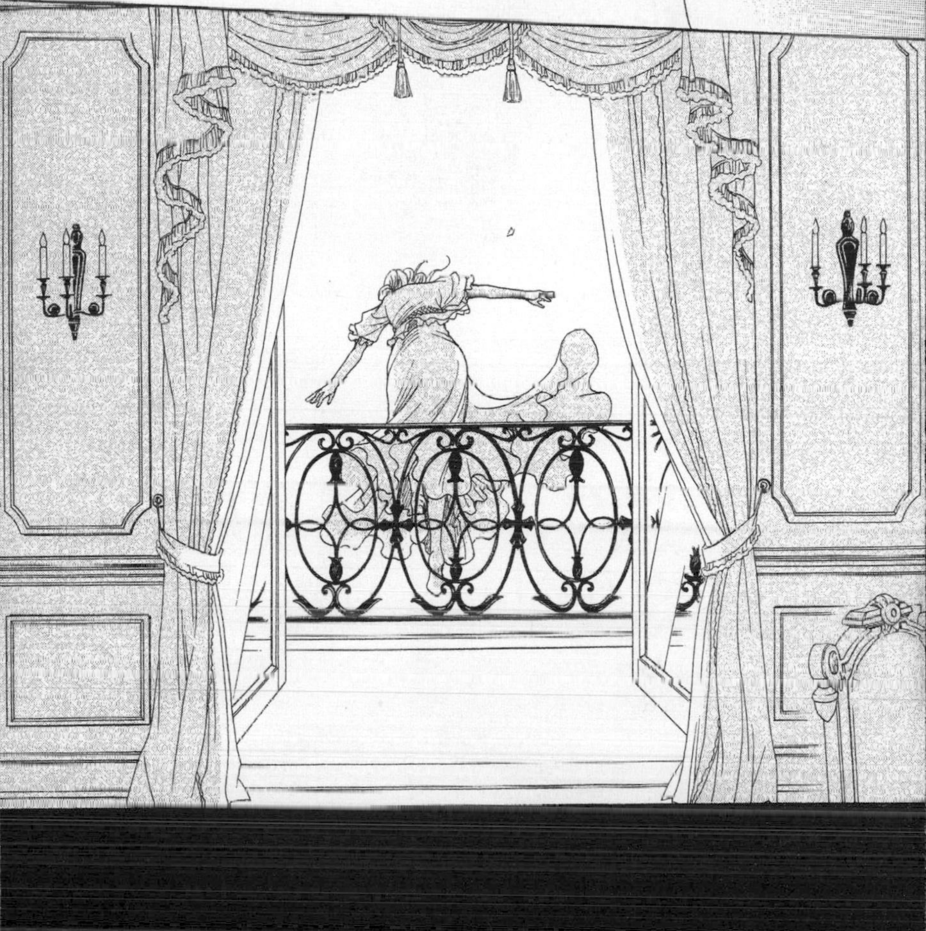

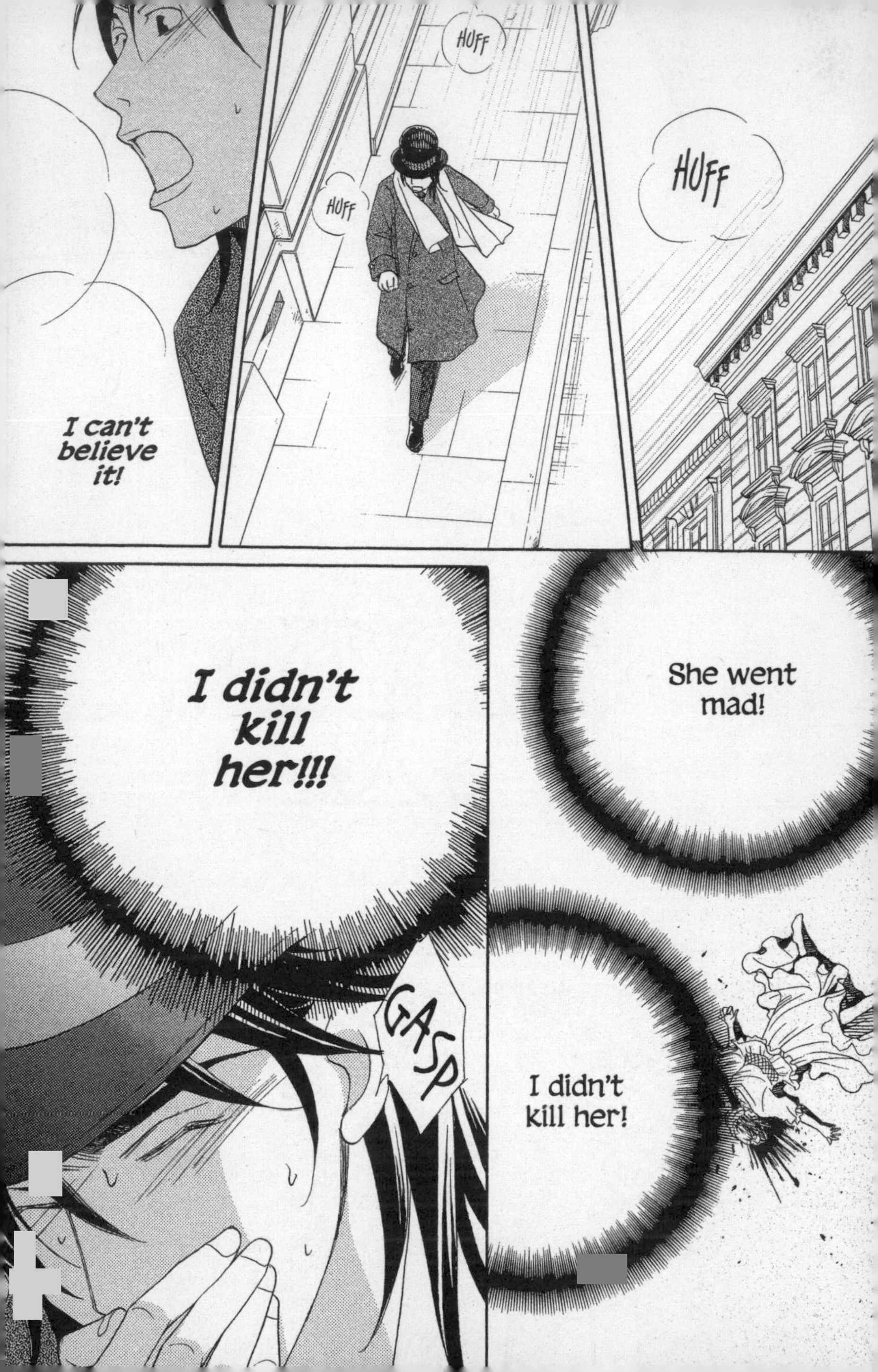
HUFF
HUFF
HUFF
I can't believe it!
She went mad!
I didn't kill her!
I didn't kill her!!!
GASP

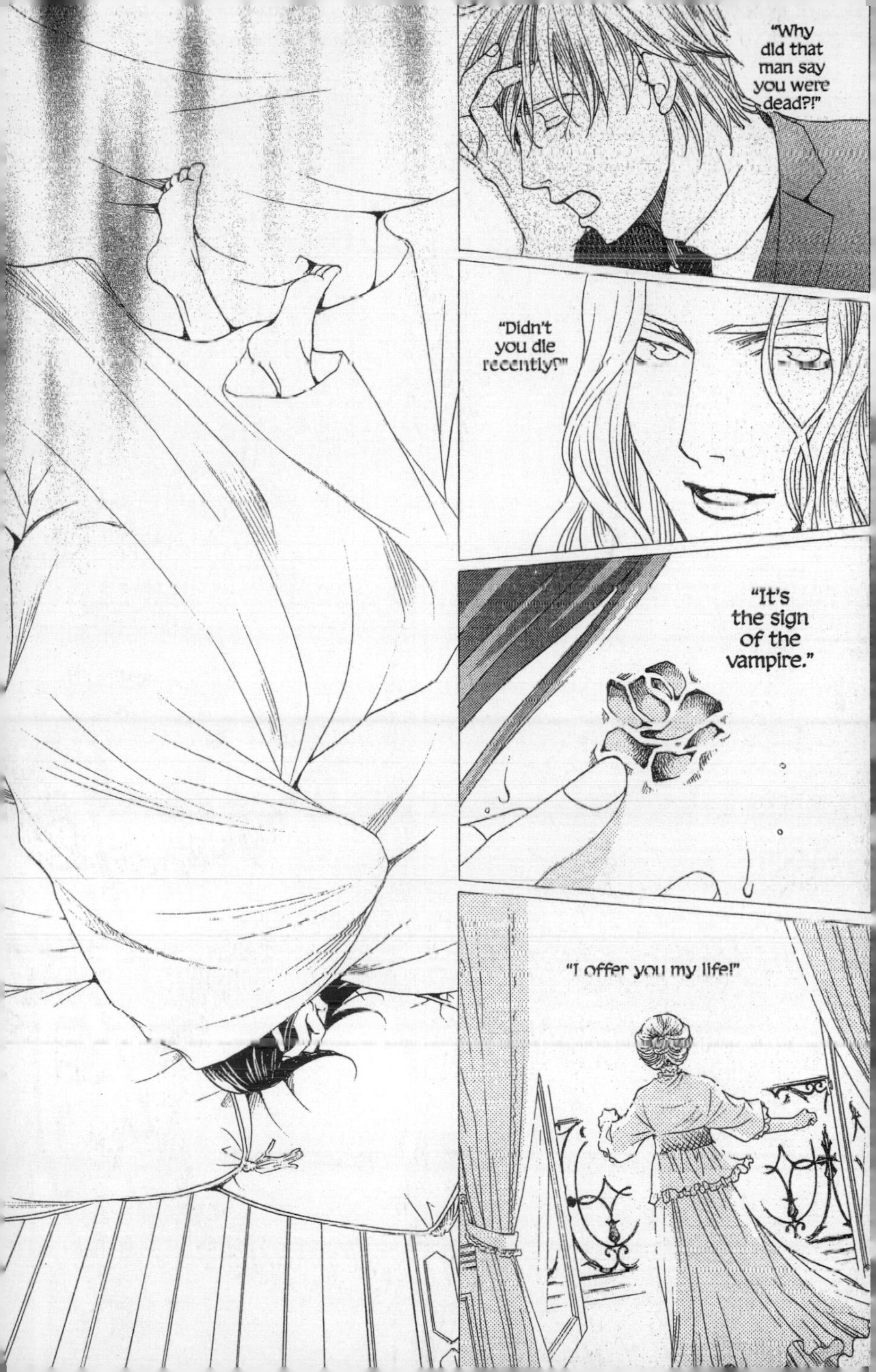
"Why did that man say you were dead?!"
"Didn't you die recently?"
"It's the sign of the vampire."
"I offer you my life!"

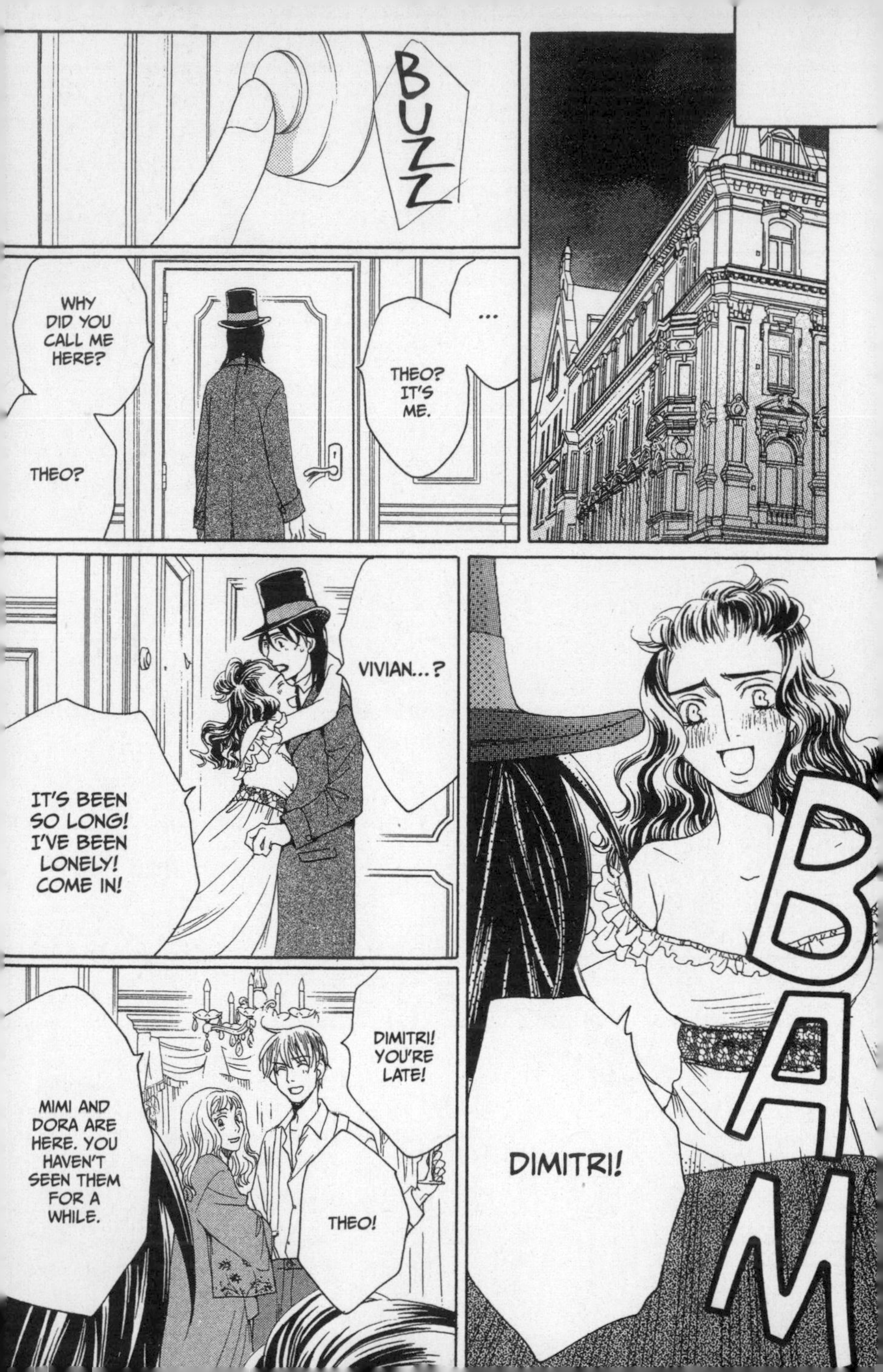
BUZZ
...
THEO? IT'S ME.
WHY DID YOU CALL ME HERE?
THEO?
BAM
DIMITRI!
VIVIAN...?
IT'S BEEN SO LONG! I'VE BEEN LONELY! COME IN!
DIMITRI! YOU'RE LATE!
THEO!
MIMI AND DORA ARE HERE. YOU HAVEN'T SEEN THEM FOR A WHILE.

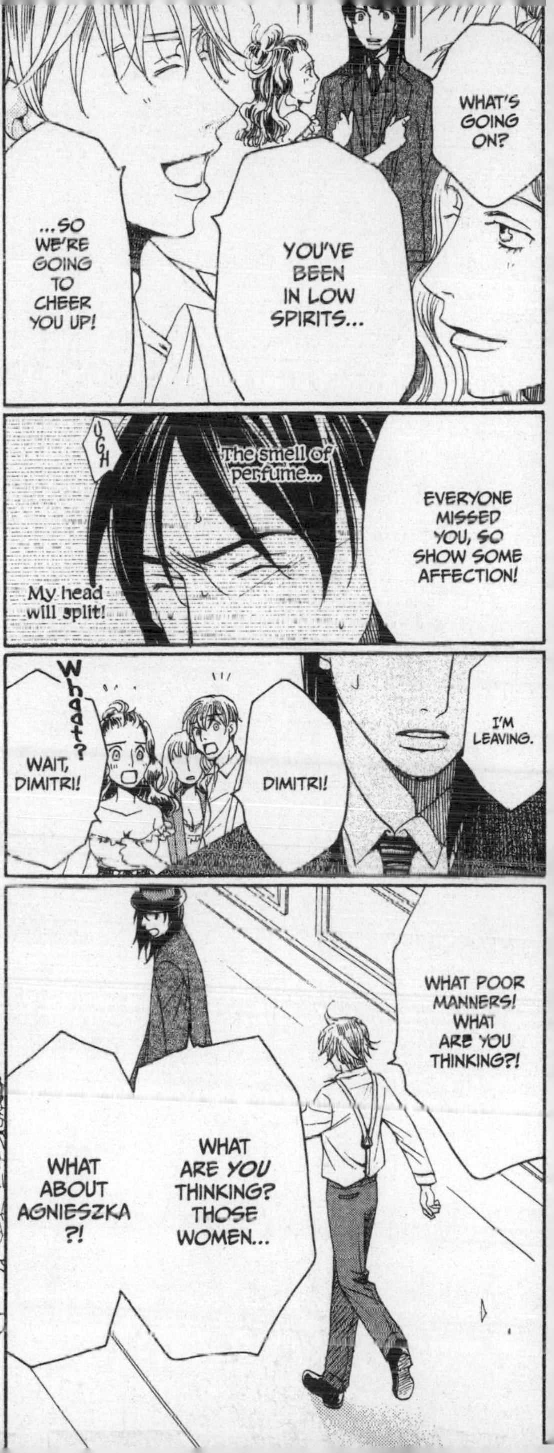
WHAT'S GOING ON?
YOU'VE BEEN IN LOW SPIRITS...
...SO WE'RE GOING TO CHEER YOU UP!
EVERYONE MISSED YOU, SO SHOW SOME AFFECTION!
The smell of perfume...
UGH
My head will split!
I'M LEAVING.
DIMITRI!
Whaat?
WAIT, DIMITRI!
WHAT POOR MANNERS! WHAT ARE YOU THINKING?!
WHAT ARE *YOU* THINKING? THOSE WOMEN...
WHAT ABOUT AGNIESZKA?!

This story begins in 1908, the age of Art Nouveau (Jugendstil) in Europe, when lots of my favorite things were in full bloom, like René Lalique, Klimt and Schiele. They're so cool! ❀ But 100 years isn't really that long ago.

I thought a rustling dress with a bustle would suit Agnieszka, but they were already out of fashion by this time. Too bad! Researching the history of clothing and accessories was fun!

I made Agnieszka's birthday party dress like something in a Mucha picture. It's probably a present from the ever-playful Theo! ♡

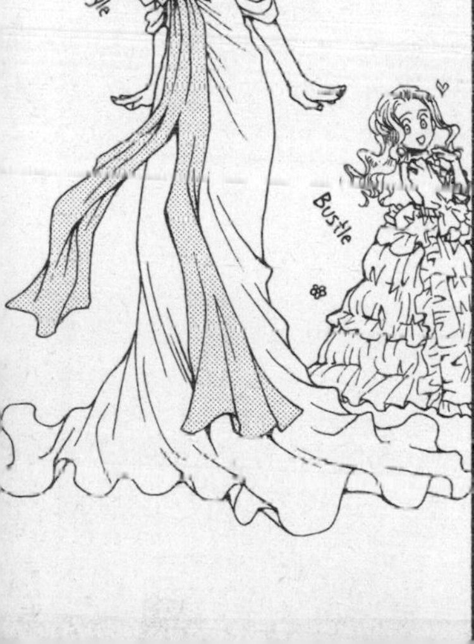
Mucha style
Bustle

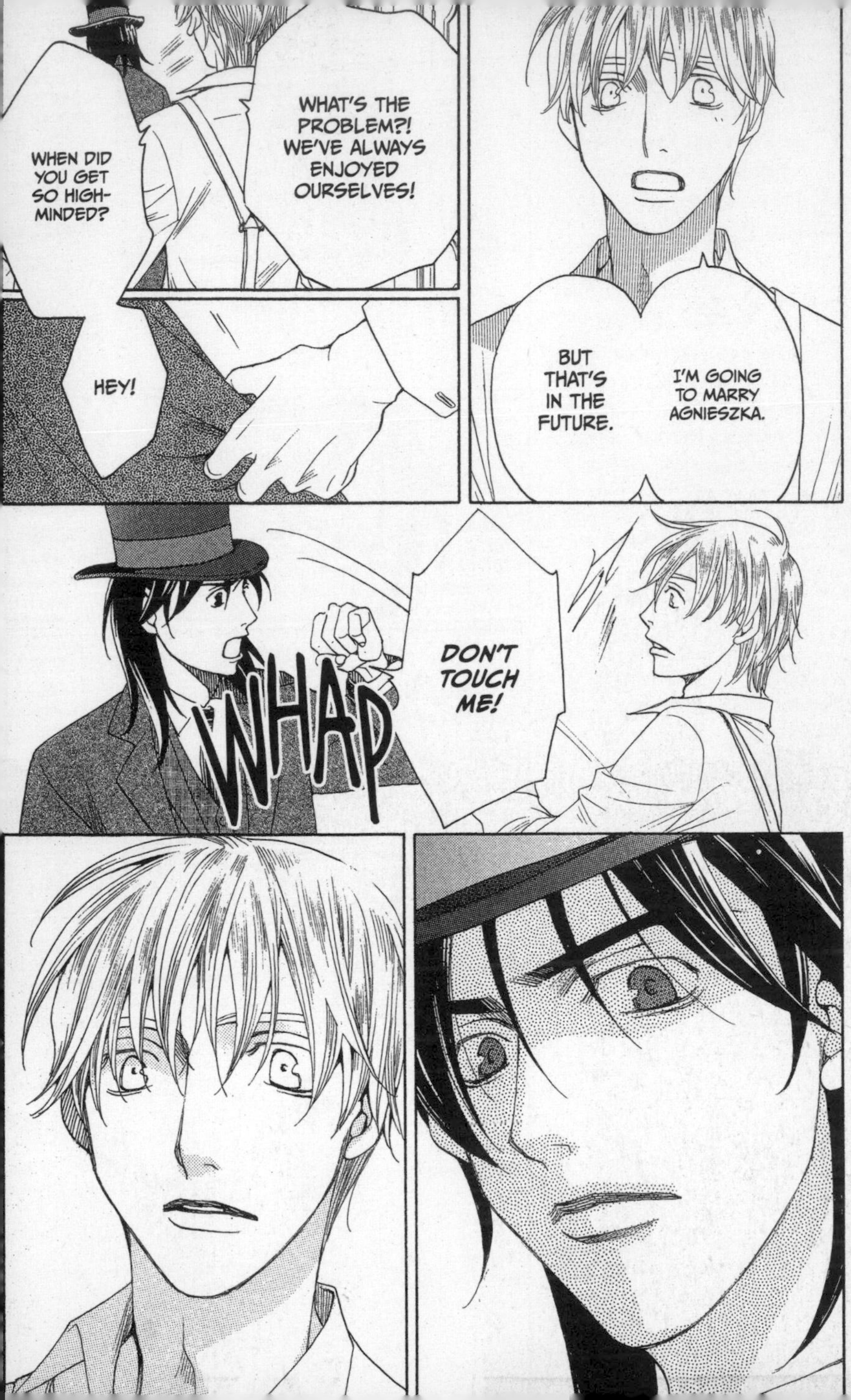
I'M GOING TO MARRY AGNIESZKA.
BUT THAT'S IN THE FUTURE.
WHAT'S THE PROBLEM?! WE'VE ALWAYS ENJOYED OURSELVES!
WHEN DID YOU GET SO HIGH-MINDED?
HEY!
DON'T TOUCH ME!
WHAP

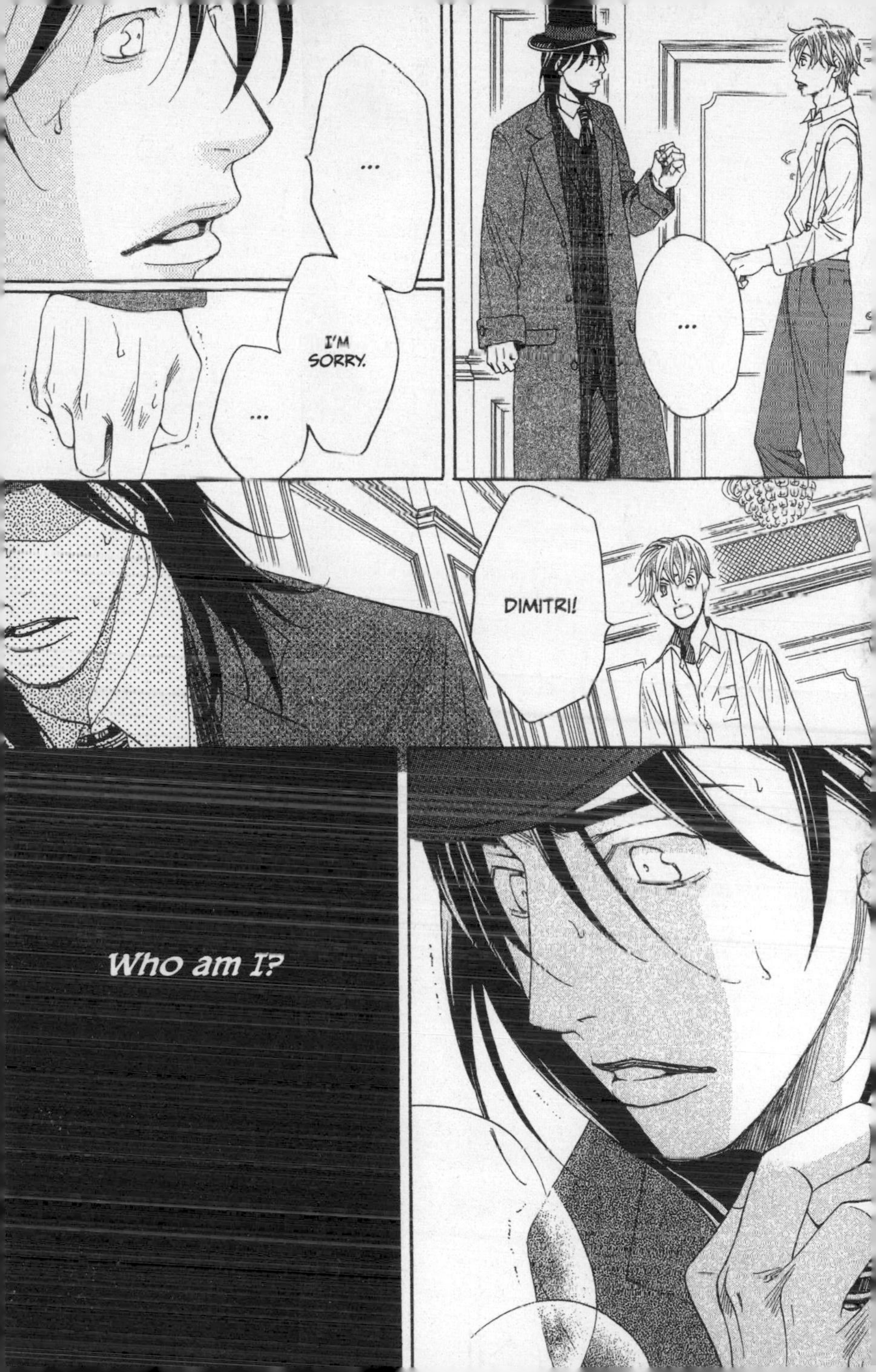
...
...
I'M SORRY.
...
DIMITRI!
Who am I?

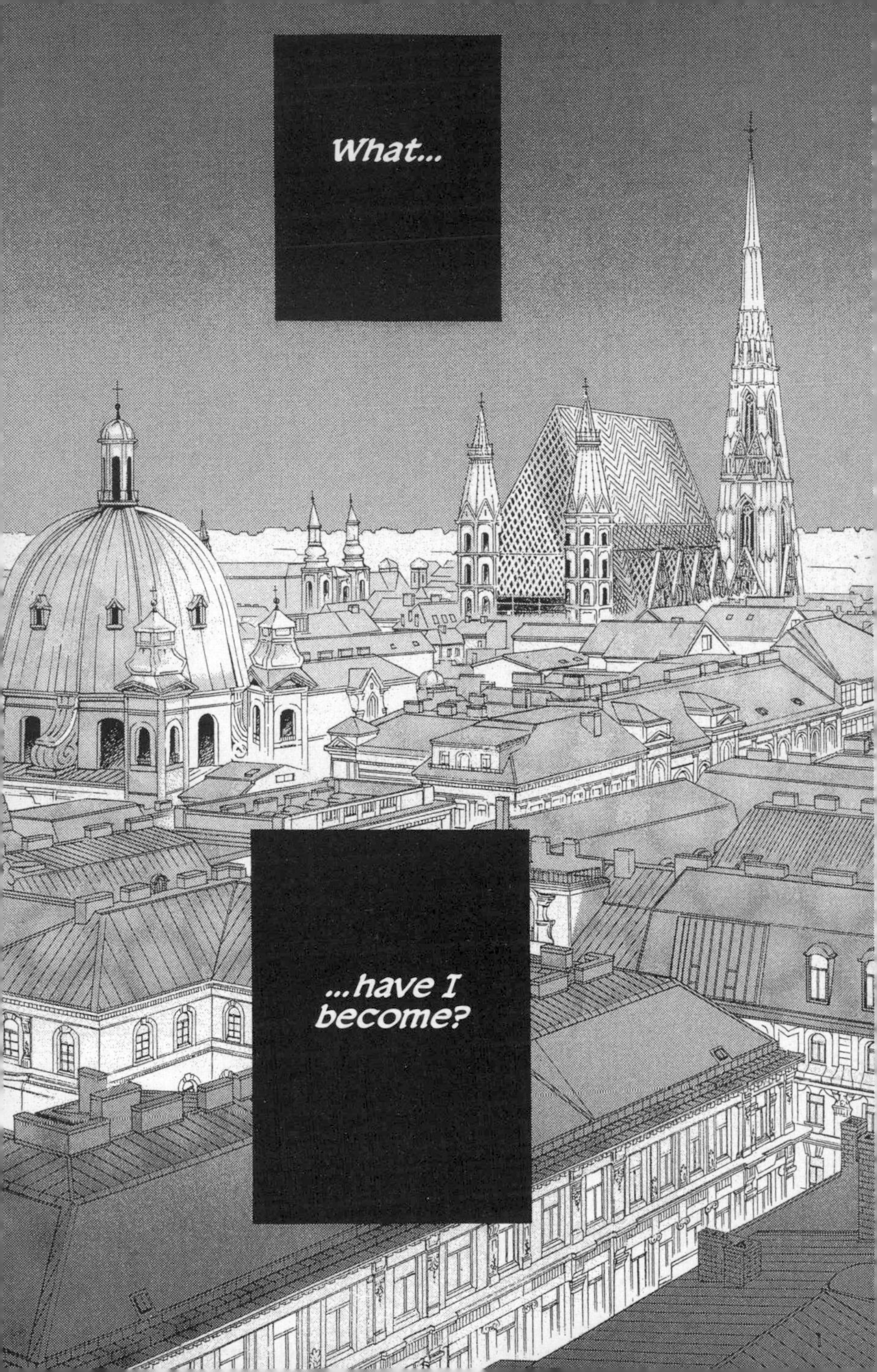
What...
...have I become?

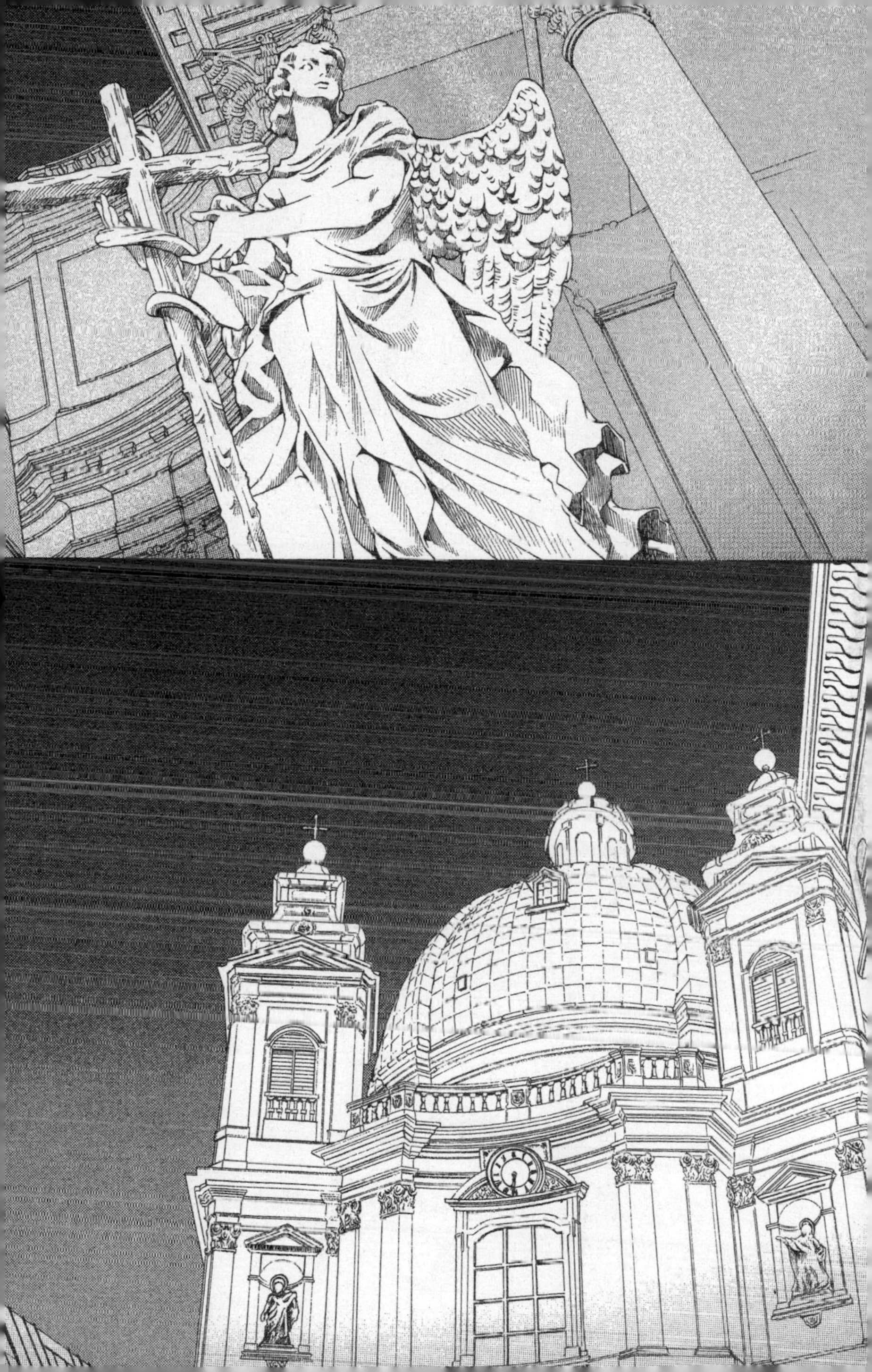

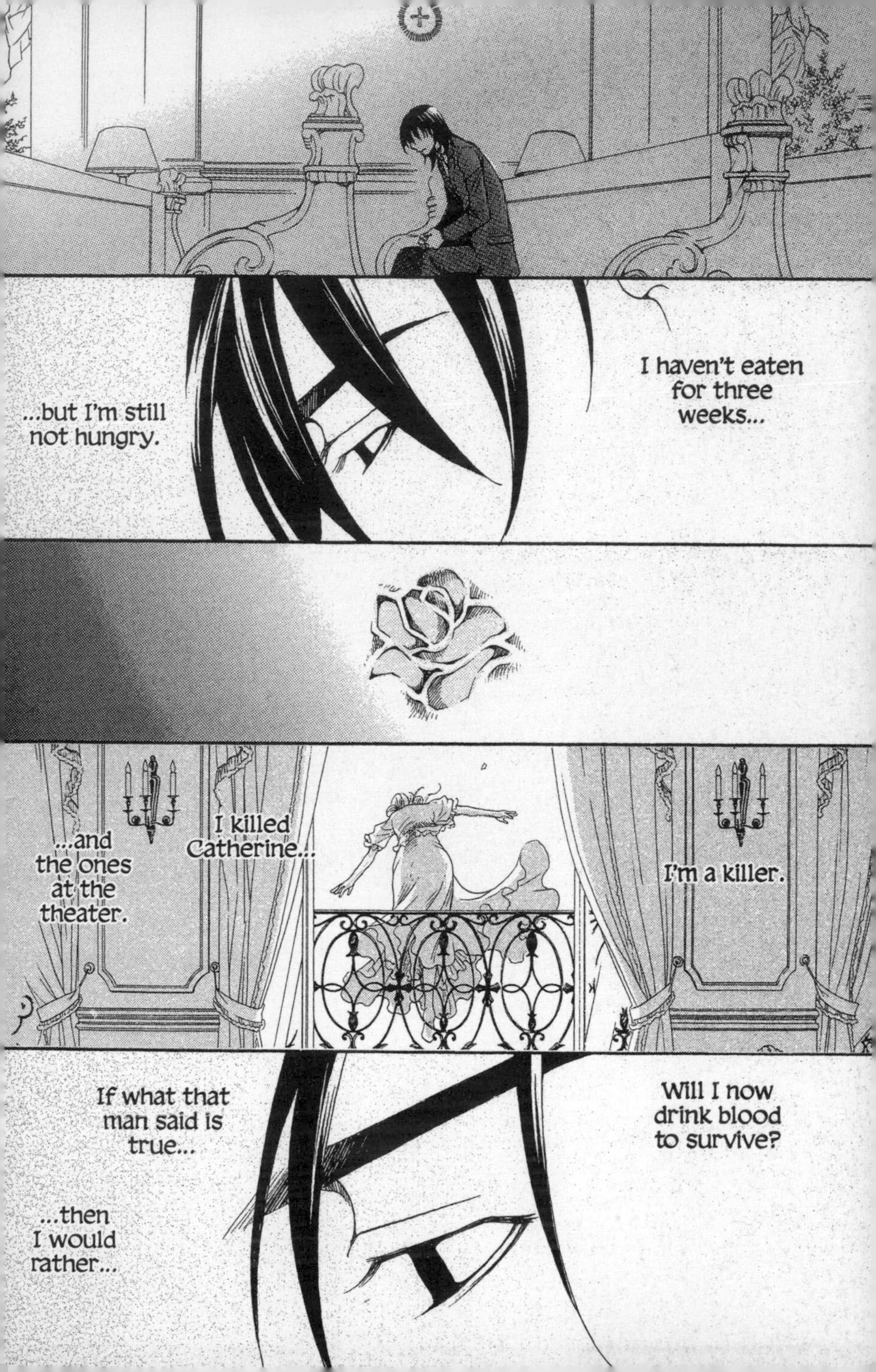
I haven't eaten for three weeks...
...but I'm still not hungry.
I'm a killer.
I killed Catherine...
...and the ones at the theater.
Will I now drink blood to survive?
If what that man said is true...
...then I would rather...

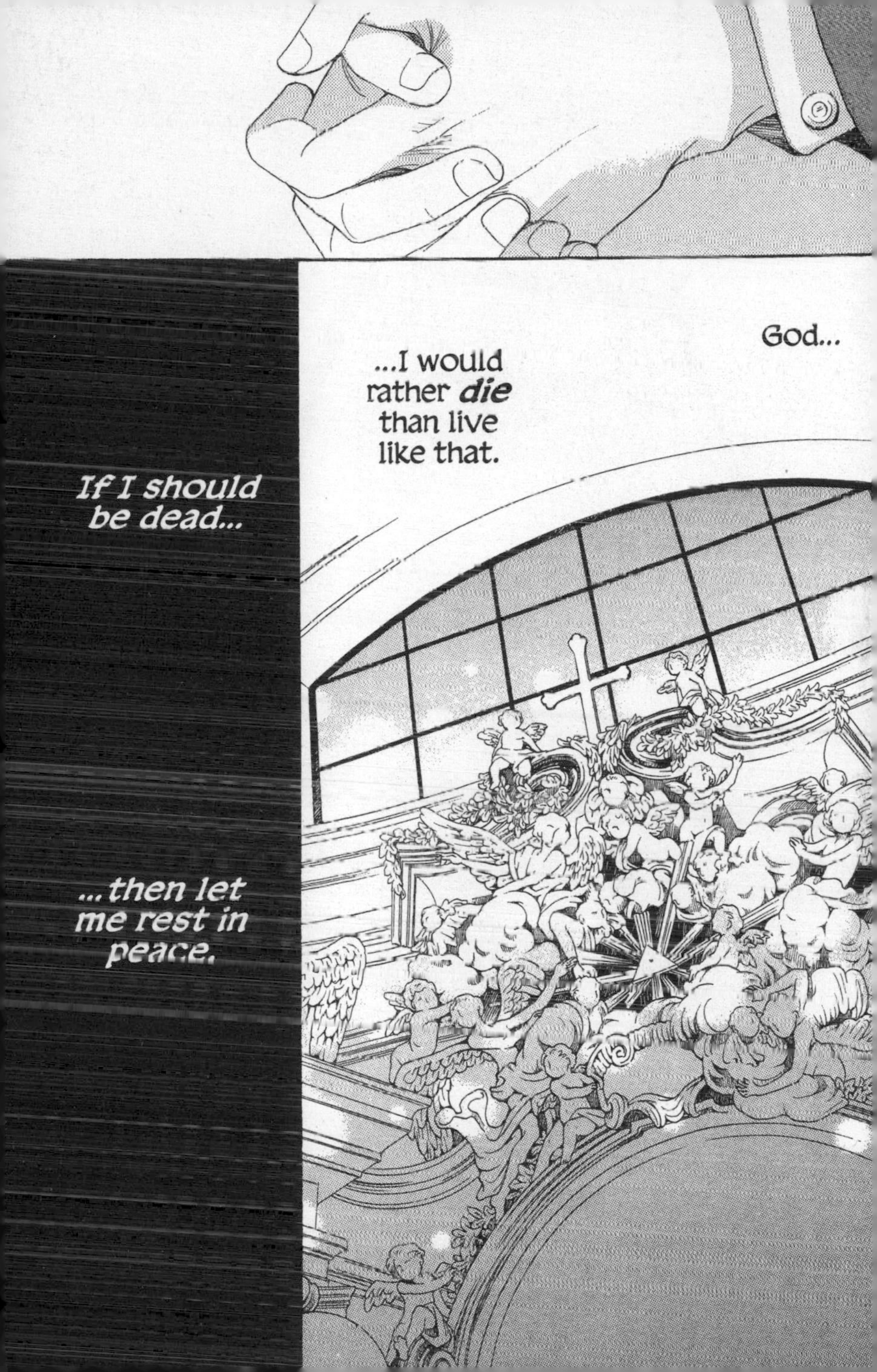
God...
...I would rather *die* than live like that.
If I should be dead...
...then let me rest in peace.

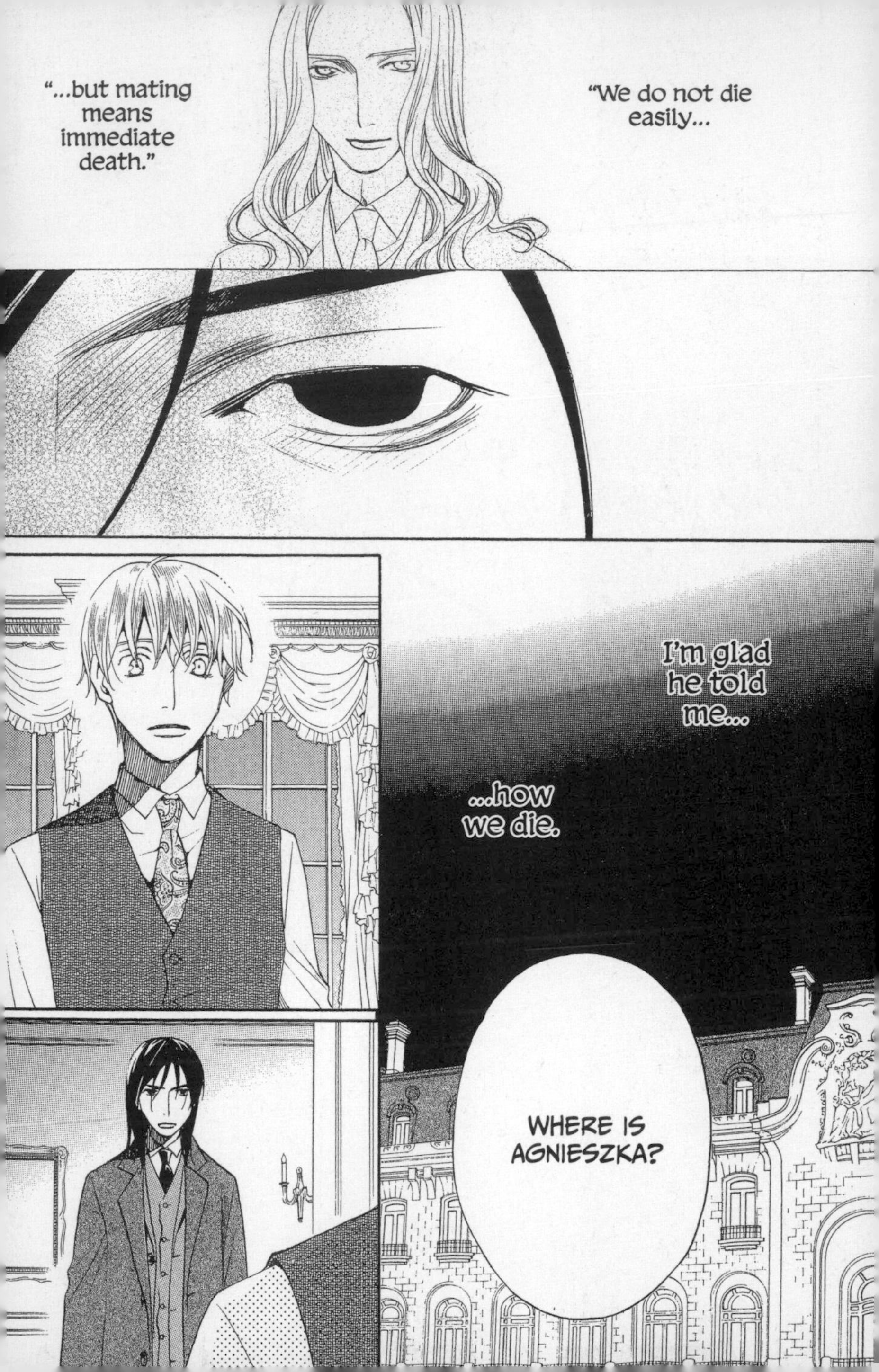
"We do not die easily...
"...but mating means immediate death."
I'm glad he told me...
...how we die.
WHERE IS AGNIESZKA?

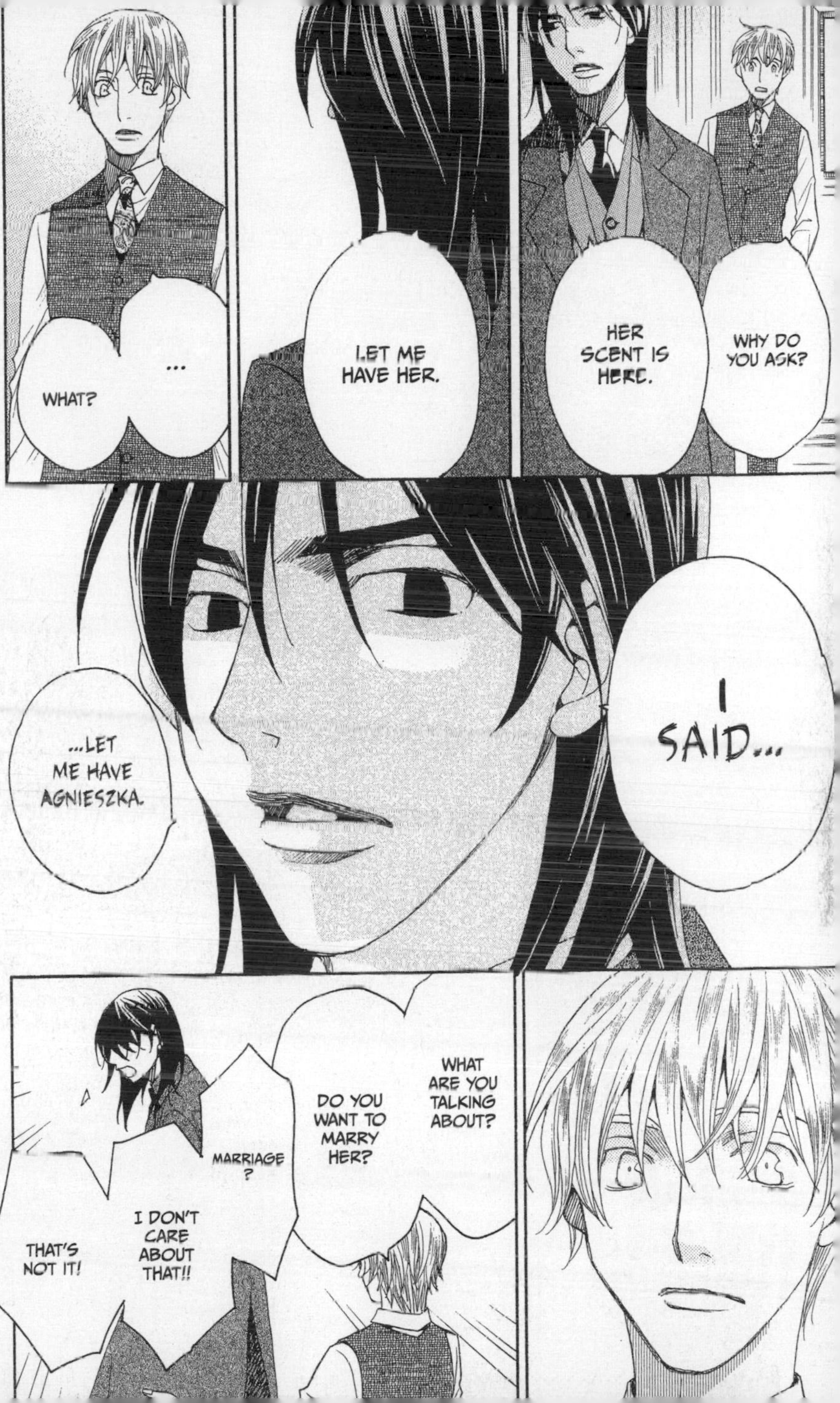
WHY DO YOU ASK?
HER SCENT IS HERE.
LET ME HAVE HER.
...
WHAT?
I SAID...
...LET ME HAVE AGNIESZKA.
WHAT ARE YOU TALKING ABOUT?
DO YOU WANT TO MARRY HER?
MARRIAGE?
I DON'T CARE ABOUT THAT!!
THAT'S NOT IT!

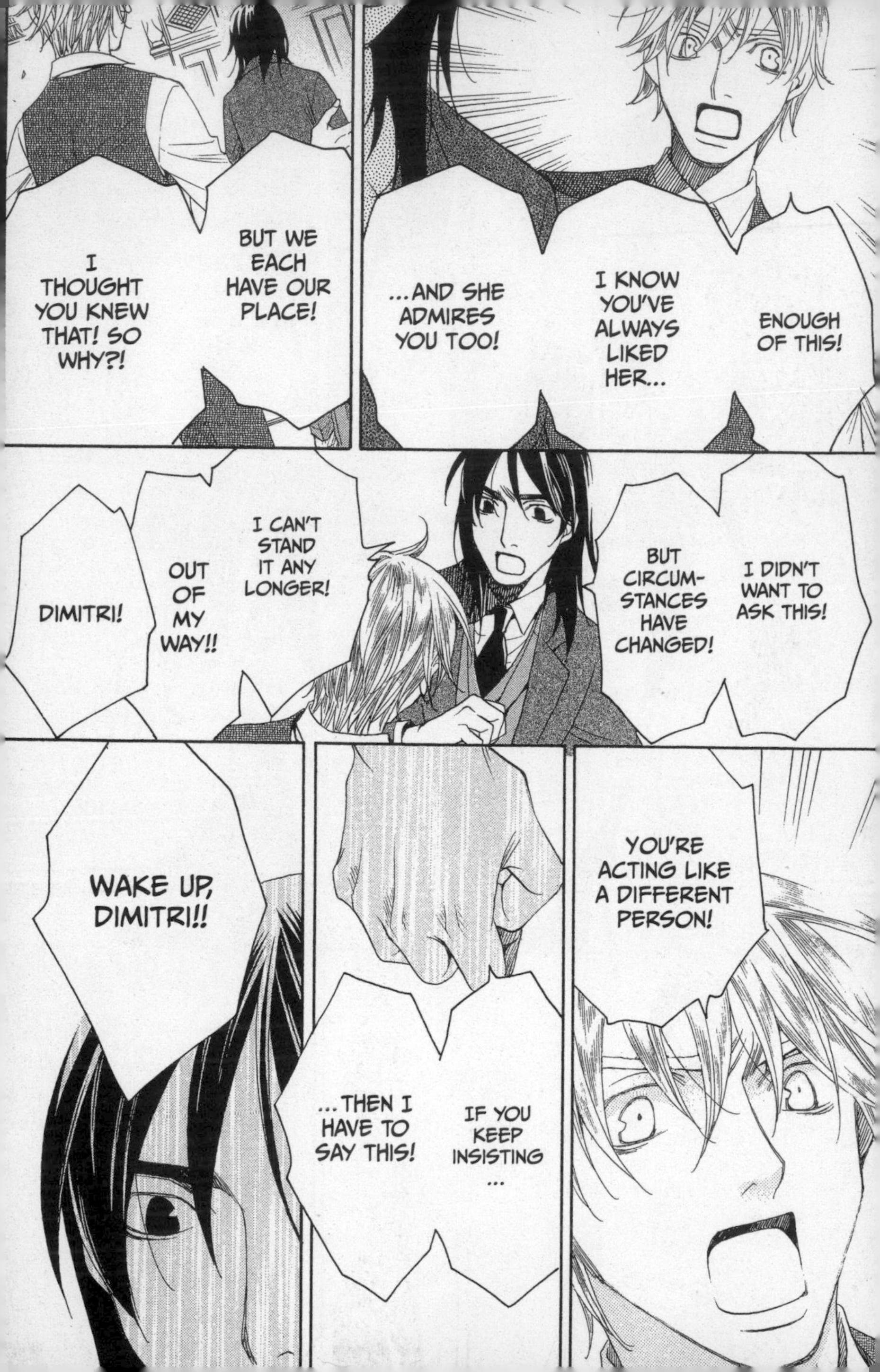
ENOUGH OF THIS!
I KNOW YOU'VE ALWAYS LIKED HER...
...AND SHE ADMIRES YOU TOO!
BUT WE EACH HAVE OUR PLACE!
I THOUGHT YOU KNEW THAT! SO WHY?!
I DIDN'T WANT TO ASK THIS!
BUT CIRCUMSTANCES HAVE CHANGED!
I CAN'T STAND IT ANY LONGER!
OUT OF MY WAY!!
DIMITRI!
YOU'RE ACTING LIKE A DIFFERENT PERSON!
IF YOU KEEP INSISTING...
...THEN I HAVE TO SAY THIS!
WAKE UP, DIMITRI!!

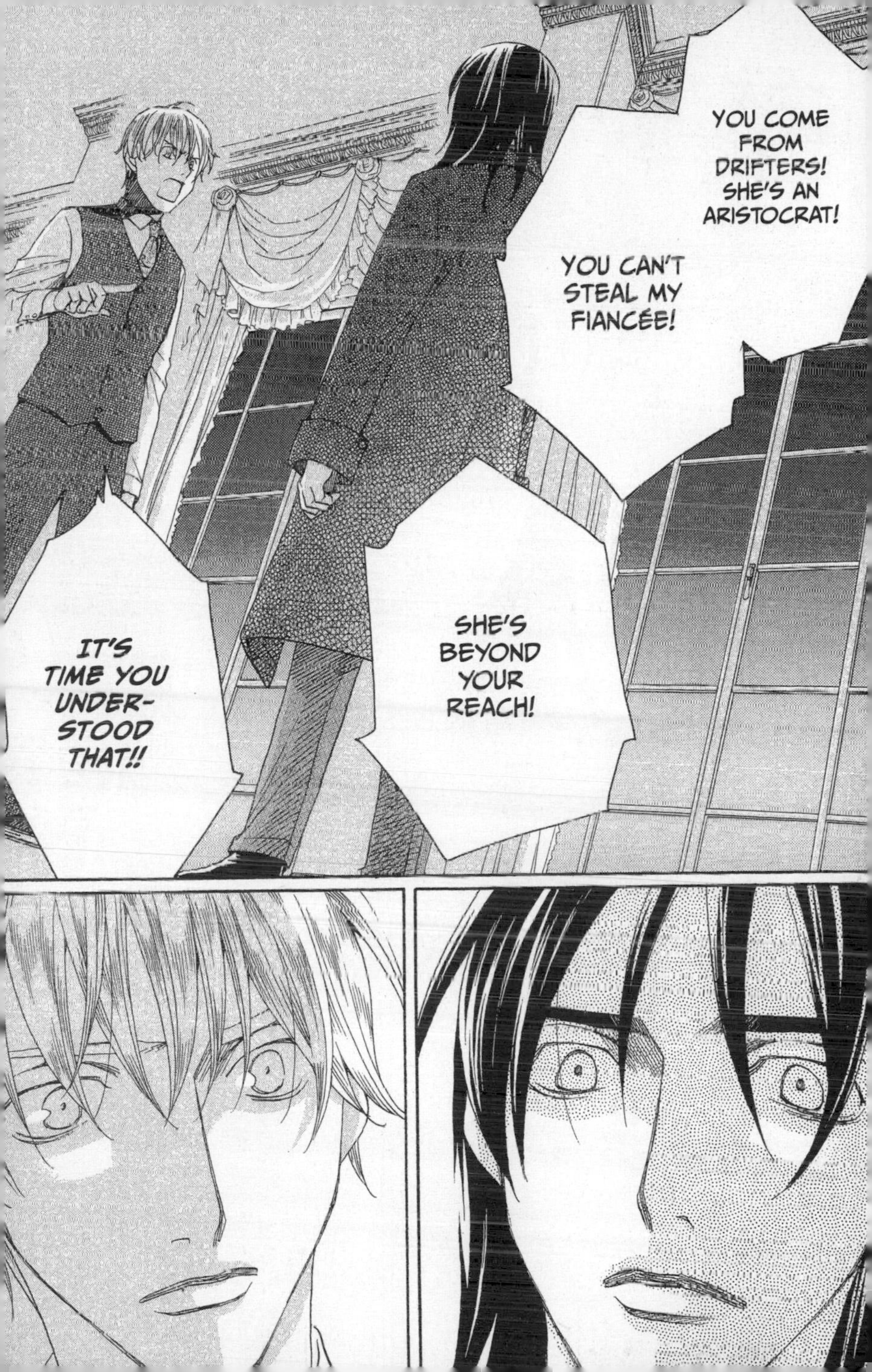
YOU COME FROM DRIFTERS! SHE'S AN ARISTOCRAT!
YOU CAN'T STEAL MY FIANCÉE!
SHE'S BEYOND YOUR REACH!
IT'S TIME YOU UNDER-STOOD THAT!!

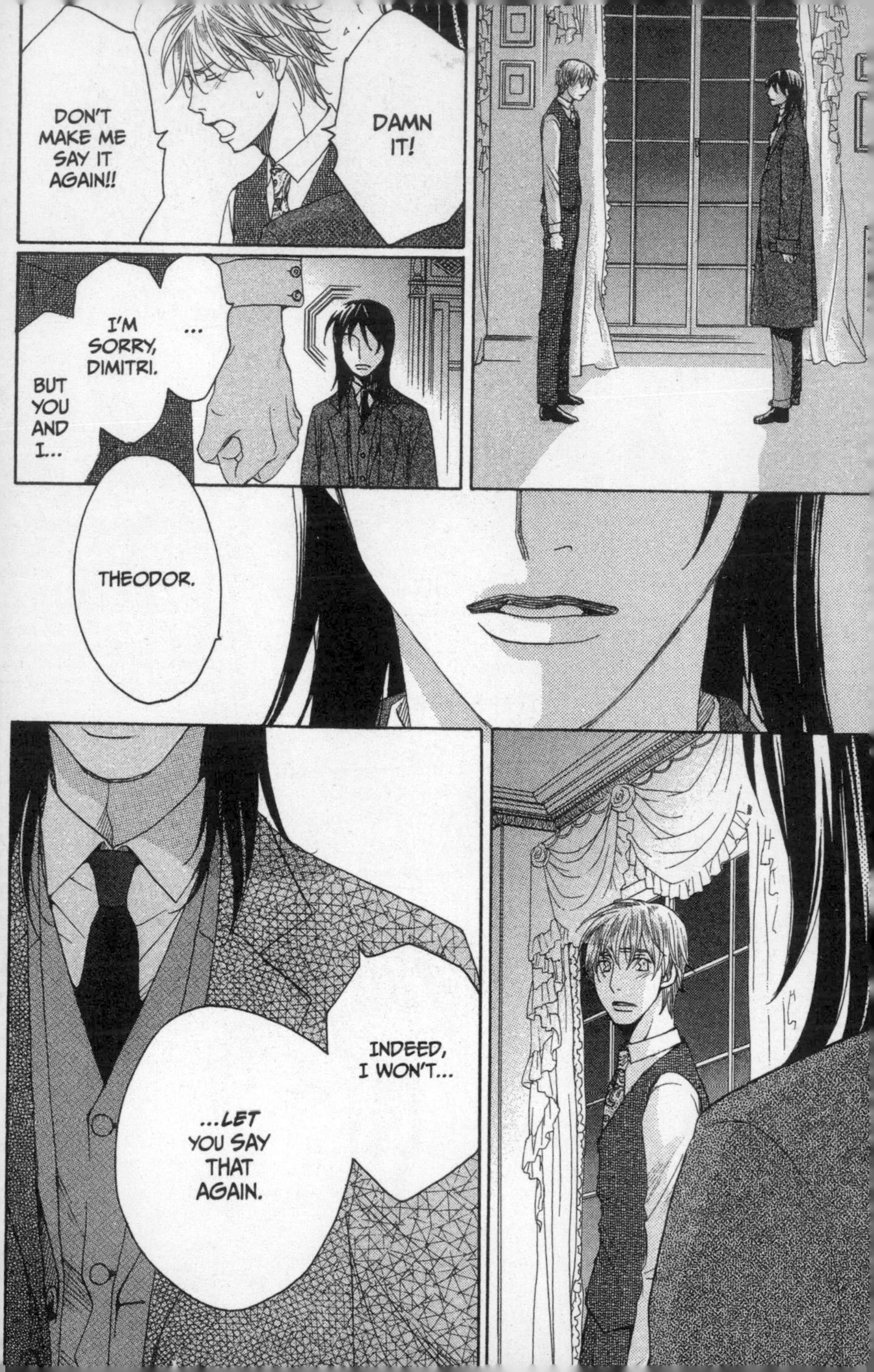
DAMN IT!
DON'T MAKE ME SAY IT AGAIN!!
...
I'M SORRY, DIMITRI.
BUT YOU AND I...
THEODOR.
INDEED, I WON'T...
...LET YOU SAY THAT AGAIN.

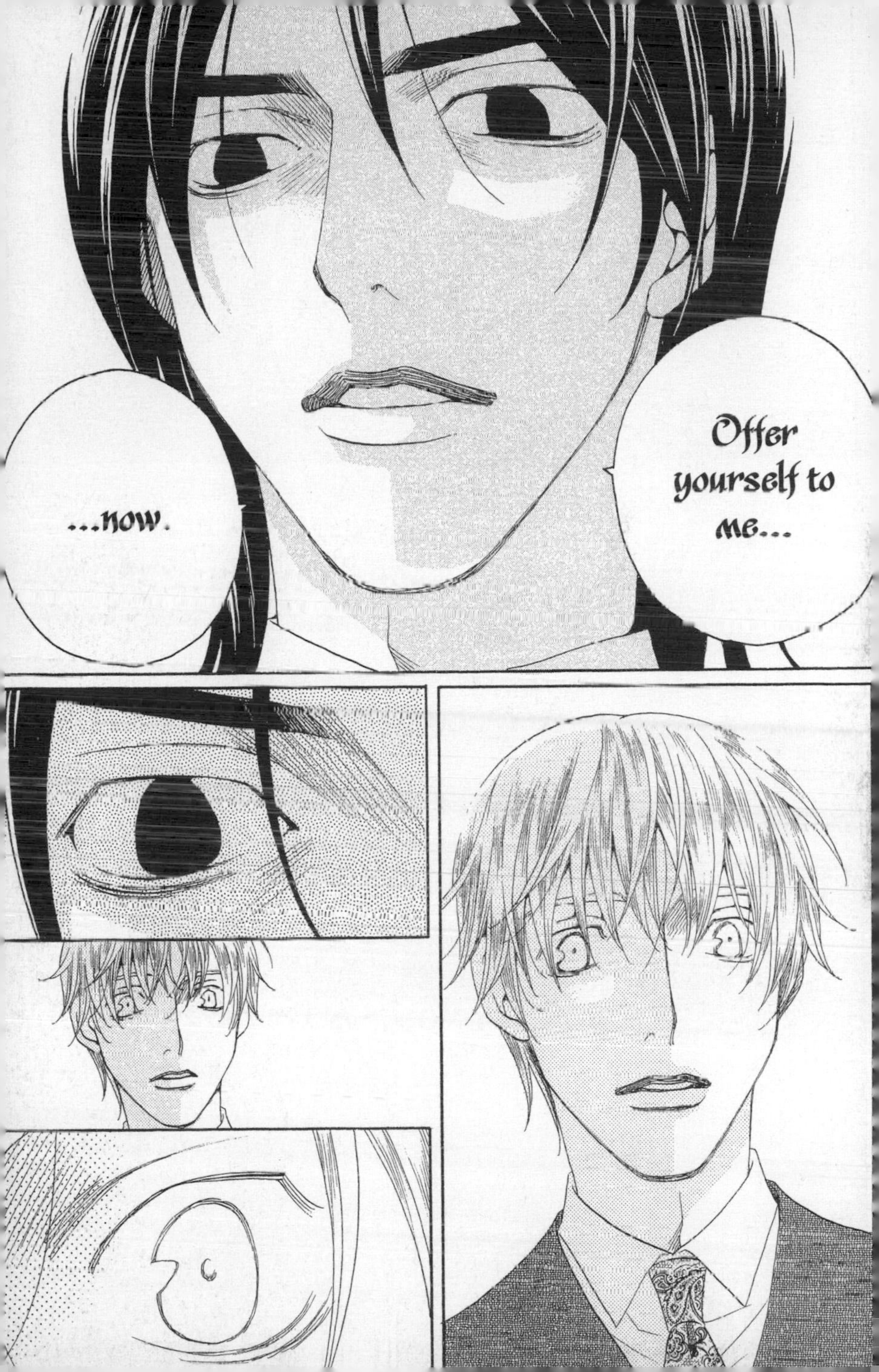
Offer yourself to me...
...now.

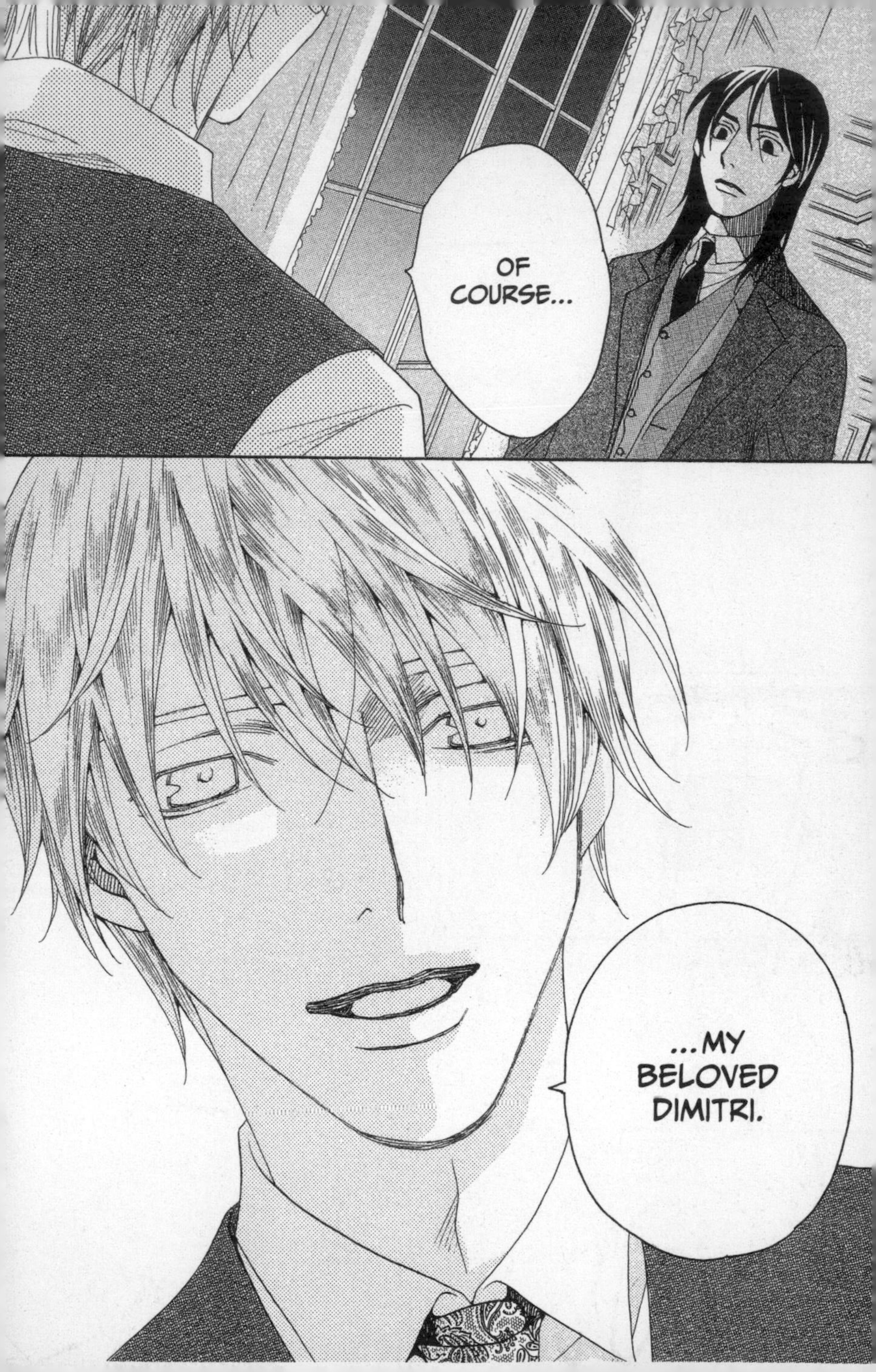
OF COURSE...
...MY BELOVED DIMITRI.

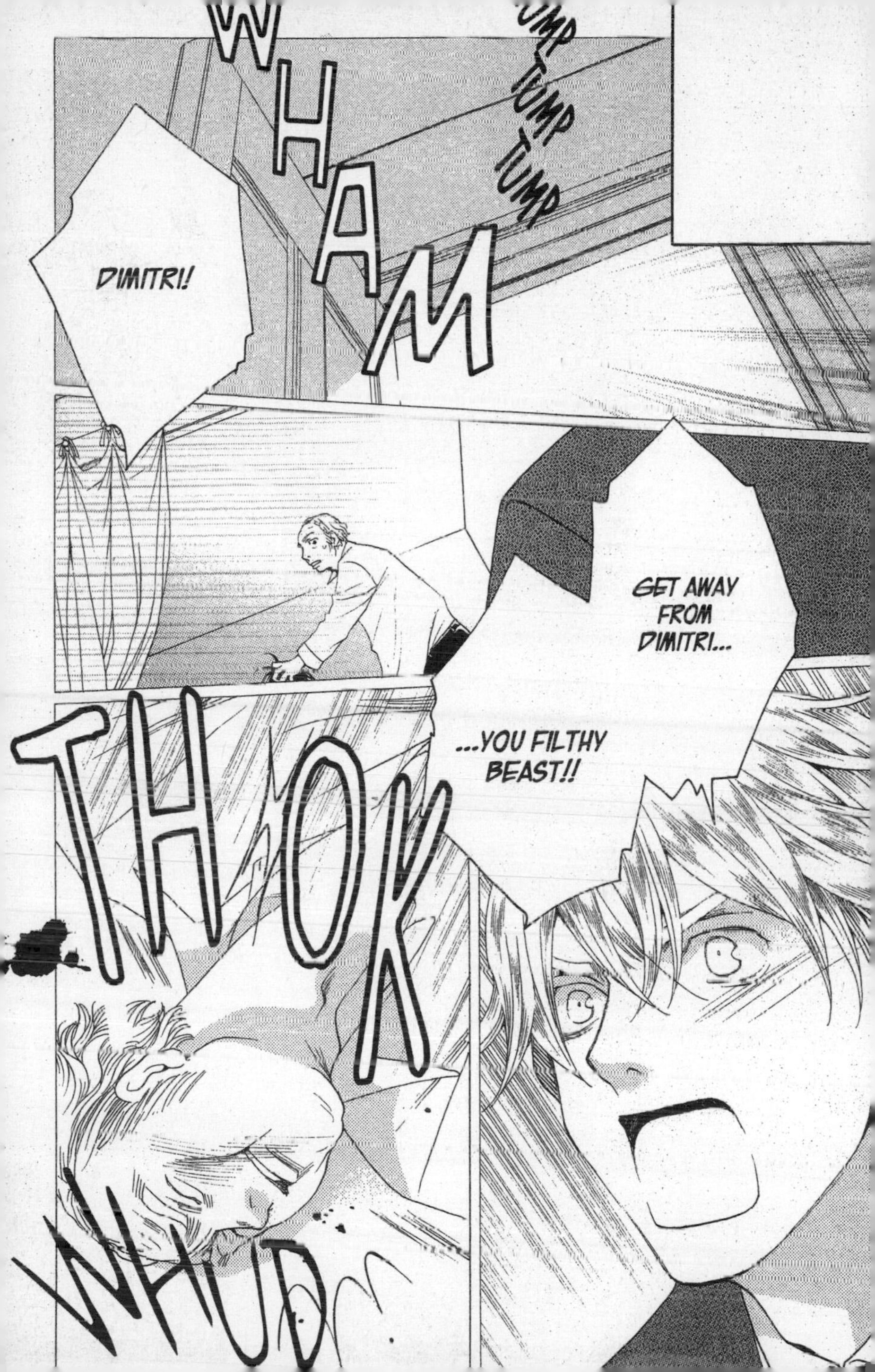
UMP THUMP THUMP
WHAM
DIMITRI!
GET AWAY FROM DIMITRI...
...YOU FILTHY BEAST!!
THOK
WHUD

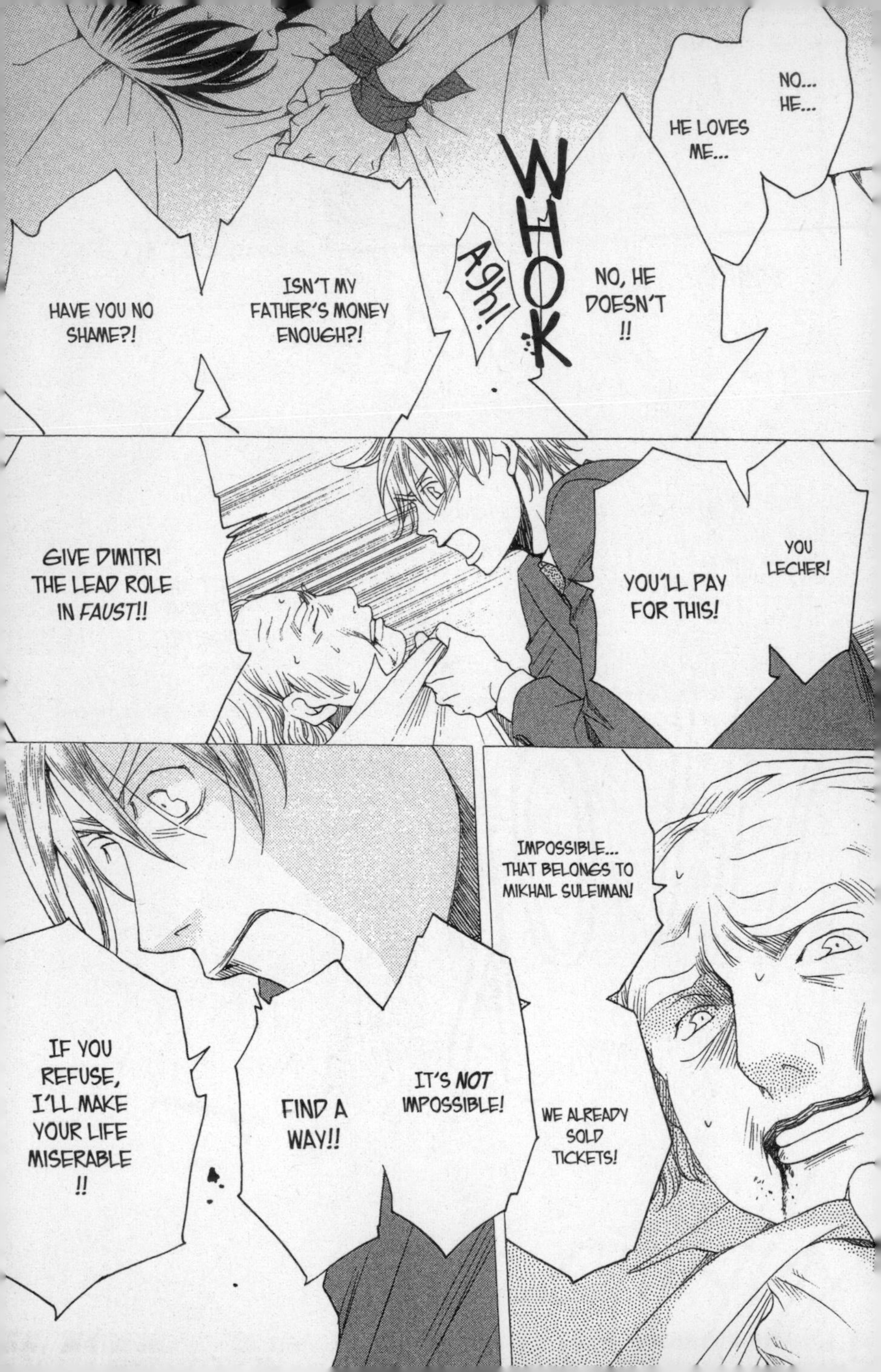
NO... HE...
HE LOVES ME...
NO, HE DOESN'T !!
WHOK
Agh!
ISN'T MY FATHER'S MONEY ENOUGH?!
HAVE YOU NO SHAME?!
YOU LECHER!
YOU'LL PAY FOR THIS!
GIVE DIMITRI THE LEAD ROLE IN *FAUST*!!
IMPOSSIBLE... THAT BELONGS TO MIKHAIL SULEIMAN!
WE ALREADY SOLD TICKETS!
IT'S *NOT* IMPOSSIBLE!
FIND A WAY!!
IF YOU REFUSE, I'LL MAKE YOUR LIFE MISERABLE !!

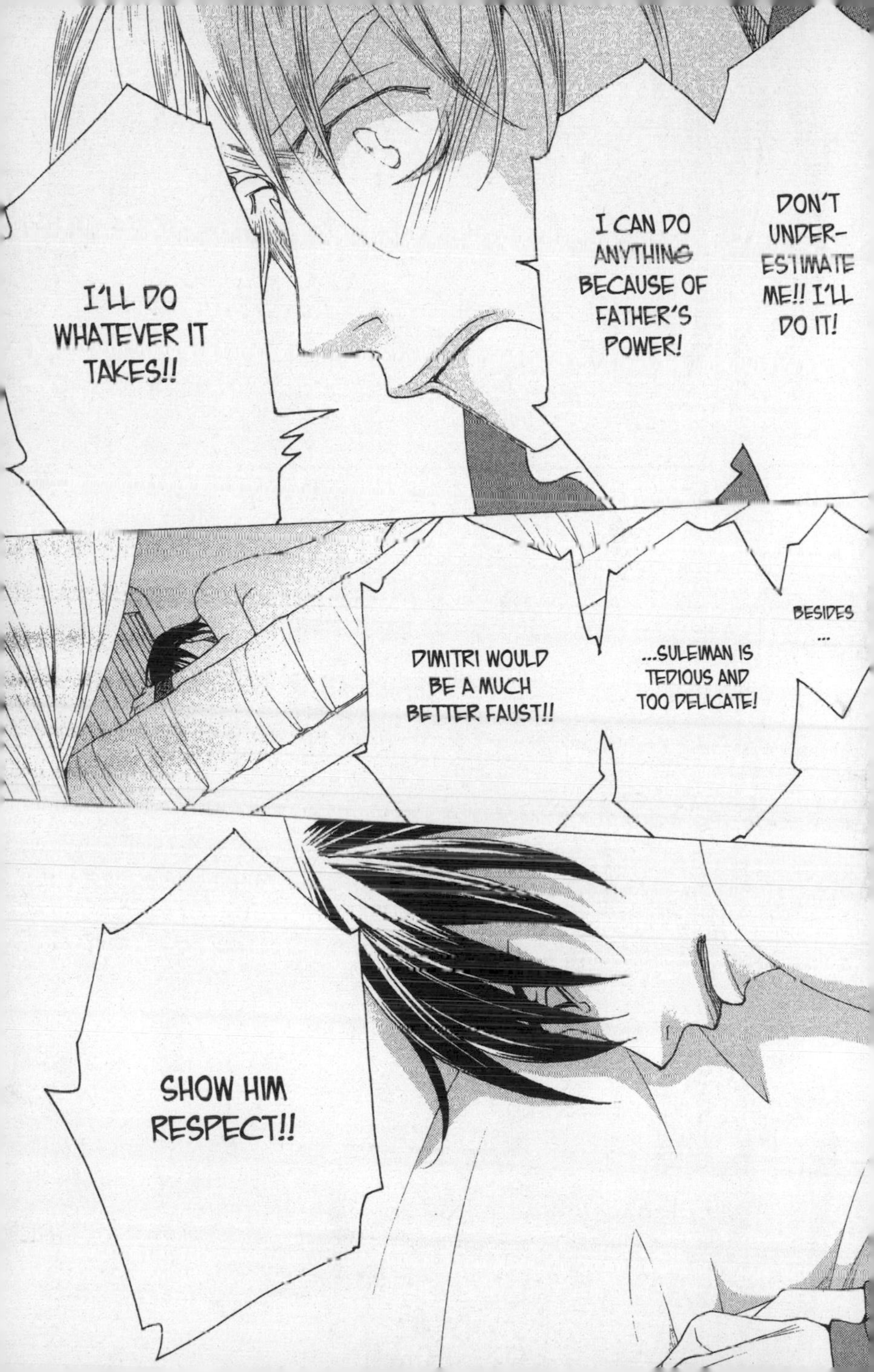
DON'T UNDER-ESTIMATE ME!! I'LL DO IT!
I CAN DO ANYTHING BECAUSE OF FATHER'S POWER!
I'LL DO WHATEVER IT TAKES!!
BESIDES ...
...SULEIMAN IS TEDIOUS AND TOO DELICATE!
DIMITRI WOULD BE A MUCH BETTER FAUST!!
SHOW HIM RESPECT!!

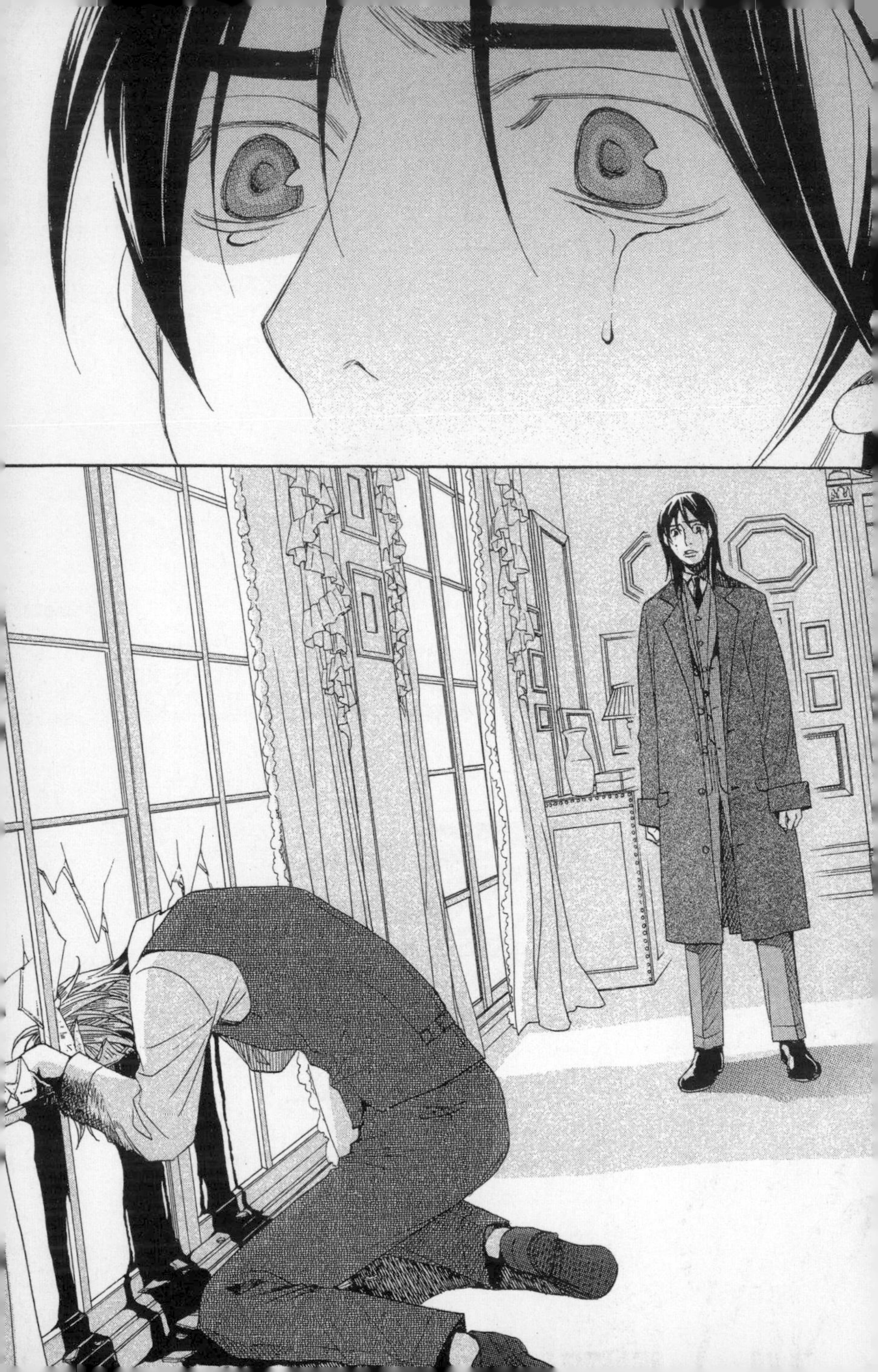

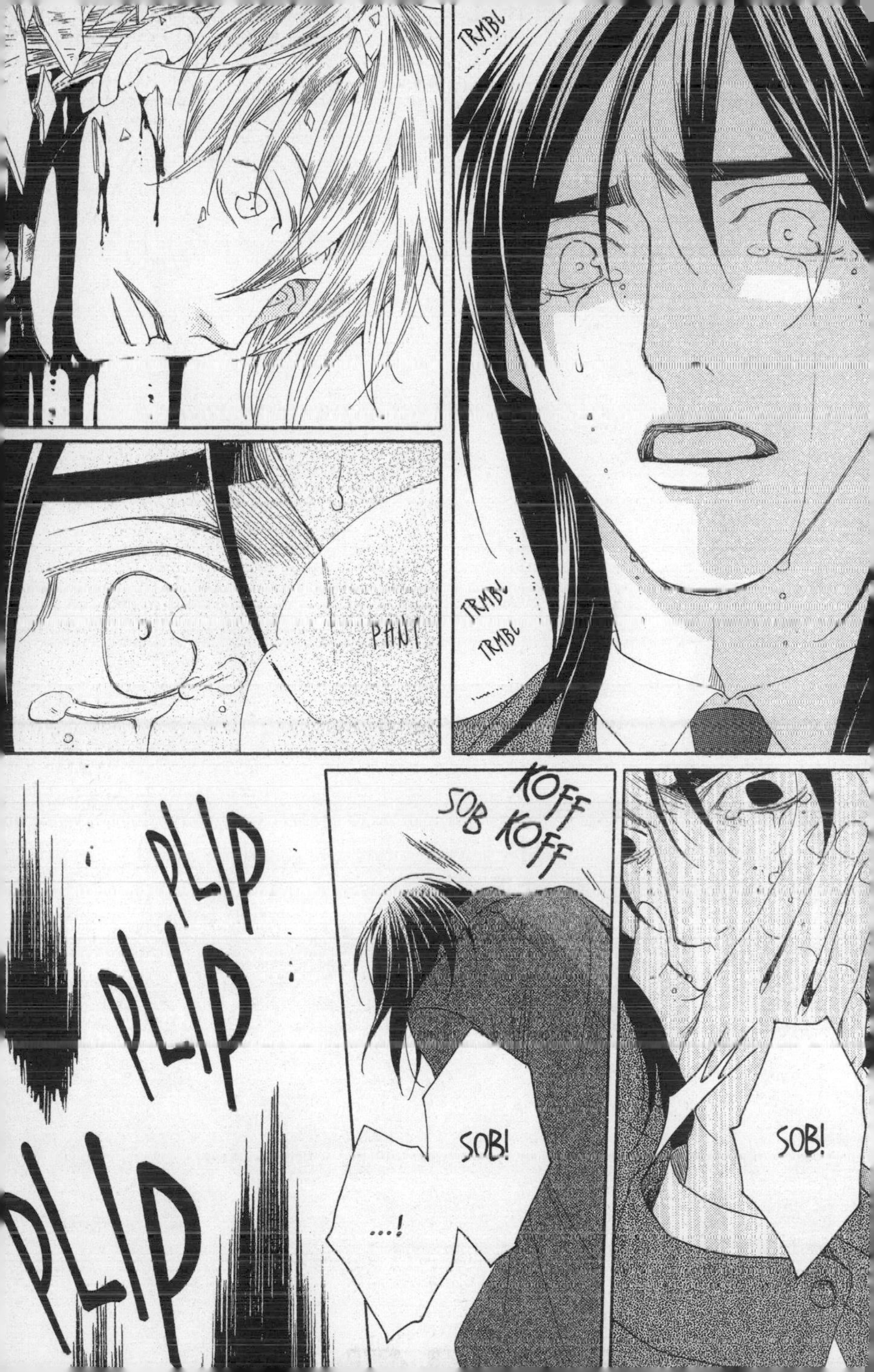
TRMBL
TRMBL
TRMBL
PANT
SOB!
KOFF
SOB KOFF
SOB!
...!
PLIP
PLIP
PLIP

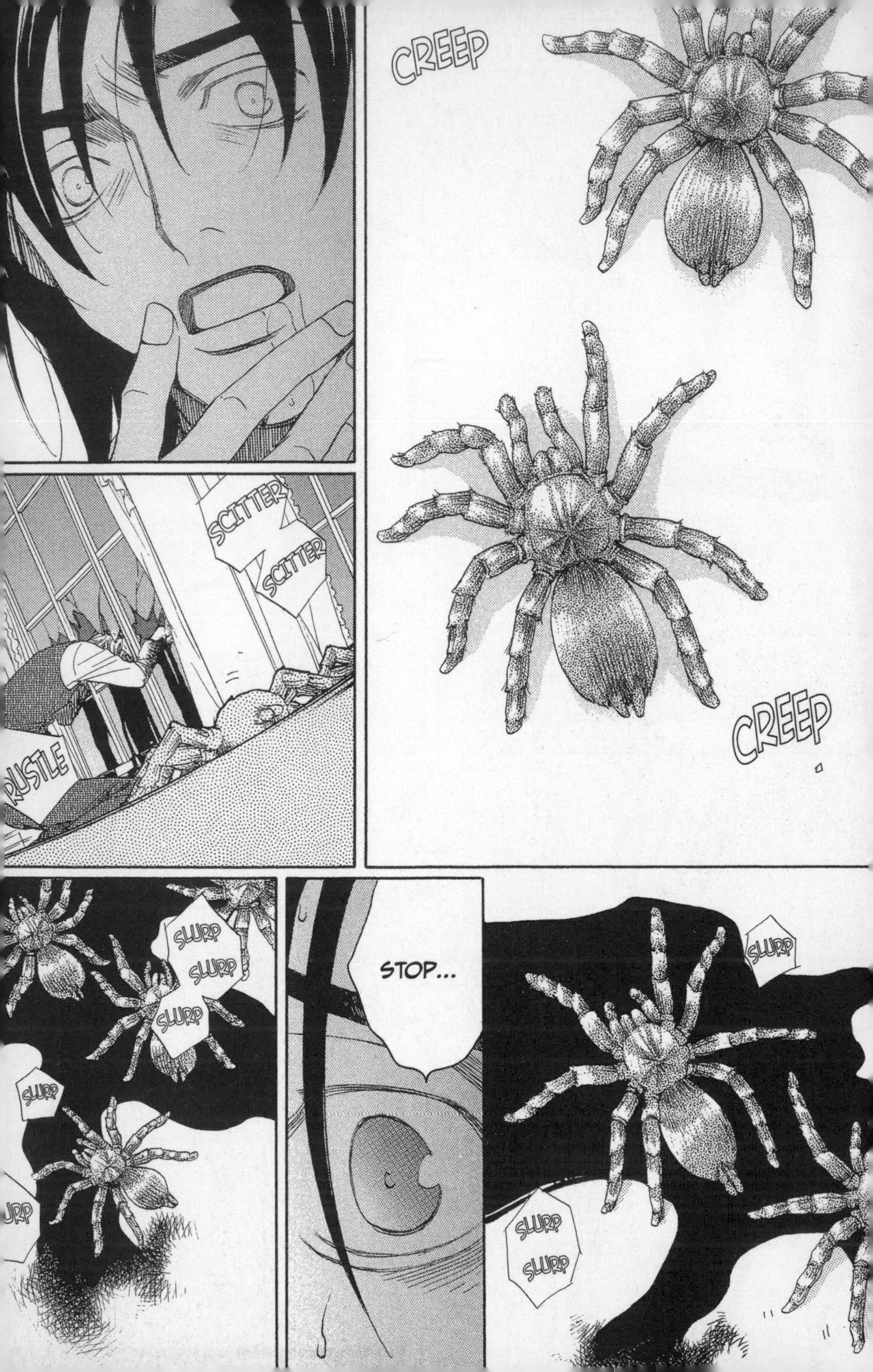
CREEP
CREEP
SCITTER
SCITTER
RUSTLE
SLURP
SLURP
SLURP
STOP...
SLURP
SLURP
SLURP
SLURP

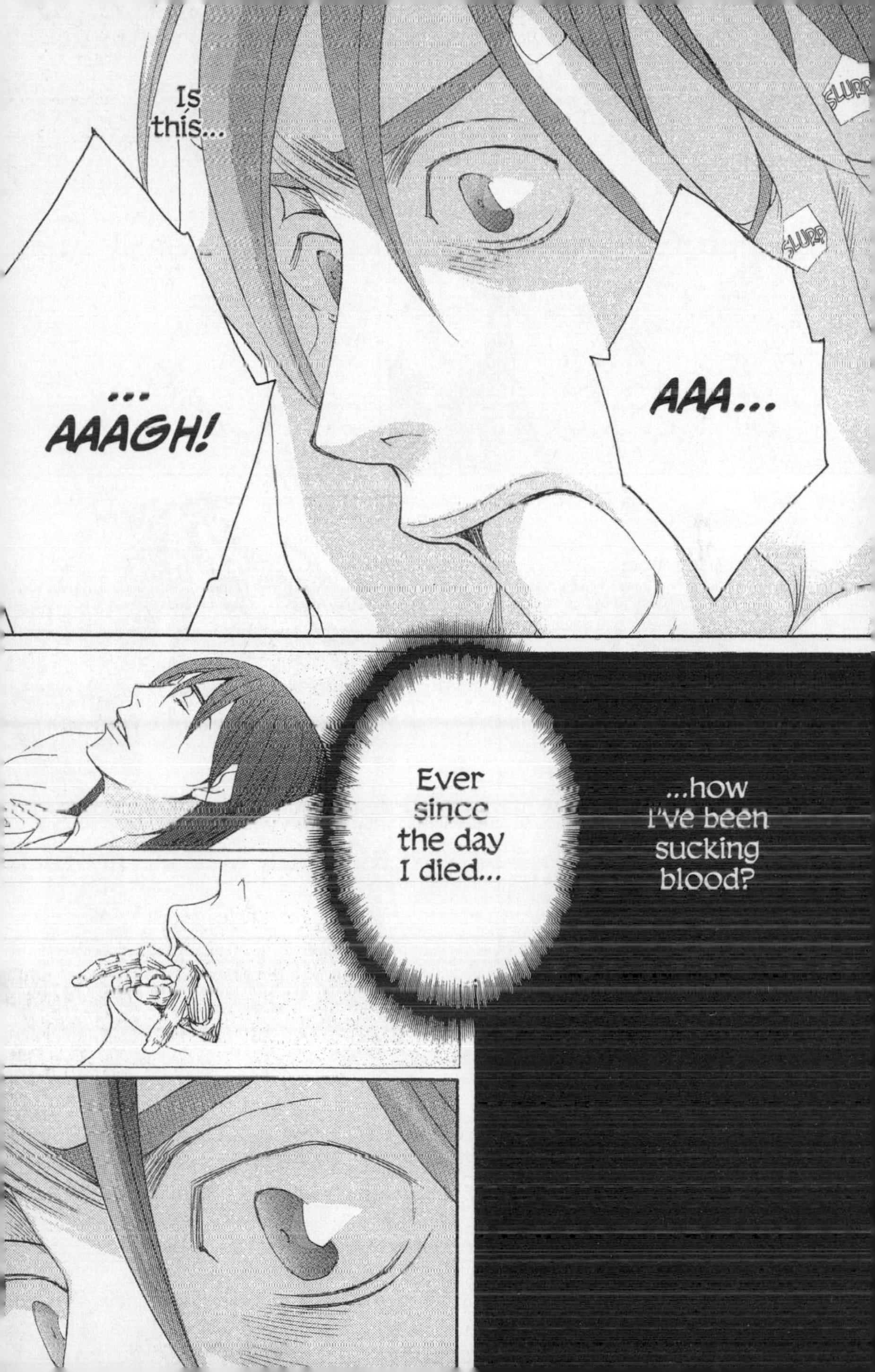
SLURP
Is this...
SLURP
AAA...
...AAÄGH!
Ever since the day I died...
...how I've been sucking blood?

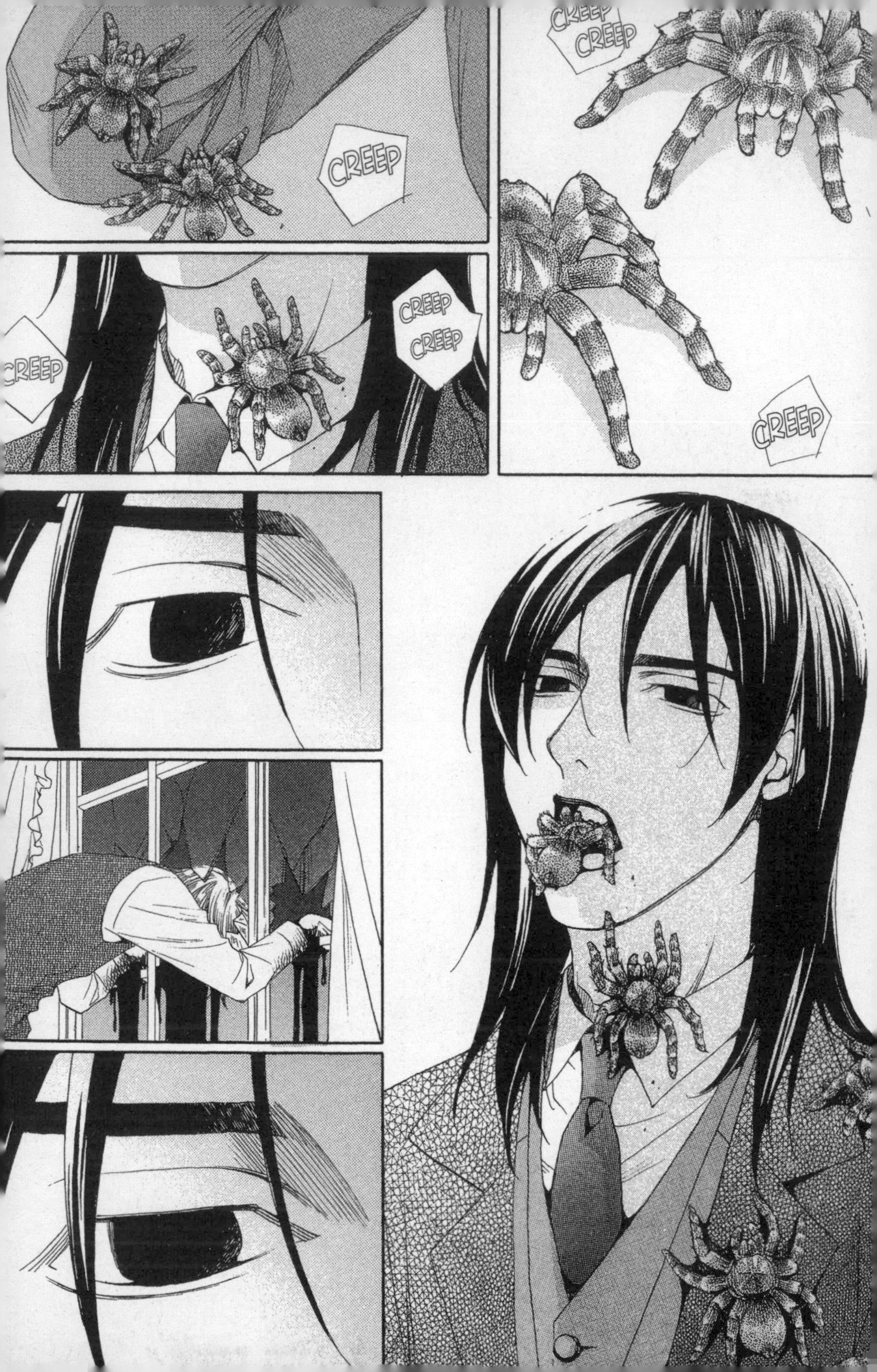
CREEP CREEP
CREEP
CREEP
CREEP CREEP
CREEP

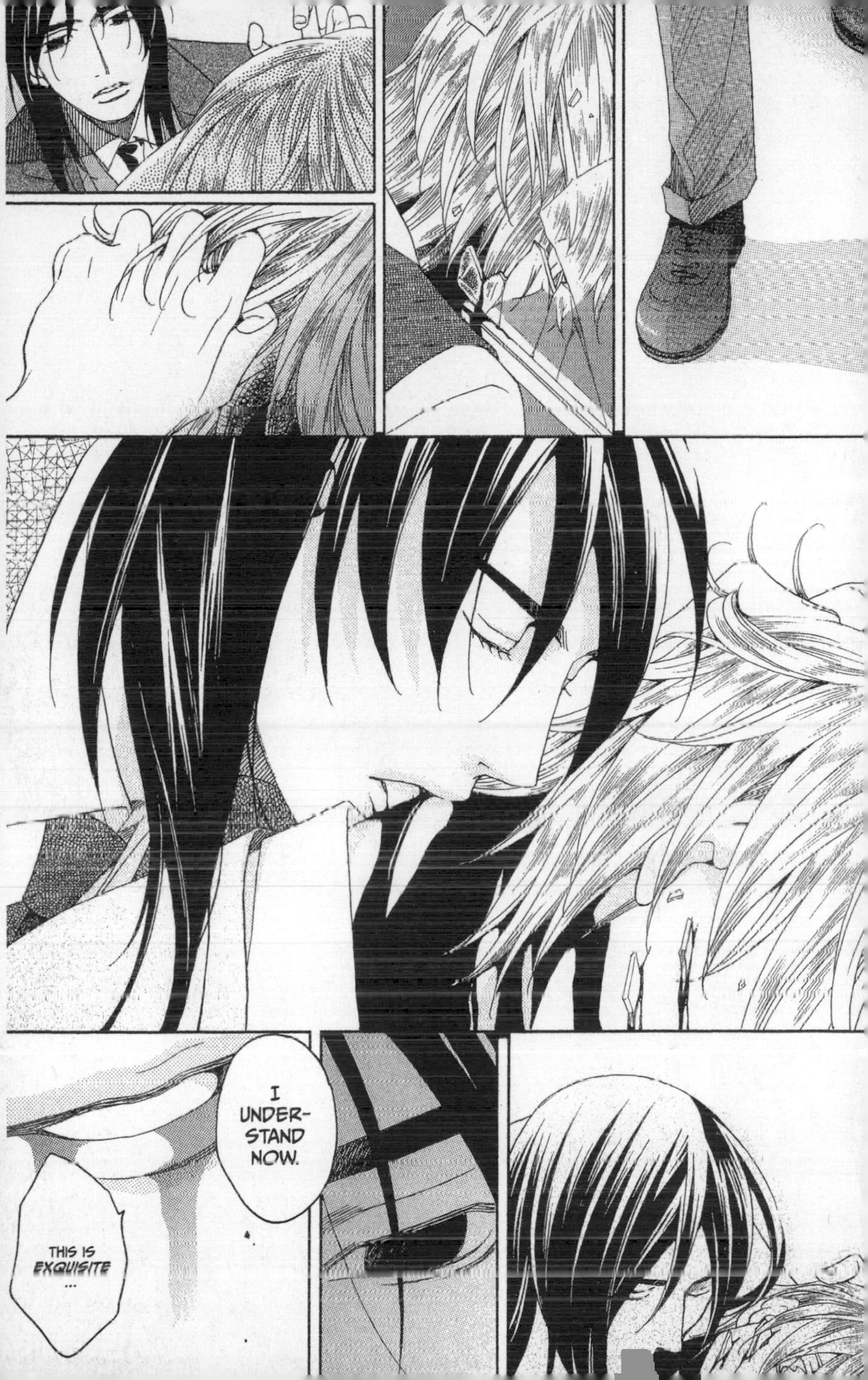
I UNDER-STAND NOW.
THIS IS EXQUISITE ...

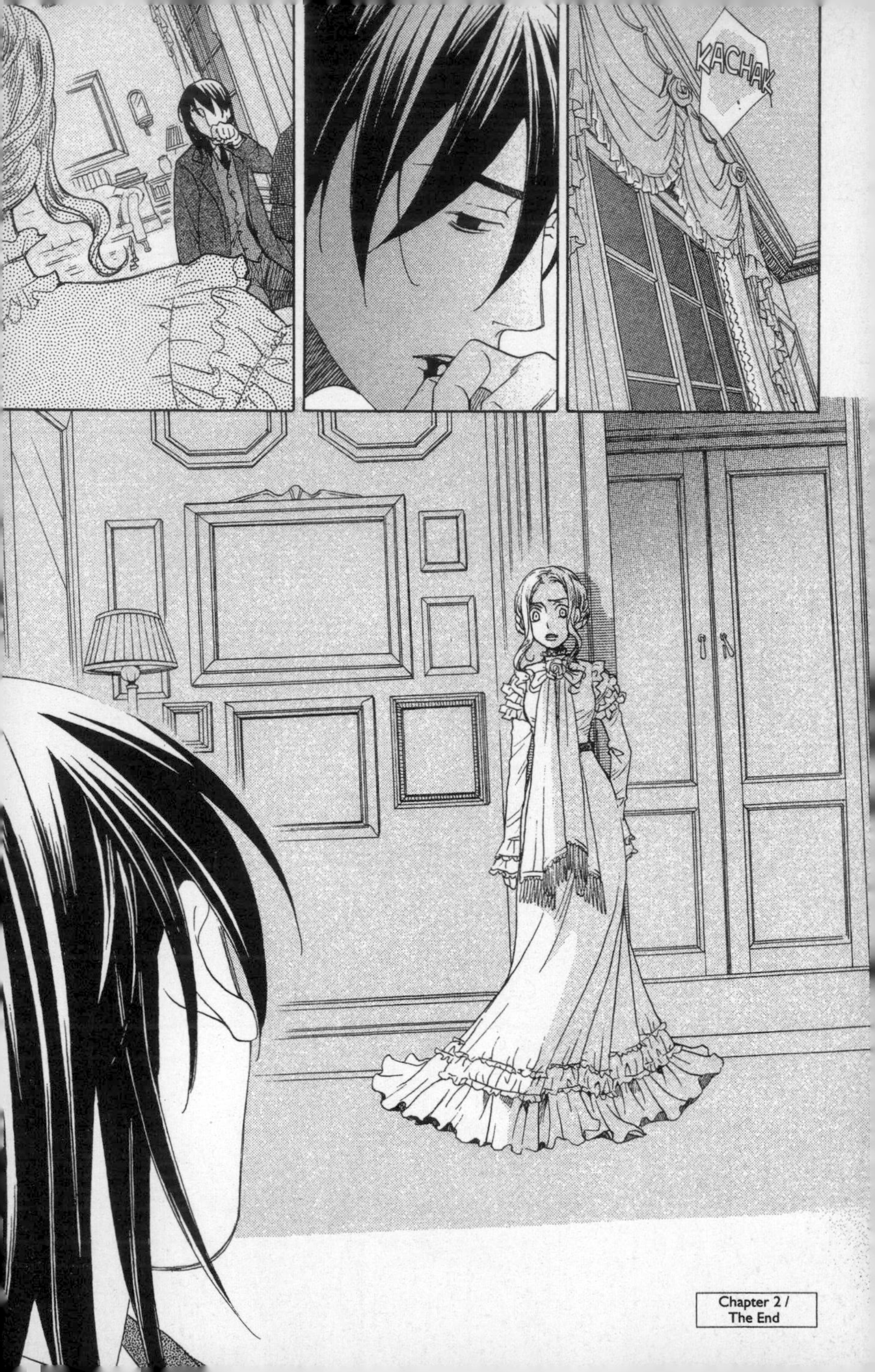
KACHAK
Chapter 2 /
The End

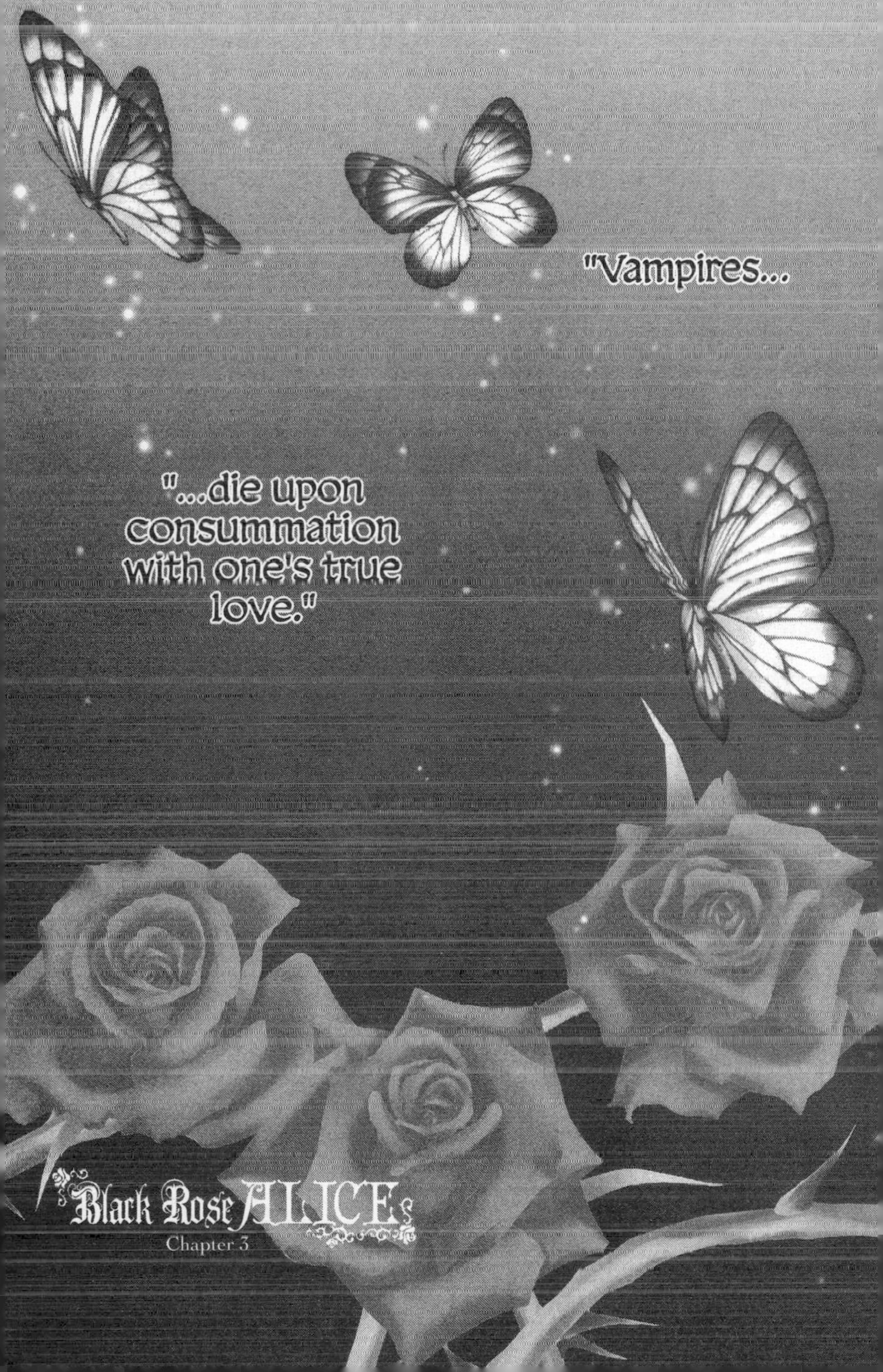
"Vampires...
"...die upon consummation with one's true love."
Black Rose Alice
Chapter 3

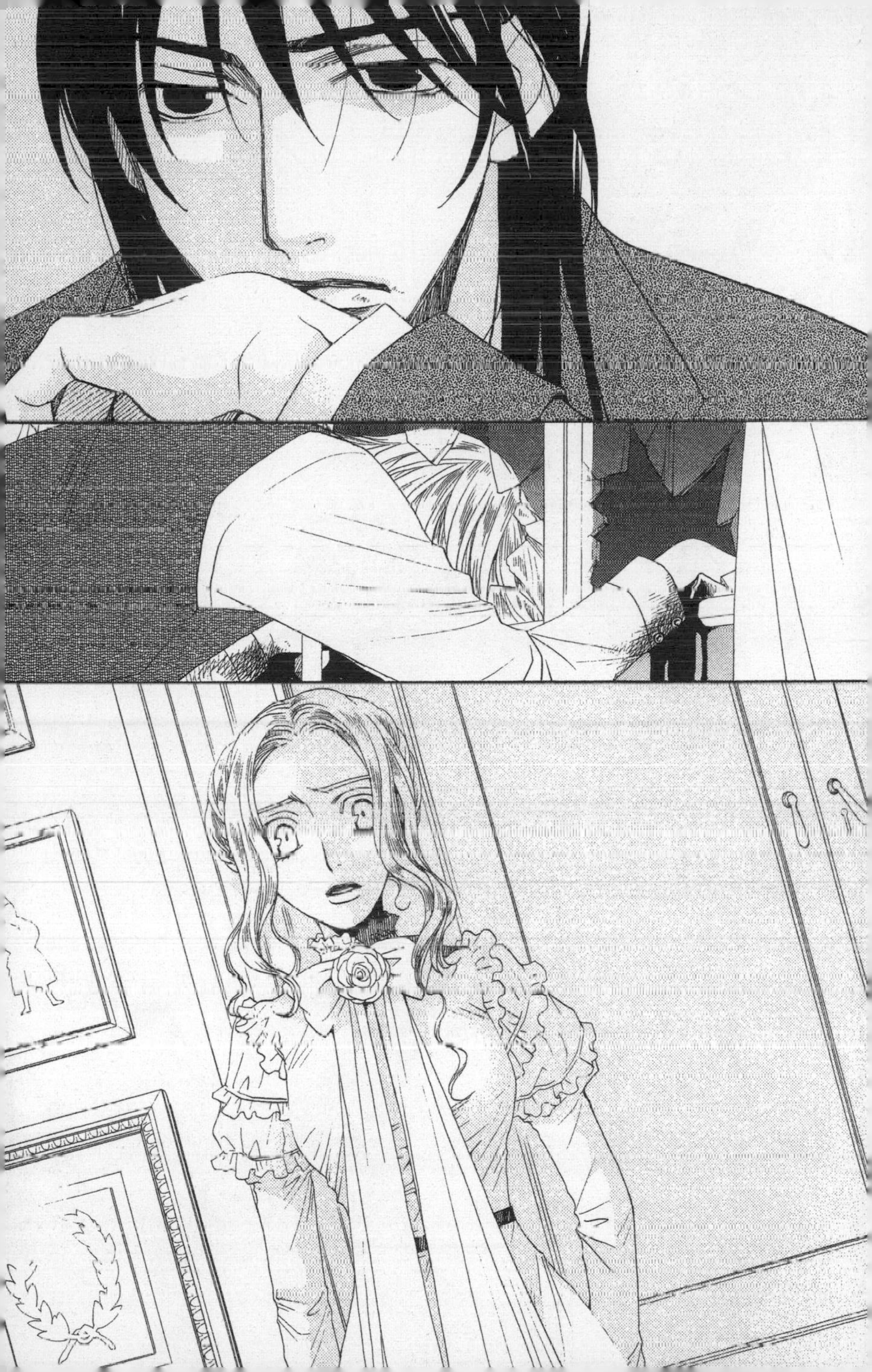

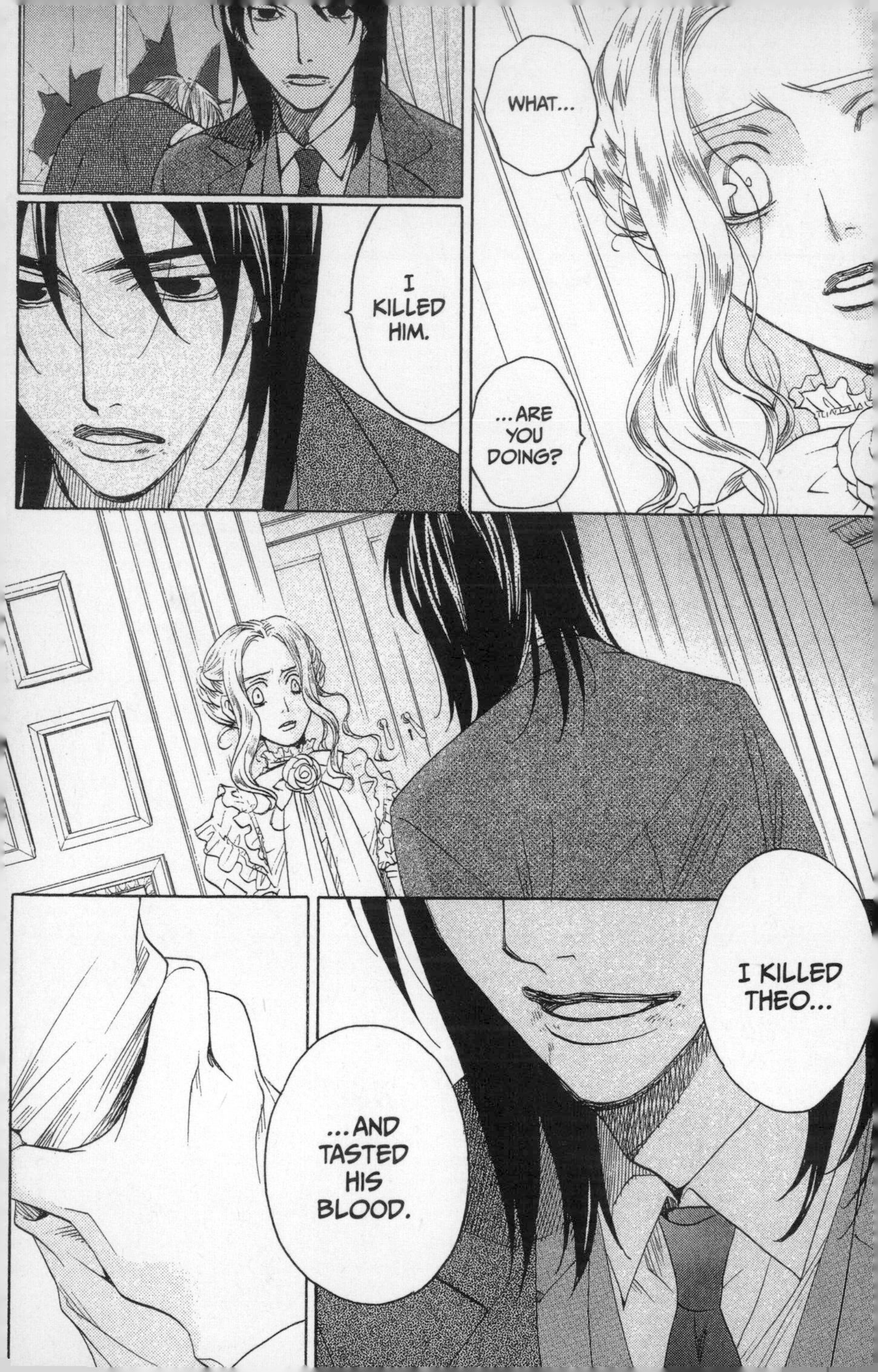
WHAT...
...ARE YOU DOING?
I KILLED HIM.
I KILLED THEO...
...AND TASTED HIS BLOOD.

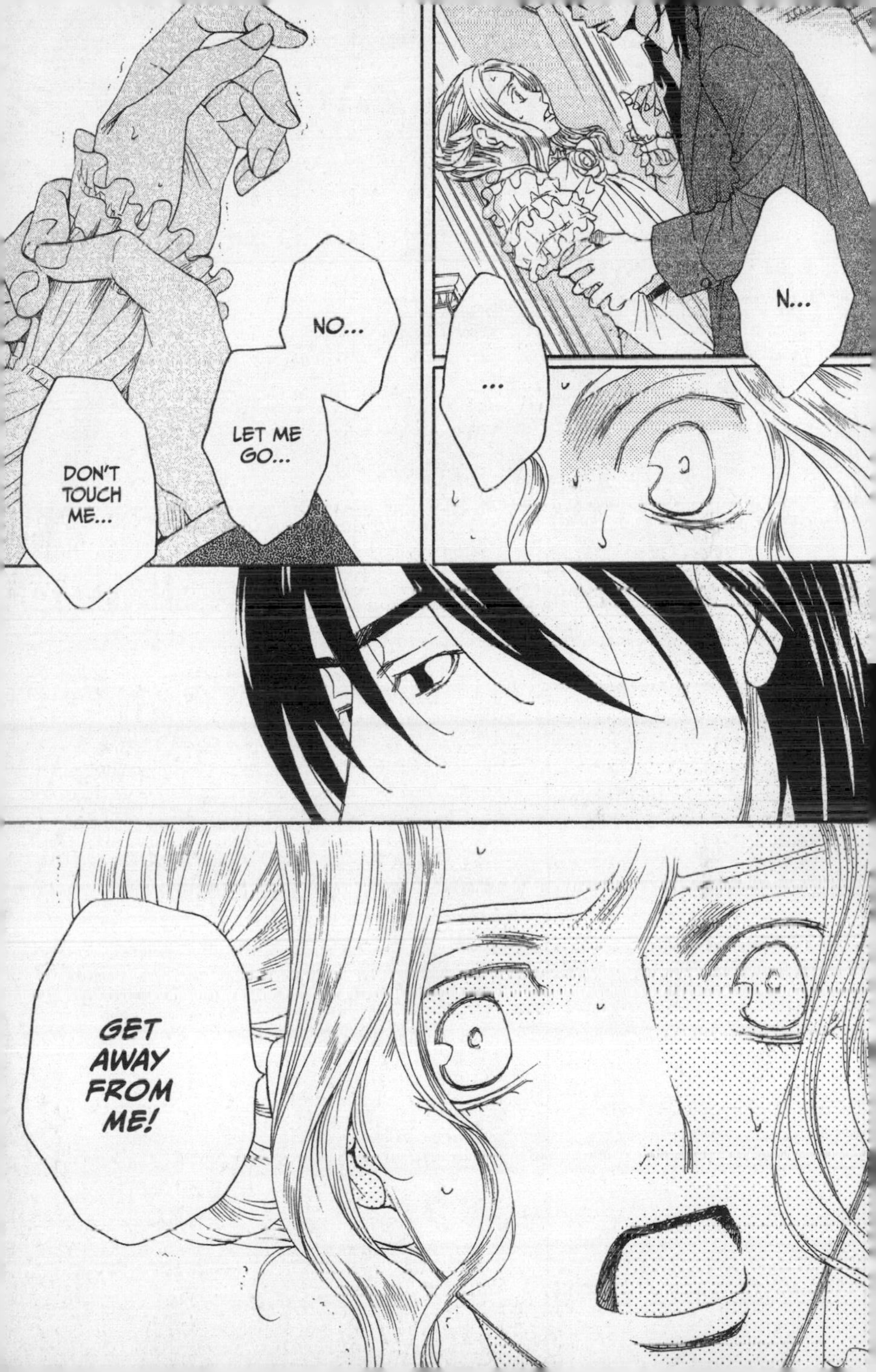
N...
...
NO...
LET ME GO...
DON'T TOUCH ME...
GET AWAY FROM ME!

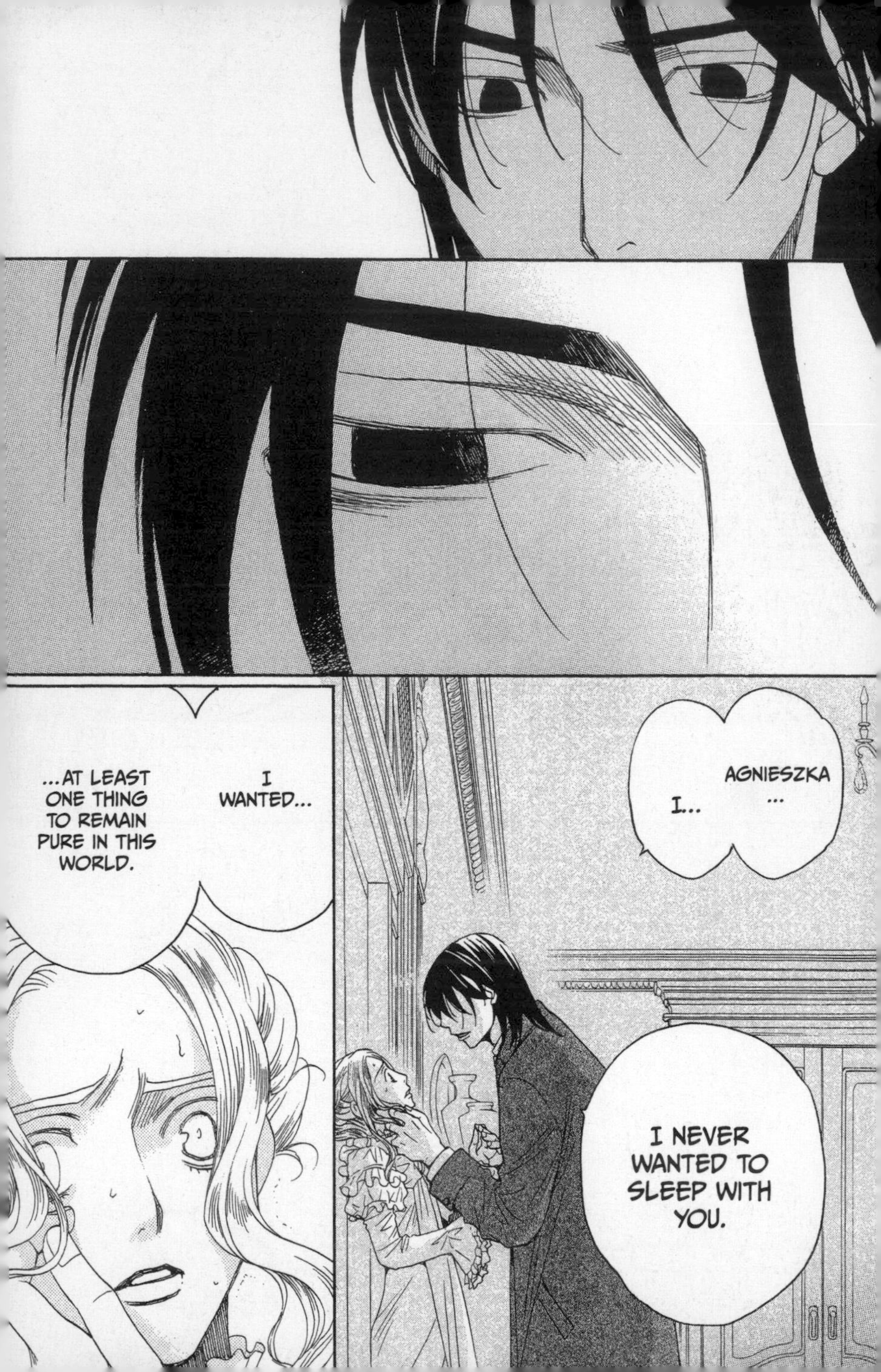
AGNIESZKA... I...
I NEVER WANTED TO SLEEP WITH YOU.
I WANTED... ...AT LEAST ONE THING TO REMAIN PURE IN THIS WORLD.

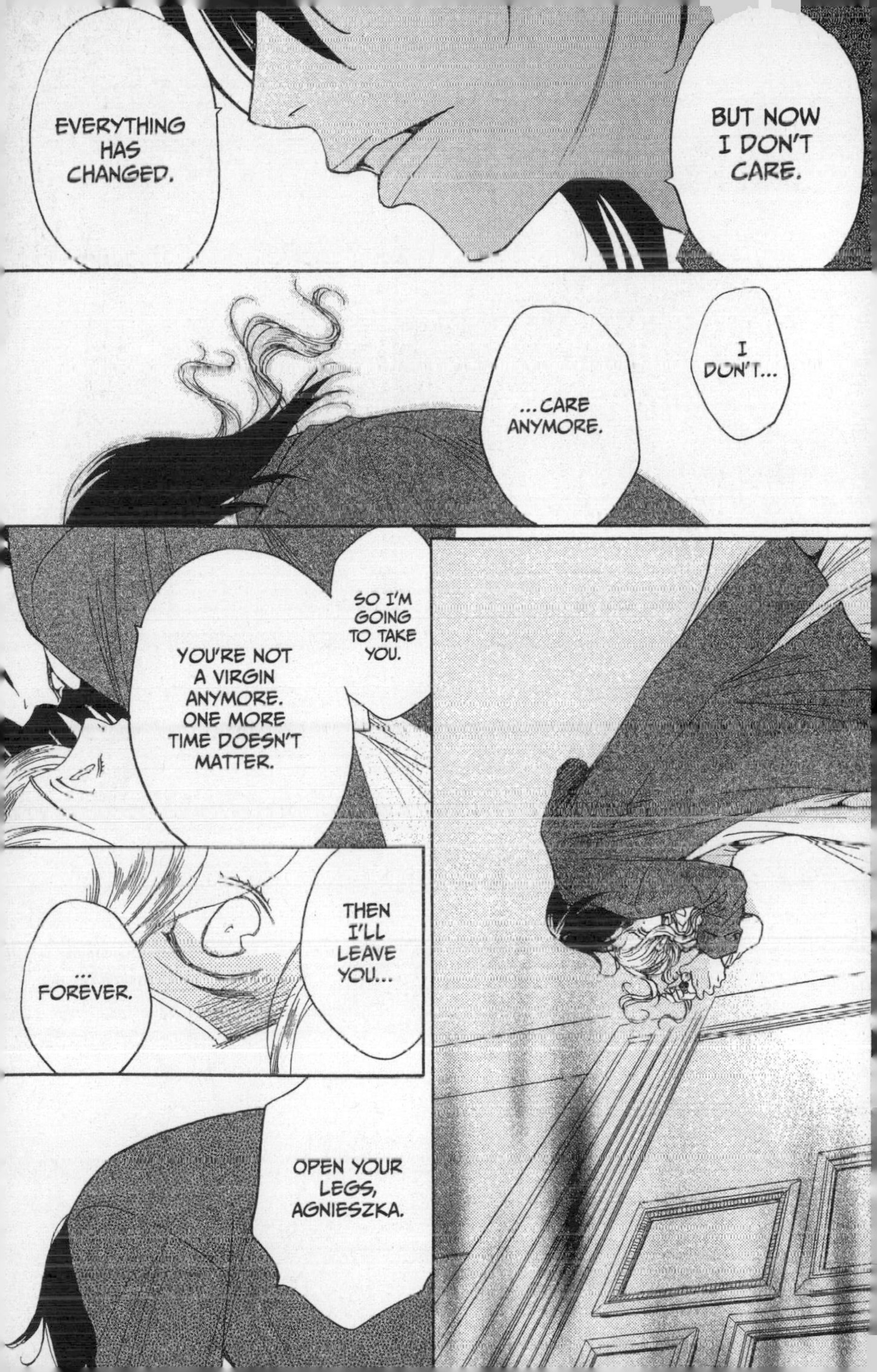
BUT NOW I DON'T CARE.
EVERYTHING HAS CHANGED.
I DON'T...
...CARE ANYMORE.
SO I'M GOING TO TAKE YOU.
YOU'RE NOT A VIRGIN ANYMORE. ONE MORE TIME DOESN'T MATTER.
THEN I'LL LEAVE YOU...
...FOREVER.
OPEN YOUR LEGS, AGNIESZKA.

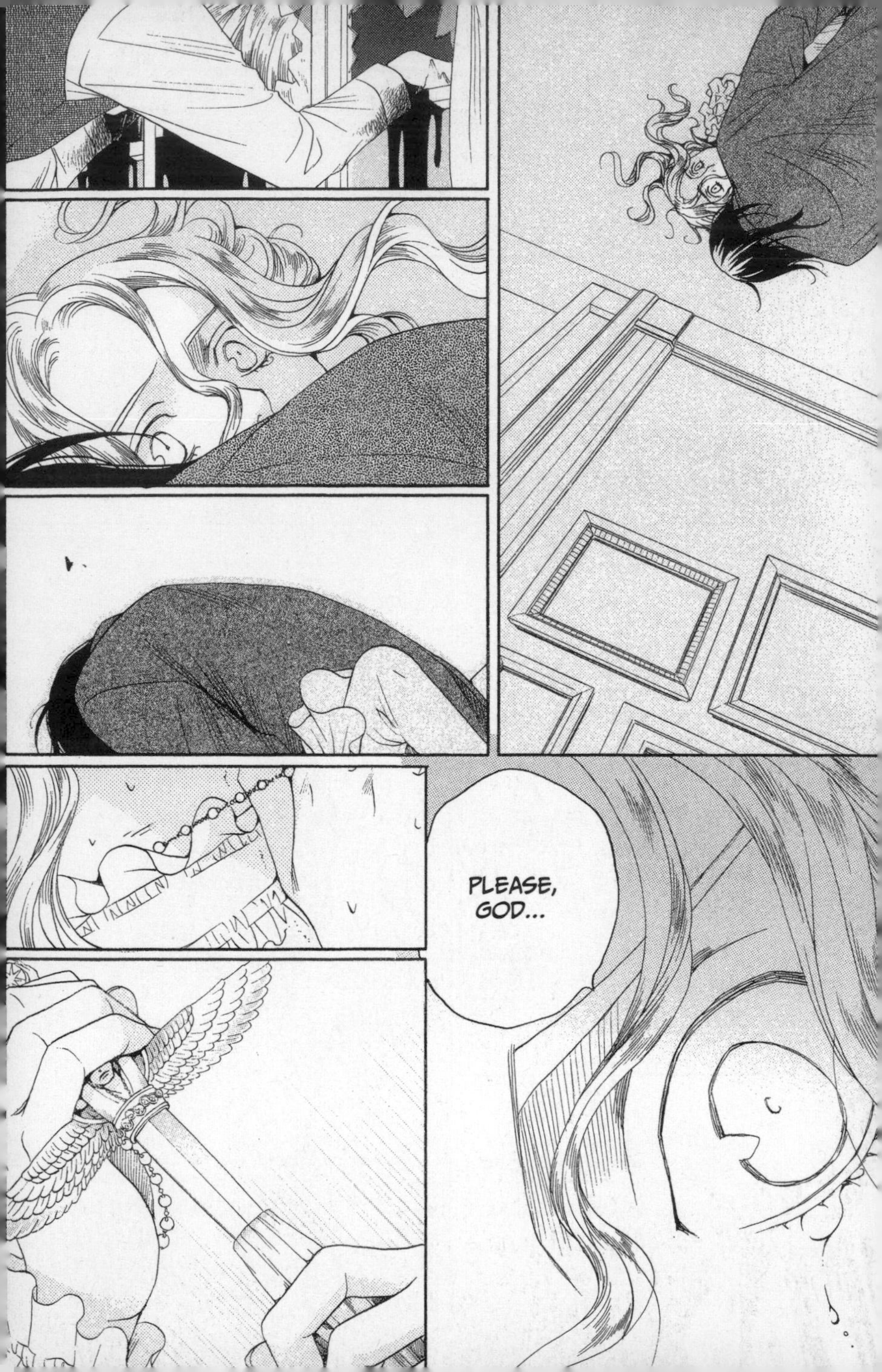
PLEASE, GOD...

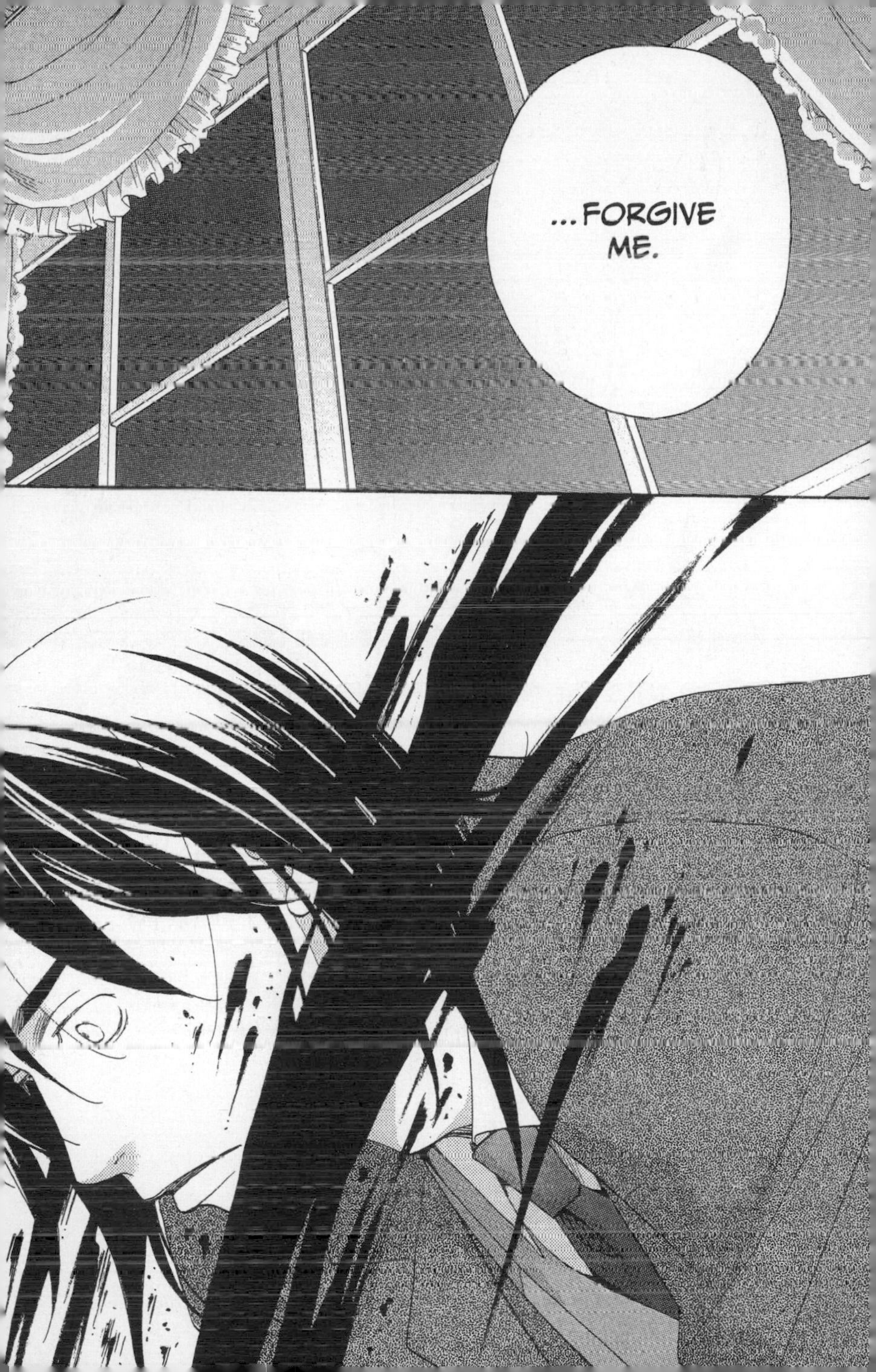
...FORGIVE ME.

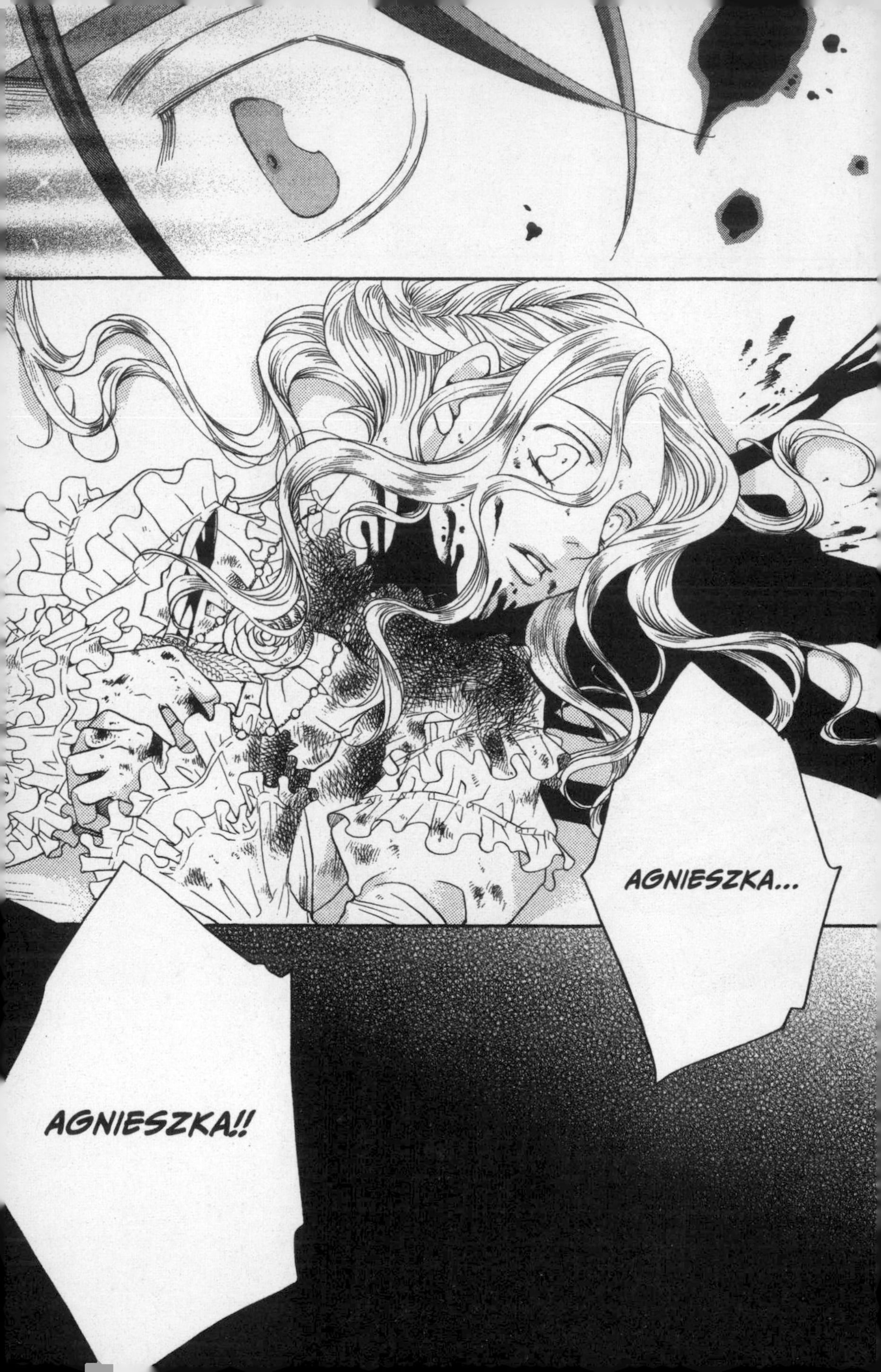
AGNIESZKA...
AGNIESZKA!!

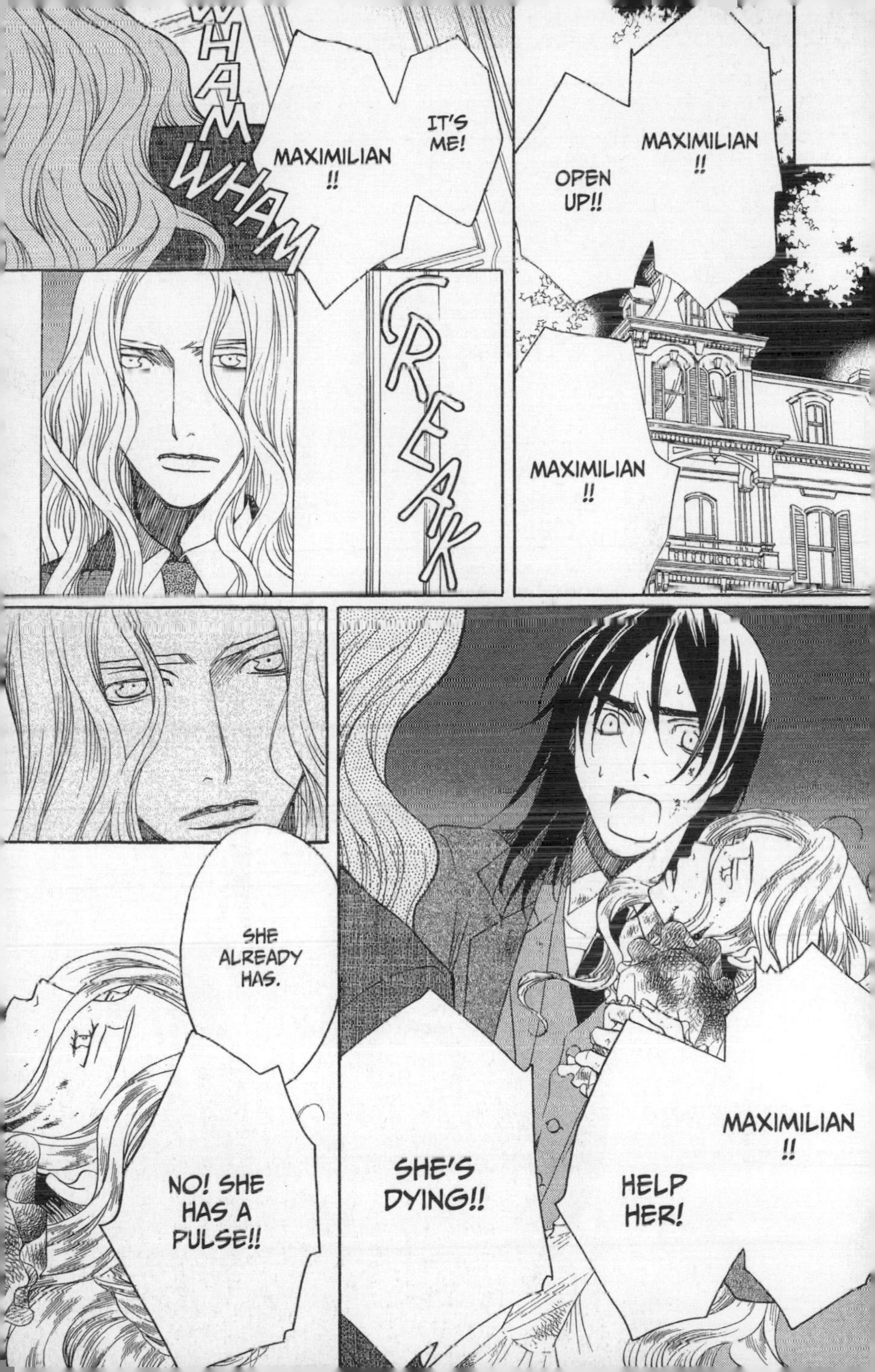
MAXIMILIAN!!
OPEN UP!!
MAXIMILIAN!!
IT'S ME!
MAXIMILIAN!!
WHAM
WHAM
CREAK
MAXIMILIAN!!
HELP HER!
SHE'S DYING!!
SHE ALREADY HAS.
NO! SHE HAS A PULSE!!

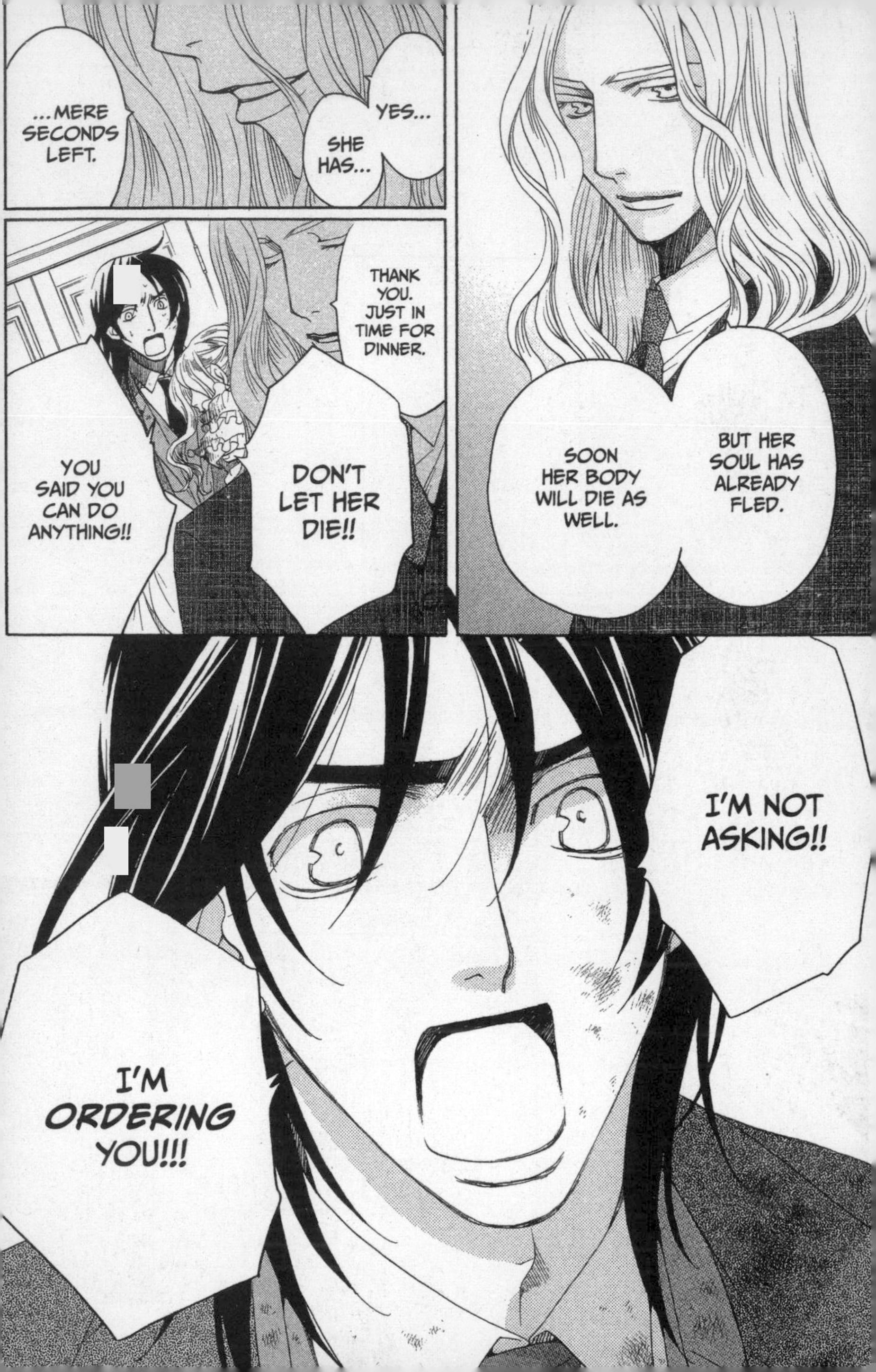
BUT HER SOUL HAS ALREADY FLED.
SOON HER BODY WILL DIE AS WELL.
YES... SHE HAS...
...MERE SECONDS LEFT.
THANK YOU. JUST IN TIME FOR DINNER.
DON'T LET HER DIE!!
YOU SAID YOU CAN DO ANYTHING!!
I'M NOT ASKING!!
I'M ORDERING YOU!!!

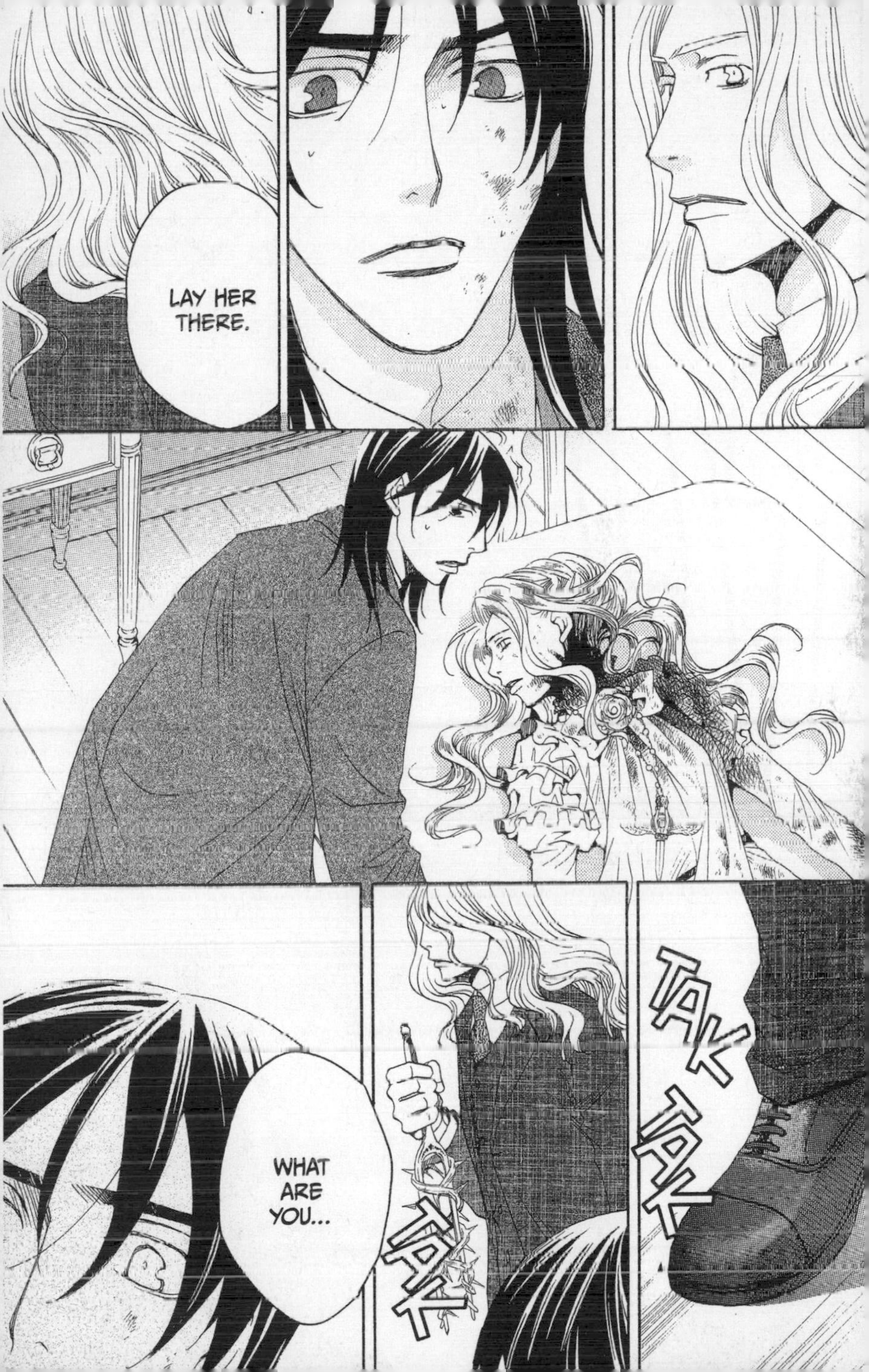
LAY HER THERE.
TAK TAK
TAK
WHAT ARE YOU...

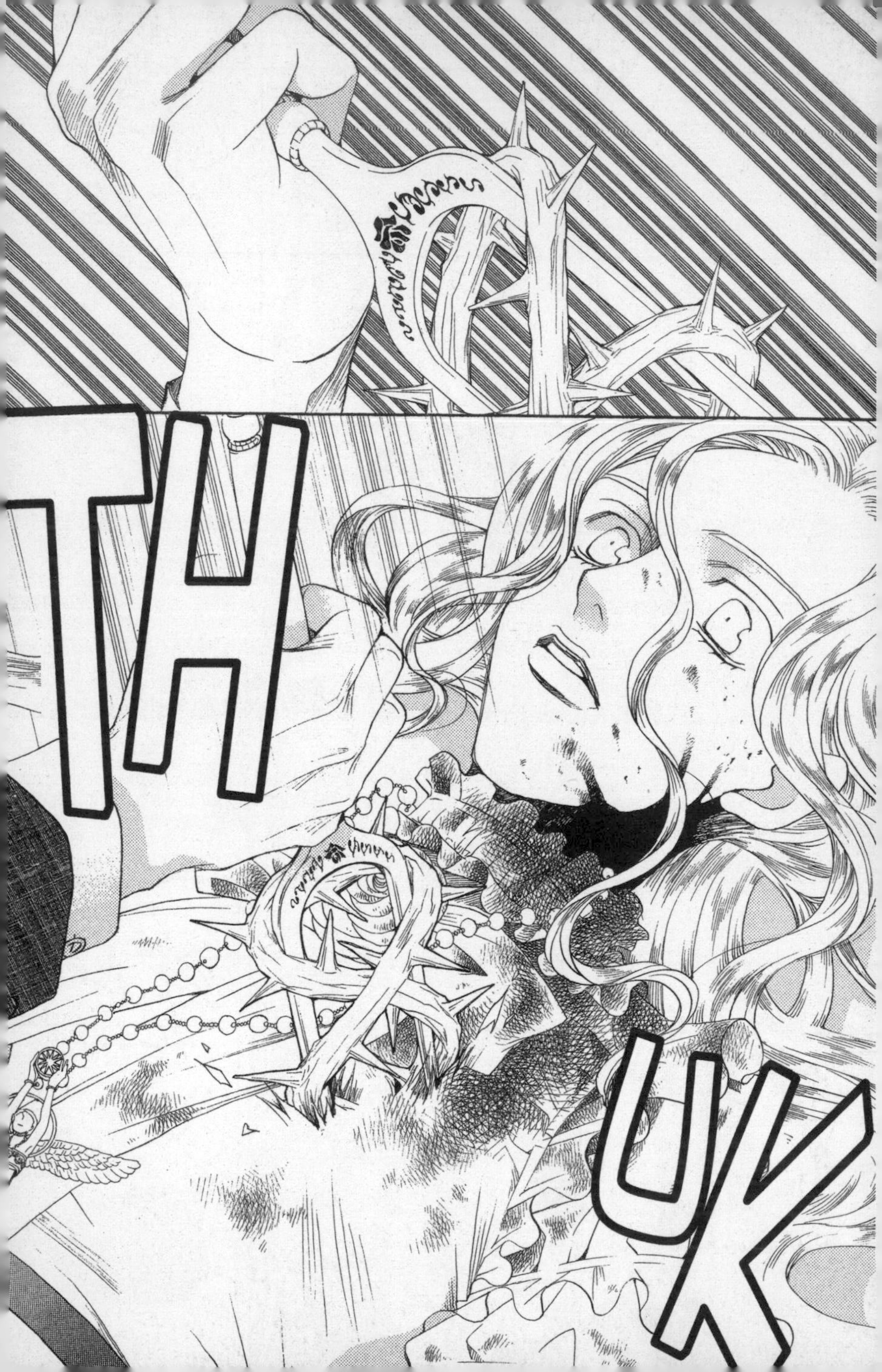
THUK

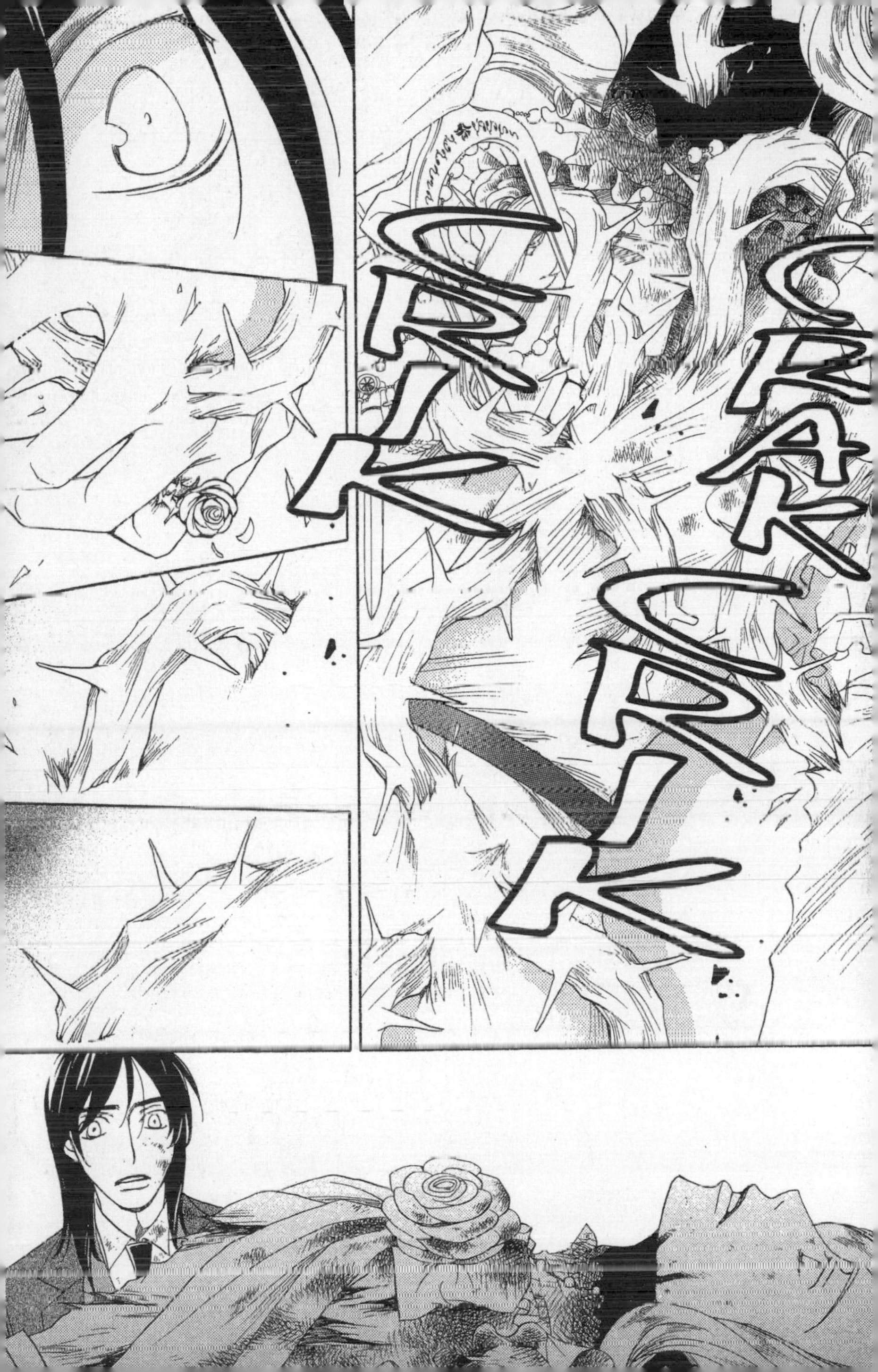
CRAK
CRIK
CRIK

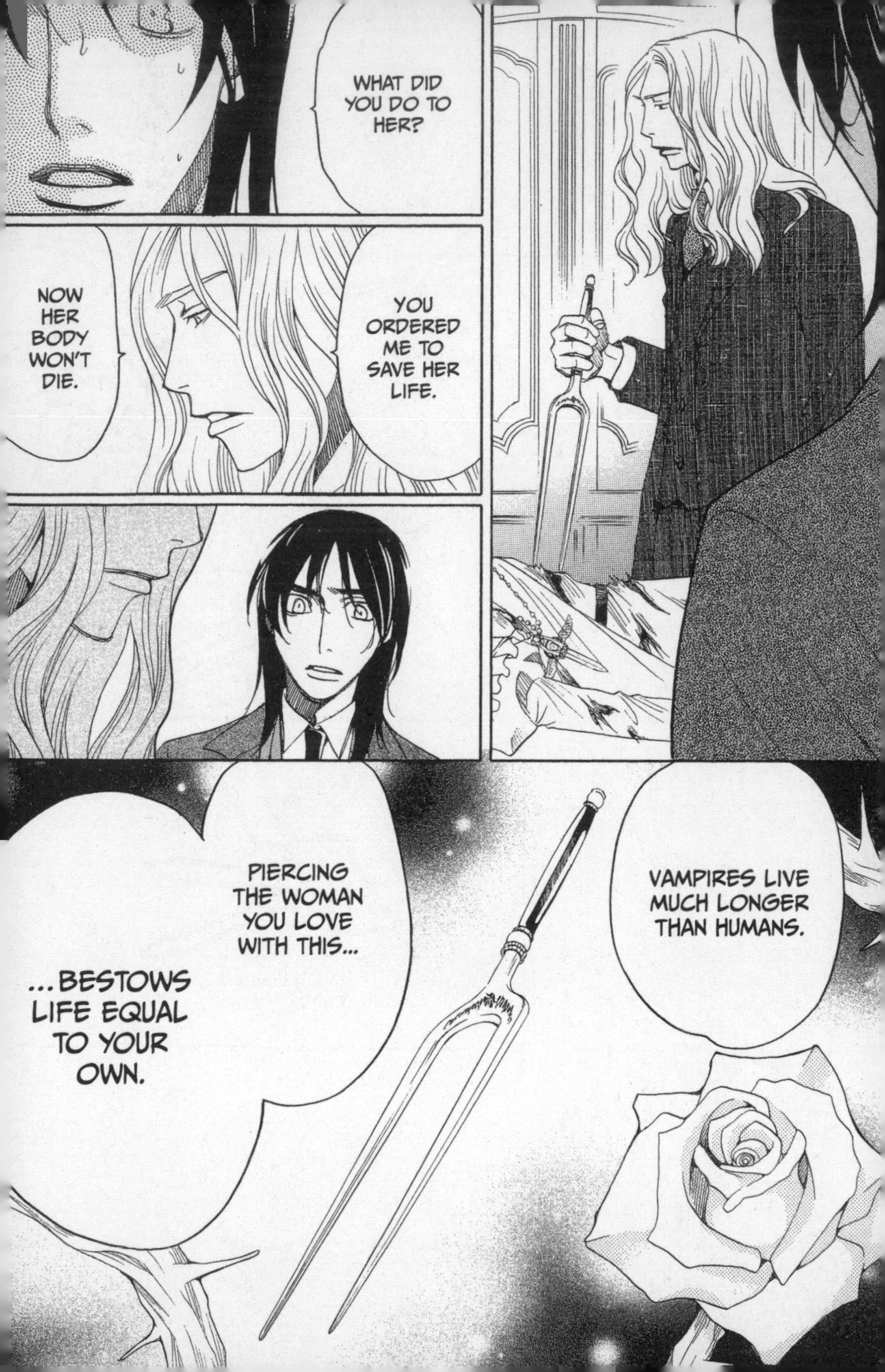
WHAT DID YOU DO TO HER?
YOU ORDERED ME TO SAVE HER LIFE.
NOW HER BODY WON'T DIE.
VAMPIRES LIVE MUCH LONGER THAN HUMANS.
PIERCING THE WOMAN YOU LOVE WITH THIS...
...BESTOWS LIFE EQUAL TO YOUR OWN.

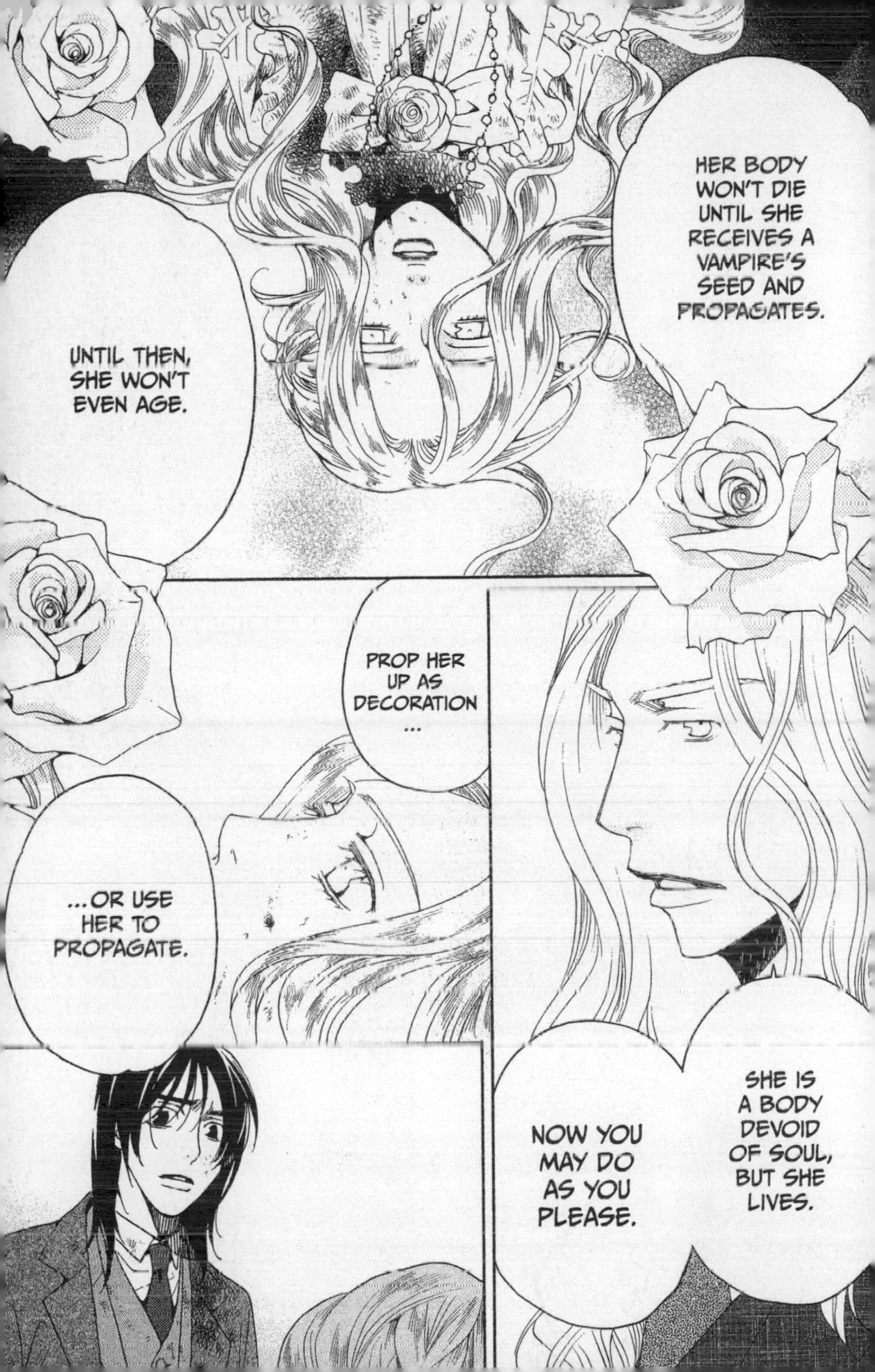
HER BODY WON'T DIE UNTIL SHE RECEIVES A VAMPIRE'S SEED AND PROPAGATES.
UNTIL THEN, SHE WON'T EVEN AGE.
PROP HER UP AS DECORATION ...
...OR USE HER TO PROPAGATE.
SHE IS A BODY DEVOID OF SOUL, BUT SHE LIVES.
NOW YOU MAY DO AS YOU PLEASE.

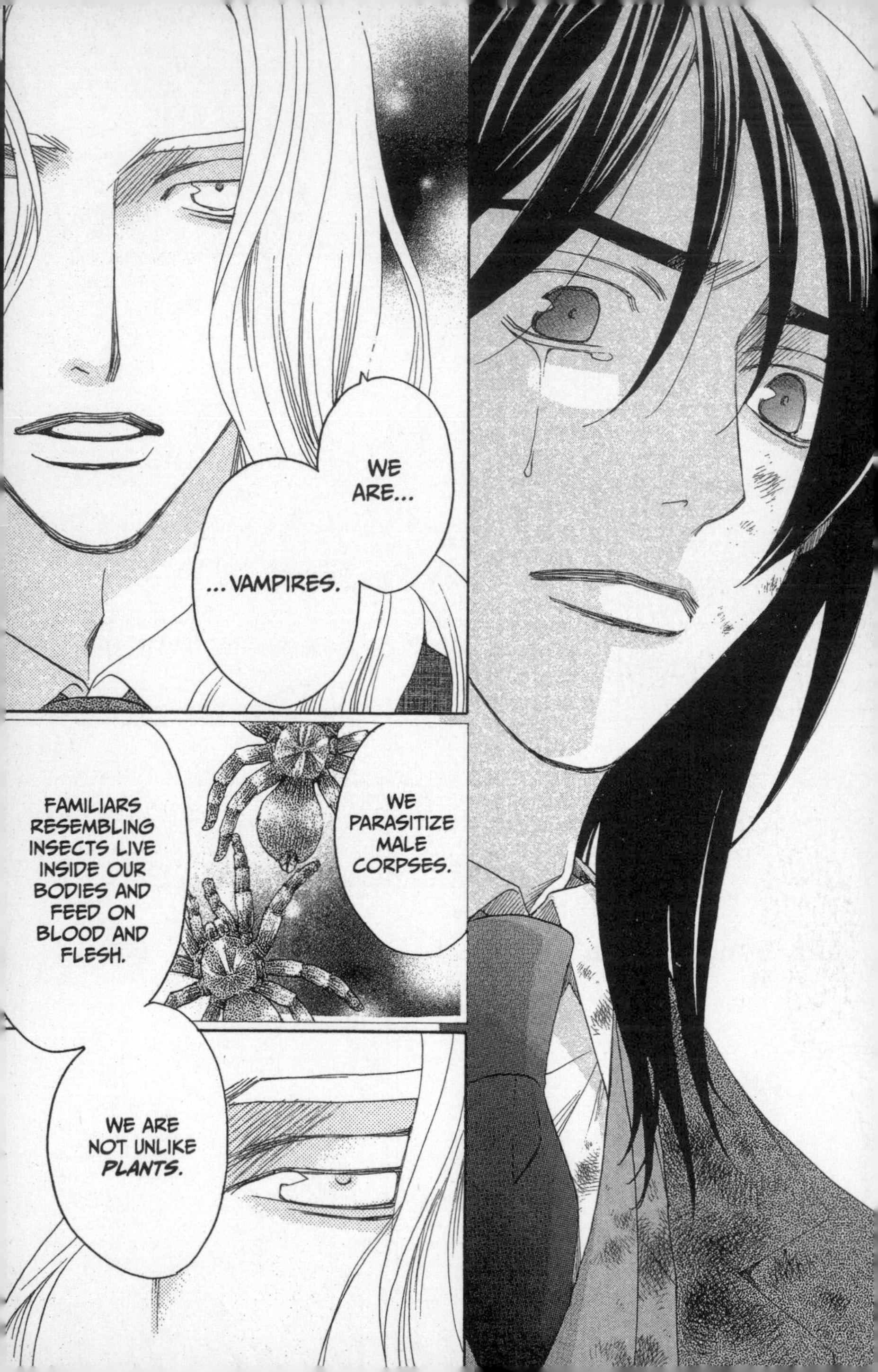
WE ARE...
...VAMPIRES.
WE PARASITIZE MALE CORPSES.
FAMILIARS RESEMBLING INSECTS LIVE INSIDE OUR BODIES AND FEED ON BLOOD AND FLESH.
WE ARE NOT UNLIKE *PLANTS*.

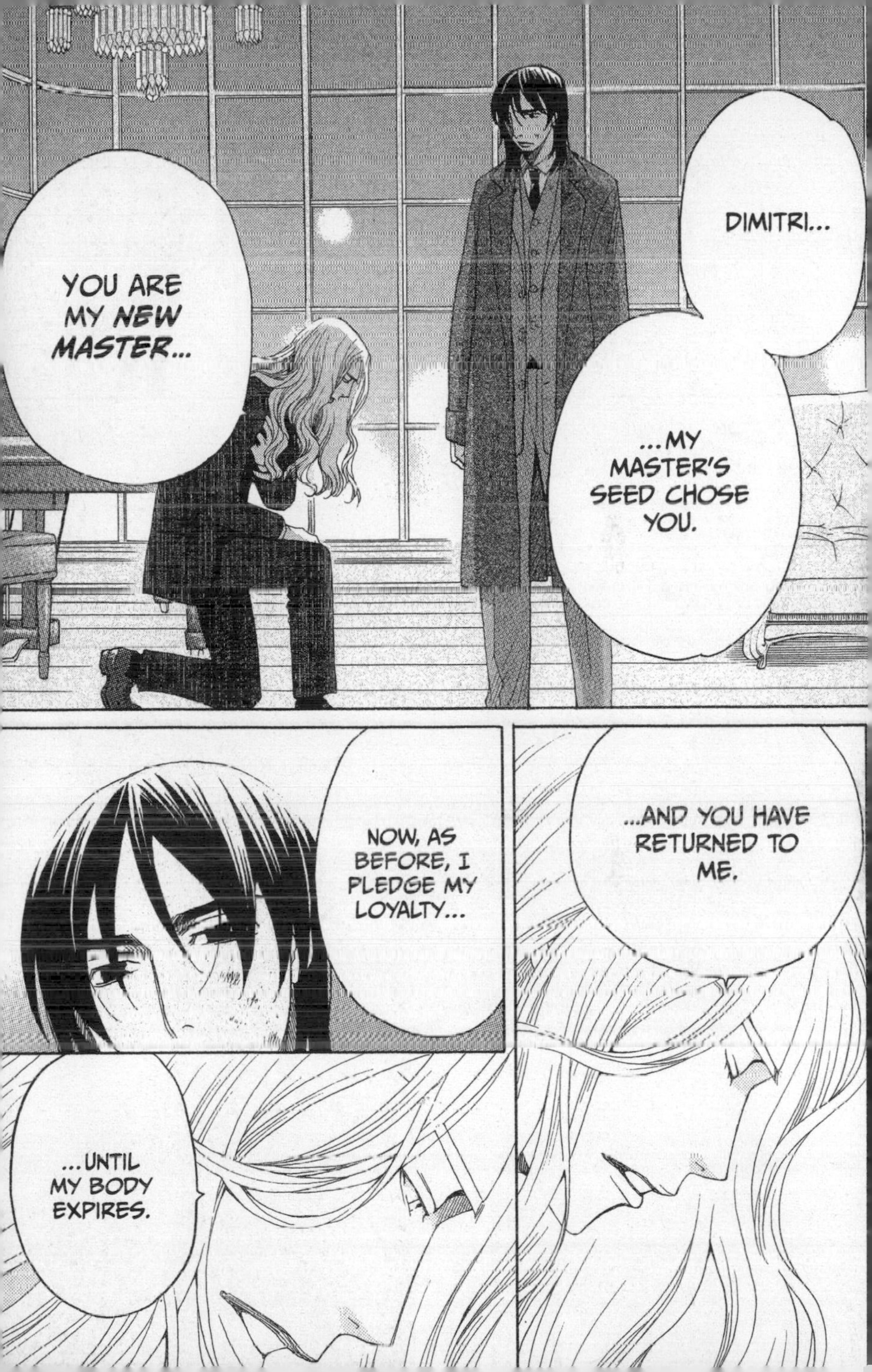
DIMITRI...
...MY MASTER'S SEED CHOSE YOU.
YOU ARE MY *NEW MASTER*...
...AND YOU HAVE RETURNED TO ME.
NOW, AS BEFORE, I PLEDGE MY LOYALTY...
...UNTIL MY BODY EXPIRES.

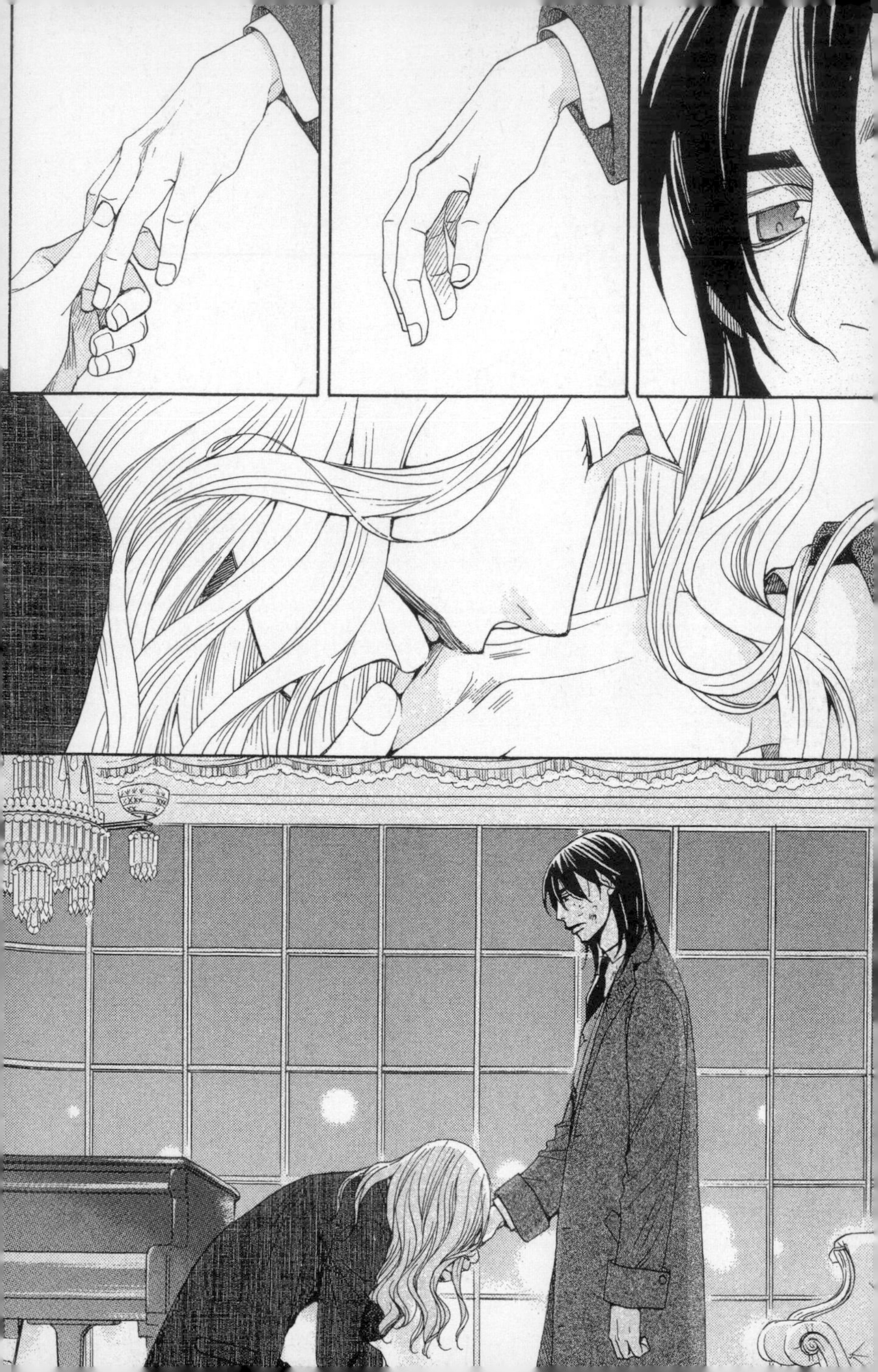

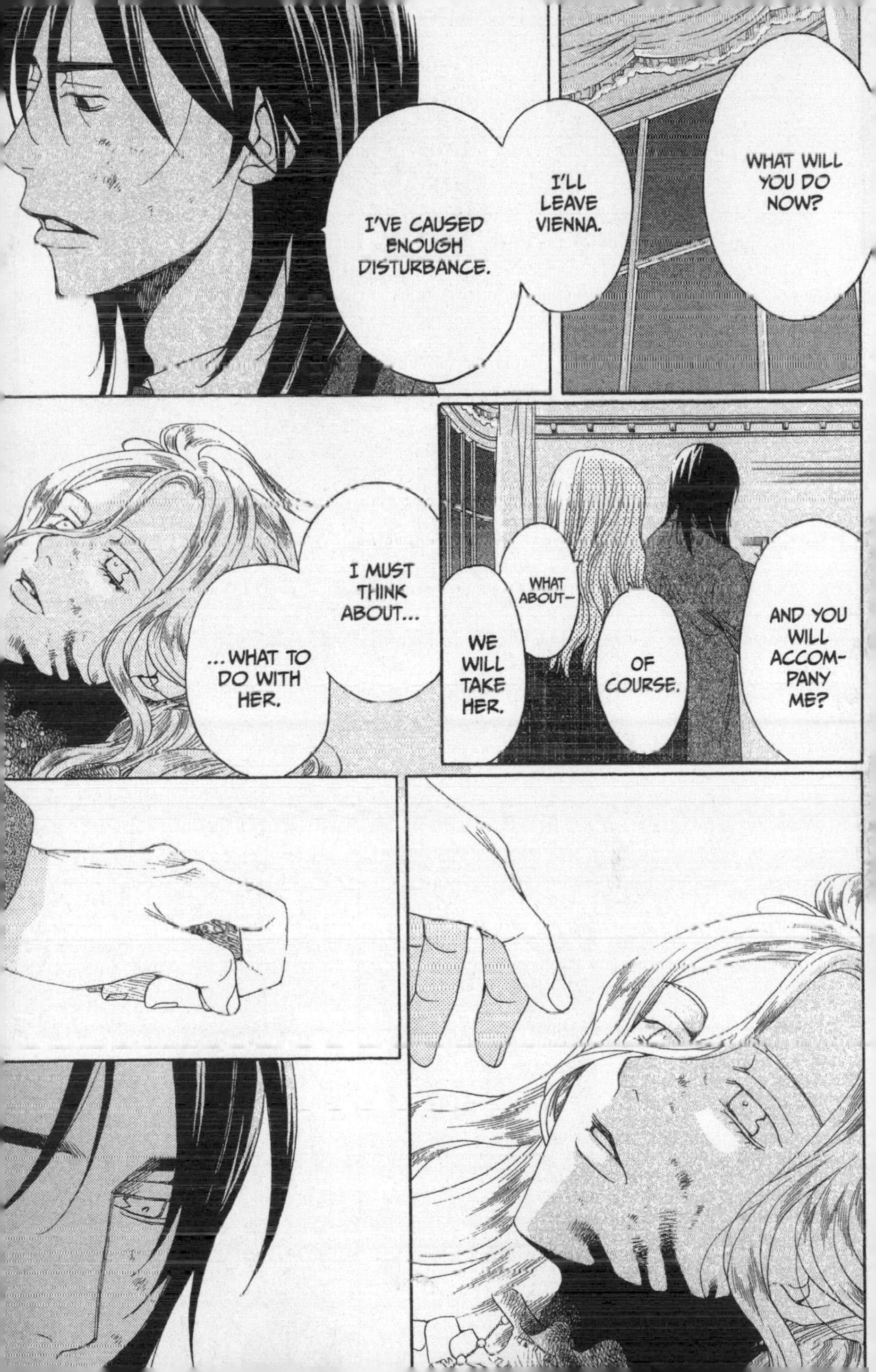
WHAT WILL YOU DO NOW?
I'LL LEAVE VIENNA.
I'VE CAUSED ENOUGH DISTURBANCE.
AND YOU WILL ACCOMPANY ME?
OF COURSE.
WHAT ABOUT—
WE WILL TAKE HER.
I MUST THINK ABOUT...
...WHAT TO DO WITH HER.

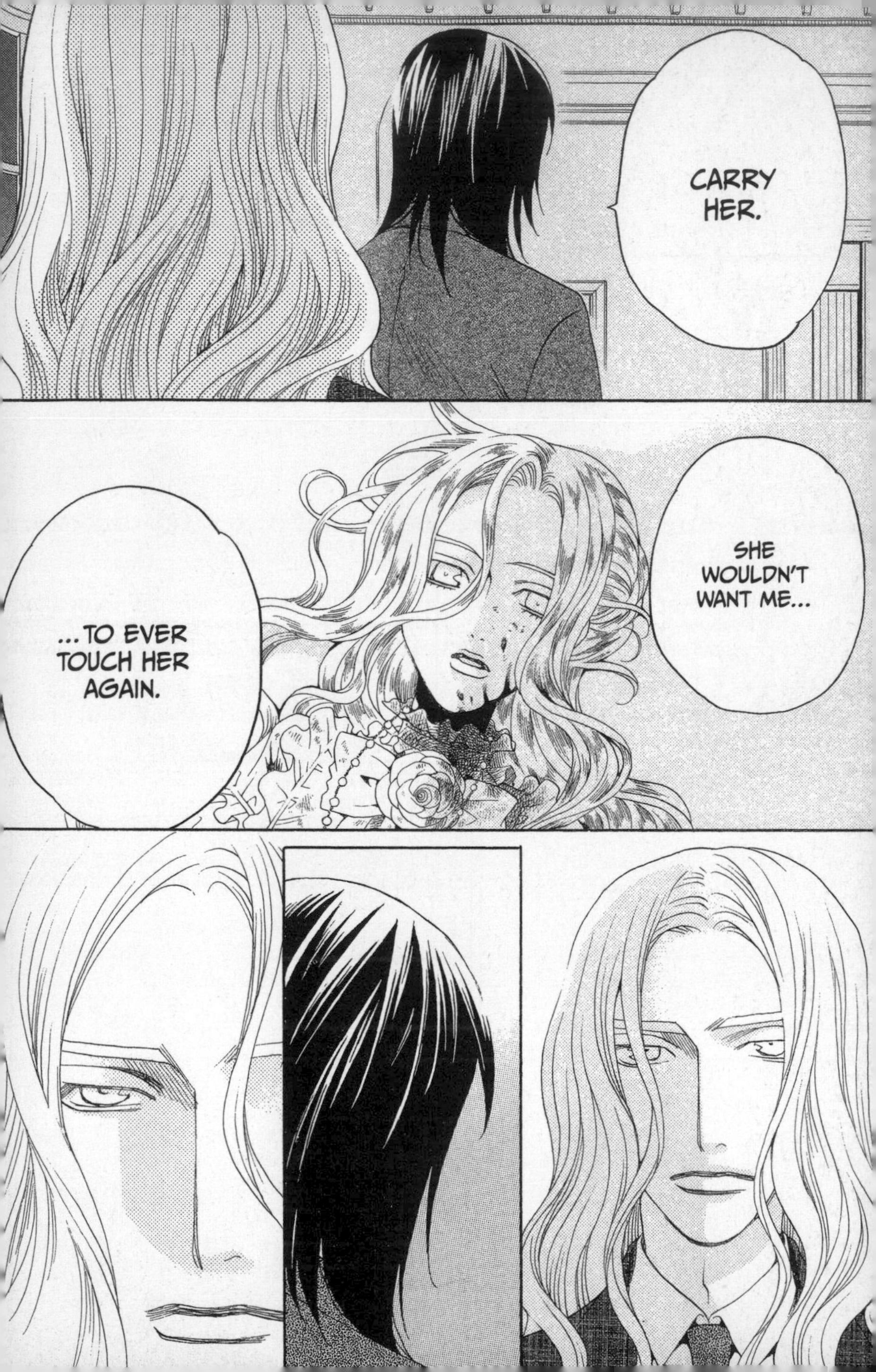
CARRY HER.
SHE WOULDN'T WANT ME...
...TO EVER TOUCH HER AGAIN.

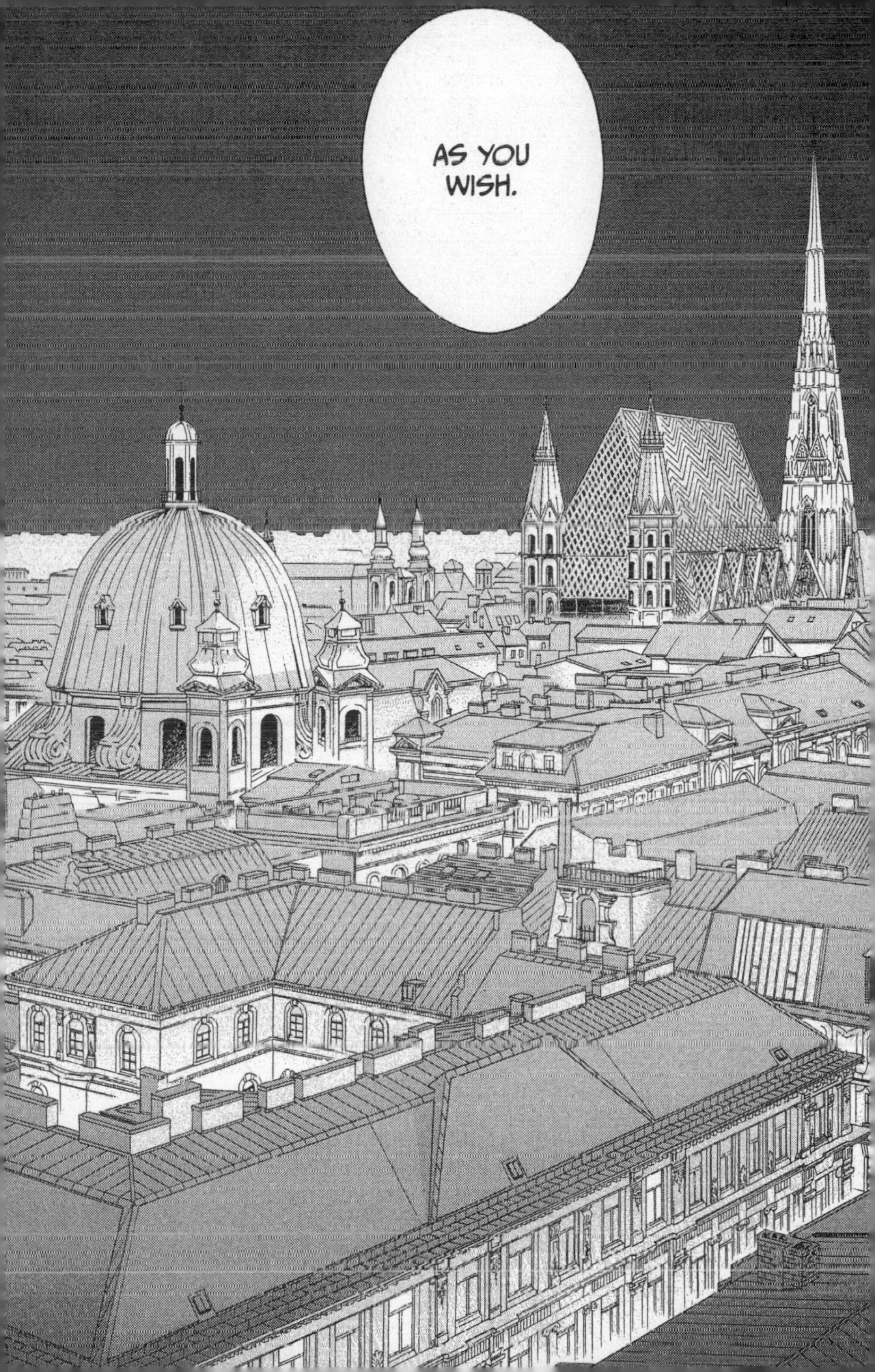
AS YOU WISH.

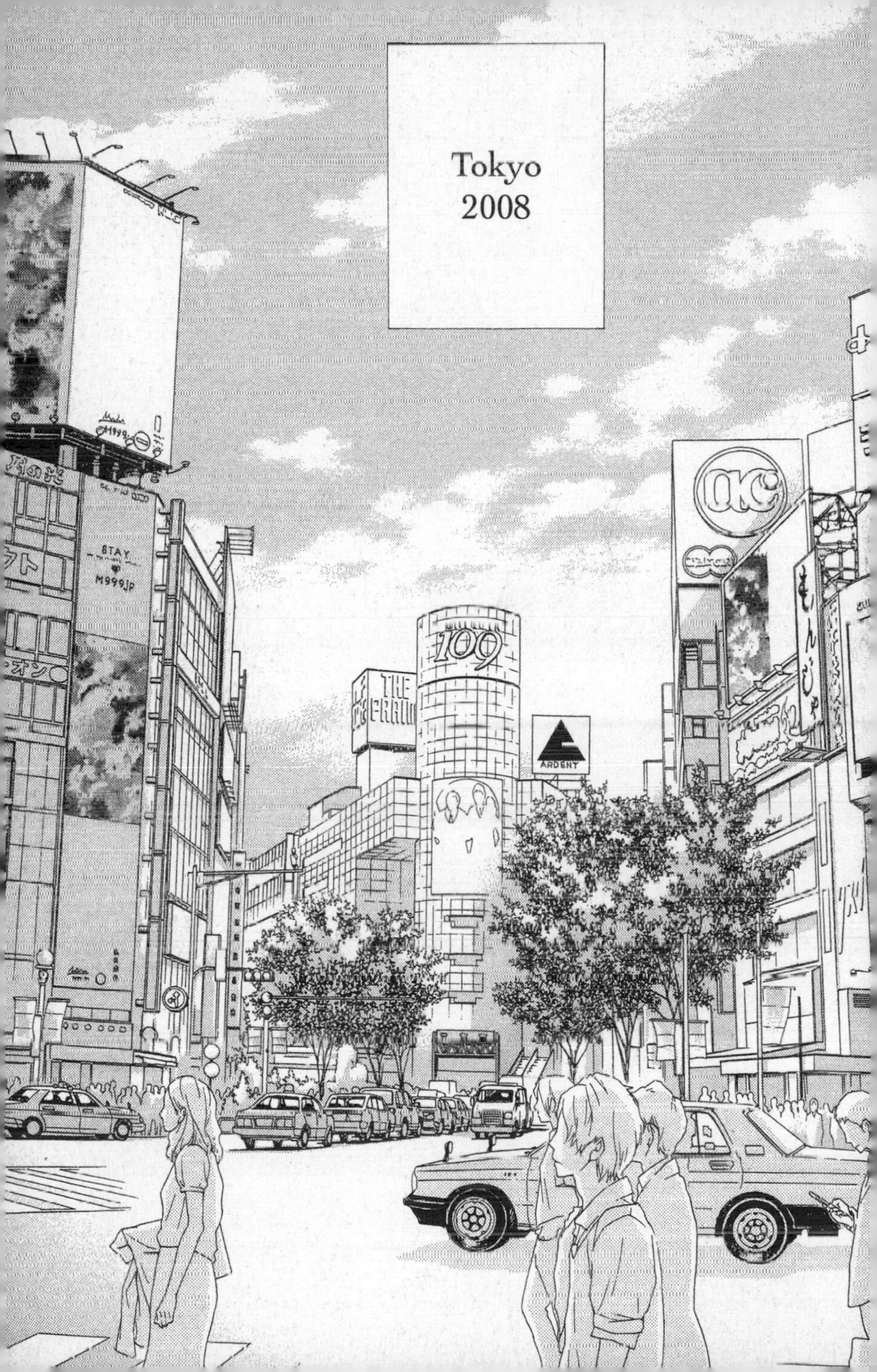
Tokyo
2008
109
ARDENT
STAY
M999jp

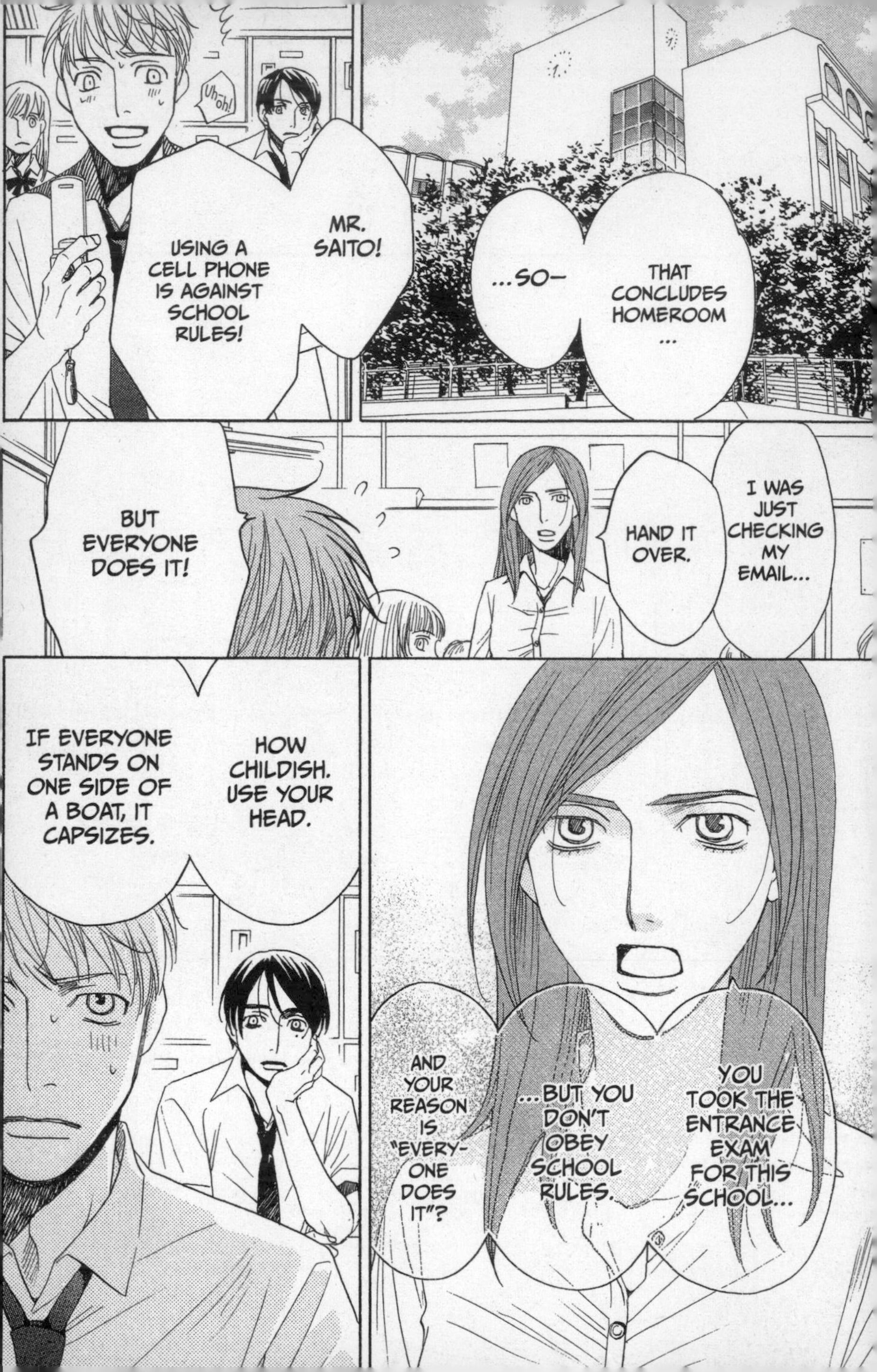
THAT CONCLUDES HOMEROOM ...
...SO—
Uh-oh!
MR. SAITO!
USING A CELL PHONE IS AGAINST SCHOOL RULES!
I WAS JUST CHECKING MY EMAIL...
HAND IT OVER.
BUT EVERYONE DOES IT!
YOU TOOK THE ENTRANCE EXAM FOR THIS SCHOOL...
...BUT YOU DON'T OBEY SCHOOL RULES.
AND YOUR REASON IS "EVERY-ONE DOES IT"?
HOW CHILDISH. USE YOUR HEAD.
IF EVERYONE STANDS ON ONE SIDE OF A BOAT, IT CAPSIZES.

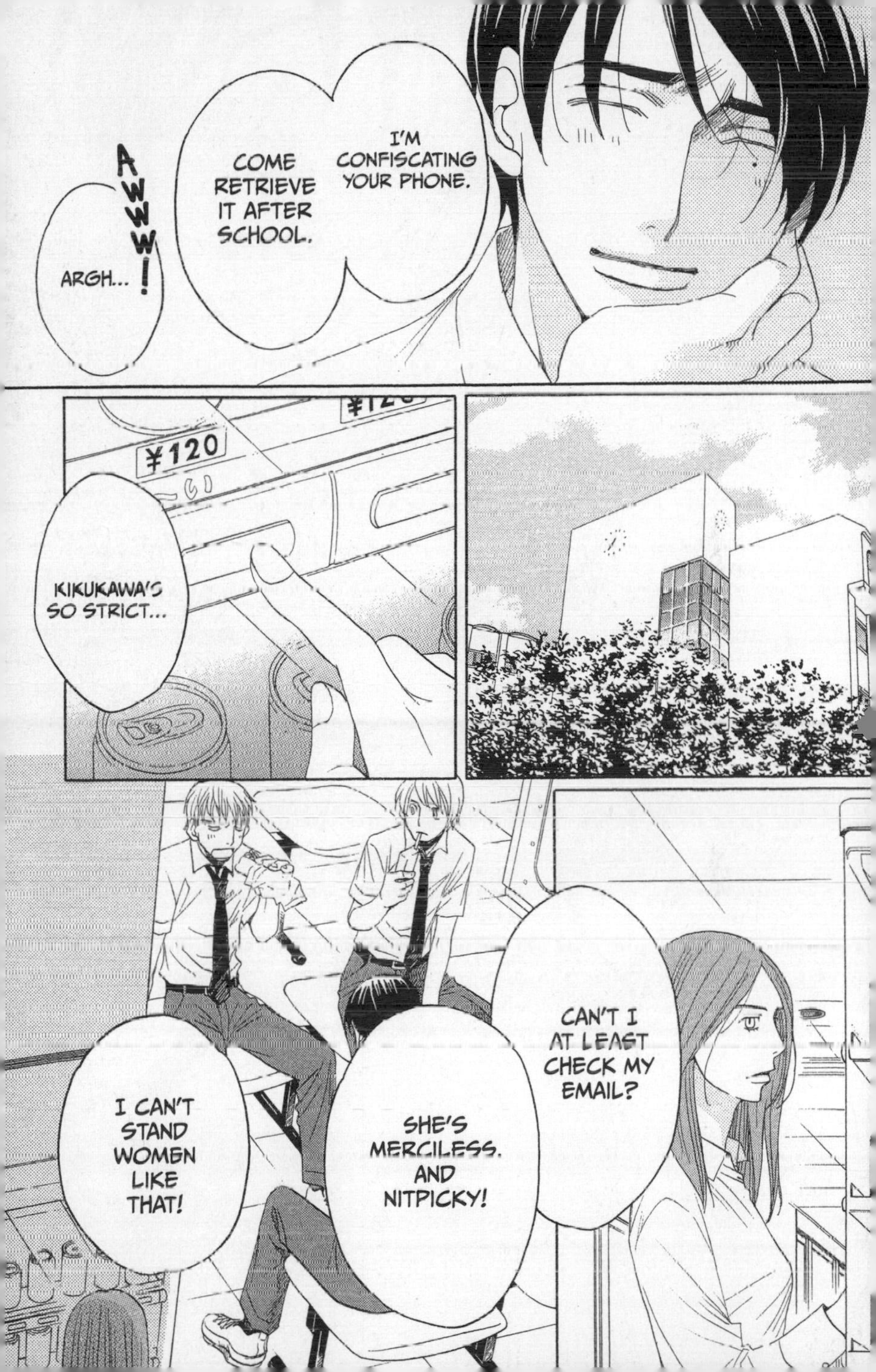
I'M CONFISCATING YOUR PHONE.
COME RETRIEVE IT AFTER SCHOOL.
AWWW!
ARGH...
¥120
KIKUKAWA'S SO STRICT...
CAN'T I AT LEAST CHECK MY EMAIL?
SHE'S MERCILESS. AND NITPICKY!
I CAN'T STAND WOMEN LIKE THAT!

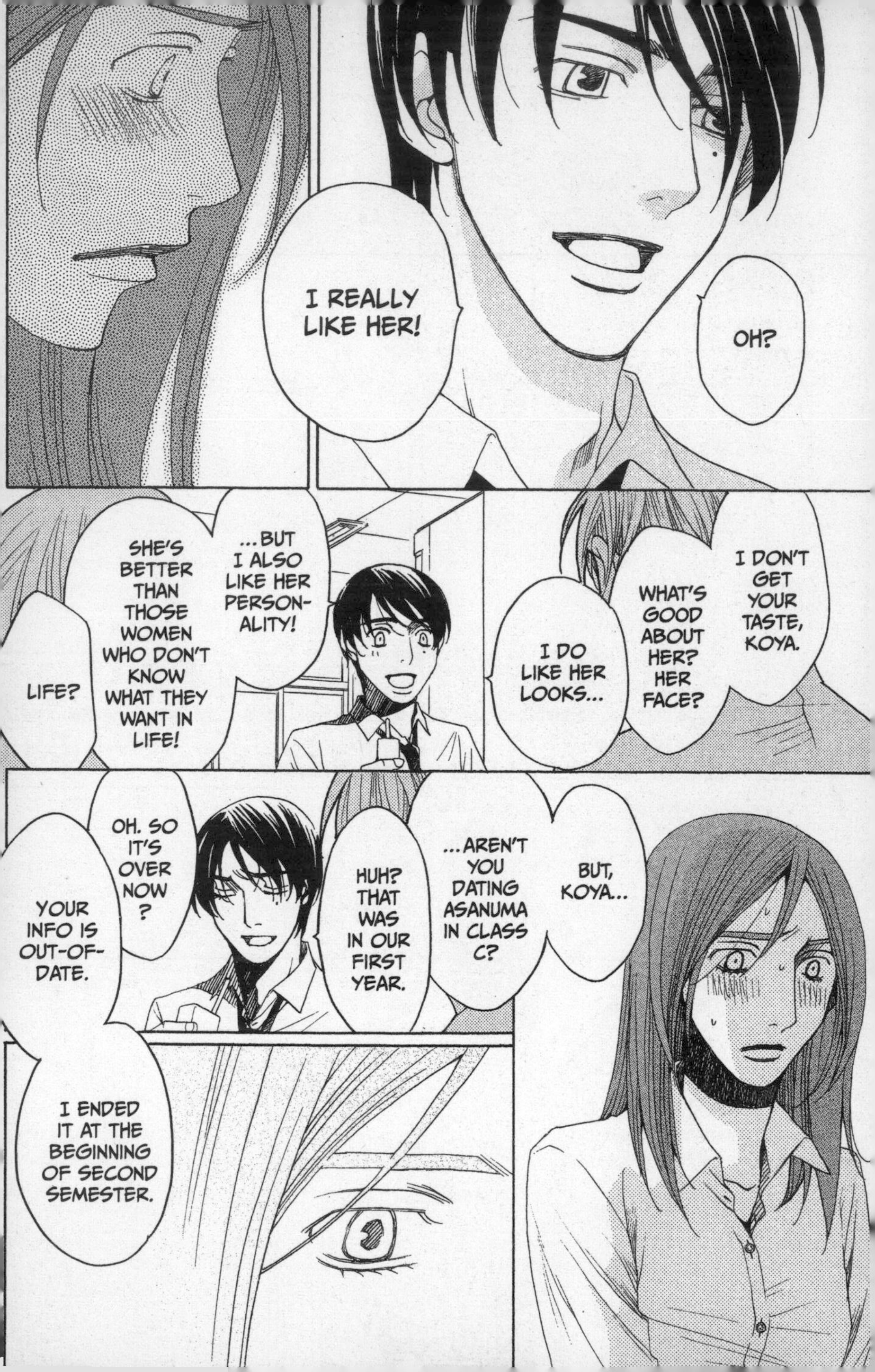
OH?
I REALLY LIKE HER!
I DON'T GET YOUR TASTE, KOYA.
WHAT'S GOOD ABOUT HER? HER FACE?
I DO LIKE HER LOOKS...
...BUT I ALSO LIKE HER PERSON-ALITY!
SHE'S BETTER THAN THOSE WOMEN WHO DON'T KNOW WHAT THEY WANT IN LIFE!
LIFE?
BUT, KOYA...
...AREN'T YOU DATING ASANUMA IN CLASS C?
HUH? THAT WAS IN OUR FIRST YEAR.
OH. SO IT'S OVER NOW?
YOUR INFO IS OUT-OF-DATE.
I ENDED IT AT THE BEGINNING OF SECOND SEMESTER.

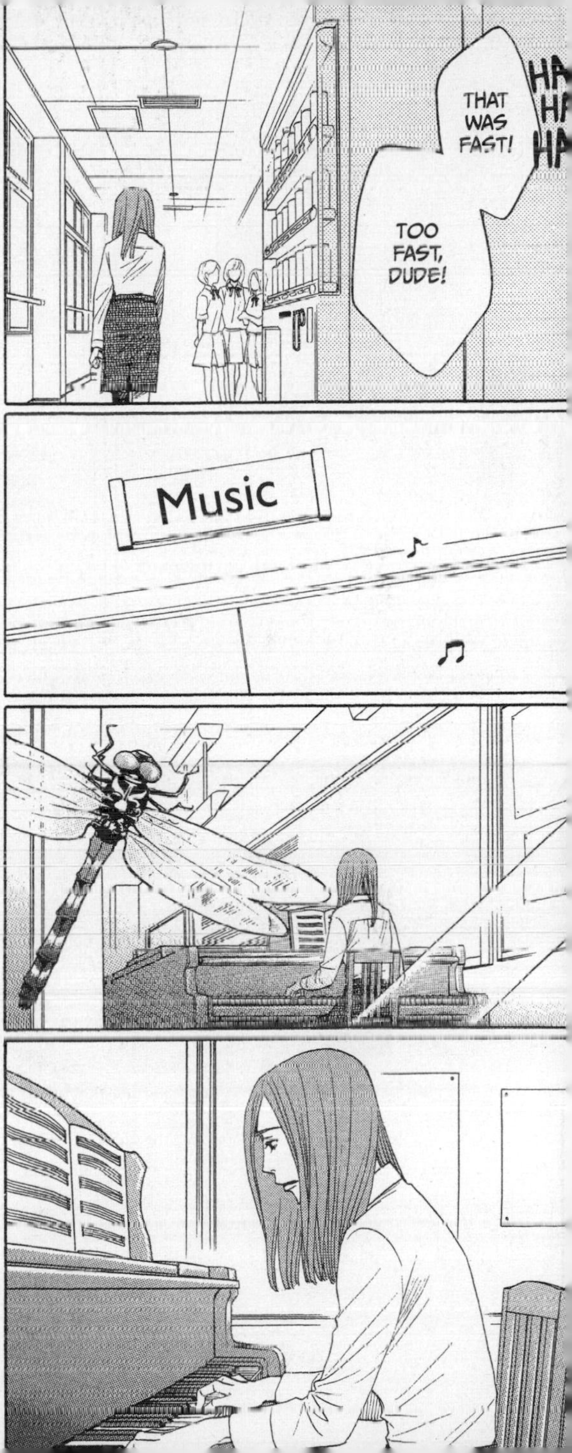
THAT WAS FAST!
TOO FAST, DUDE!
Music

Before beginning this series, I traveled alone to Vienna. I wandered around town and visited the churches and cafes and took lots of pictures and tried to imagine how Dimitri and the others would have lived 100 years ago.

The city is full of relics from the past, and time passes slowly there, so it seemed like a great place to live. I'd love to go again! And the food's great! ♡

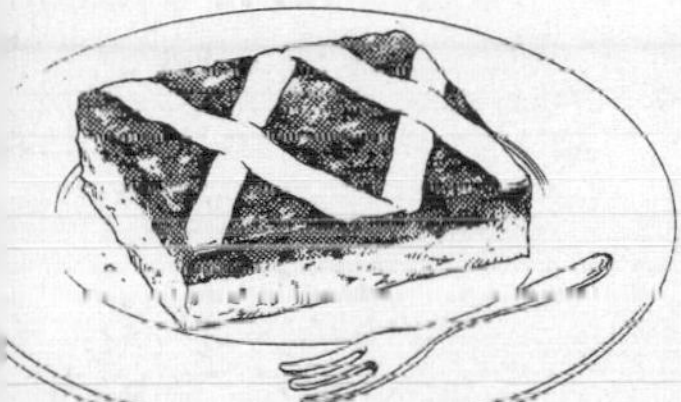

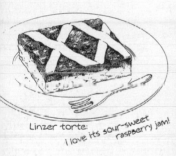

Linzer torte: I love its sour-sweet raspberry jam!

But the pieces of cake were huge! About 1 1/2-2 times a serving in Japan! Wherever I went, lots of cake and sweets were lined up in showcases. They're all cute and have a nice old-fashioned air about them.

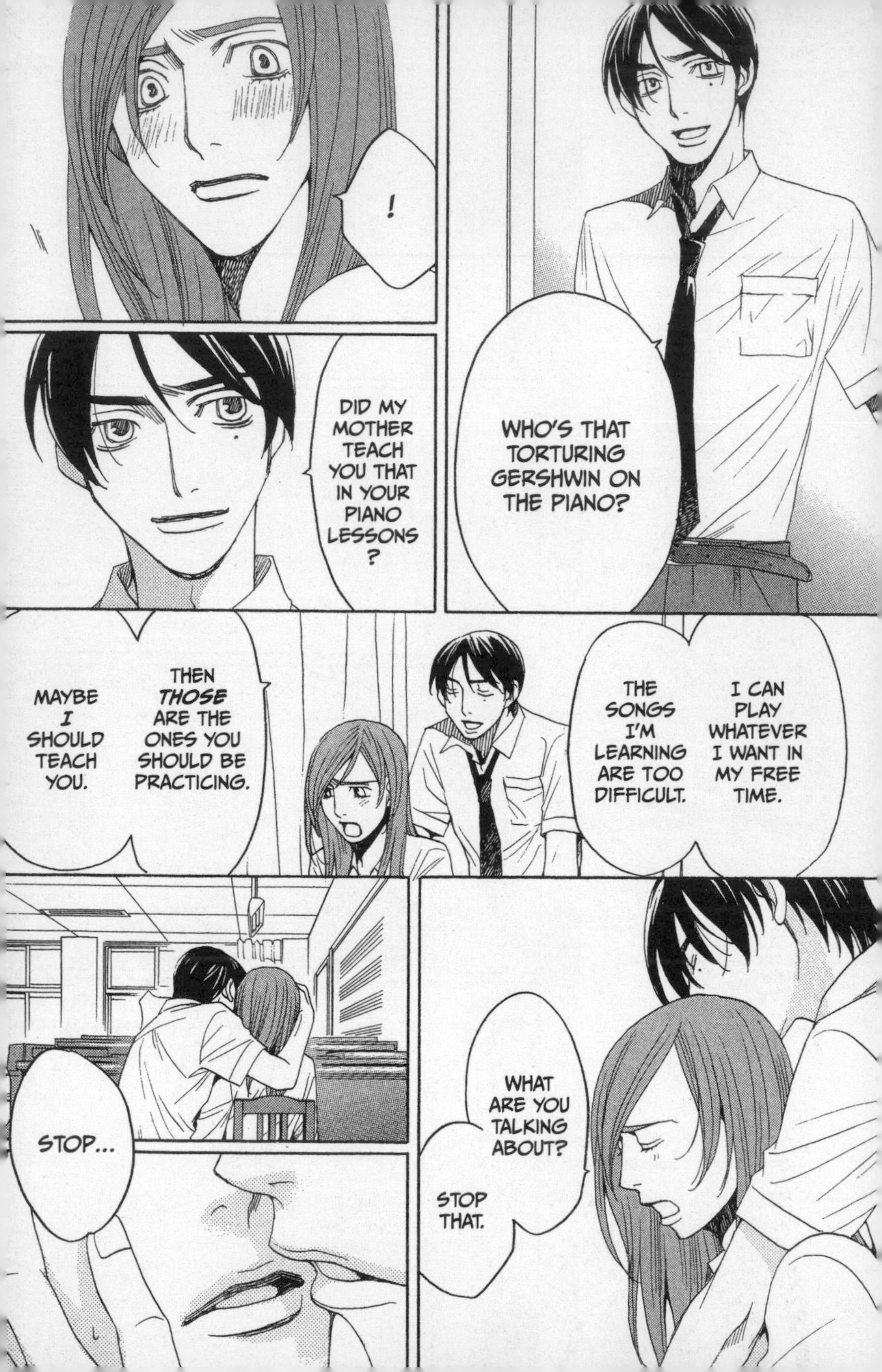
WHO'S THAT TORTURING GERSHWIN ON THE PIANO?
!
DID MY MOTHER TEACH YOU THAT IN YOUR PIANO LESSONS?
I CAN PLAY WHATEVER I WANT IN MY FREE TIME.
THE SONGS I'M LEARNING ARE TOO DIFFICULT.
THEN *THOSE* ARE THE ONES YOU SHOULD BE PRACTICING.
MAYBE *I* SHOULD TEACH YOU.
WHAT ARE YOU TALKING ABOUT?
STOP THAT.
STOP...

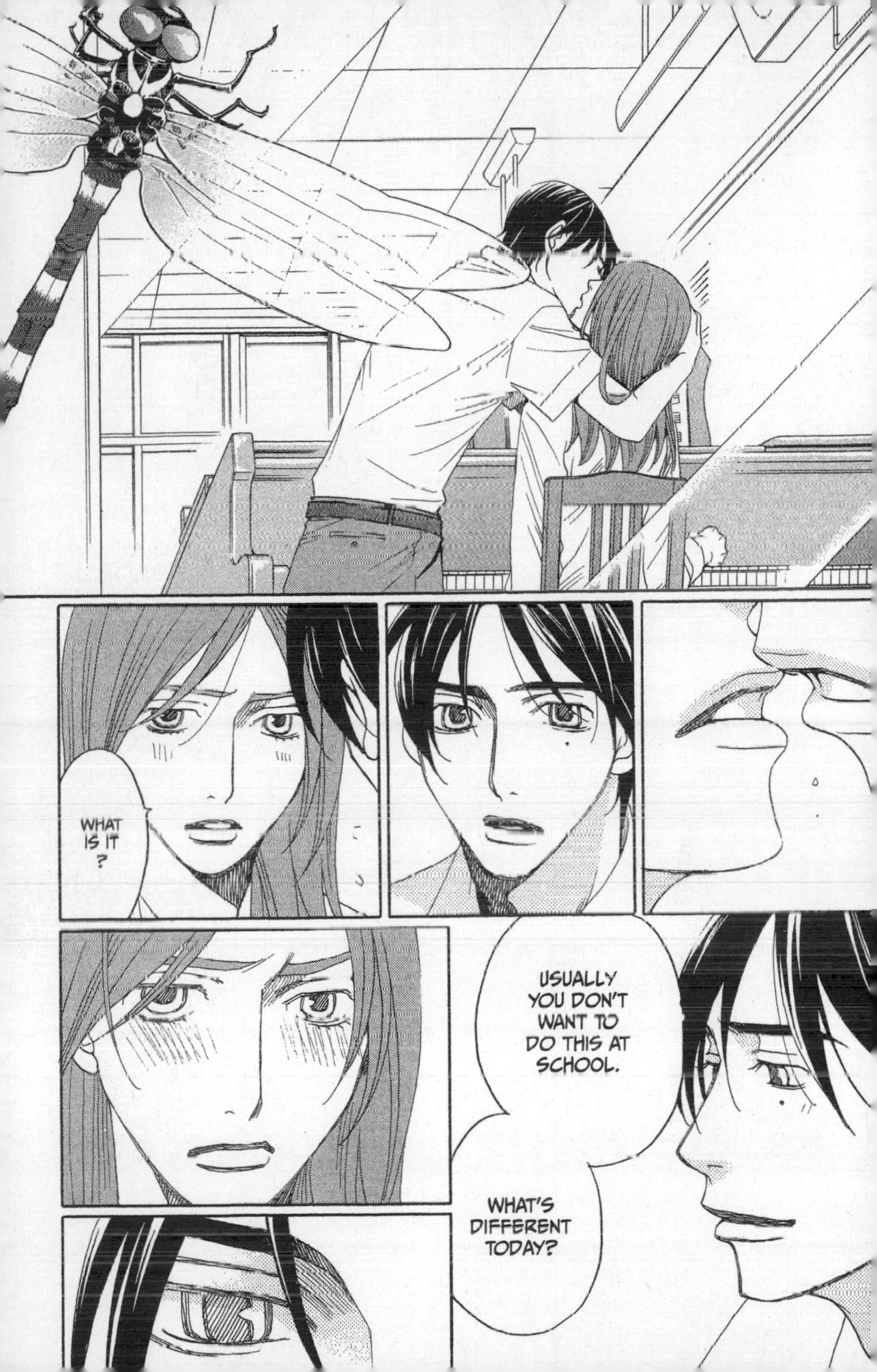
WHAT IS IT ?
USUALLY YOU DON'T WANT TO DO THIS AT SCHOOL.
WHAT'S DIFFERENT TODAY?

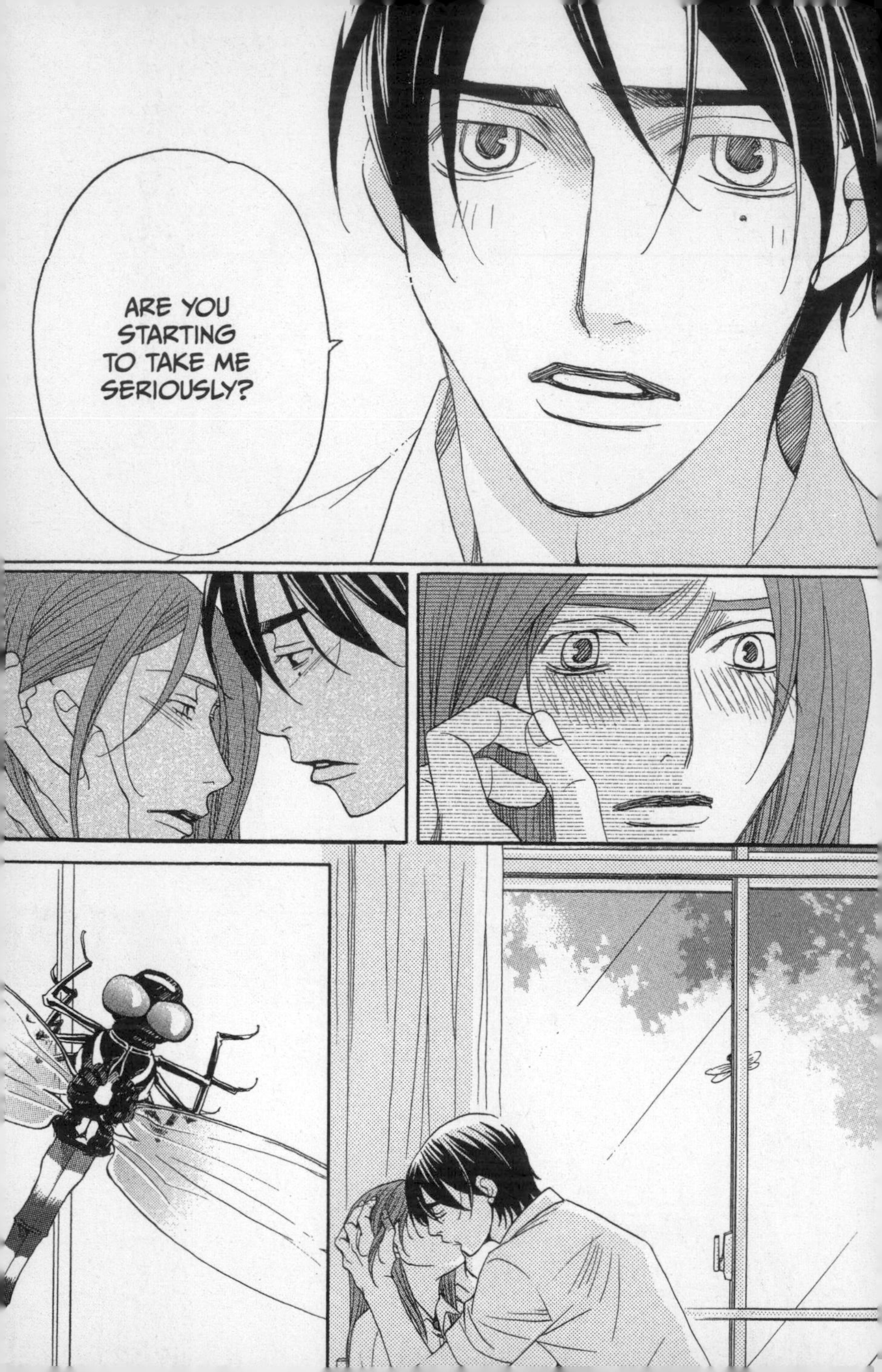
ARE YOU STARTING TO TAKE ME SERIOUSLY?

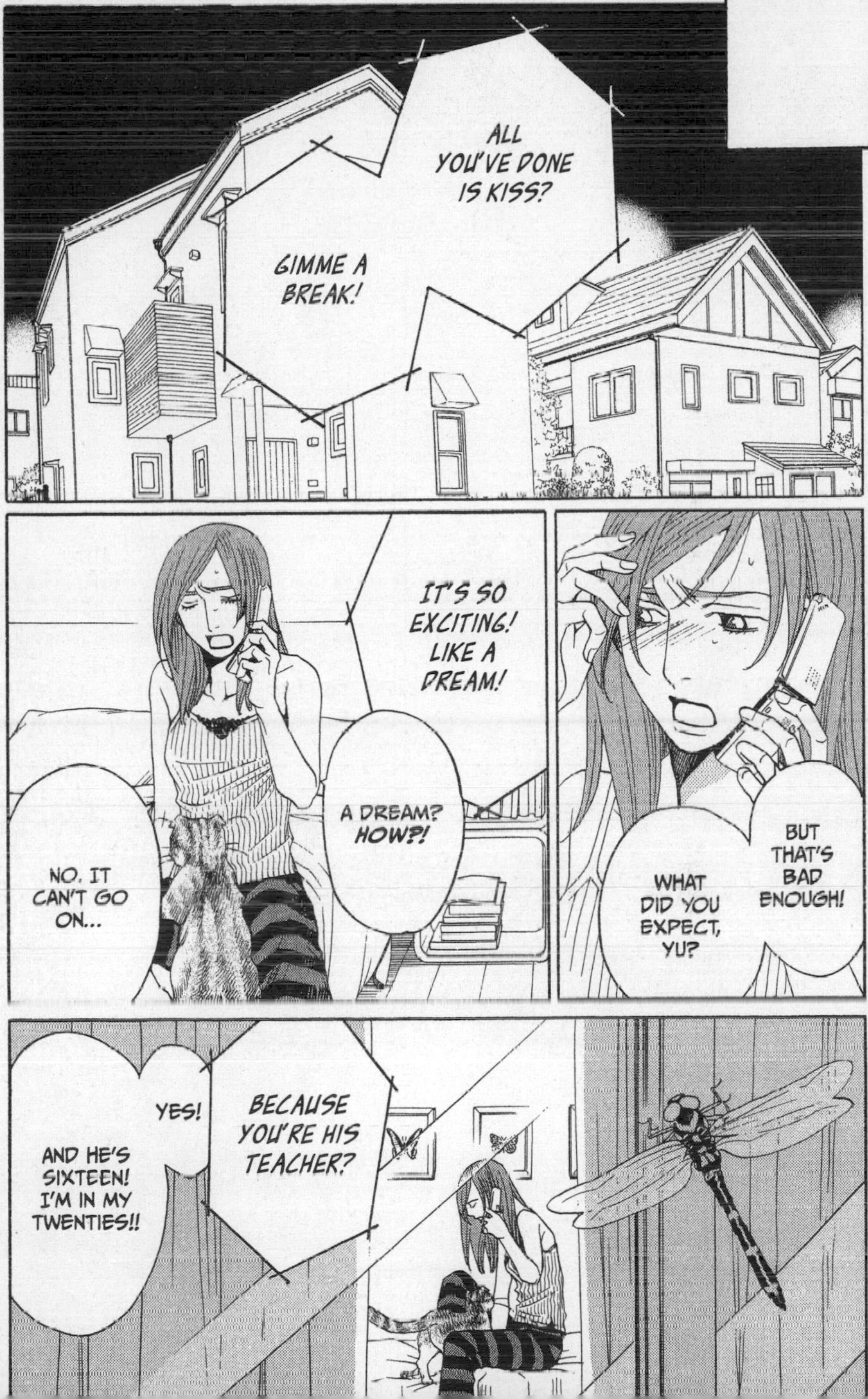
ALL YOU'VE DONE IS KISS?
GIMME A BREAK!
BUT THAT'S BAD ENOUGH!
WHAT DID YOU EXPECT, YU?
IT'S SO EXCITING! LIKE A DREAM!
A DREAM? HOW?!
NO. IT CAN'T GO ON...
BECAUSE YOU'RE HIS TEACHER?
YES!
AND HE'S SIXTEEN! I'M IN MY TWENTIES!!

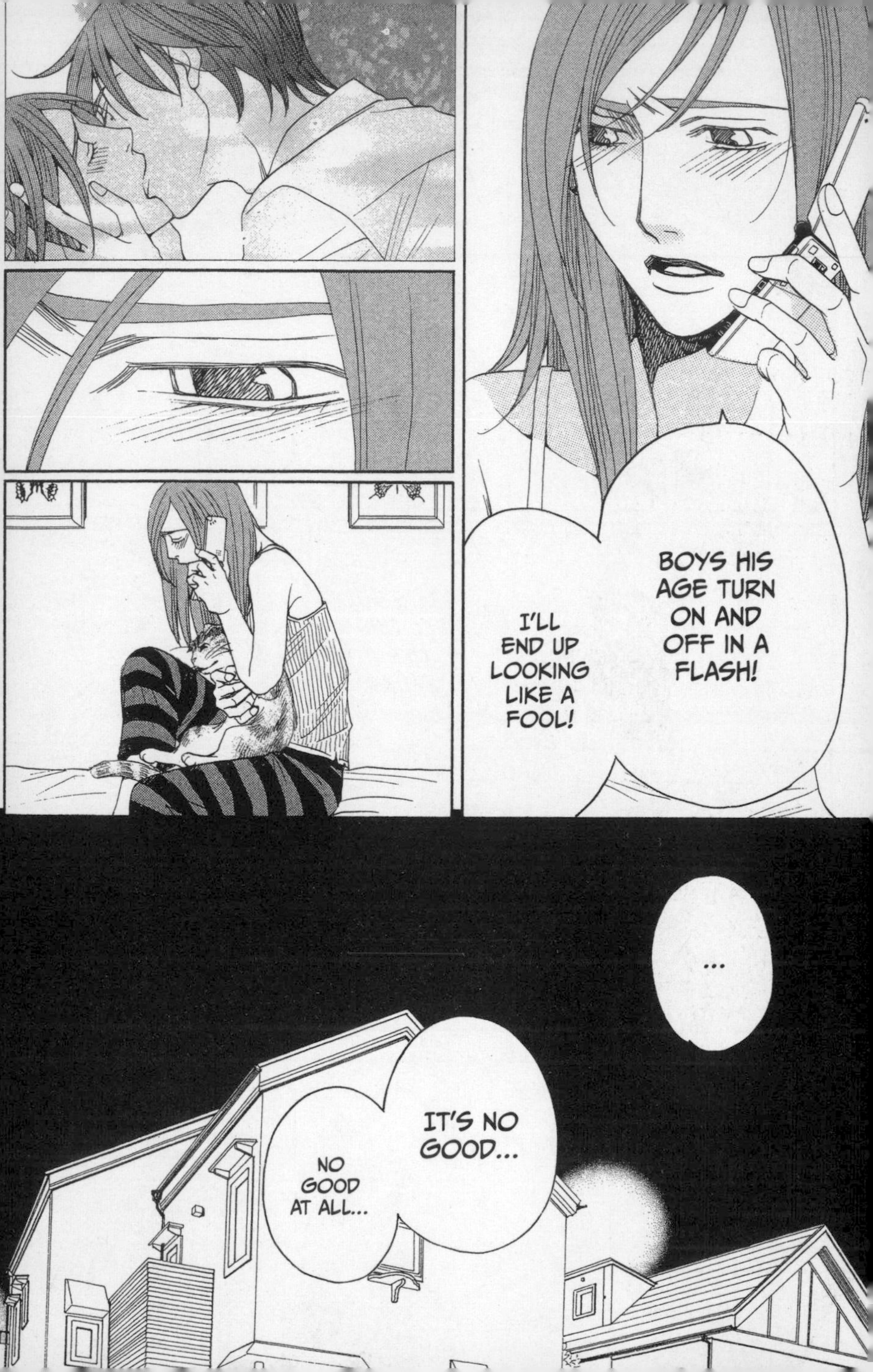
BOYS HIS AGE TURN ON AND OFF IN A FLASH!
I'LL END UP LOOKING LIKE A FOOL!
...
IT'S NO GOOD...
NO GOOD AT ALL...

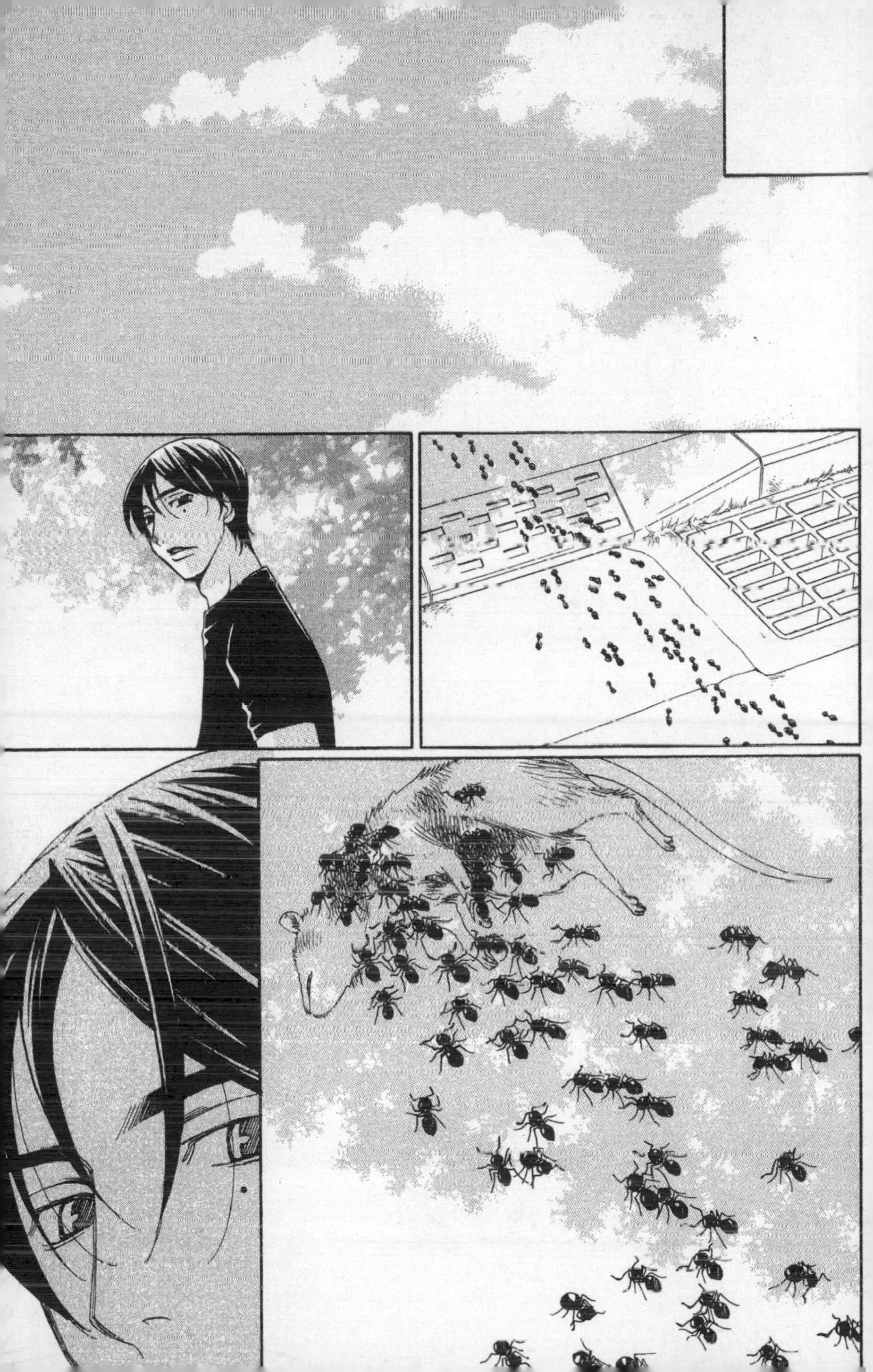

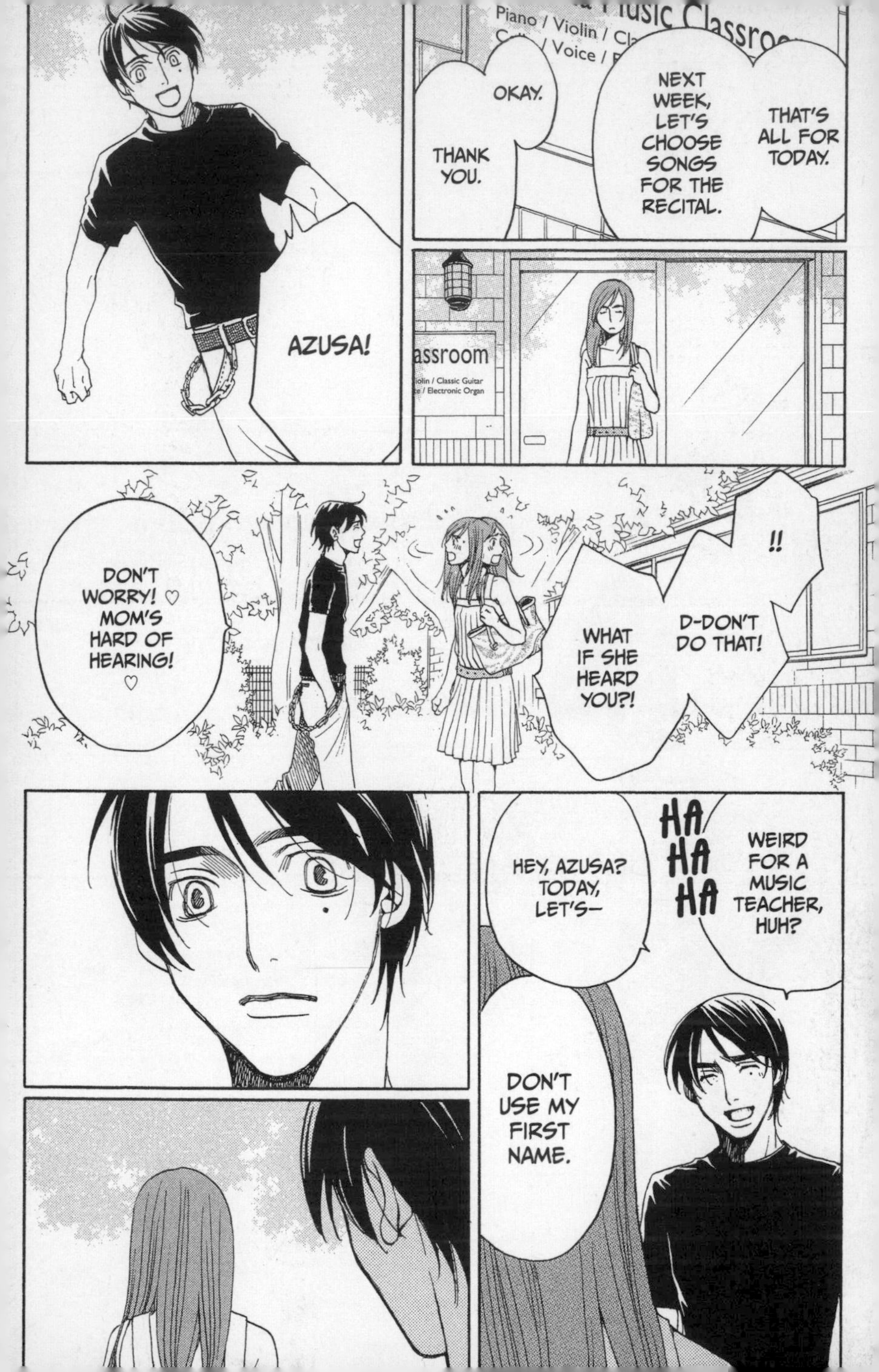
usic Classroo
Piano / Violin / Cla
/ Voice /
THAT'S ALL FOR TODAY.
NEXT WEEK, LET'S CHOOSE SONGS FOR THE RECITAL.
OKAY.
THANK YOU.
assroom
iolin / Classic Guitar
e / Electronic Organ
AZUSA!
!!
D-DON'T DO THAT!
WHAT IF SHE HEARD YOU?!
DON'T WORRY! ♡ MOM'S HARD OF HEARING! ♡
WEIRD FOR A MUSIC TEACHER, HUH?
HA HA HA
HEY, AZUSA? TODAY, LET'S—
DON'T USE MY FIRST NAME.

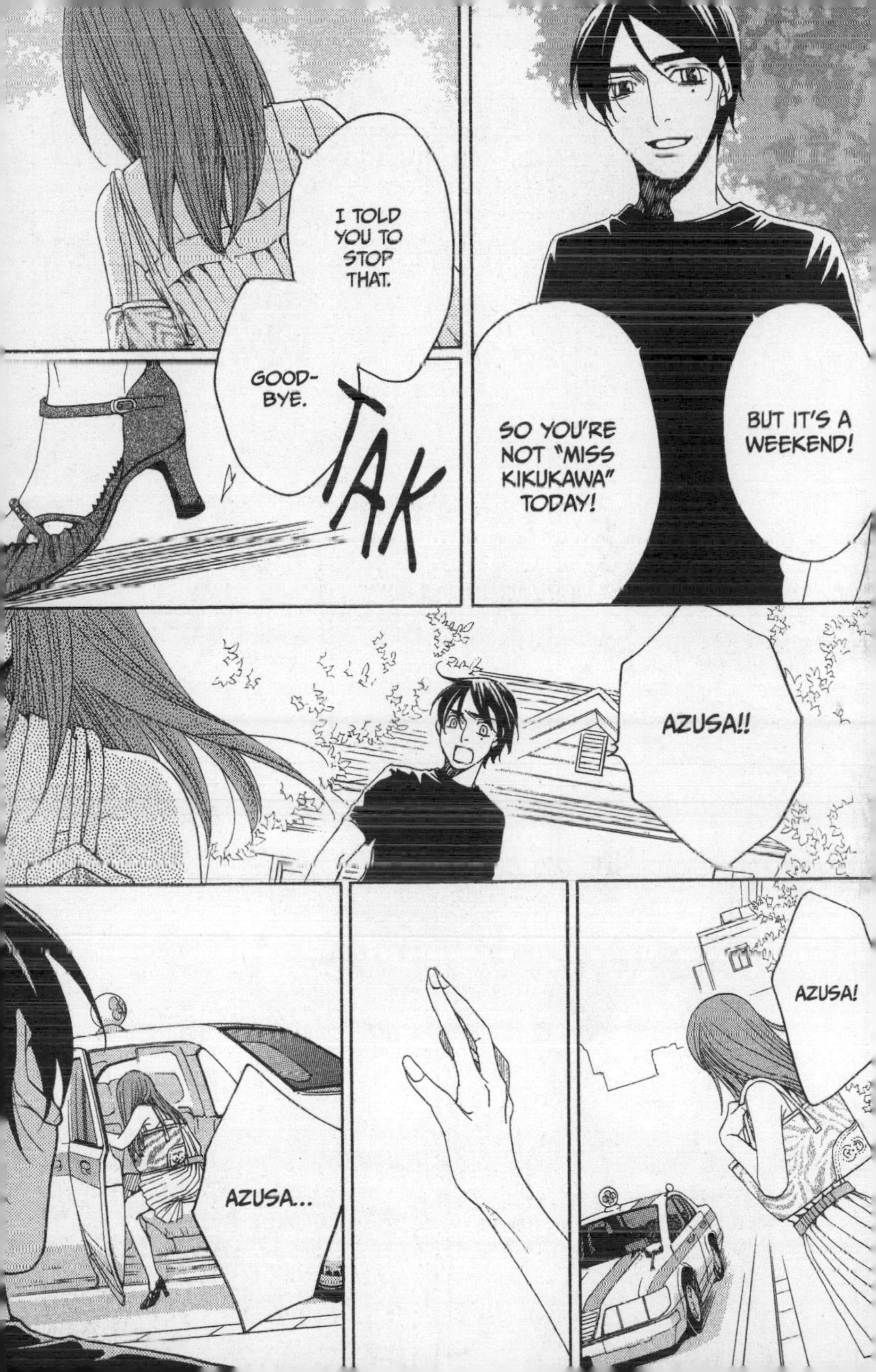
BUT IT'S A WEEKEND!
SO YOU'RE NOT "MISS KIKUKAWA" TODAY!
I TOLD YOU TO STOP THAT.
GOOD-BYE.
TAK
AZUSA!!
AZUSA!
AZUSA...

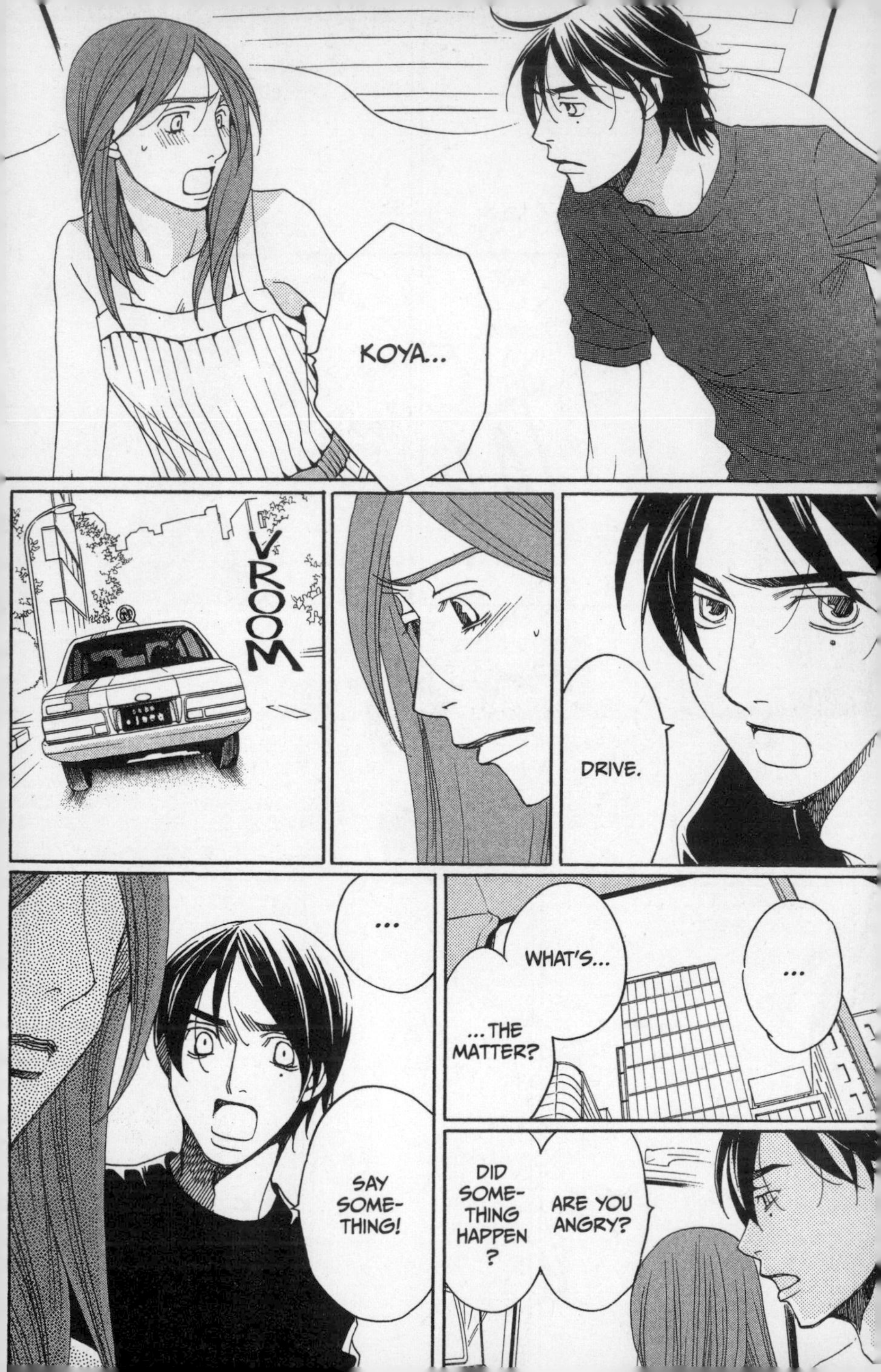
KOYA...
DRIVE.
VROOM
...
WHAT'S...
...THE MATTER?
ARE YOU ANGRY?
DID SOME-THING HAPPEN?
...
SAY SOME-THING!

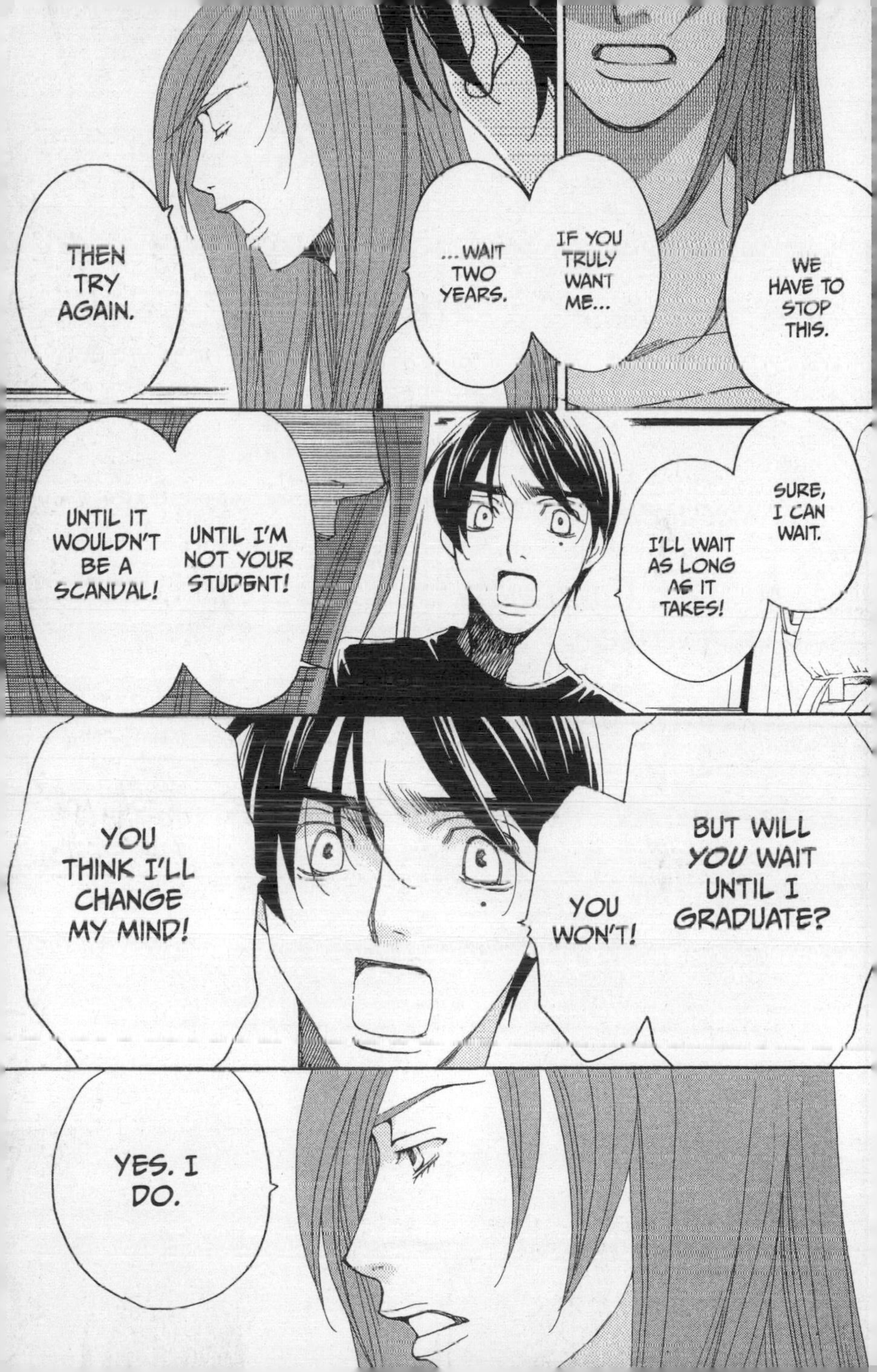
WE HAVE TO STOP THIS.
IF YOU TRULY WANT ME...
...WAIT TWO YEARS.
THEN TRY AGAIN.
SURE, I CAN WAIT.
I'LL WAIT AS LONG AS IT TAKES!
UNTIL I'M NOT YOUR STUDENT!
UNTIL IT WOULDN'T BE A SCANDAL!
BUT WILL *YOU* WAIT UNTIL I GRADUATE?
YOU WON'T!
YOU THINK I'LL CHANGE MY MIND!
YES. I DO.

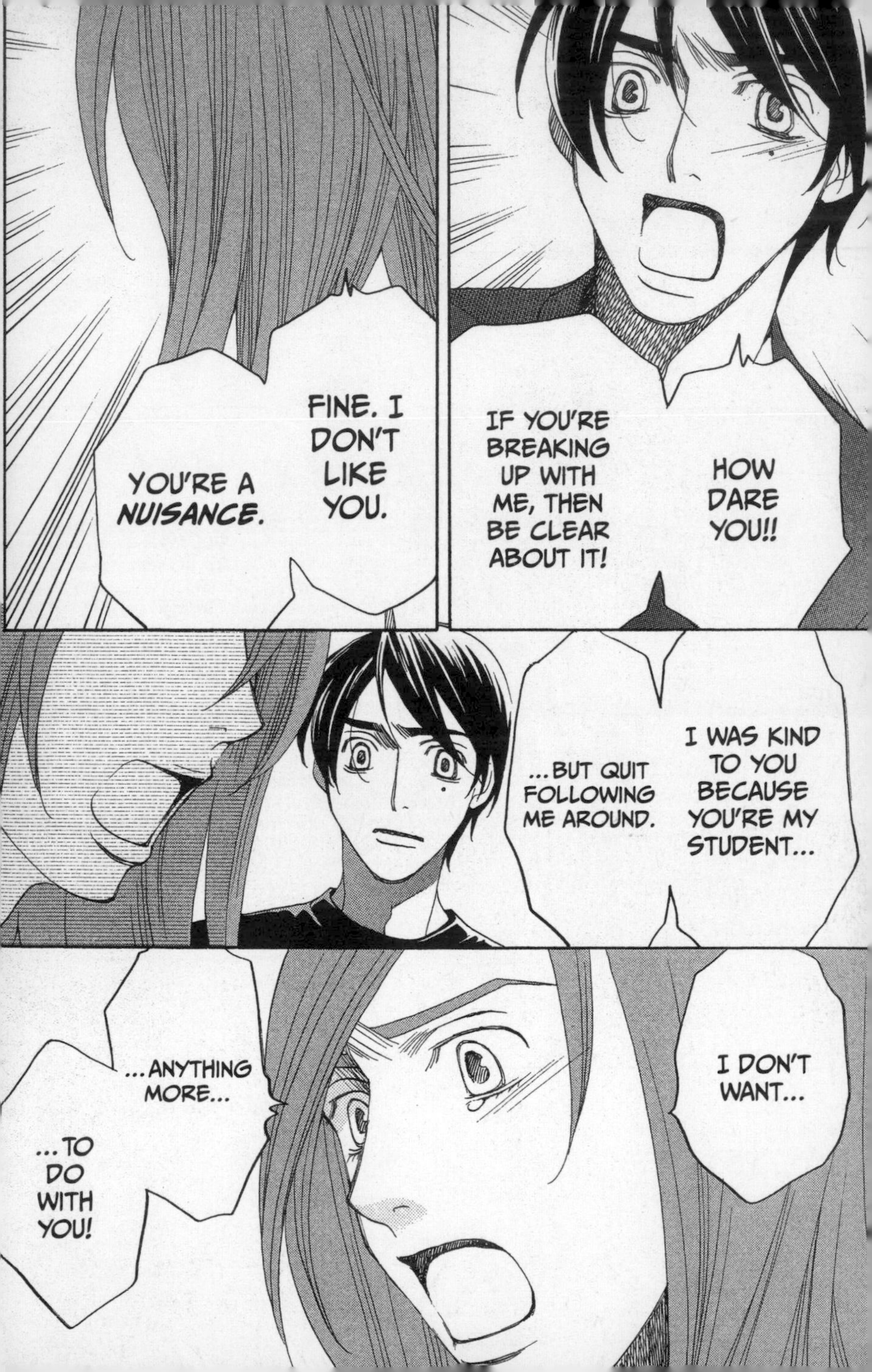
HOW DARE YOU!!
IF YOU'RE BREAKING UP WITH ME, THEN BE CLEAR ABOUT IT!
FINE. I DON'T LIKE YOU.
YOU'RE A *NUISANCE*.
I WAS KIND TO YOU BECAUSE YOU'RE MY STUDENT...
...BUT QUIT FOLLOWING ME AROUND.
I DON'T WANT...
...ANYTHING MORE...
...TO DO WITH YOU!

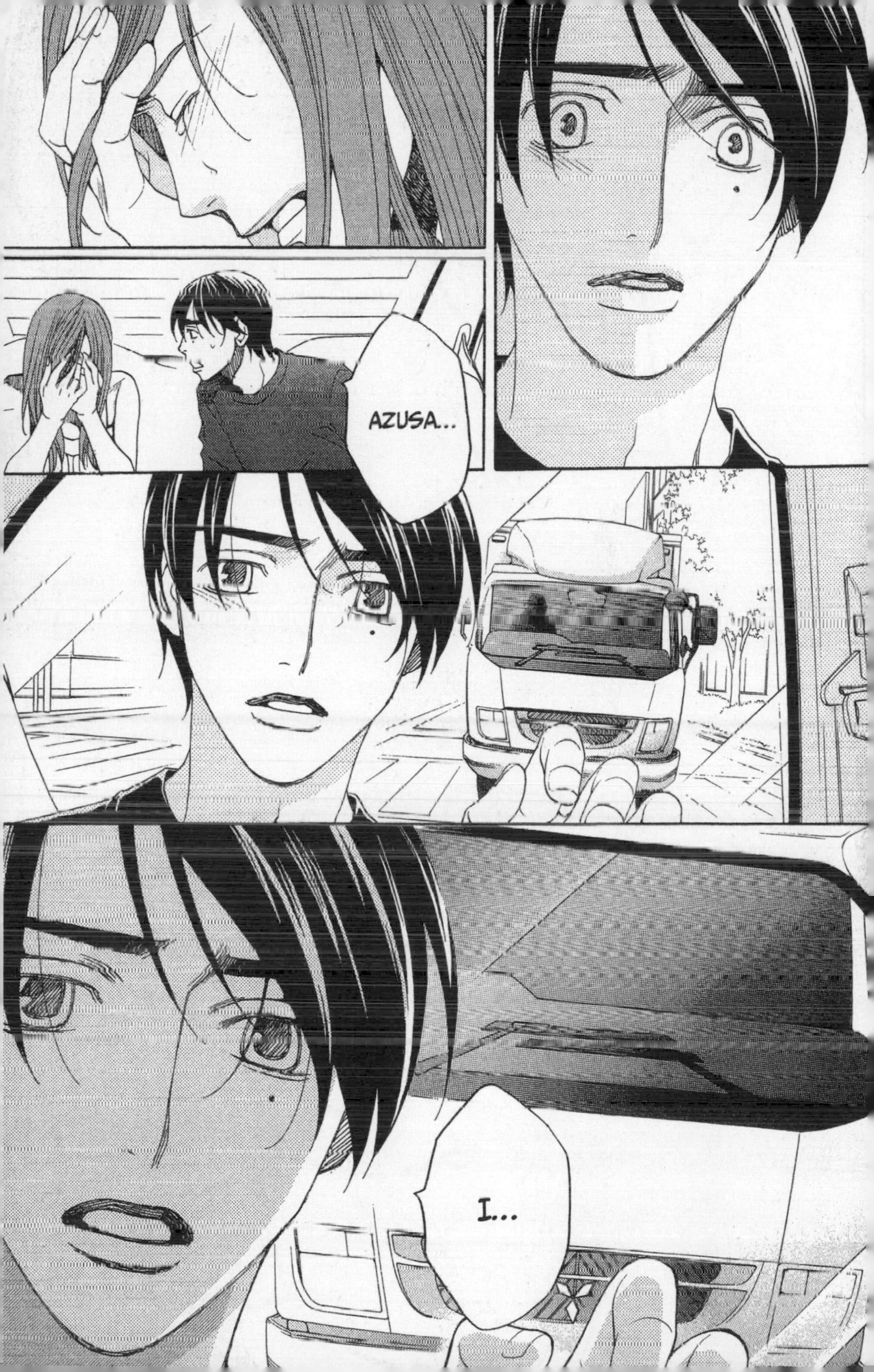
AZUSA...
I...

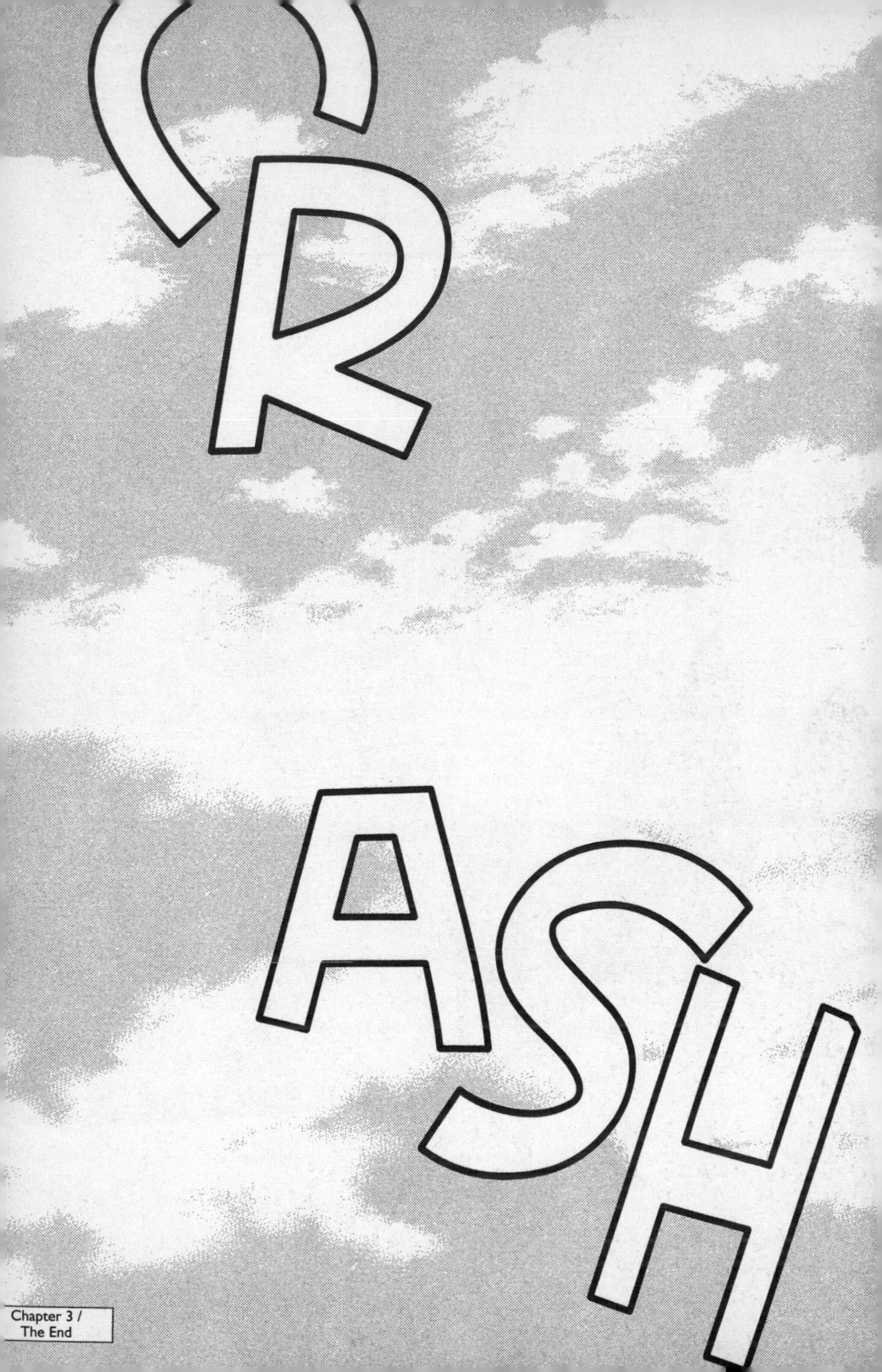
CRASH

Chapter 3 /
The End

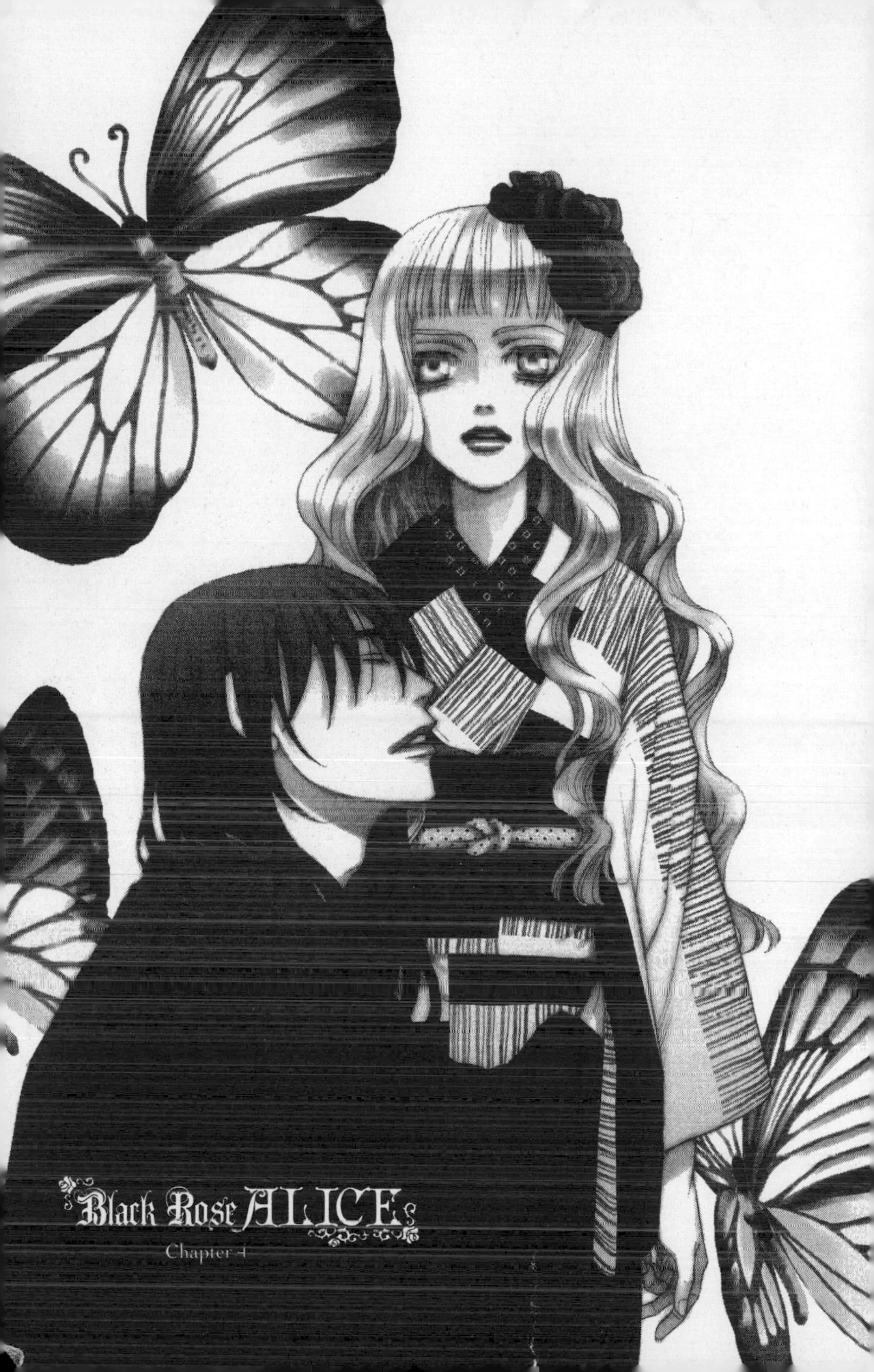
Black Rose ALICE
Chapter 4

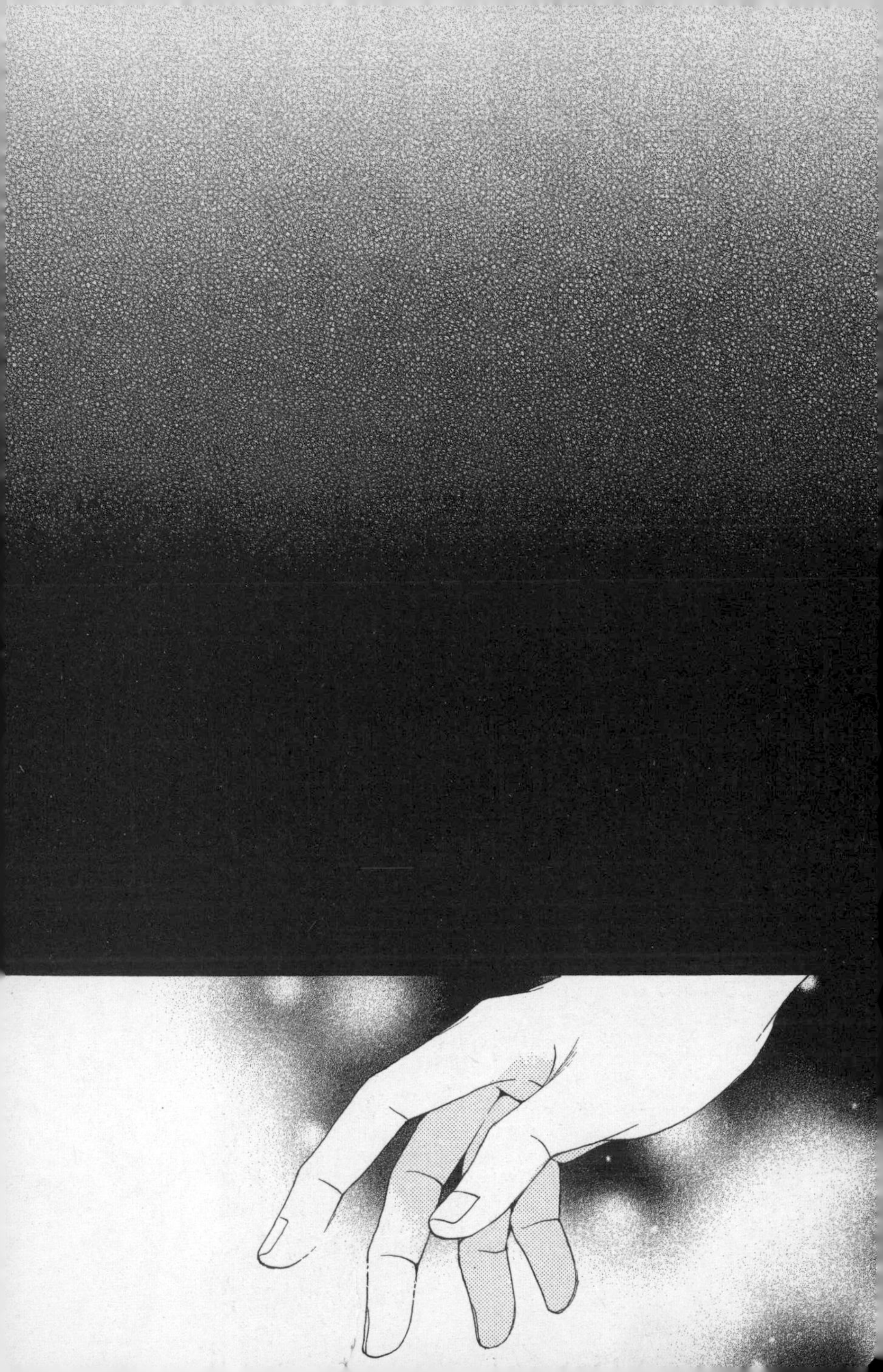

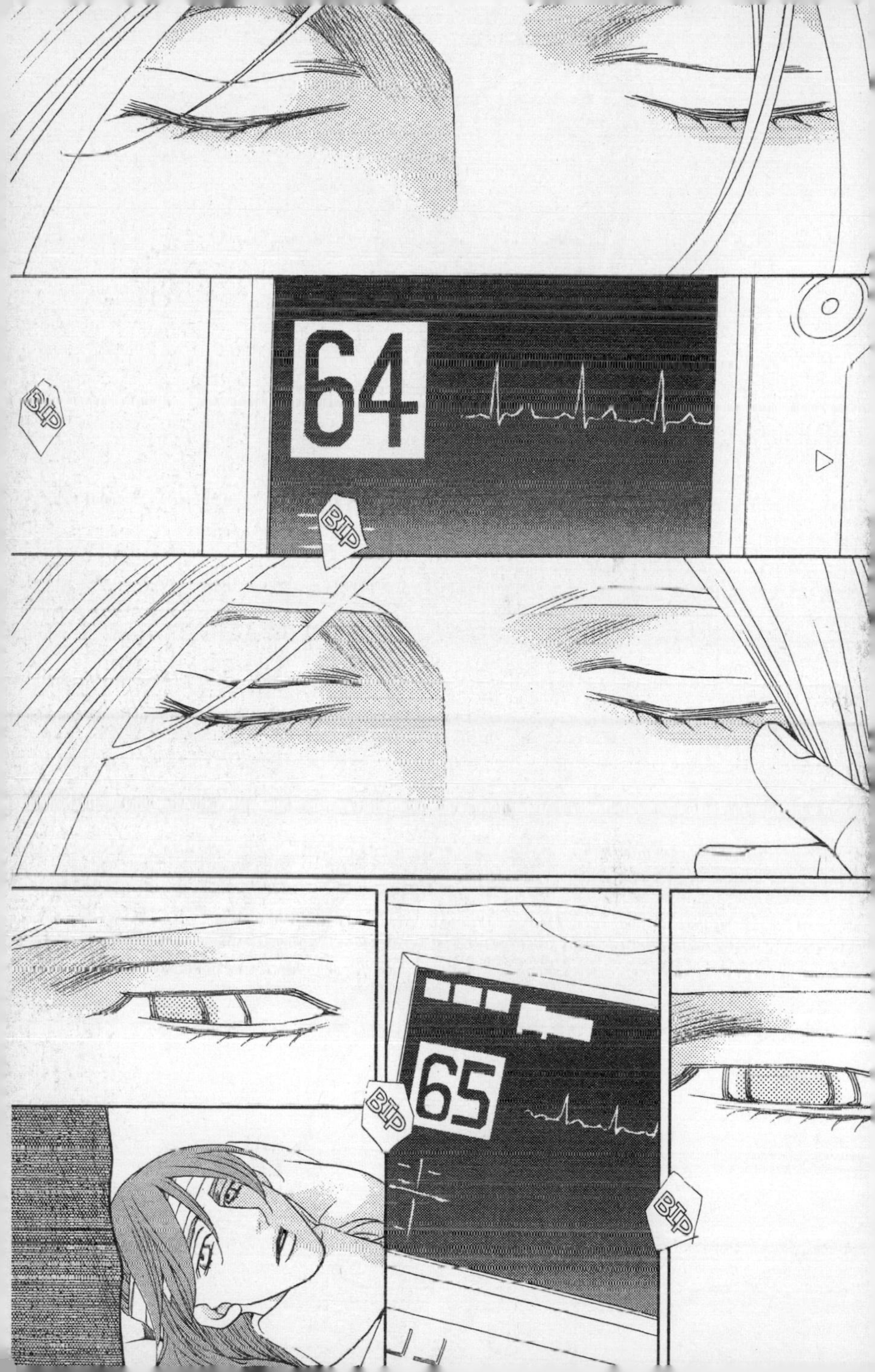
64
BIP
BIP
BIP
65
BIP

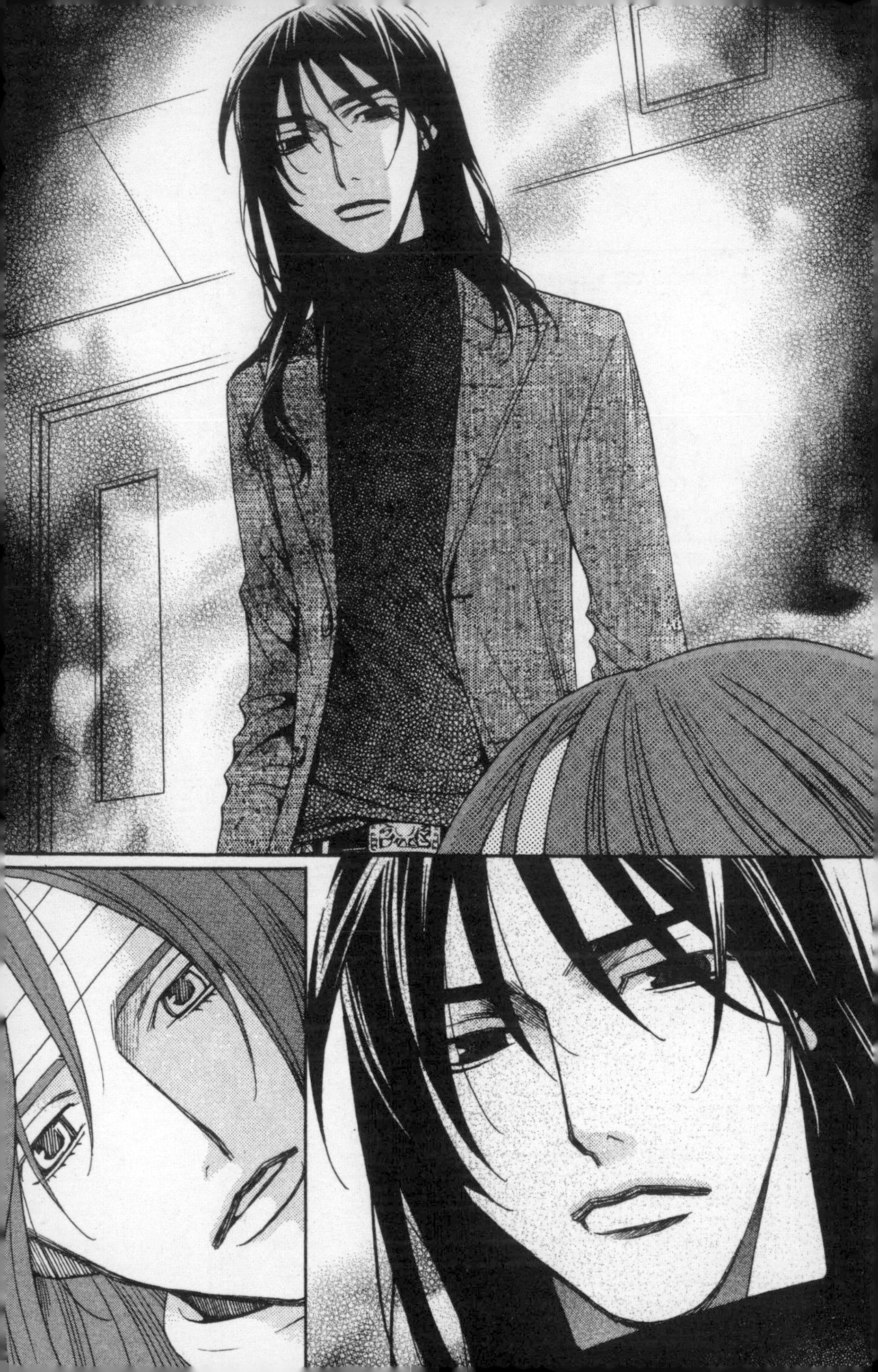

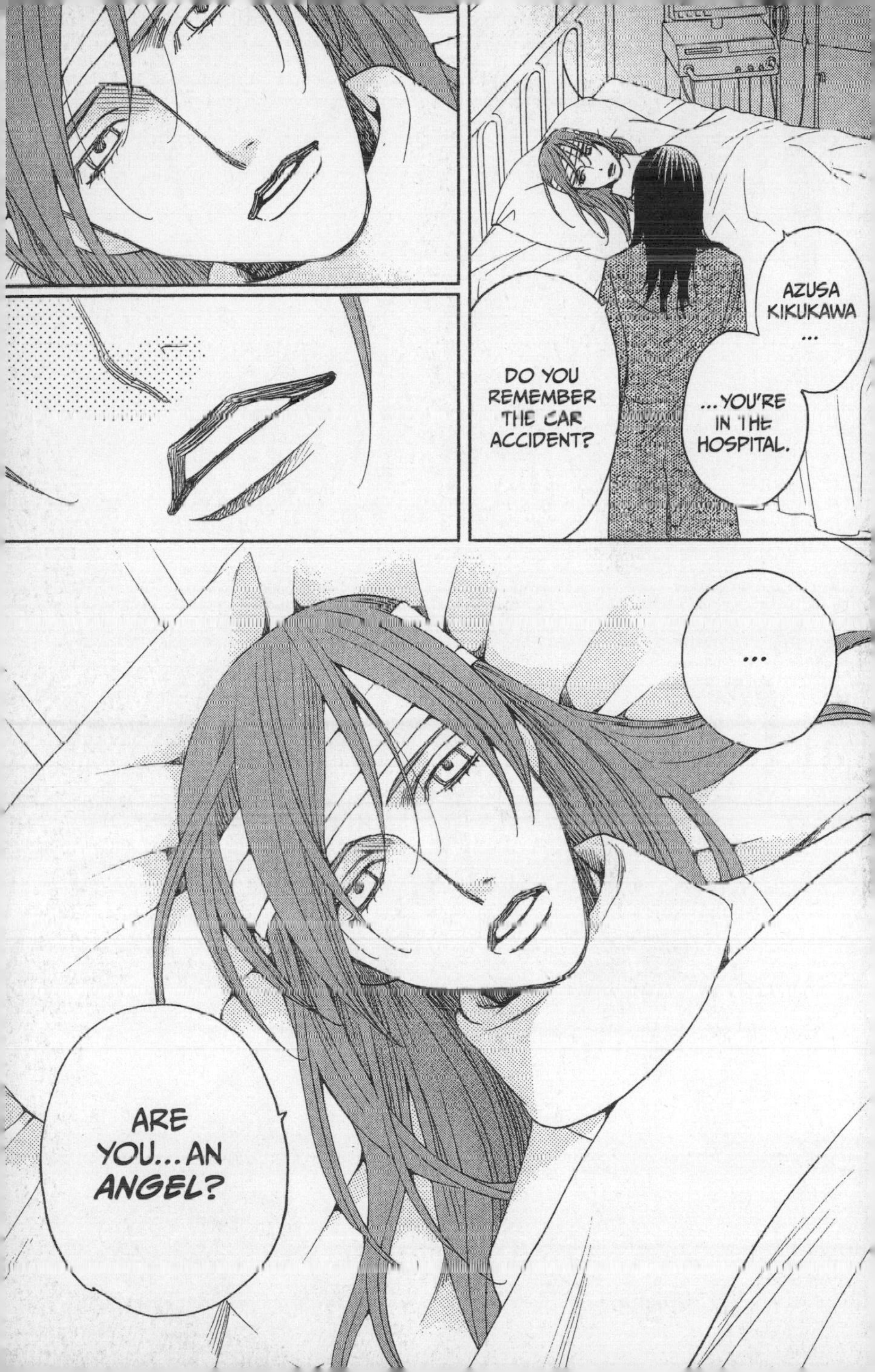
AZUSA KIKUKAWA ...
...YOU'RE IN THE HOSPITAL.
DO YOU REMEMBER THE CAR ACCIDENT?
...
ARE YOU...AN *ANGEL*?

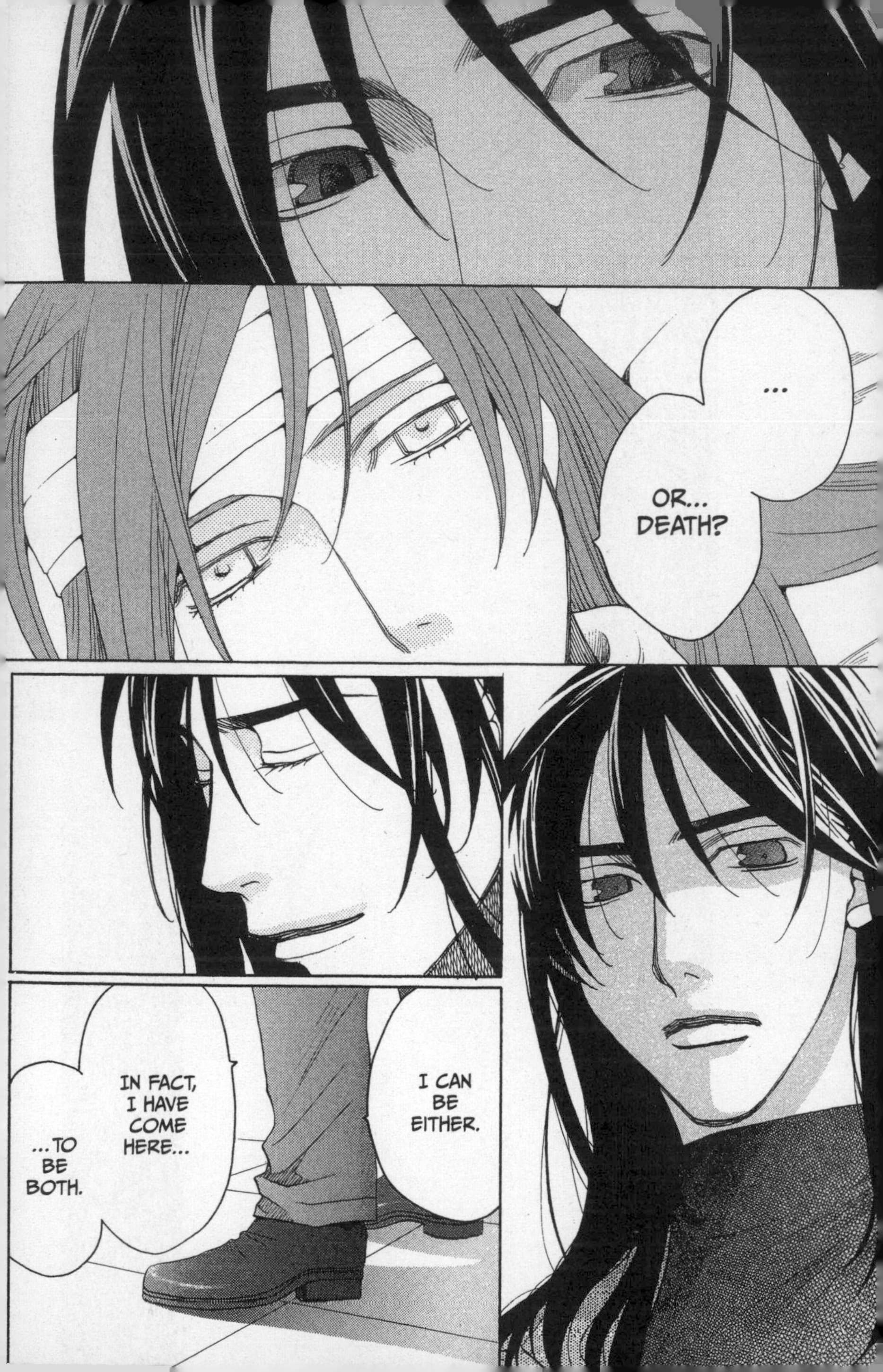
... OR... DEATH?
I CAN BE EITHER.
IN FACT, I HAVE COME HERE...
...TO BE BOTH.

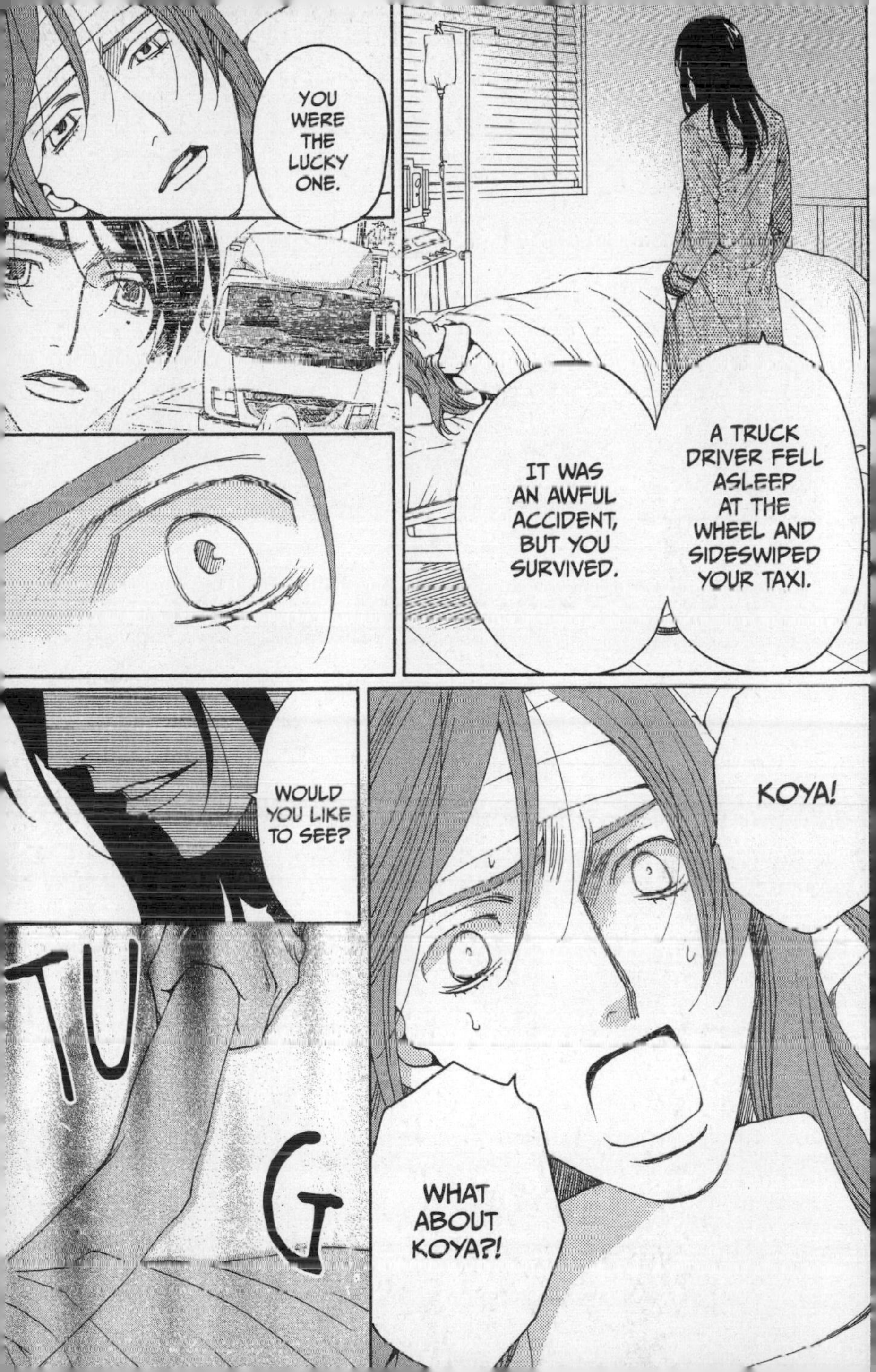
A TRUCK DRIVER FELL ASLEEP AT THE WHEEL AND SIDESWIPED YOUR TAXI.
IT WAS AN AWFUL ACCIDENT, BUT YOU SURVIVED.
YOU WERE THE LUCKY ONE.
KOYA!
WHAT ABOUT KOYA?!
WOULD YOU LIKE TO SEE?
TUG

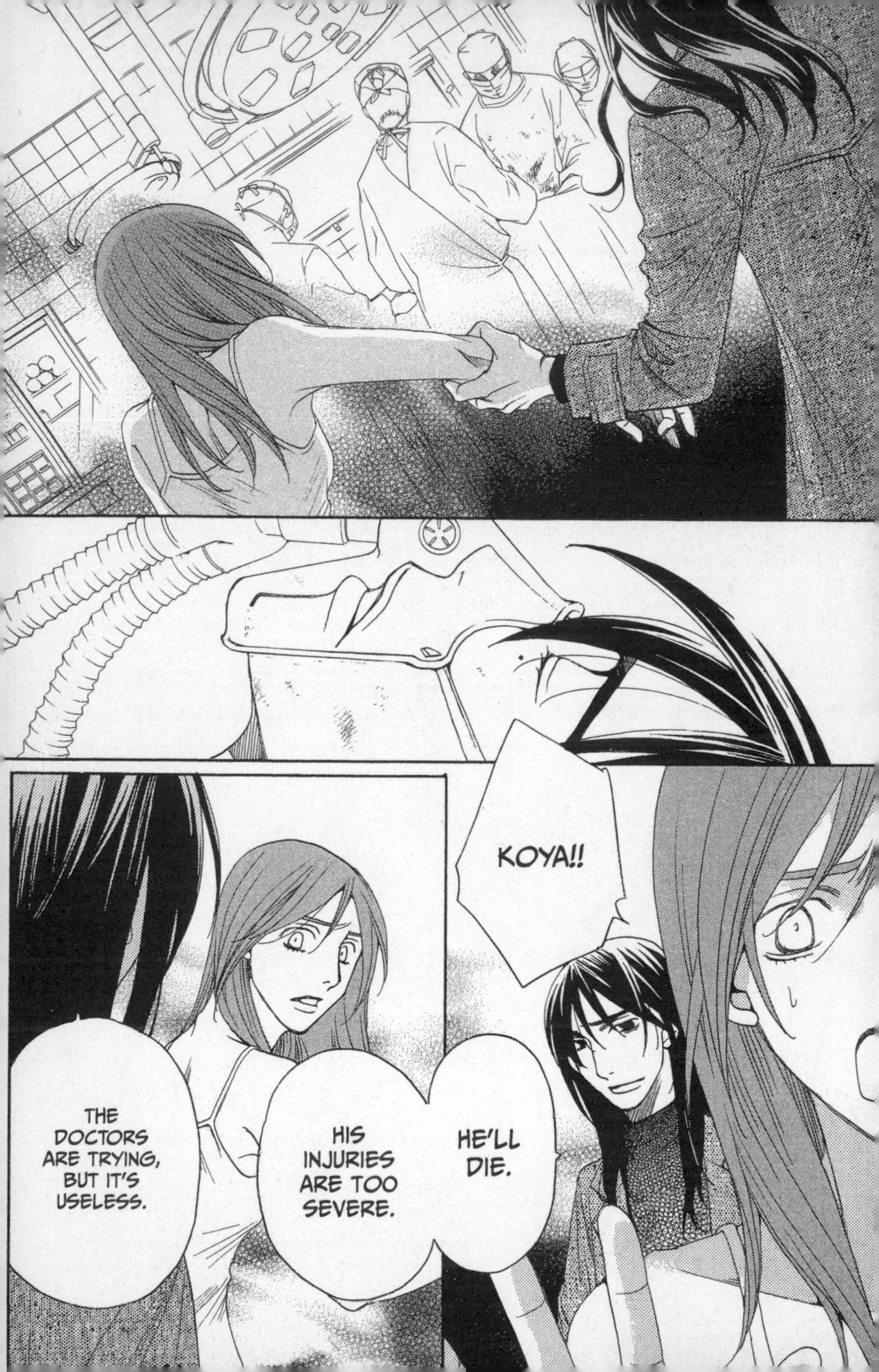
KOYA!!
HE'LL DIE.
HIS INJURIES ARE TOO SEVERE.
THE DOCTORS ARE TRYING, BUT IT'S USELESS.

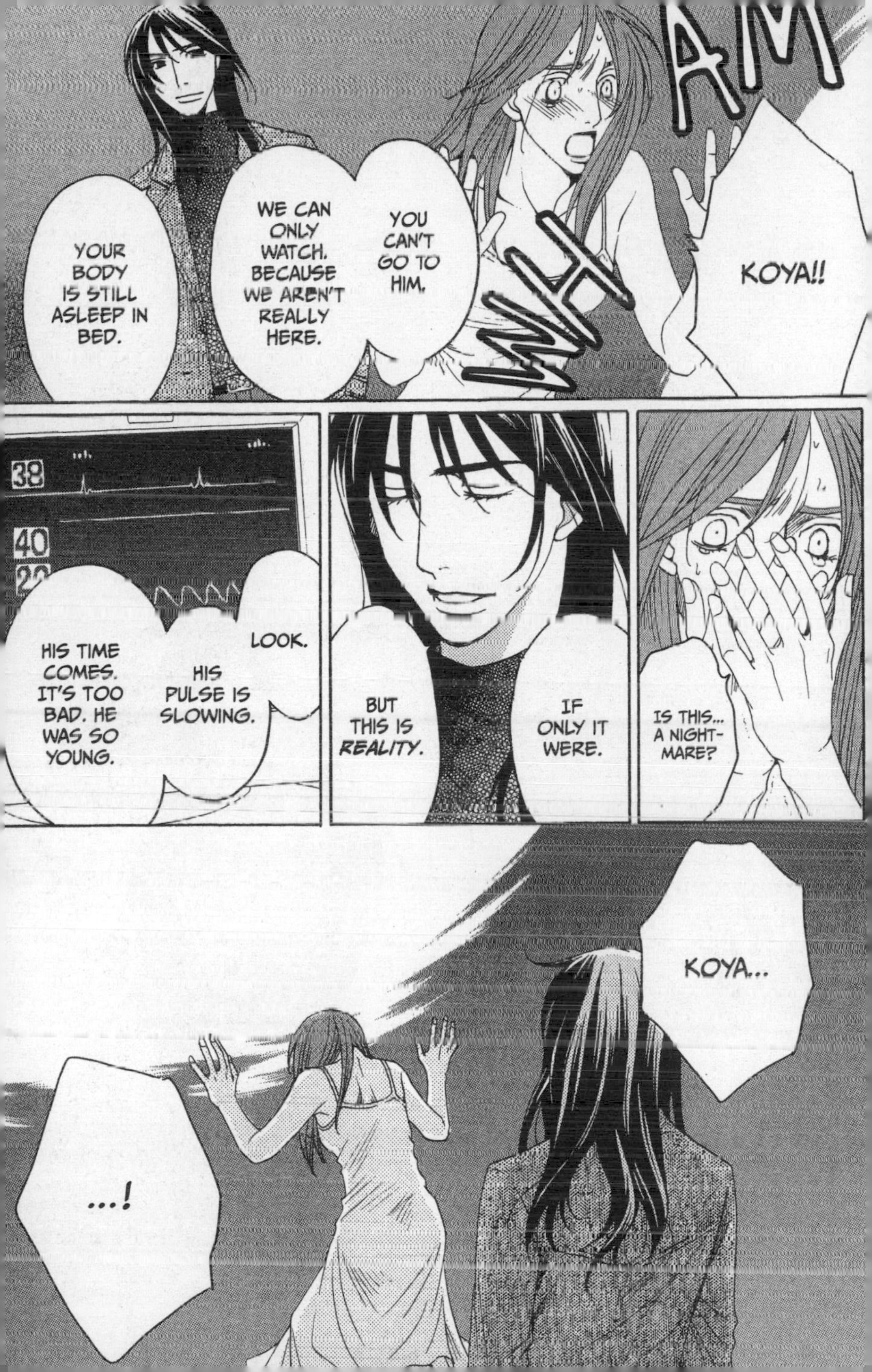
KOYA!!
WH
AM
YOU CAN'T GO TO HIM.
WE CAN ONLY WATCH. BECAUSE WE AREN'T REALLY HERE.
YOUR BODY IS STILL ASLEEP IN BED.
IS THIS... A NIGHT-MARE?
IF ONLY IT WERE.
BUT THIS IS *REALITY*.
LOOK.
HIS PULSE IS SLOWING.
HIS TIME COMES. IT'S TOO BAD. HE WAS SO YOUNG.
KOYA...
...!

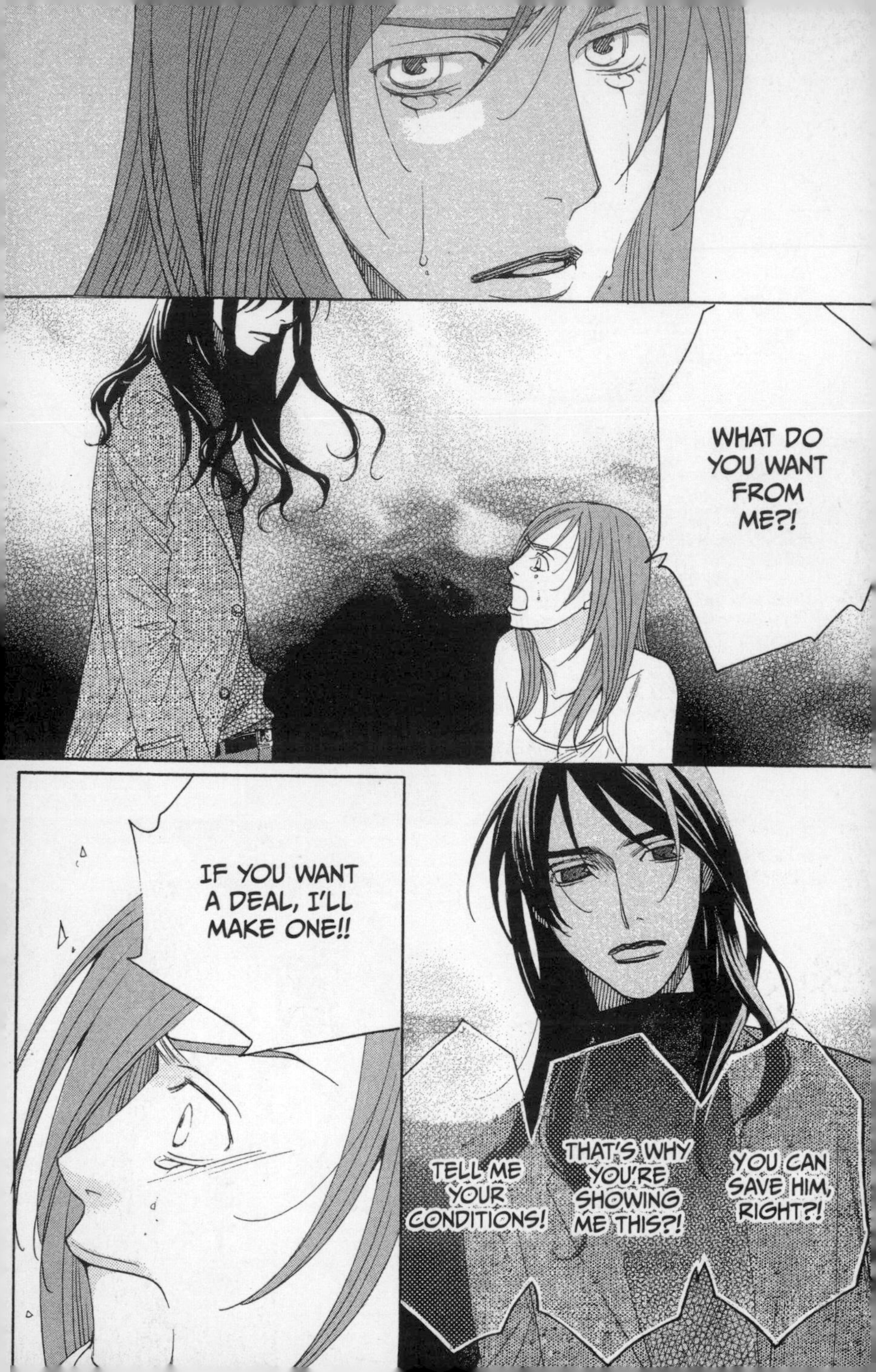
WHAT DO YOU WANT FROM ME?!
YOU CAN SAVE HIM, RIGHT?!
THAT'S WHY YOU'RE SHOWING ME THIS?!
TELL ME YOUR CONDITIONS!
IF YOU WANT A DEAL, I'LL MAKE ONE!!

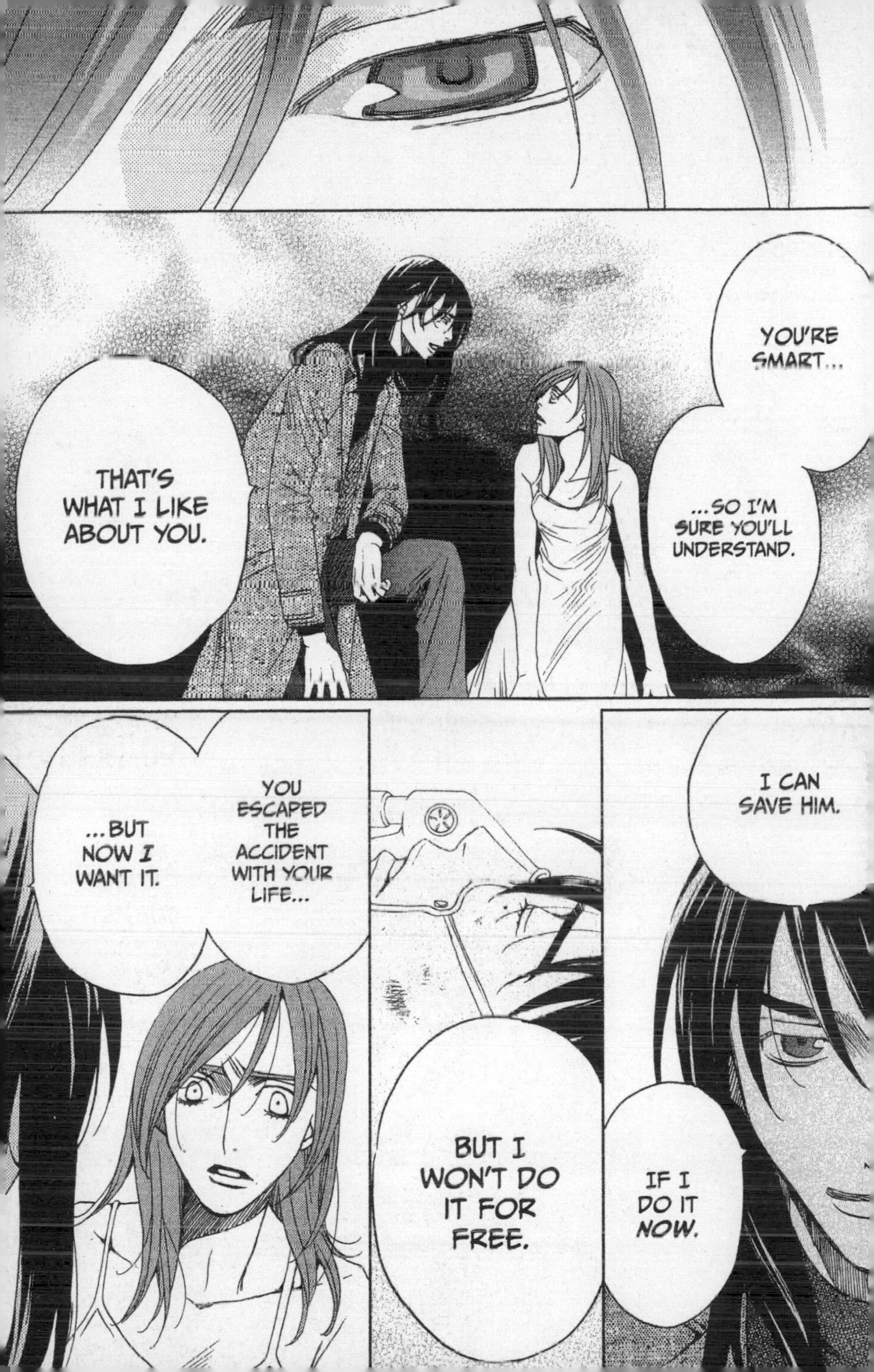
YOU'RE SMART...
...SO I'M SURE YOU'LL UNDERSTAND.
THAT'S WHAT I LIKE ABOUT YOU.
I CAN SAVE HIM.
IF I DO IT *NOW*.
BUT I WON'T DO IT FOR FREE.
YOU ESCAPED THE ACCIDENT WITH YOUR LIFE...
...BUT NOW *I* WANT IT.

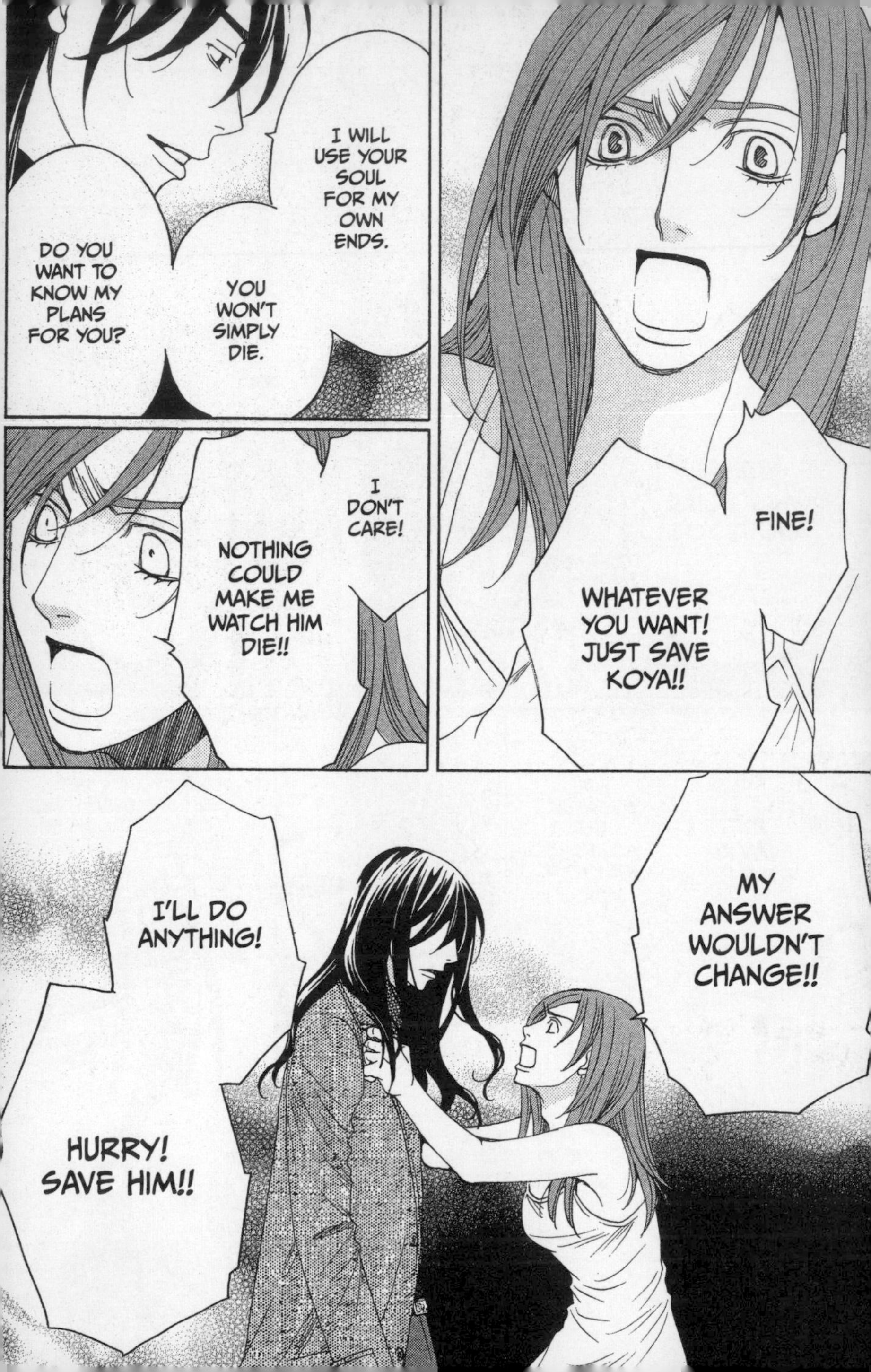
FINE!
WHATEVER YOU WANT! JUST SAVE KOYA!!
I WILL USE YOUR SOUL FOR MY OWN ENDS.
YOU WON'T SIMPLY DIE.
DO YOU WANT TO KNOW MY PLANS FOR YOU?
I DON'T CARE!
NOTHING COULD MAKE ME WATCH HIM DIE!!
MY ANSWER WOULDN'T CHANGE!!
I'LL DO ANYTHING!
HURRY! SAVE HIM!!

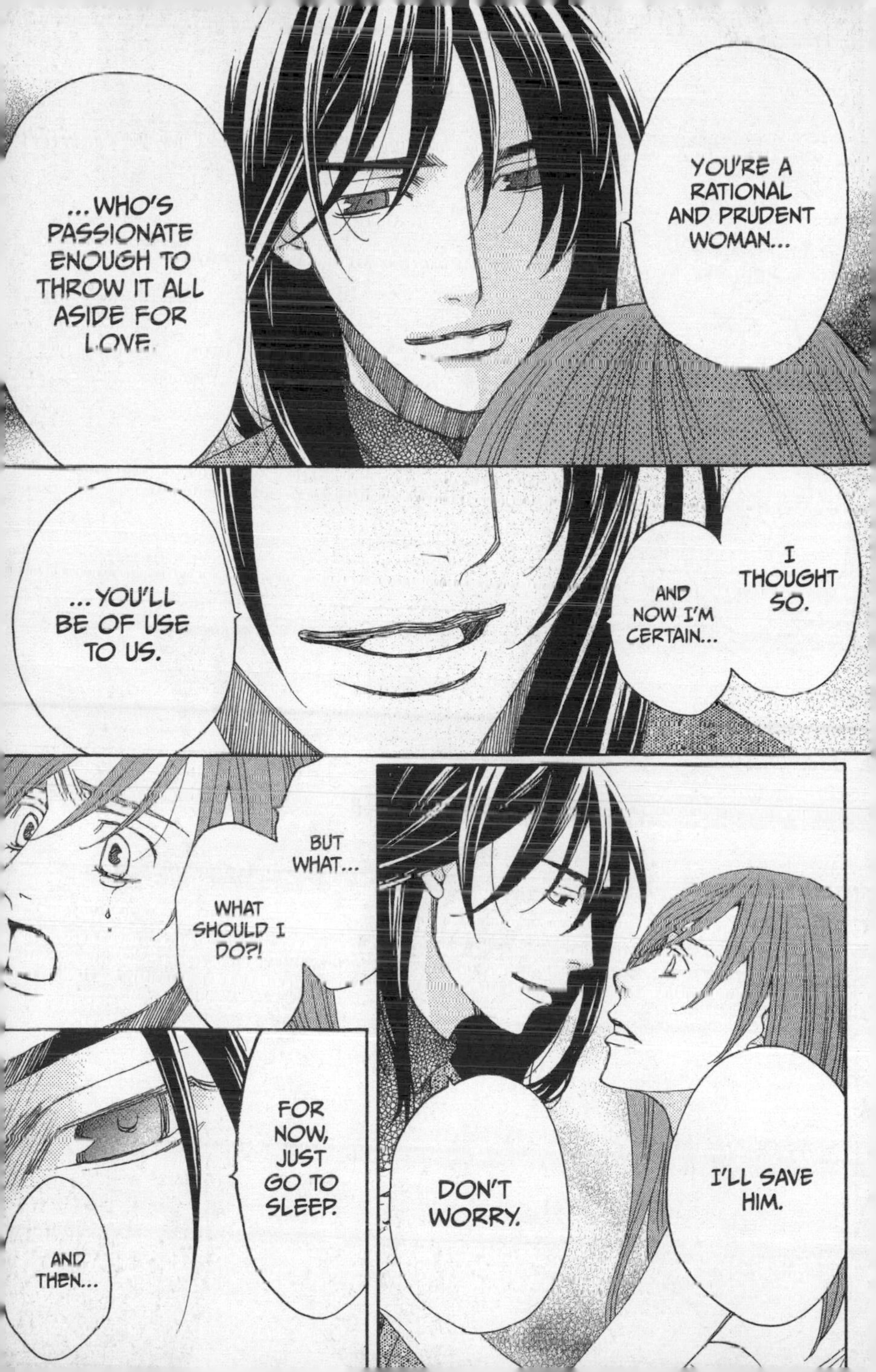
YOU'RE A RATIONAL AND PRUDENT WOMAN...
...WHO'S PASSIONATE ENOUGH TO THROW IT ALL ASIDE FOR LOVE.
I THOUGHT SO.
AND NOW I'M CERTAIN...
...YOU'LL BE OF USE TO US.
I'LL SAVE HIM.
DON'T WORRY.
BUT WHAT...
WHAT SHOULD I DO?!
FOR NOW, JUST GO TO SLEEP.
AND THEN...

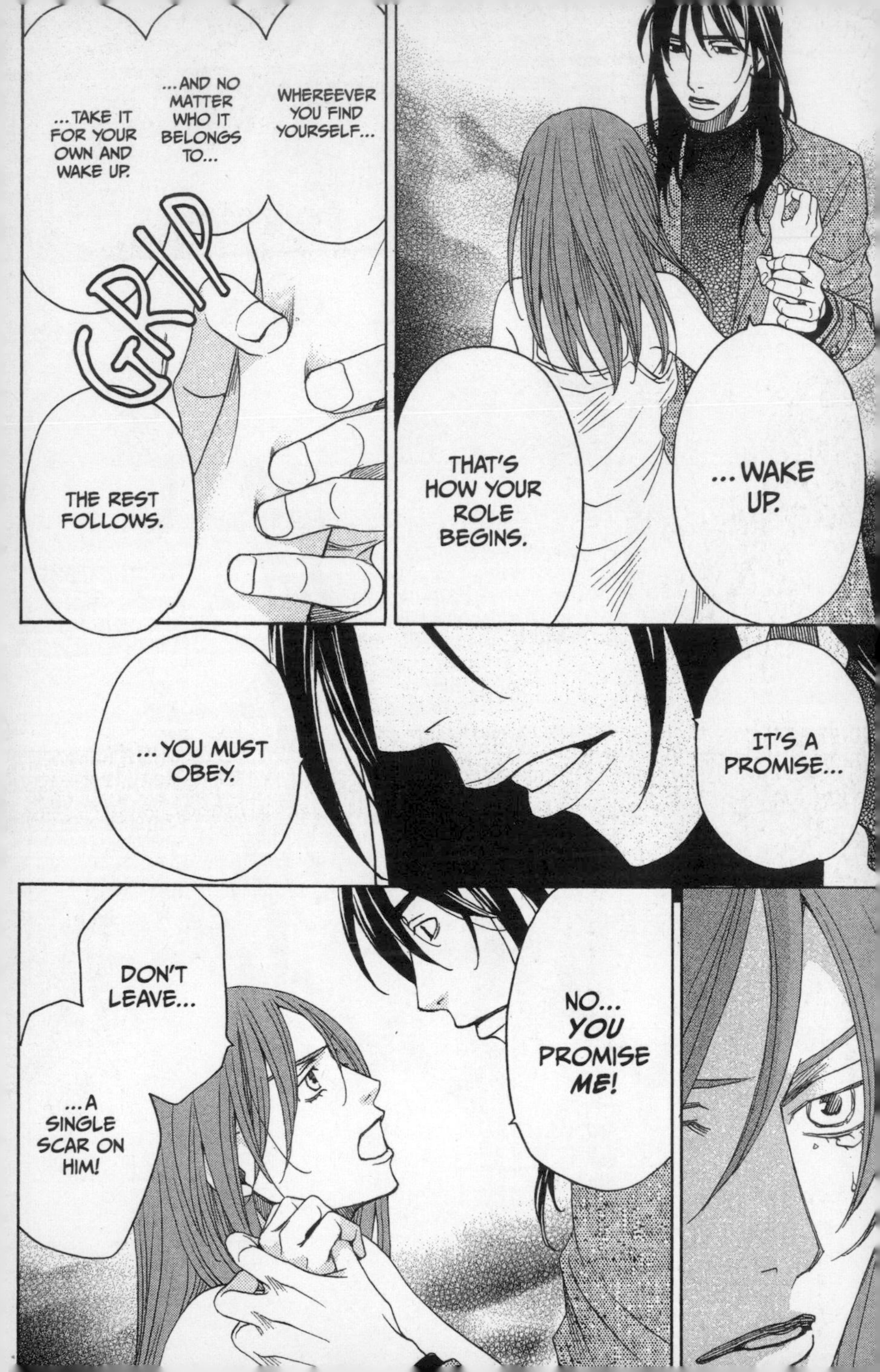
...WAKE UP.
THAT'S HOW YOUR ROLE BEGINS.
WHEREEVER YOU FIND YOURSELF...
...AND NO MATTER WHO IT BELONGS TO...
...TAKE IT FOR YOUR OWN AND WAKE UP.
GRIP
THE REST FOLLOWS.
IT'S A PROMISE...
...YOU MUST OBEY.
NO... *YOU* PROMISE *ME!*
DON'T LEAVE...
...A SINGLE SCAR ON HIM!

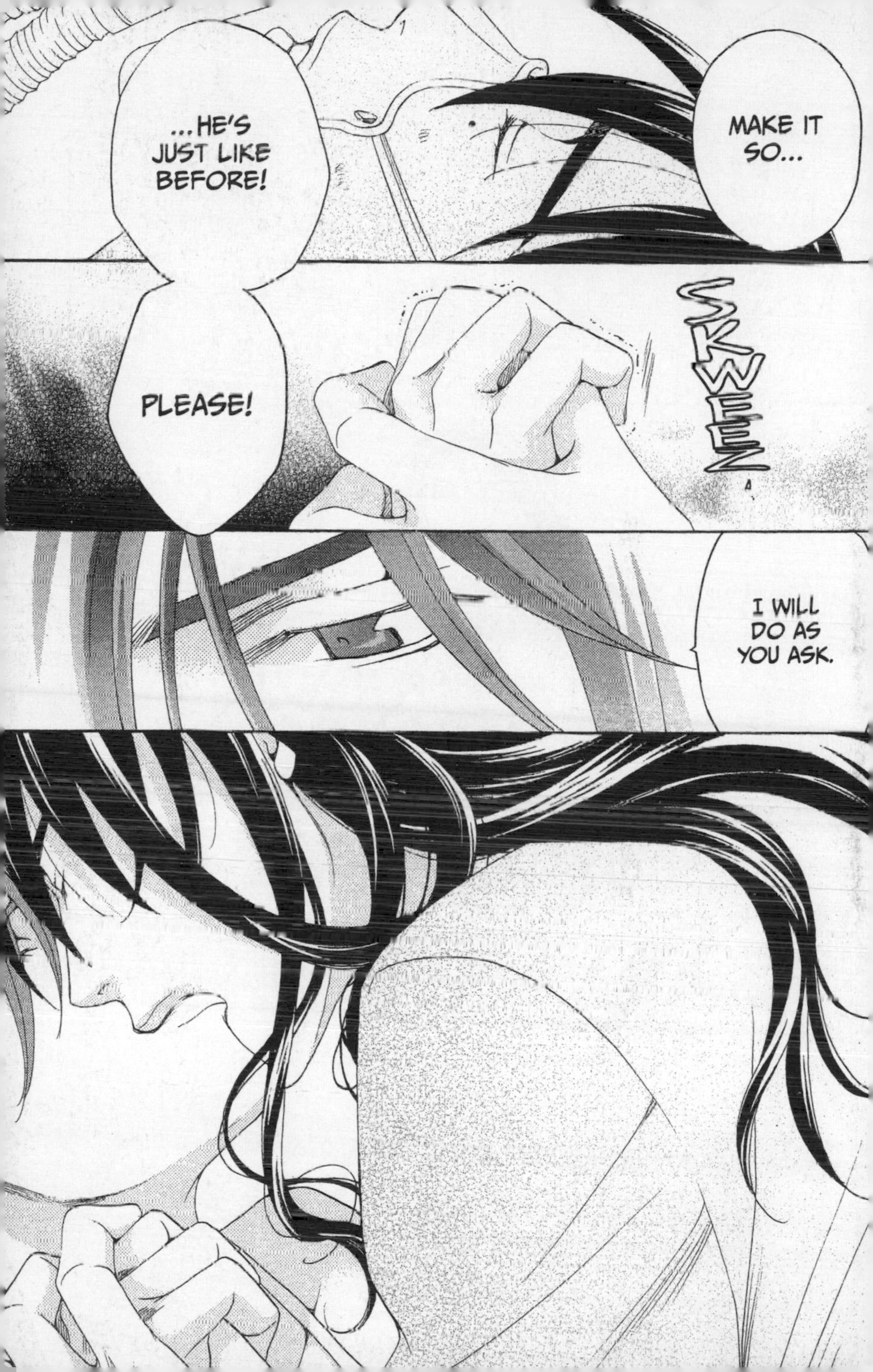
MAKE IT SO...
...HE'S JUST LIKE BEFORE!
SKWEEZ
PLEASE!
I WILL DO AS YOU ASK.

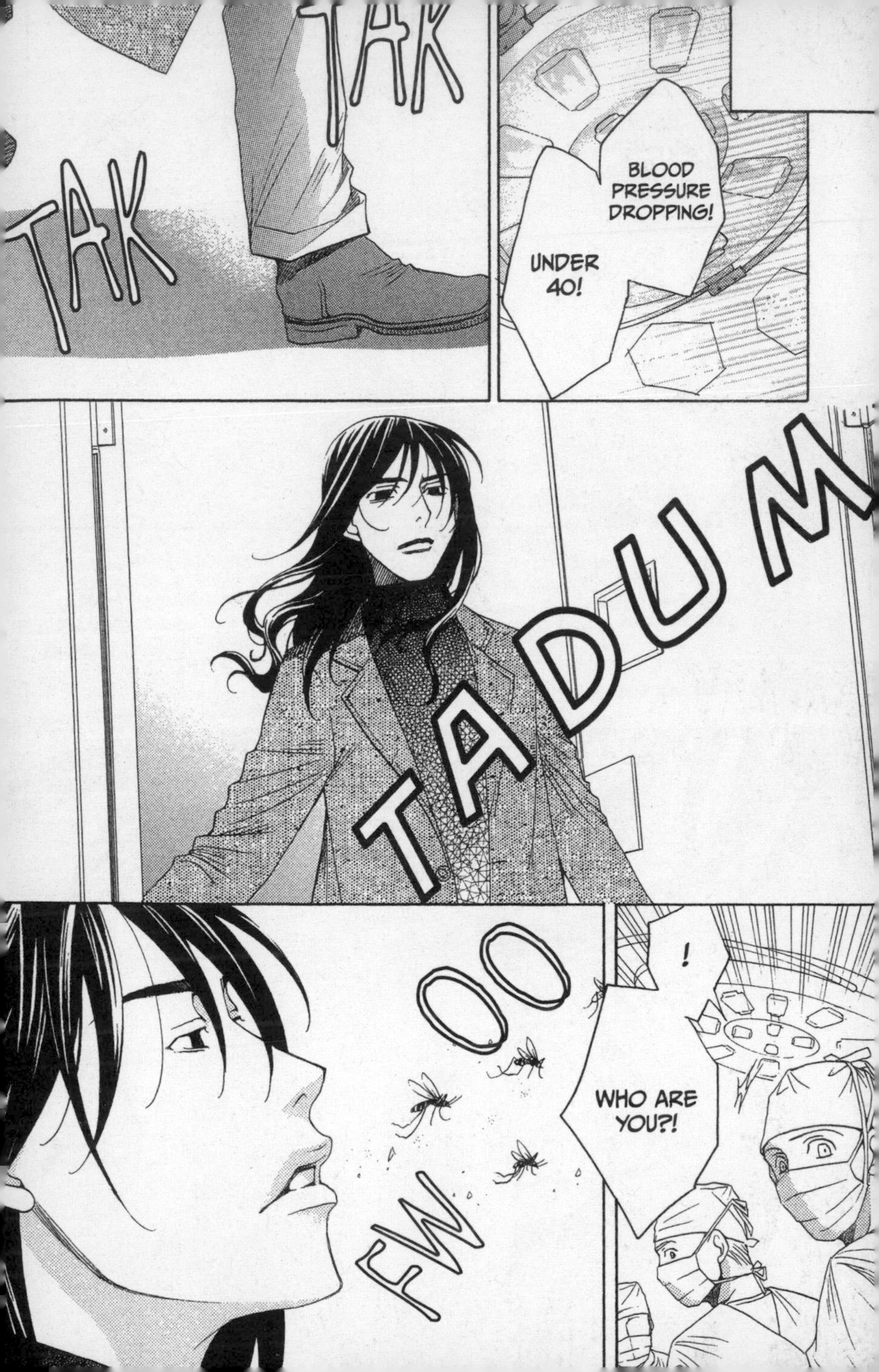
BLOOD PRESSURE DROPPING!
UNDER 40!
TAK
TAK
TADUM
!
WHO ARE YOU?!
FWOO

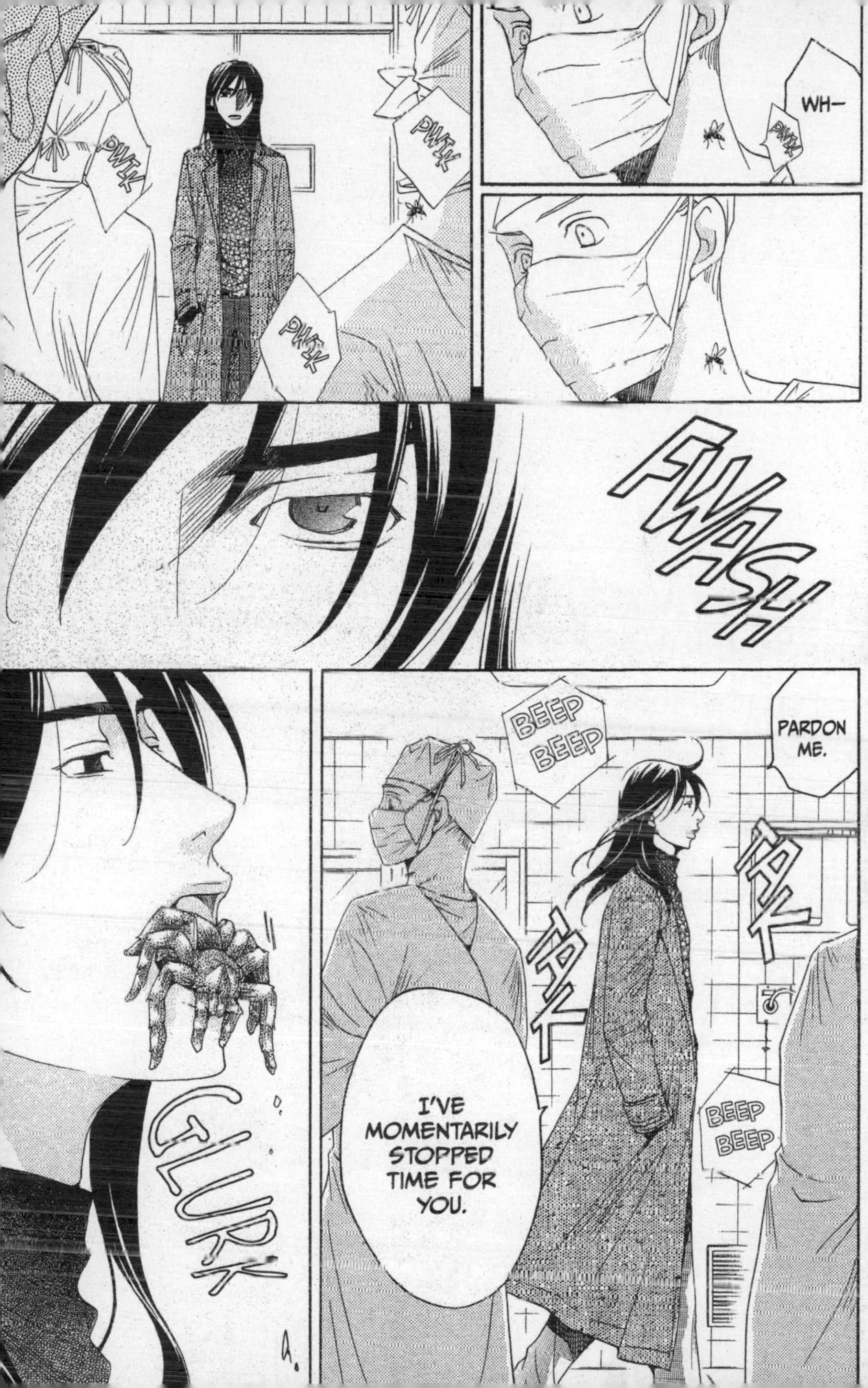
WH—
PWIK
PWIK
PWIK
PWIK
FWASH
PARDON ME.
BEEP BEEP
TAK
TAK
BEEP BEEP
I'VE MOMENTARILY STOPPED TIME FOR YOU.
GLURK

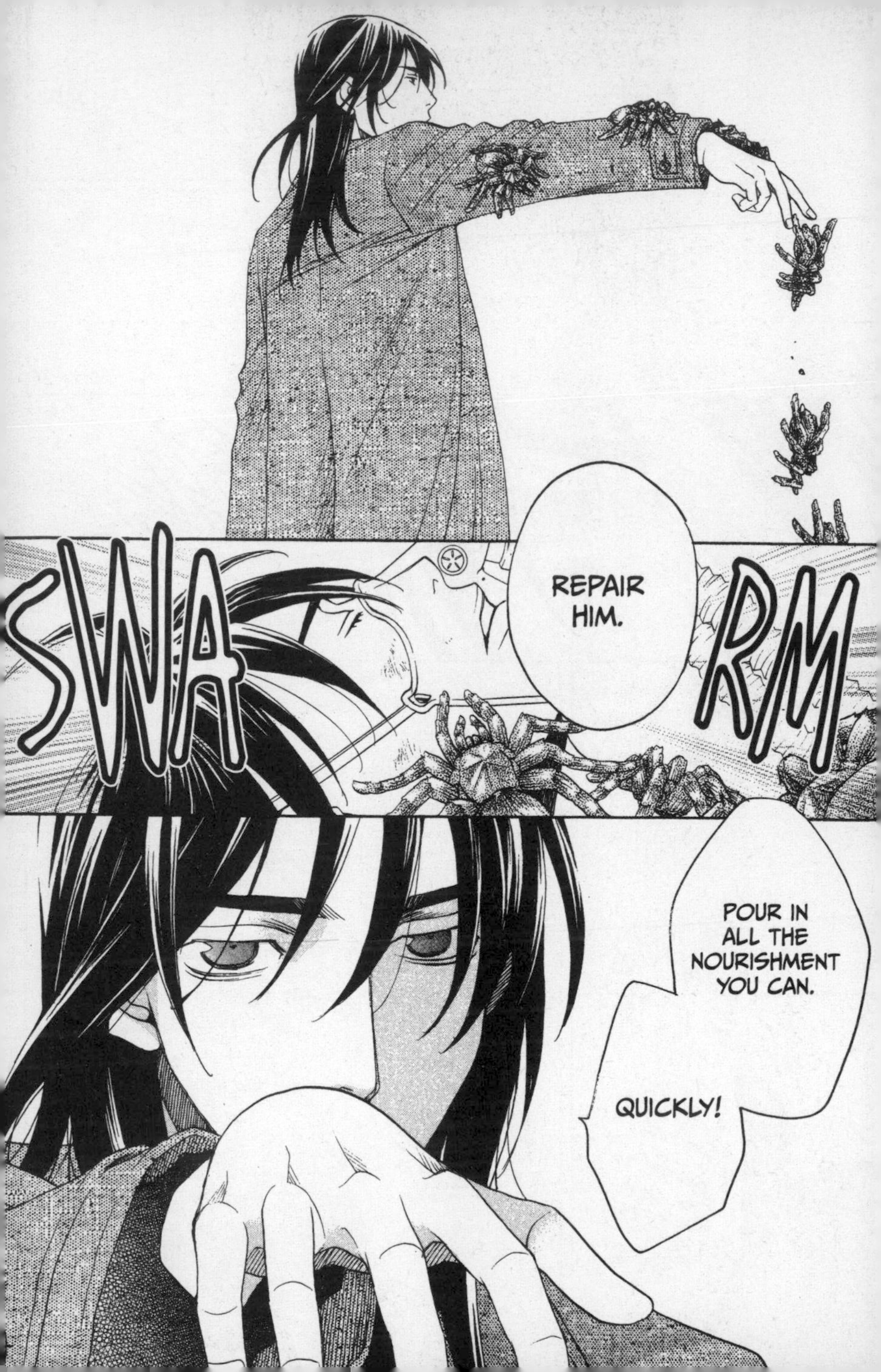
REPAIR HIM.
SWA RM
POUR IN ALL THE NOURISHMENT YOU CAN.
QUICKLY!

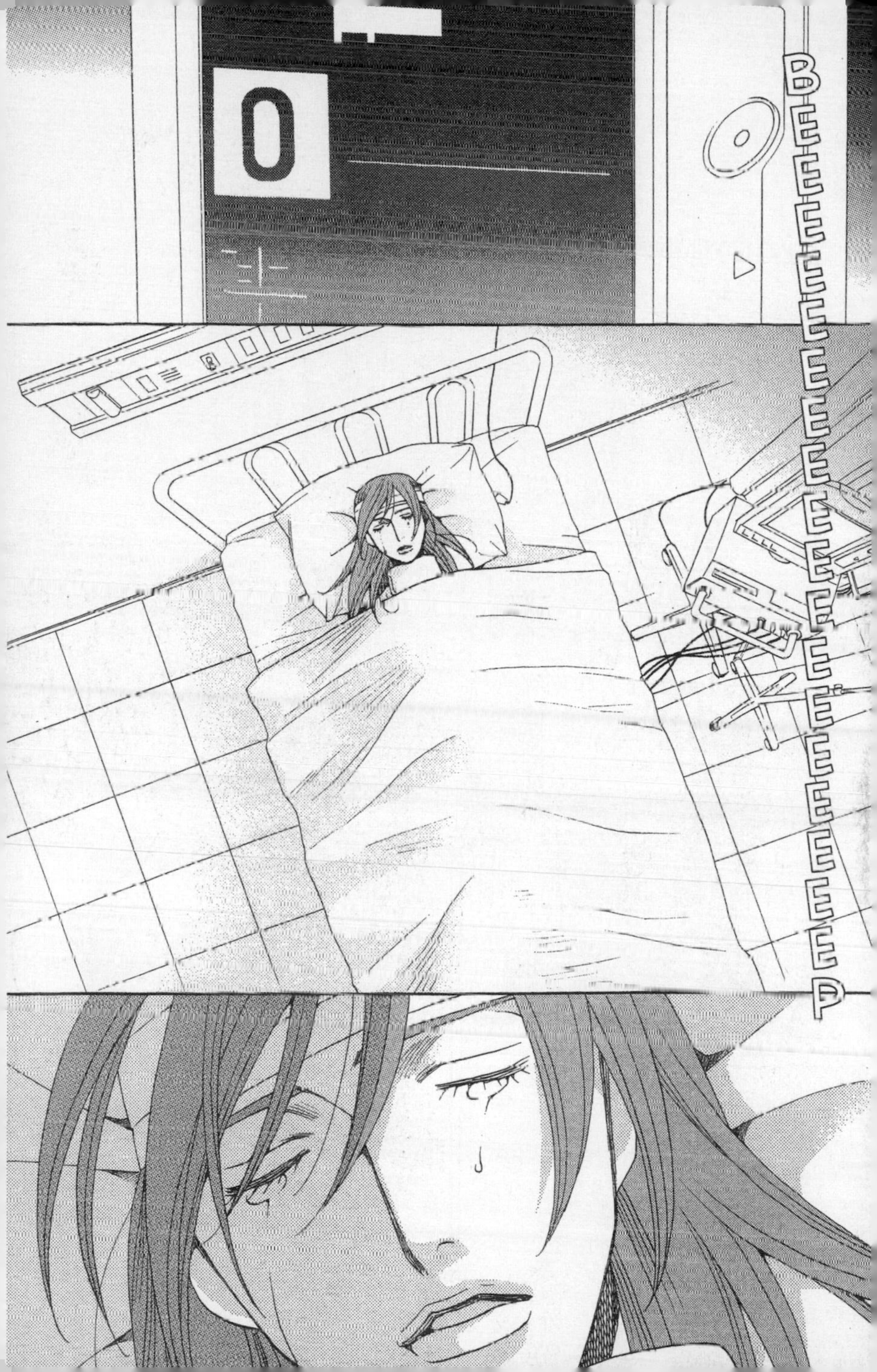
0
BEEEEEEEEEEEEEEEEP

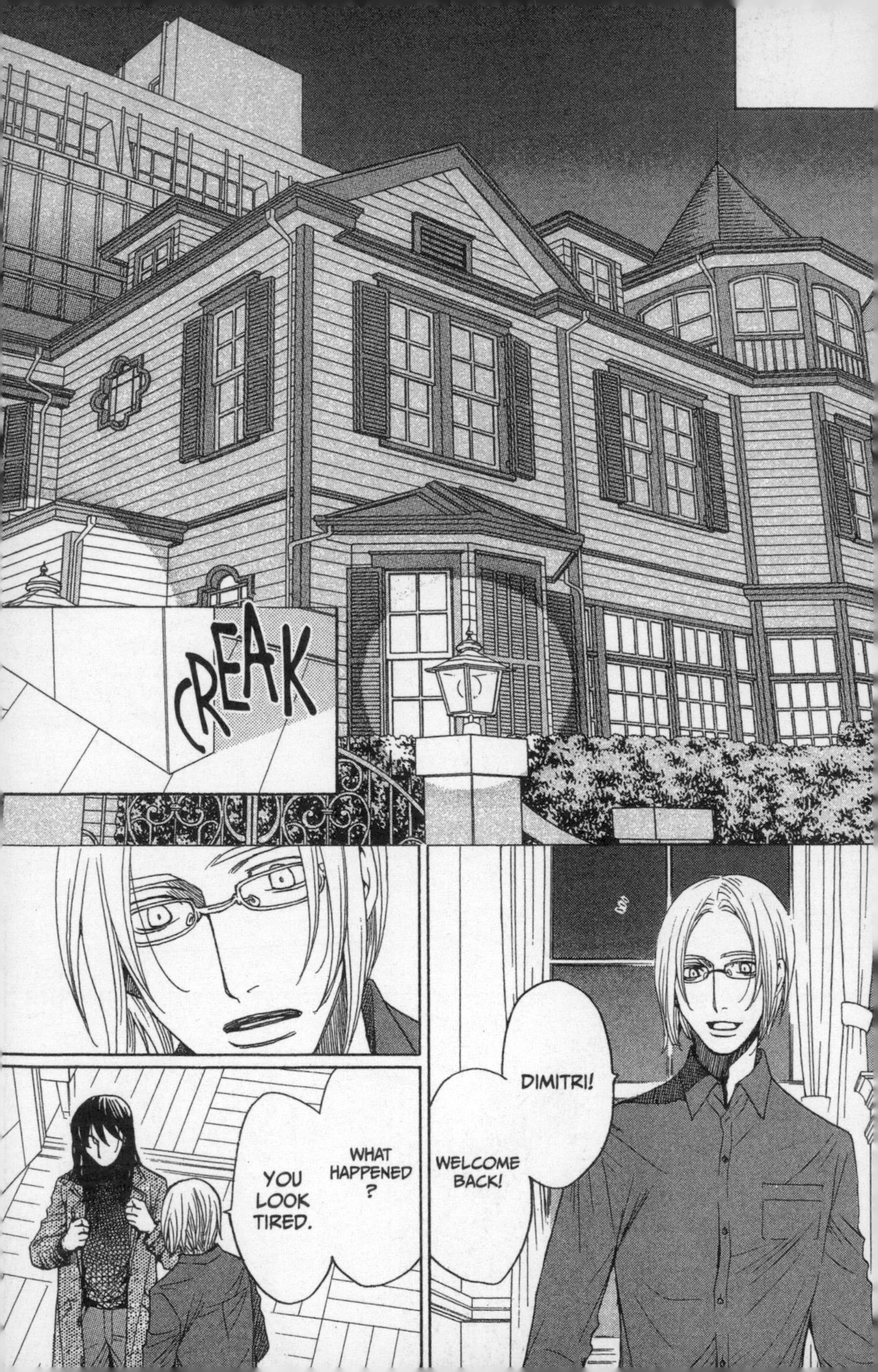
CREAK
DIMITRI! WELCOME BACK!
WHAT HAPPENED? YOU LOOK TIRED.

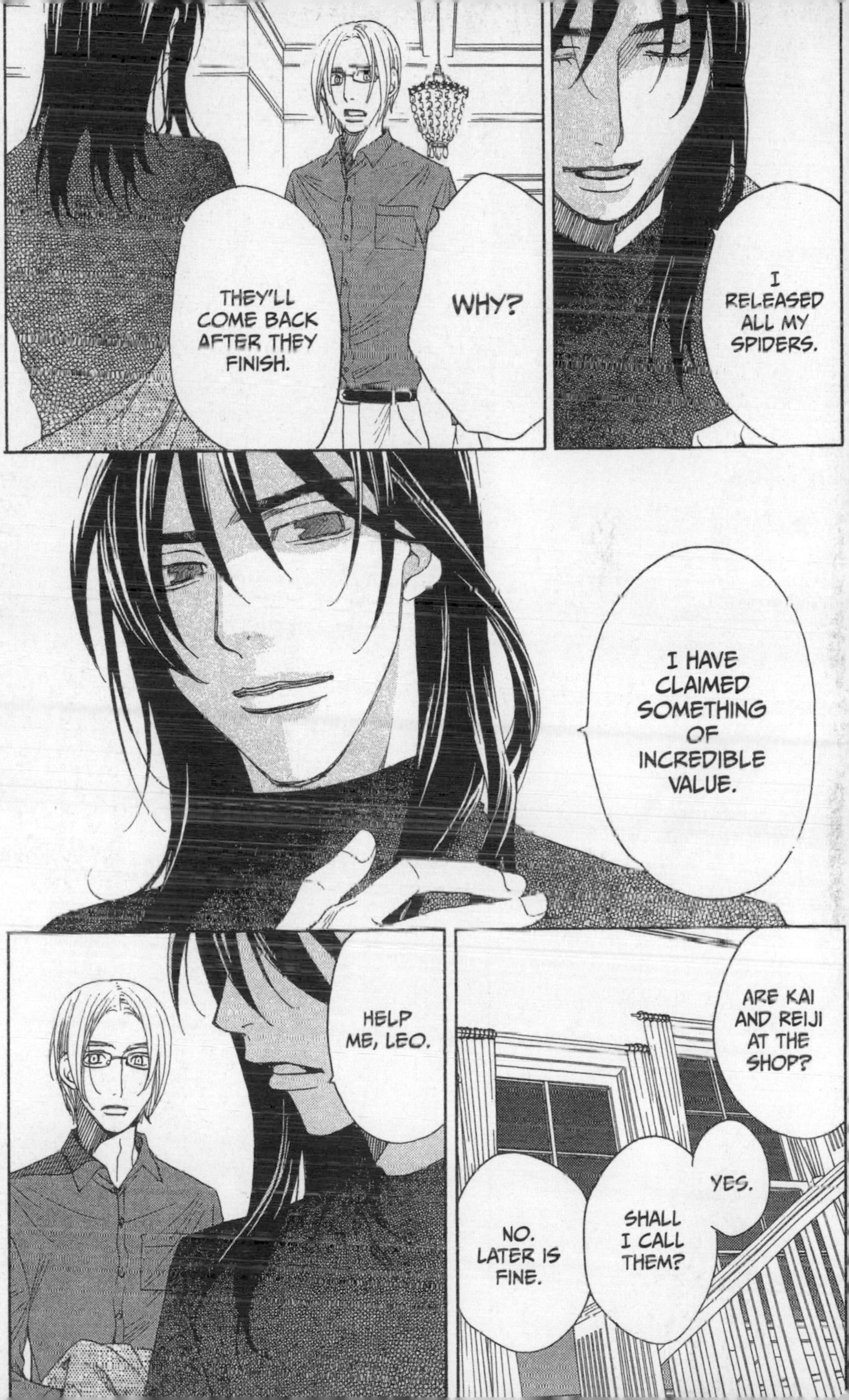
I RELEASED ALL MY SPIDERS.
WHY?
THEY'LL COME BACK AFTER THEY FINISH.
I HAVE CLAIMED SOMETHING OF INCREDIBLE VALUE.
ARE KAI AND REIJI AT THE SHOP?
YES.
SHALL I CALL THEM?
NO. LATER IS FINE.
HELP ME, LEO.

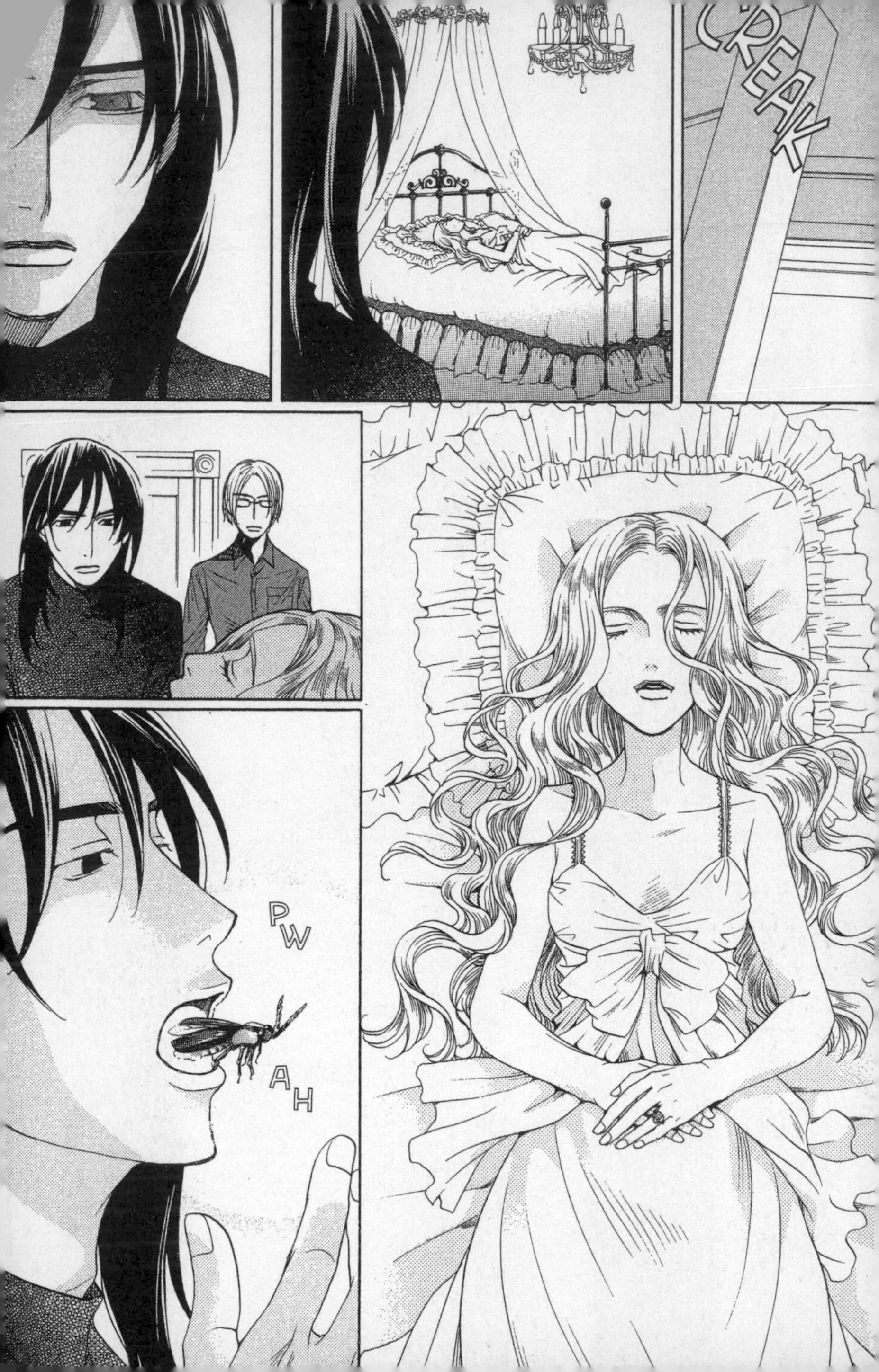
CREAK
PWAH

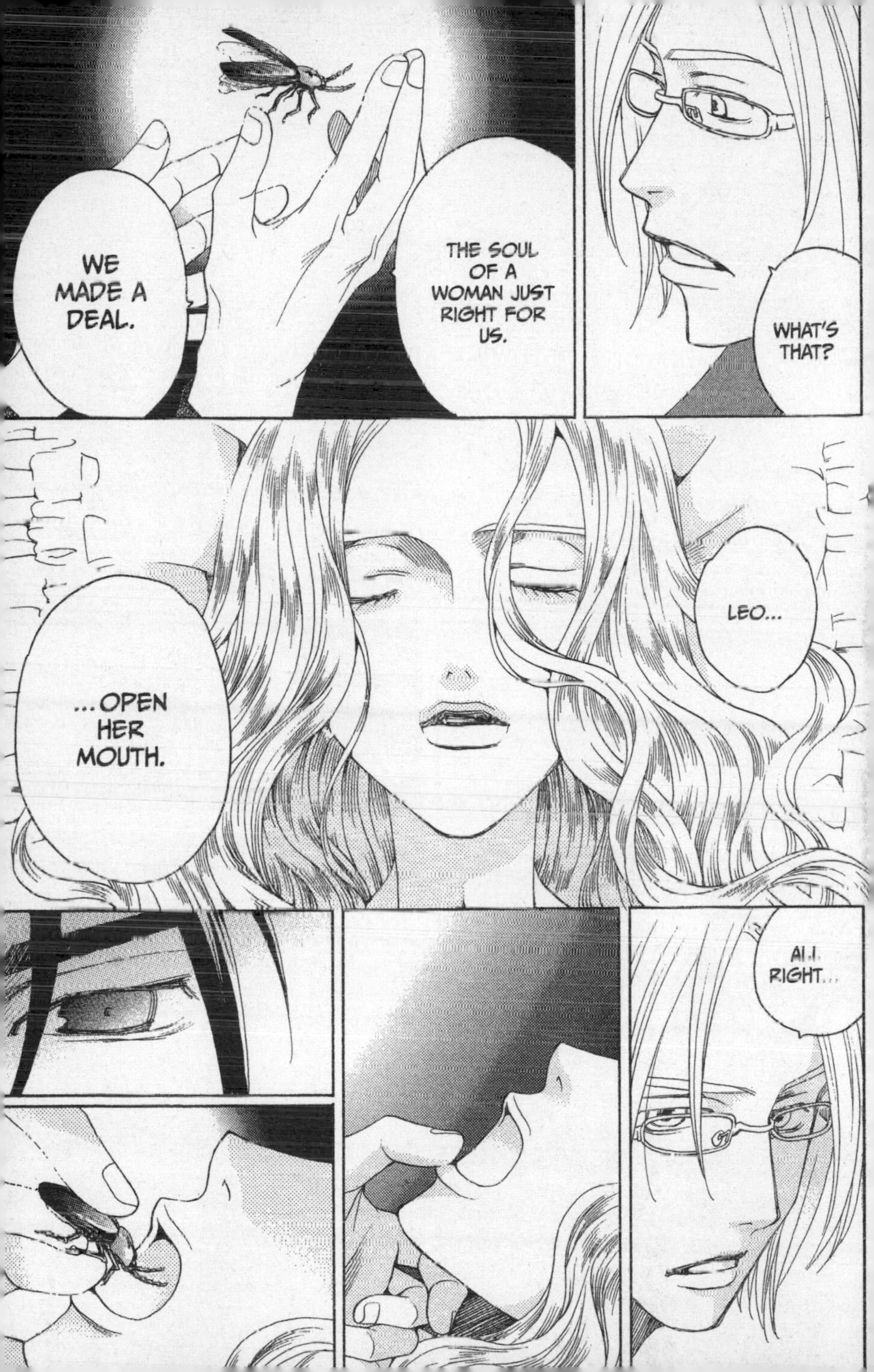
WHAT'S THAT?
THE SOUL OF A WOMAN JUST RIGHT FOR US.
WE MADE A DEAL.
LEO...
...OPEN HER MOUTH.
ALL RIGHT...

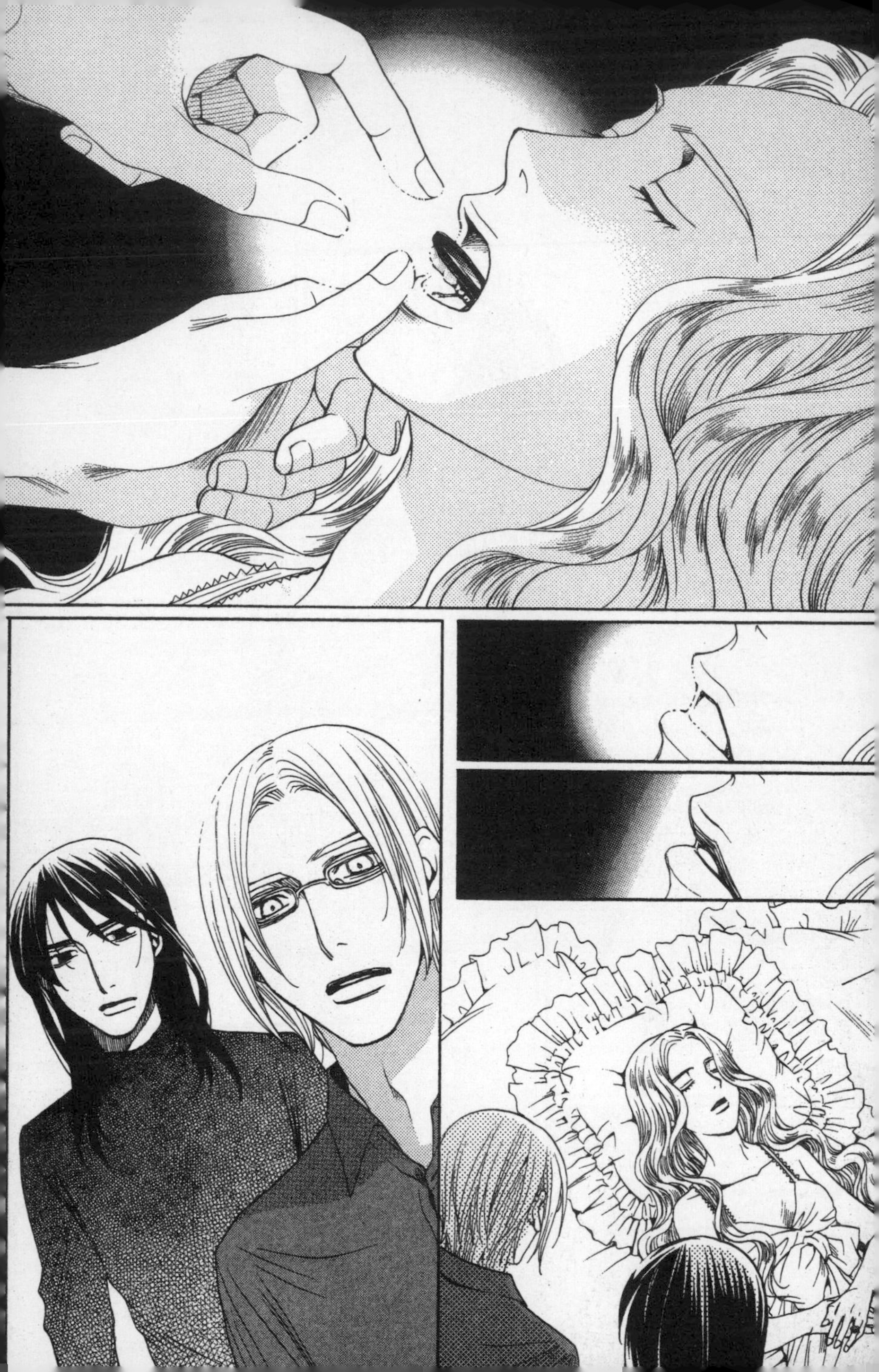

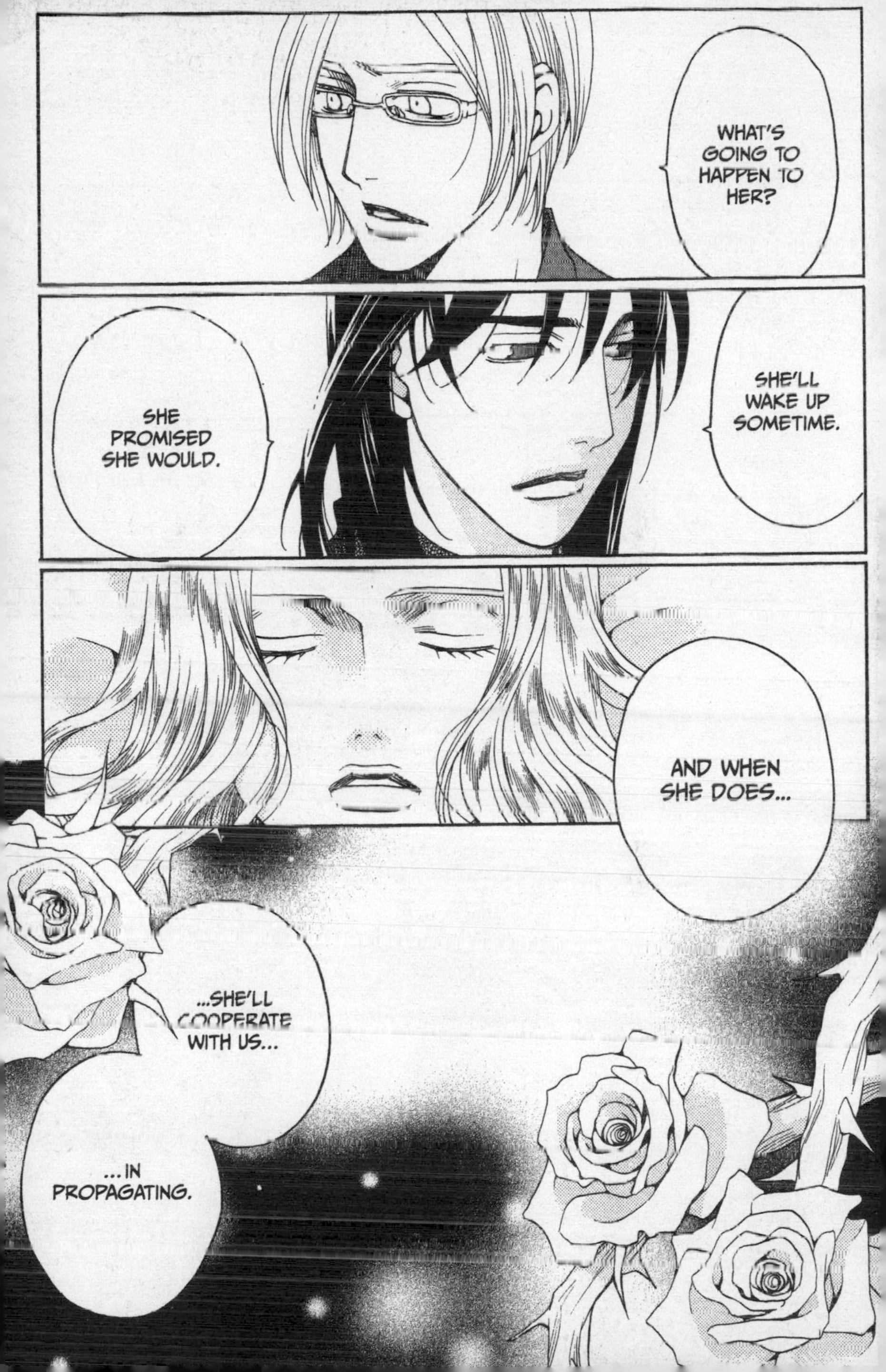
WHAT'S GOING TO HAPPEN TO HER?
SHE'LL WAKE UP SOMETIME.
SHE PROMISED SHE WOULD.
AND WHEN SHE DOES...
...SHE'LL COOPERATE WITH US...
...IN PROPAGATING.

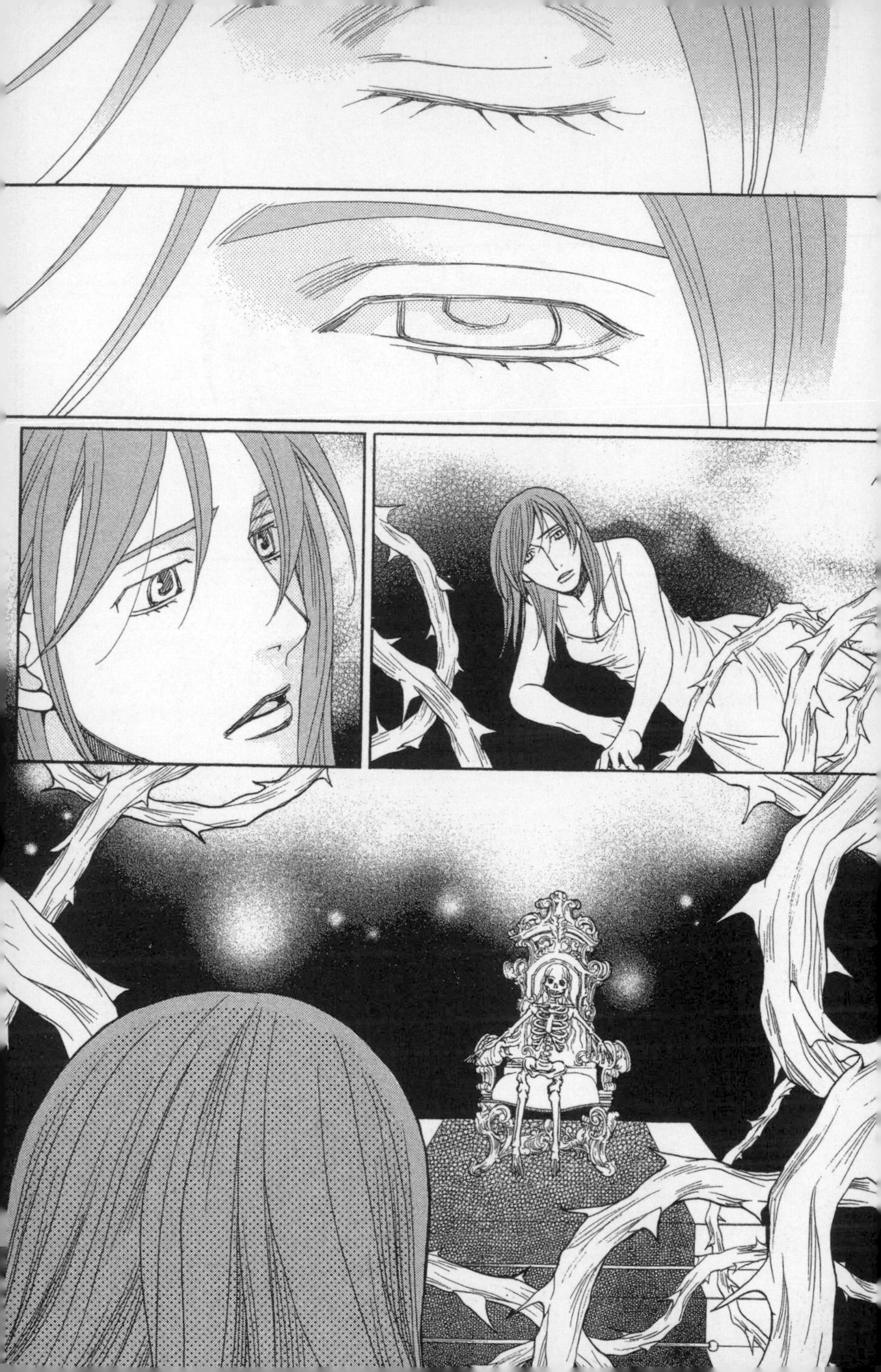

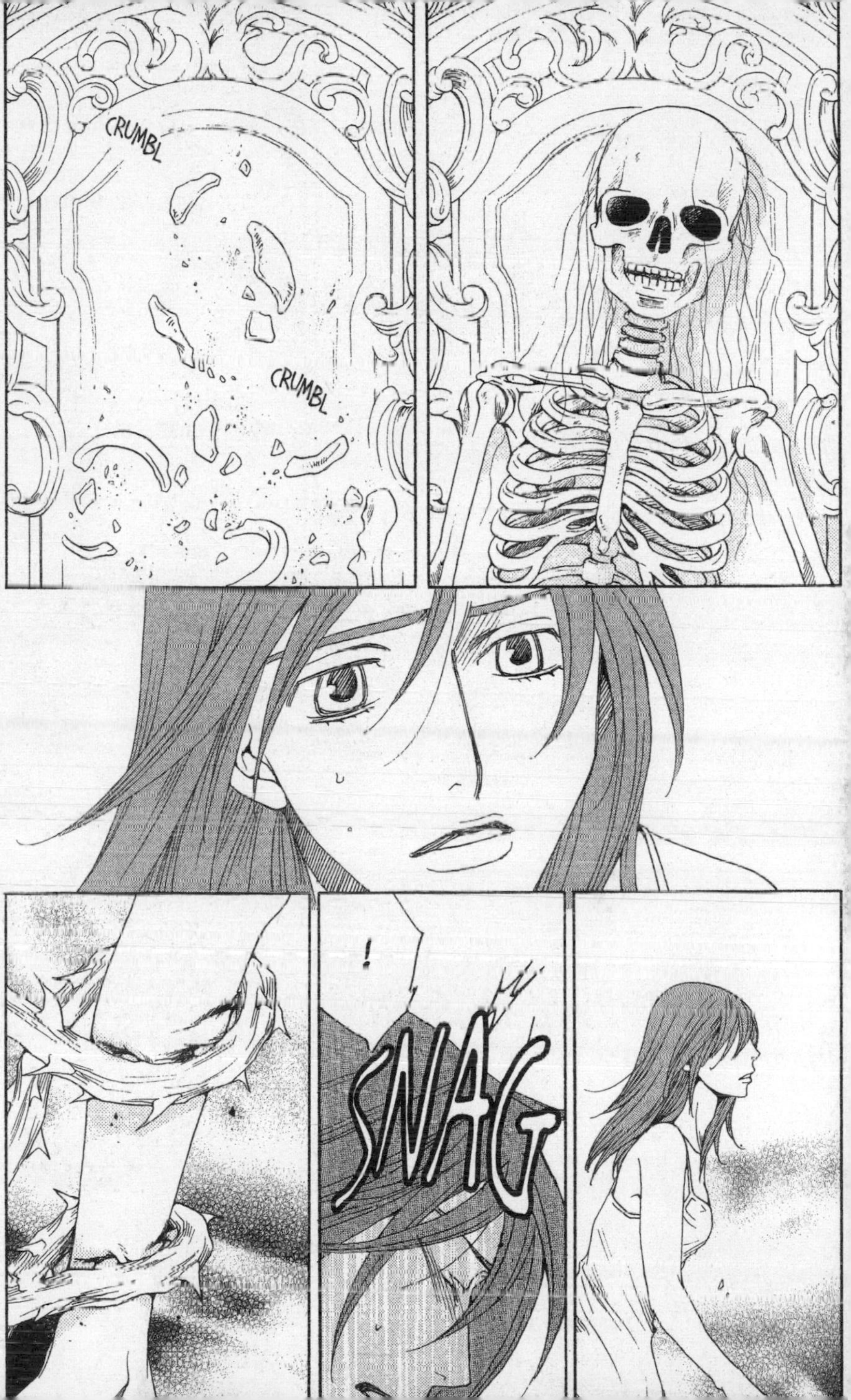
CRUMBL
CRUMBL
!
SNAG

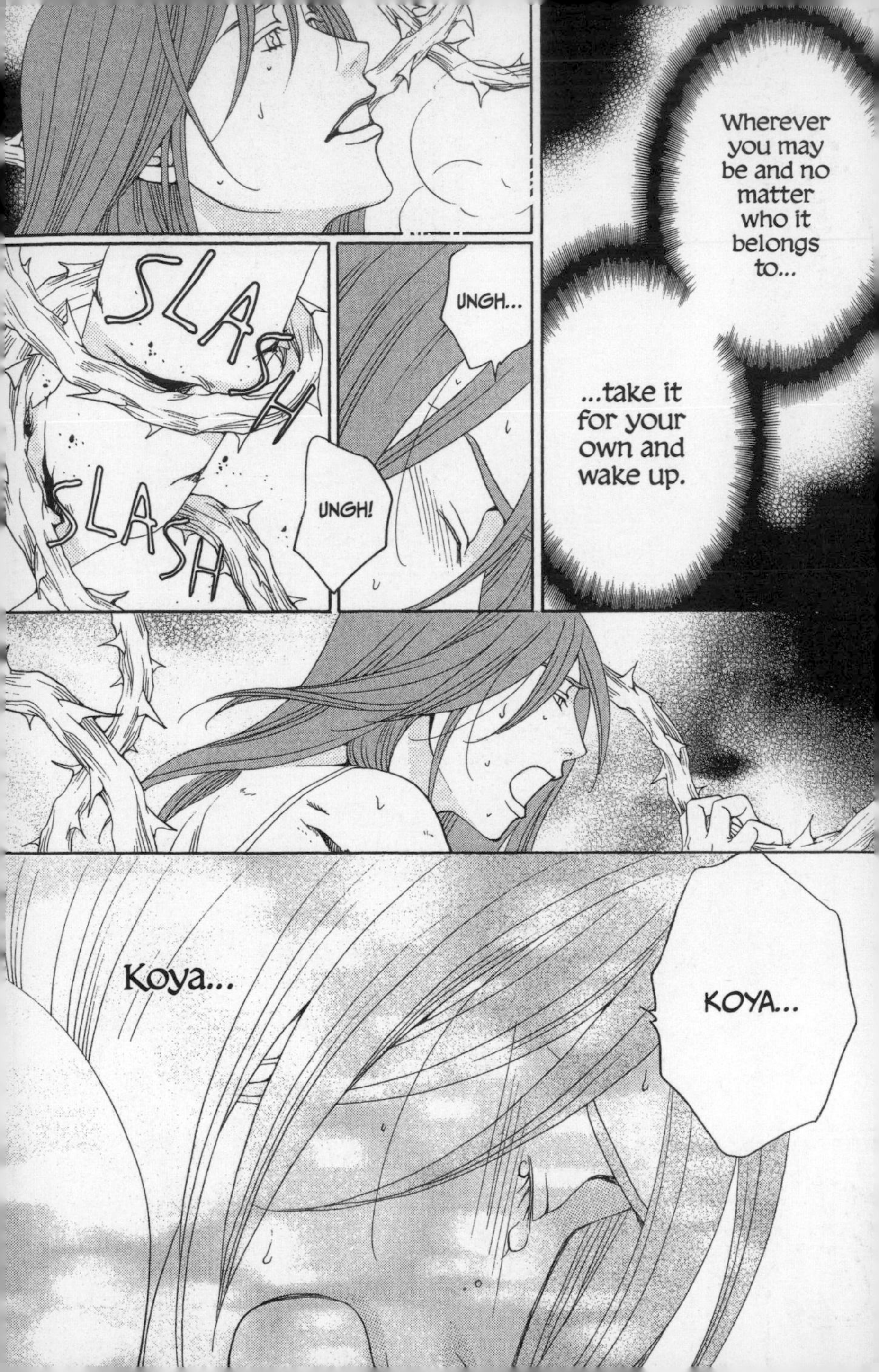
Wherever you may be and no matter who it belongs to...
...take it for your own and wake up.
UNGH...
UNGH!
SLASH
SLASH
KOYA...
Koya...

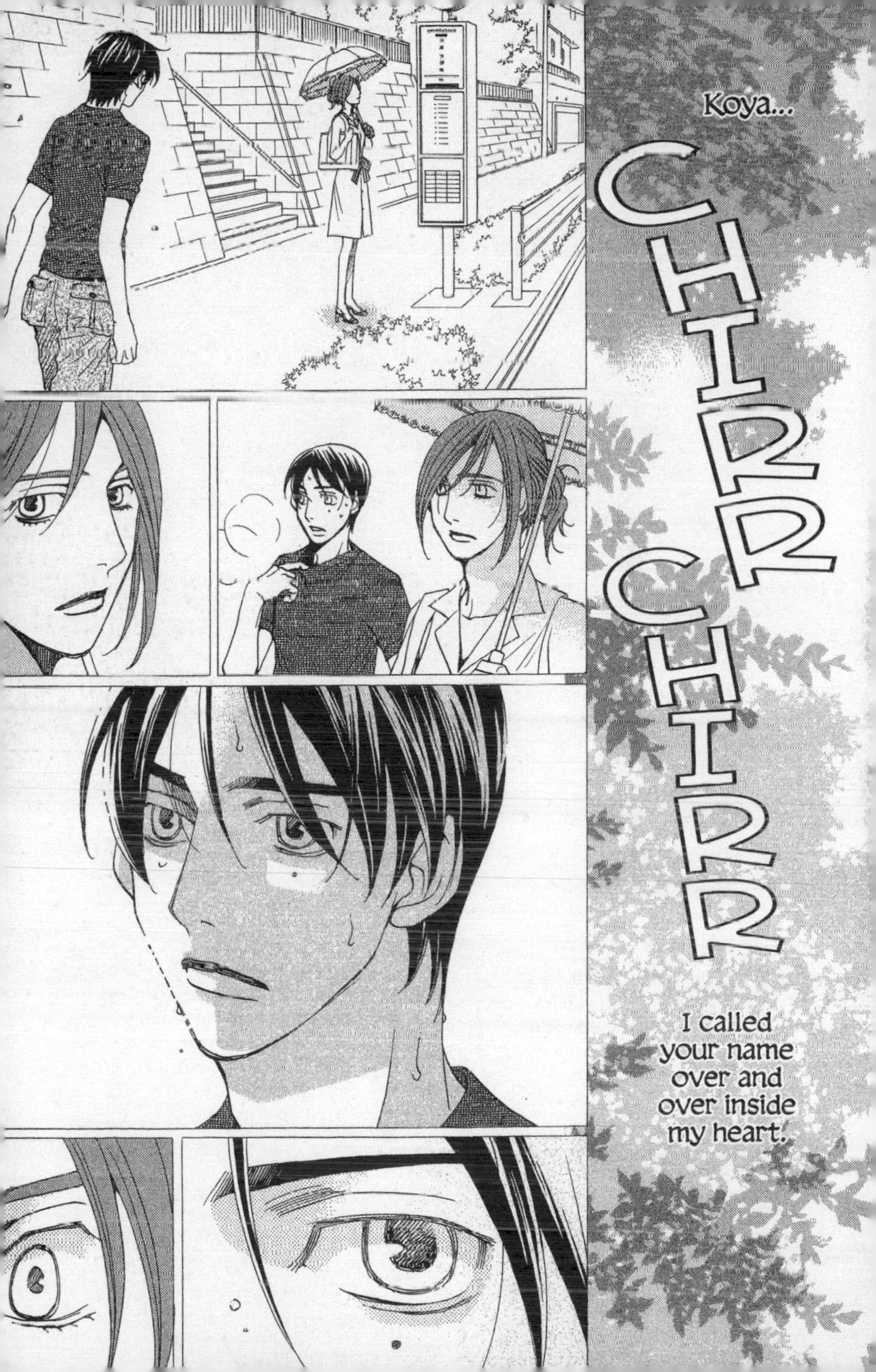
Koya...
CHIRR CHIRR
I called your name over and over inside my heart.

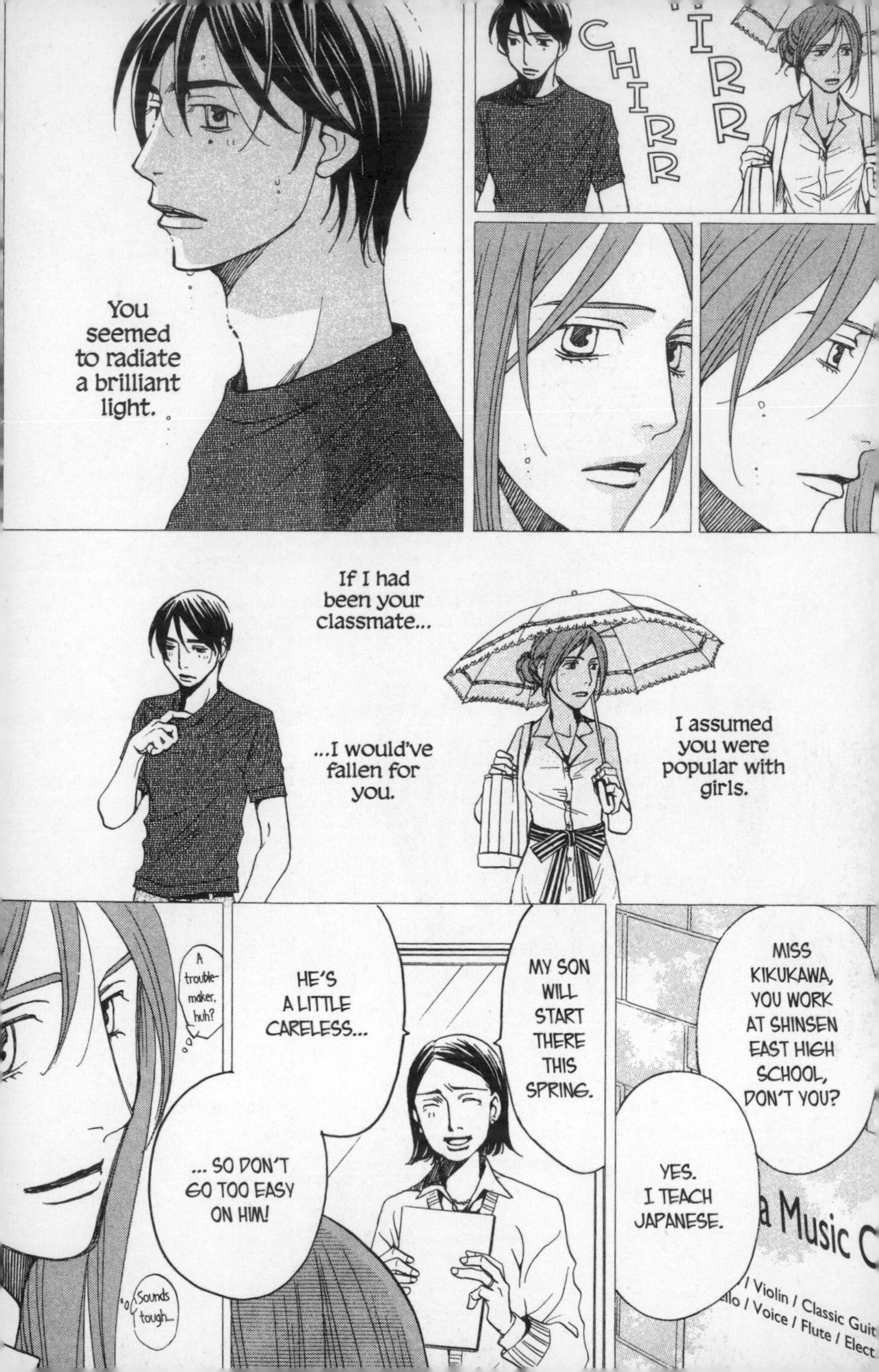
CHIRR IRR
You seemed to radiate a brilliant light.
If I had been your classmate...
...I would've fallen for you.
I assumed you were popular with girls.
MISS KIKUKAWA, YOU WORK AT SHINSEN EAST HIGH SCHOOL, DON'T YOU?
YES. I TEACH JAPANESE.
a Music C
/ Violin / Classic Guit
ello / Voice / Flute / Elect
MY SON WILL START THERE THIS SPRING.
HE'S A LITTLE CARELESS...
... SO DON'T GO TOO EASY ON HIM!
Sounds tough...
A trouble-maker, huh?

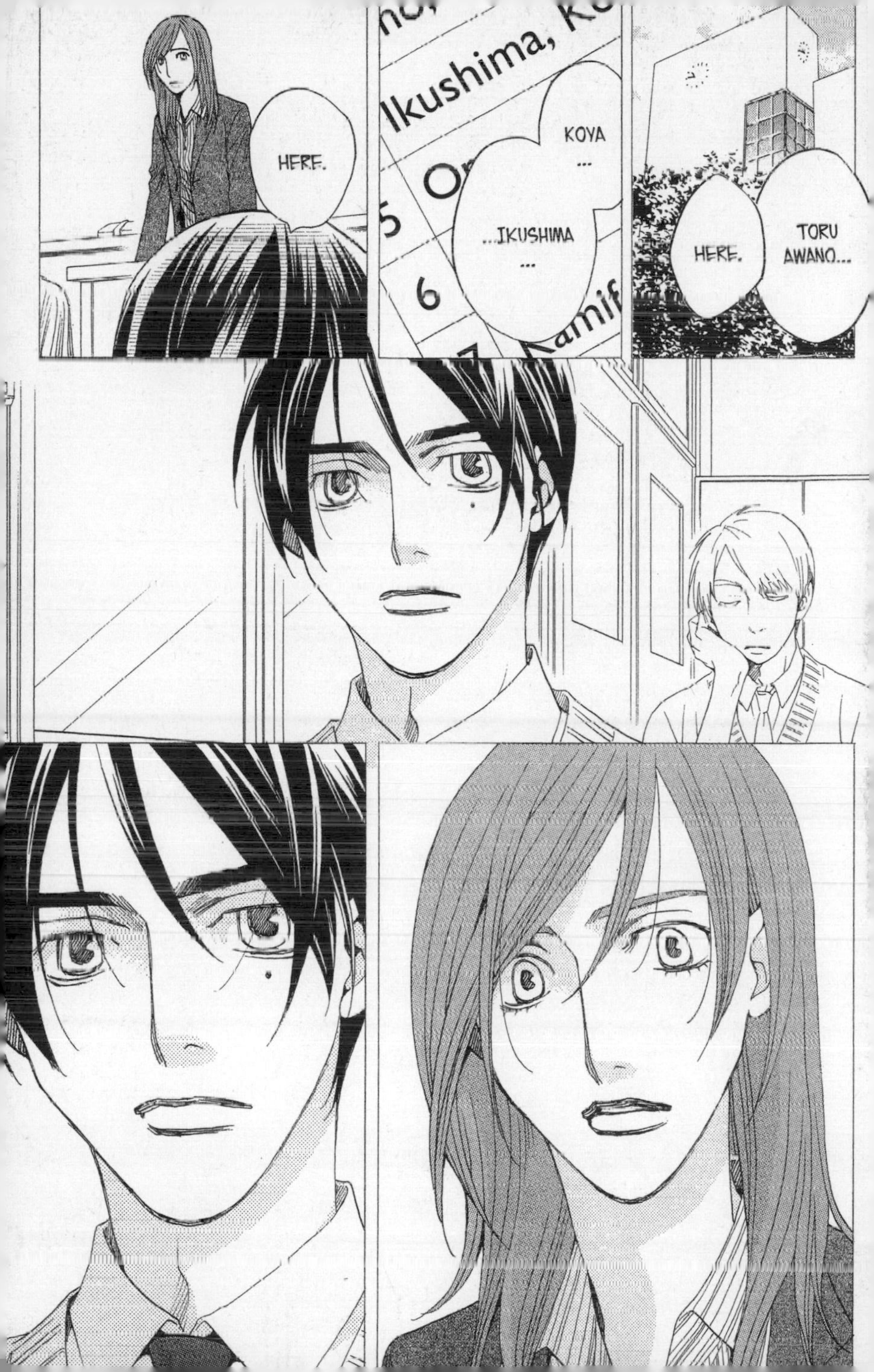
TORU AWANO...
HERE.
KOYA ...
...IKUSHIMA ...
HERE.

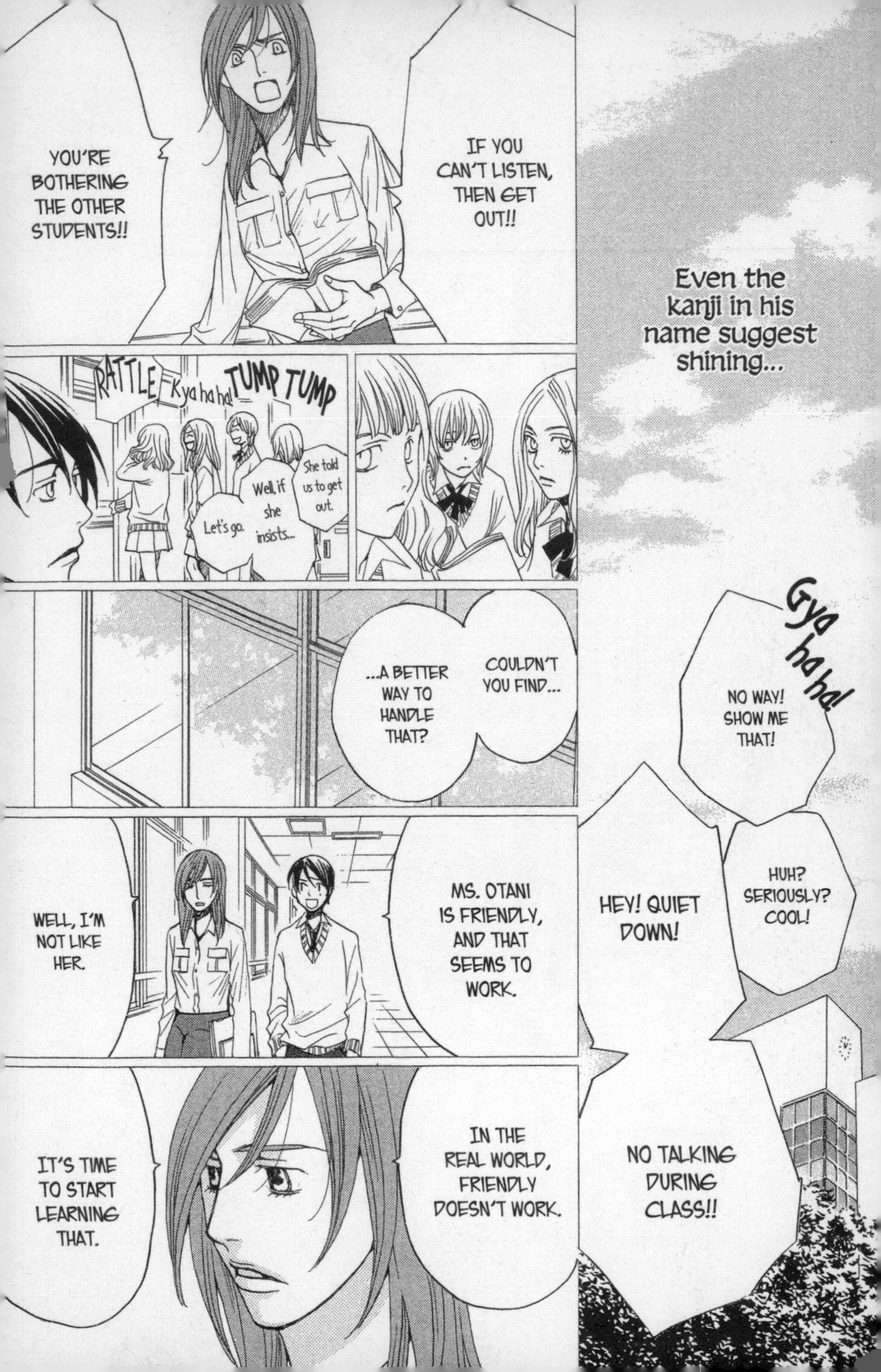
Even the kanji in his name suggest shining...
Gya ha ha!
NO WAY! SHOW ME THAT!
HUH? SERIOUSLY? COOL!
HEY! QUIET DOWN!
NO TALKING DURING CLASS!!
IF YOU CAN'T LISTEN, THEN GET OUT!!
YOU'RE BOTHERING THE OTHER STUDENTS!!
TUMP TUMP
Kya ha ha!
RATTLE
She told us to get out.
Well, if she insists...
Let's go.
COULDN'T YOU FIND...
...A BETTER WAY TO HANDLE THAT?
MS. OTANI IS FRIENDLY, AND THAT SEEMS TO WORK.
WELL, I'M NOT LIKE HER.
IN THE REAL WORLD, FRIENDLY DOESN'T WORK.
IT'S TIME TO START LEARNING THAT.

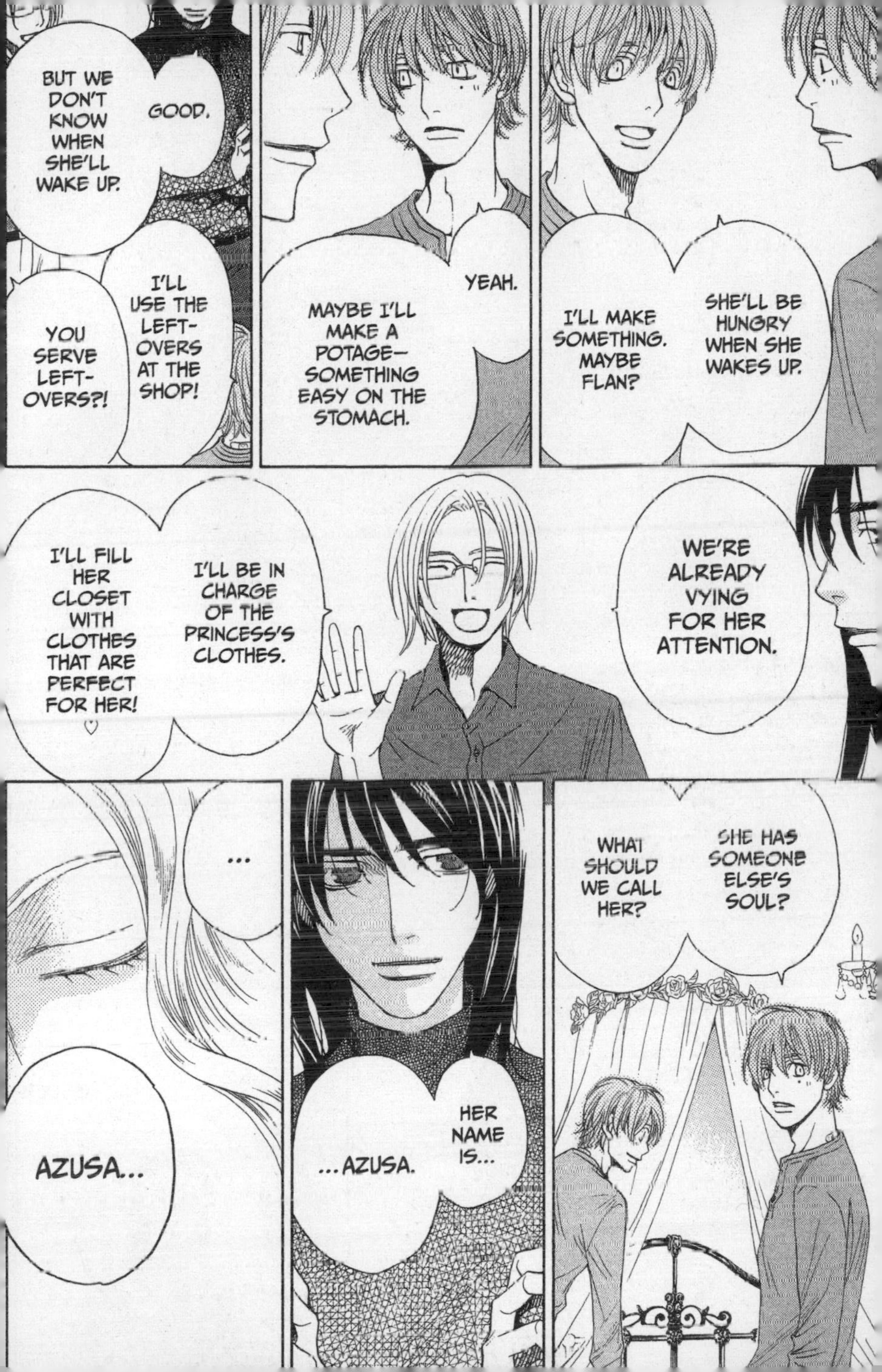
SHE'LL BE HUNGRY WHEN SHE WAKES UP.
I'LL MAKE SOMETHING. MAYBE FLAN?
YEAH.
MAYBE I'LL MAKE A POTAGE—SOMETHING EASY ON THE STOMACH.
GOOD.
BUT WE DON'T KNOW WHEN SHE'LL WAKE UP.
I'LL USE THE LEFT-OVERS AT THE SHOP!
YOU SERVE LEFT-OVERS?!
WE'RE ALREADY VYING FOR HER ATTENTION.
I'LL BE IN CHARGE OF THE PRINCESS'S CLOTHES.
I'LL FILL HER CLOSET WITH CLOTHES THAT ARE PERFECT FOR HER! ♡
SHE HAS SOMEONE ELSE'S SOUL?
WHAT SHOULD WE CALL HER?
HER NAME IS...
...AZUSA.
...
AZUSA...

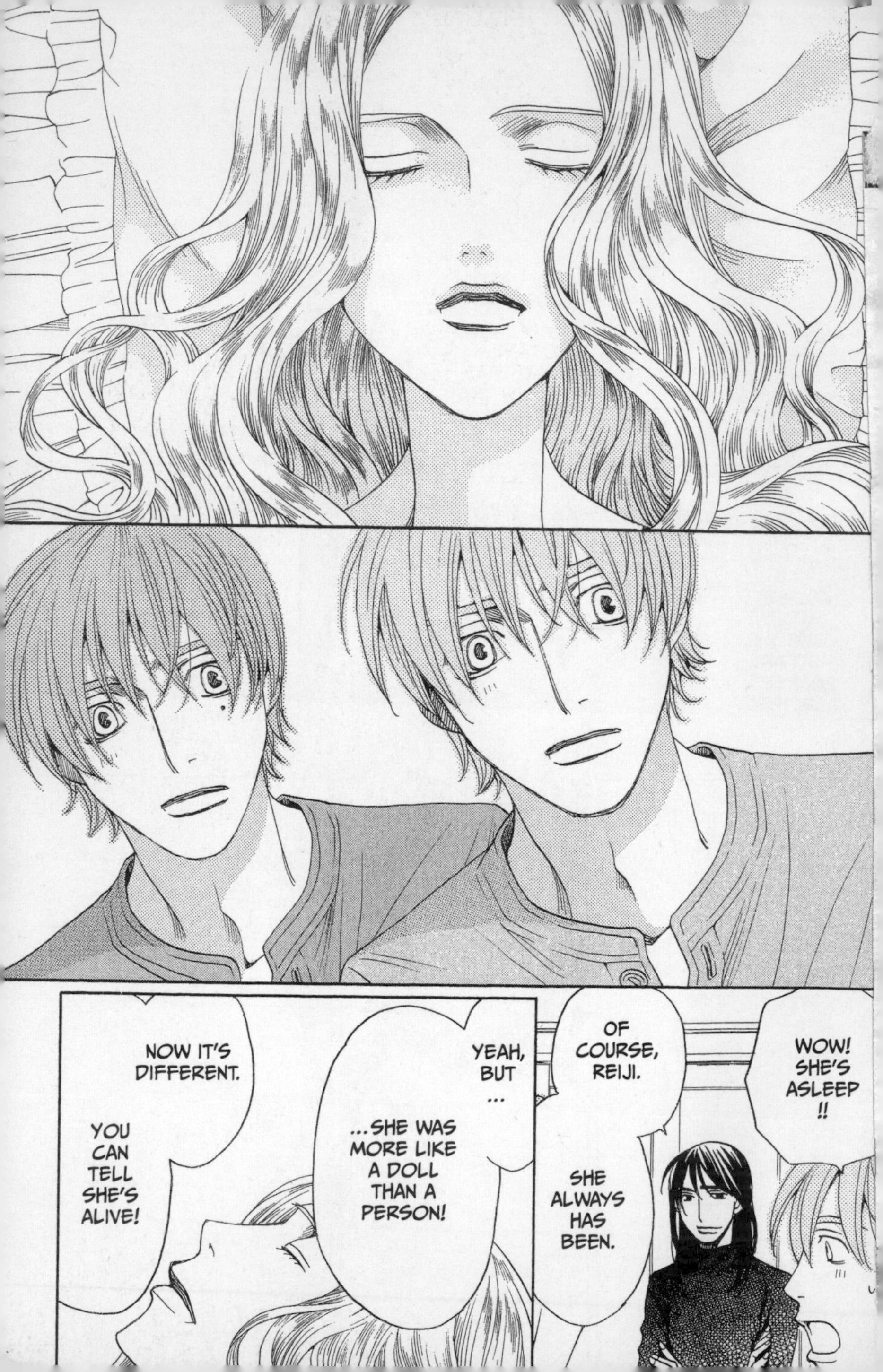
WOW! SHE'S ASLEEP!!
OF COURSE, REIJI.
SHE ALWAYS HAS BEEN.
YEAH, BUT ...
...SHE WAS MORE LIKE A DOLL THAN A PERSON!
NOW IT'S DIFFERENT.
YOU CAN TELL SHE'S ALIVE!

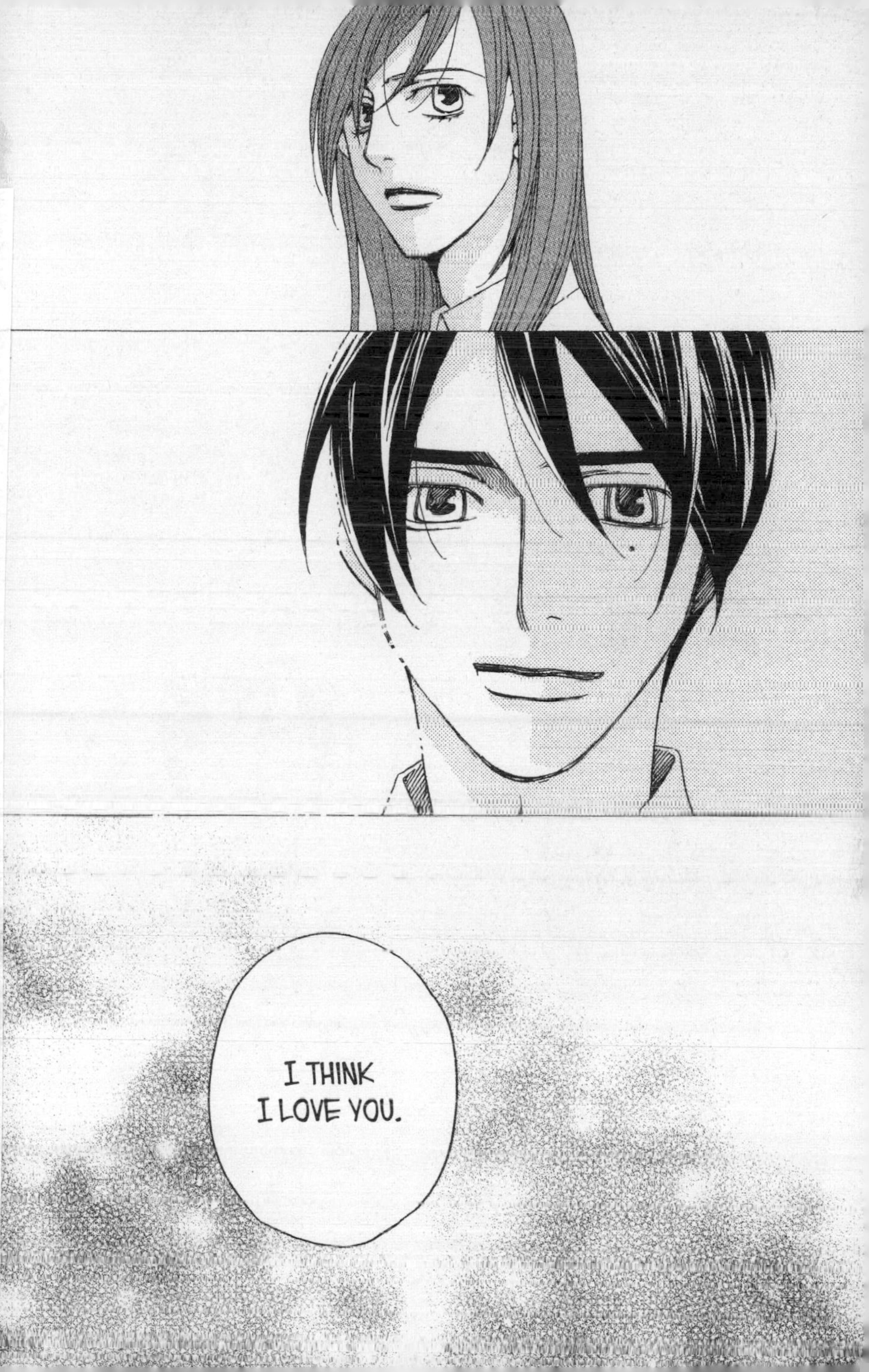
I THINK I LOVE YOU.

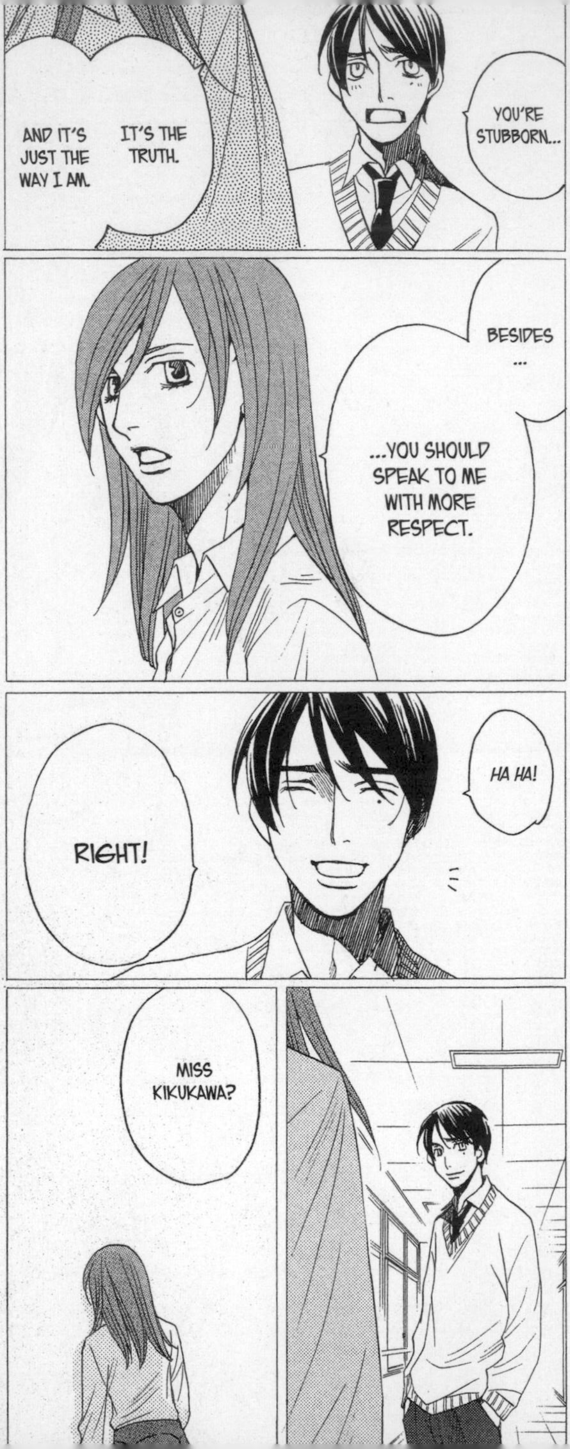
YOU'RE STUBBORN...
IT'S THE TRUTH.
AND IT'S JUST THE WAY I AM.
BESIDES...
...YOU SHOULD SPEAK TO ME WITH MORE RESPECT.
HA HA!
RIGHT!
MISS KIKUKAWA?

I actually can't stand bugs. Spiders are out of the question. I mean, they've got eight legs!!! Or rather, that's how I used to be...

...but looking at illustrated guides and enlarged photos to help with my drawing, they started looking like finely crafted mechanisms! Now they look cute to me!

If I think back, when we were kids we used to catch bugs like grasshoppers with our bare hands and play with them...

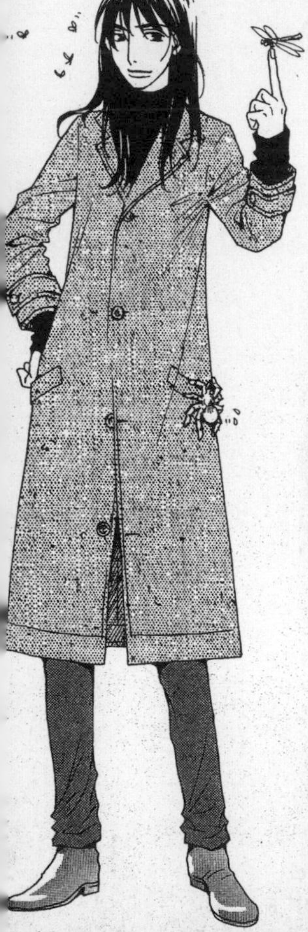

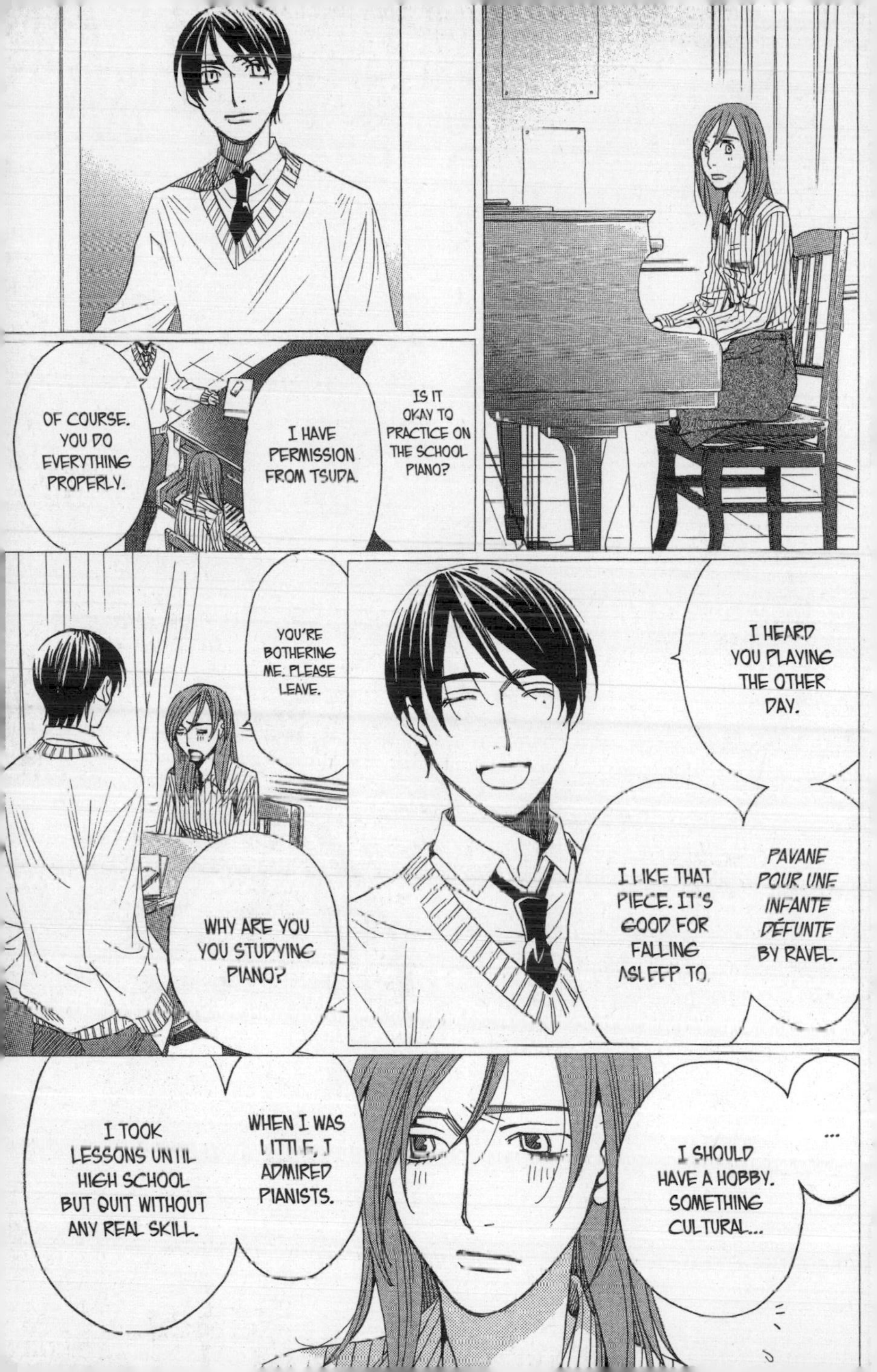
IS IT OKAY TO PRACTICE ON THE SCHOOL PIANO?
I HAVE PERMISSION FROM TSUDA.
OF COURSE. YOU DO EVERYTHING PROPERLY.
I HEARD YOU PLAYING THE OTHER DAY.
PAVANE POUR UNE INFANTE DÉFUNTE BY RAVEL.
I LIKE THAT PIECE. IT'S GOOD FOR FALLING ASLEEP TO.
YOU'RE BOTHERING ME. PLEASE LEAVE.
WHY ARE YOU YOU STUDYING PIANO?
...
I SHOULD HAVE A HOBBY. SOMETHING CULTURAL...
WHEN I WAS LITTLE, I ADMIRED PIANISTS.
I TOOK LESSONS UNTIL HIGH SCHOOL BUT QUIT WITHOUT ANY REAL SKILL.

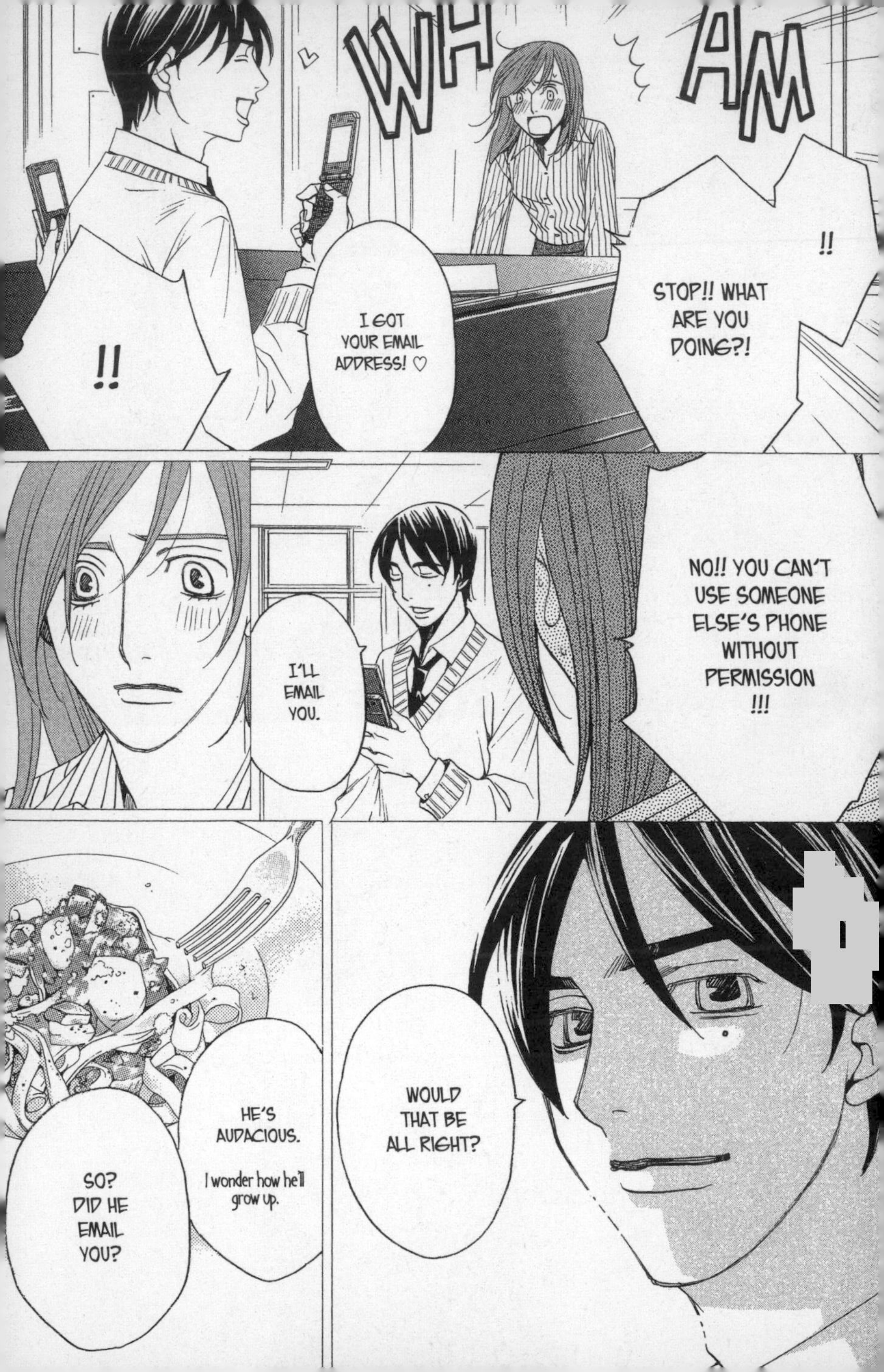
WH AM
!!
STOP!! WHAT ARE YOU DOING?!
I GOT YOUR EMAIL ADDRESS! ♡
!!
NO!! YOU CAN'T USE SOMEONE ELSE'S PHONE WITHOUT PERMISSION !!!
I'LL EMAIL YOU.
WOULD THAT BE ALL RIGHT?
HE'S AUDACIOUS.
I wonder how he'll grow up.
SO? DID HE EMAIL YOU?

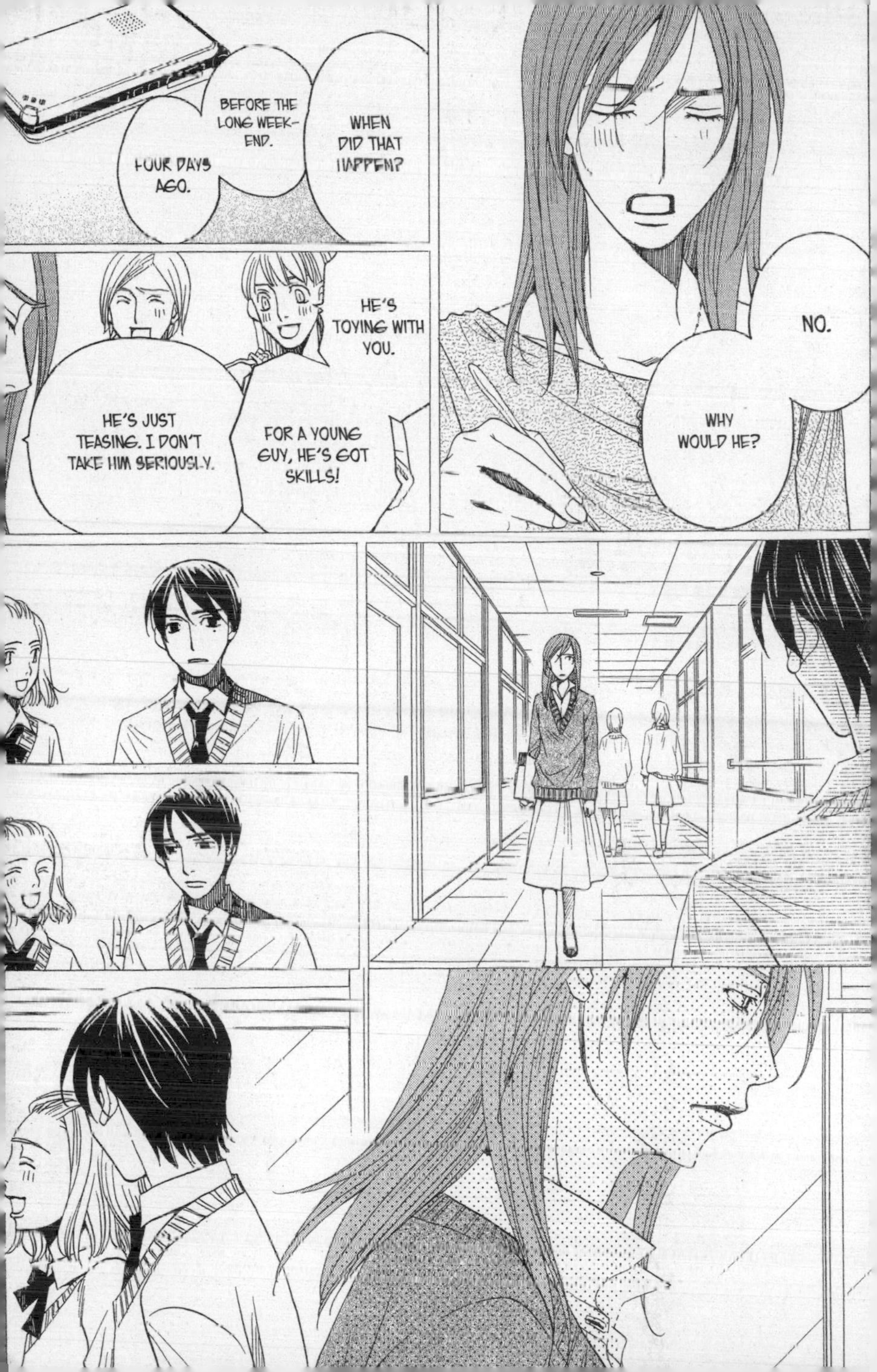
NO.
WHY WOULD HE?
WHEN DID THAT HAPPEN?
BEFORE THE LONG WEEK-END.
FOUR DAYS AGO.
HE'S TOYING WITH YOU.
FOR A YOUNG GUY, HE'S GOT SKILLS!
HE'S JUST TEASING. I DON'T TAKE HIM SERIOUSLY.

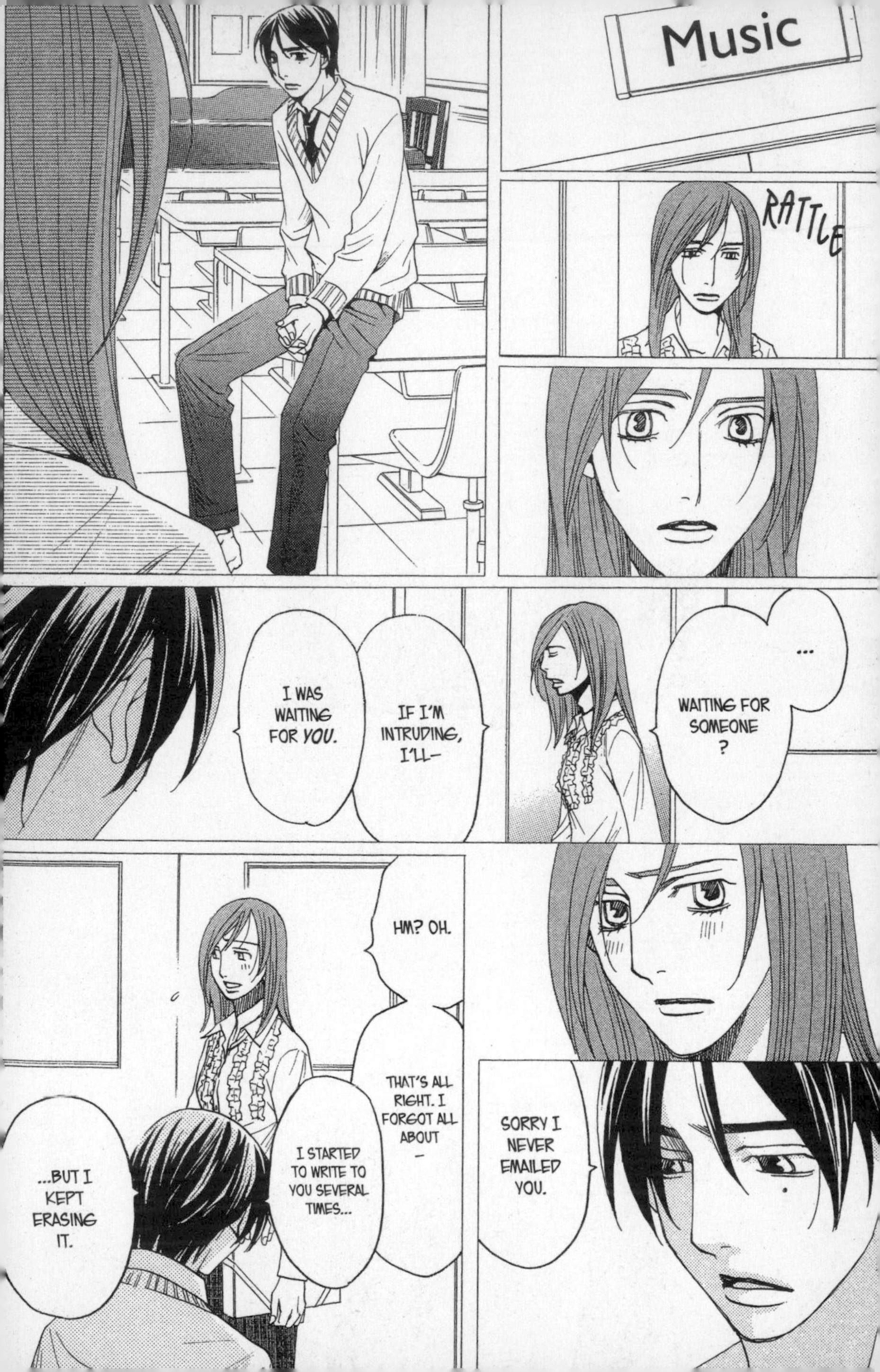
Music
RATTLE
...
WAITING FOR SOMEONE ?
IF I'M INTRUDING, I'LL-
I WAS WAITING FOR *YOU*.
SORRY I NEVER EMAILED YOU.
HM? OH.
THAT'S ALL RIGHT. I FORGOT ALL ABOUT —
I STARTED TO WRITE TO YOU SEVERAL TIMES...
...BUT I KEPT ERASING IT.

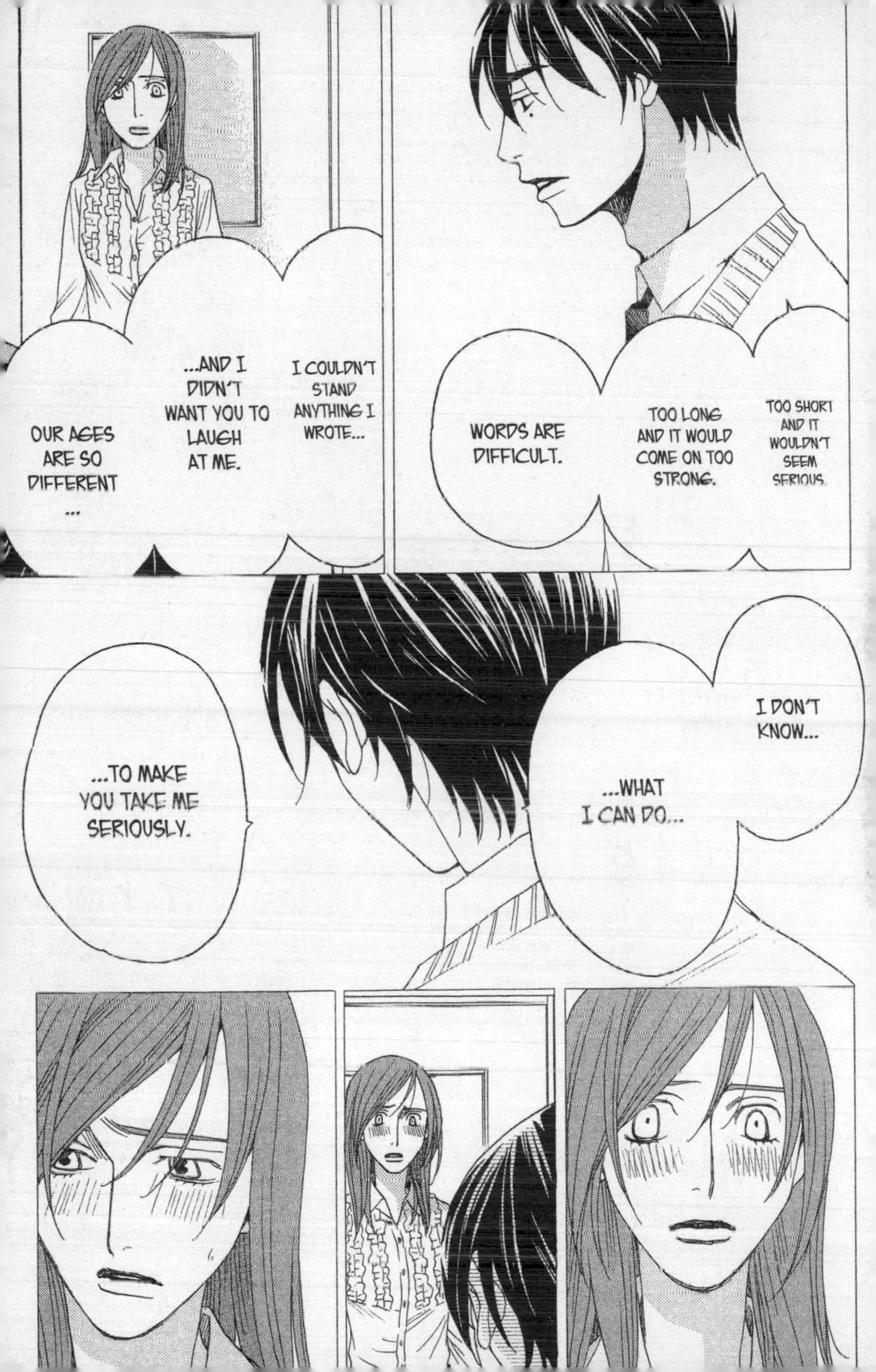
TOO SHORT AND IT WOULDN'T SEEM SERIOUS.
TOO LONG AND IT WOULD COME ON TOO STRONG.
WORDS ARE DIFFICULT.
I COULDN'T STAND ANYTHING I WROTE...
...AND I DIDN'T WANT YOU TO LAUGH AT ME.
OUR AGES ARE SO DIFFERENT ...
I DON'T KNOW...
...WHAT I CAN DO...
...TO MAKE YOU TAKE ME SERIOUSLY.

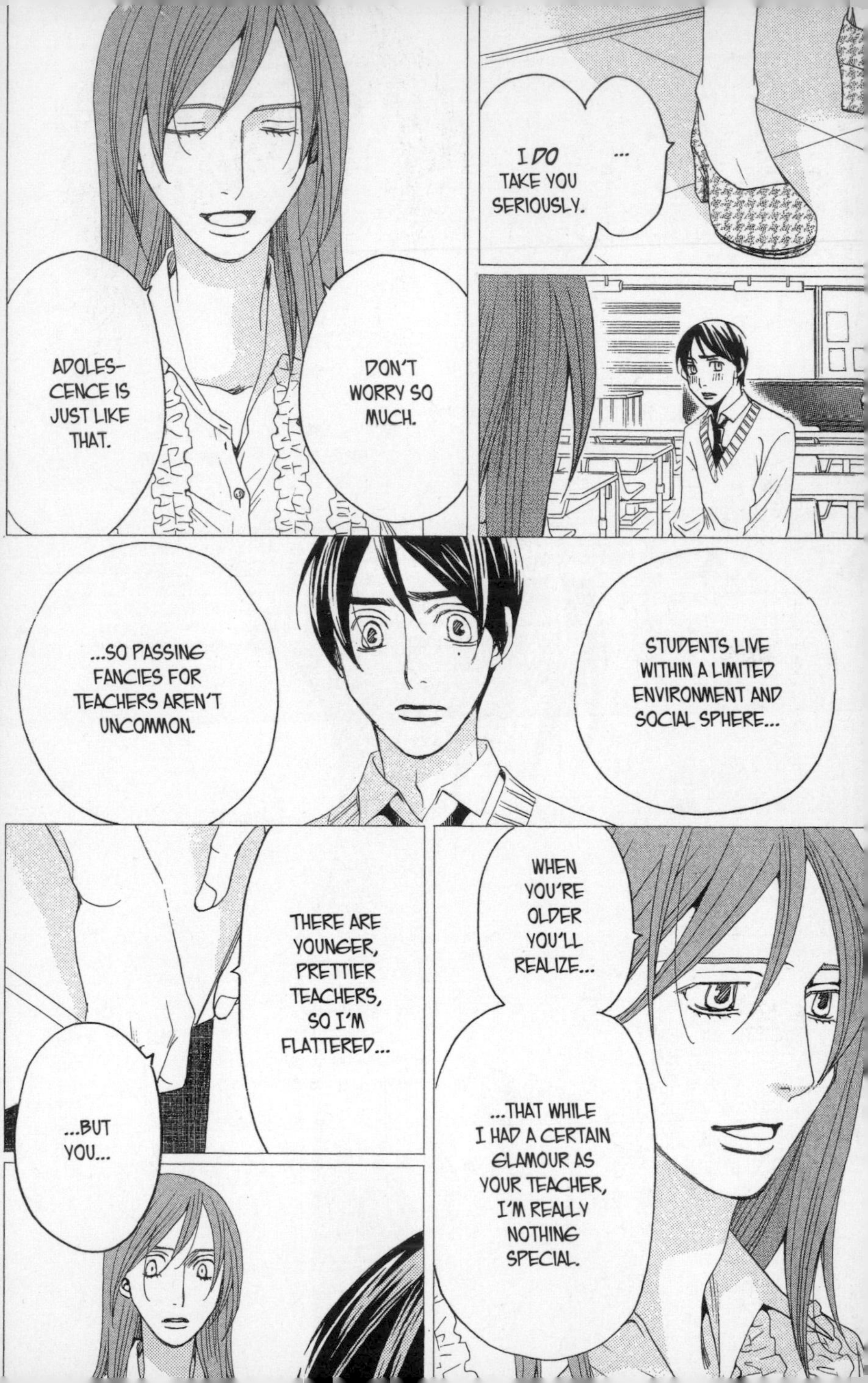
I DO... TAKE YOU SERIOUSLY.
DON'T WORRY SO MUCH.
ADOLES-CENCE IS JUST LIKE THAT.
STUDENTS LIVE WITHIN A LIMITED ENVIRONMENT AND SOCIAL SPHERE...
...SO PASSING FANCIES FOR TEACHERS AREN'T UNCOMMON.
WHEN YOU'RE OLDER YOU'LL REALIZE...
...THAT WHILE I HAD A CERTAIN GLAMOUR AS YOUR TEACHER, I'M REALLY NOTHING SPECIAL.
THERE ARE YOUNGER, PRETTIER TEACHERS, SO I'M FLATTERED...
...BUT YOU...

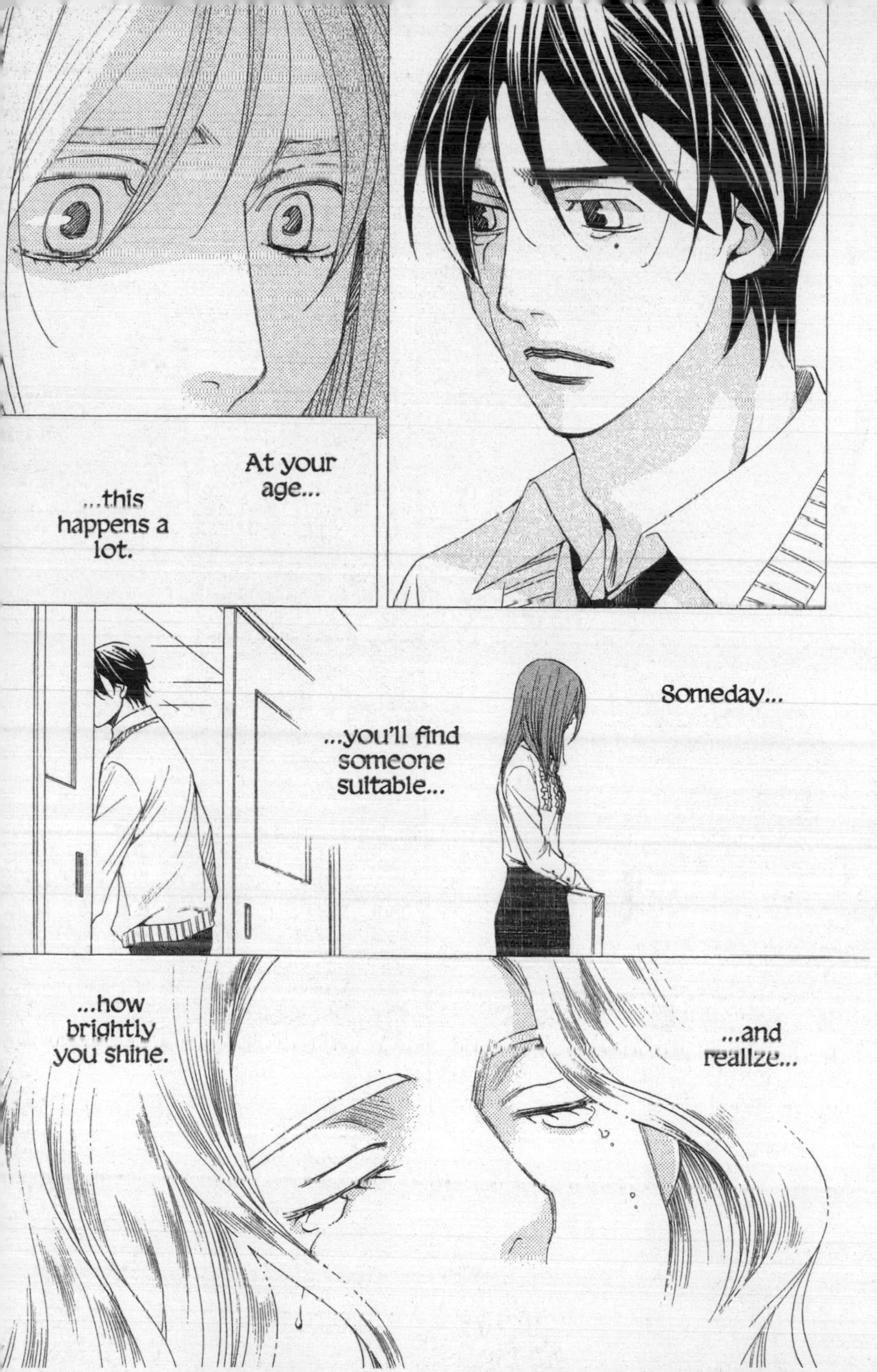
At your age...
...this happens a lot.
Someday...
...you'll find someone suitable...
...and realize...
...how brightly you shine.

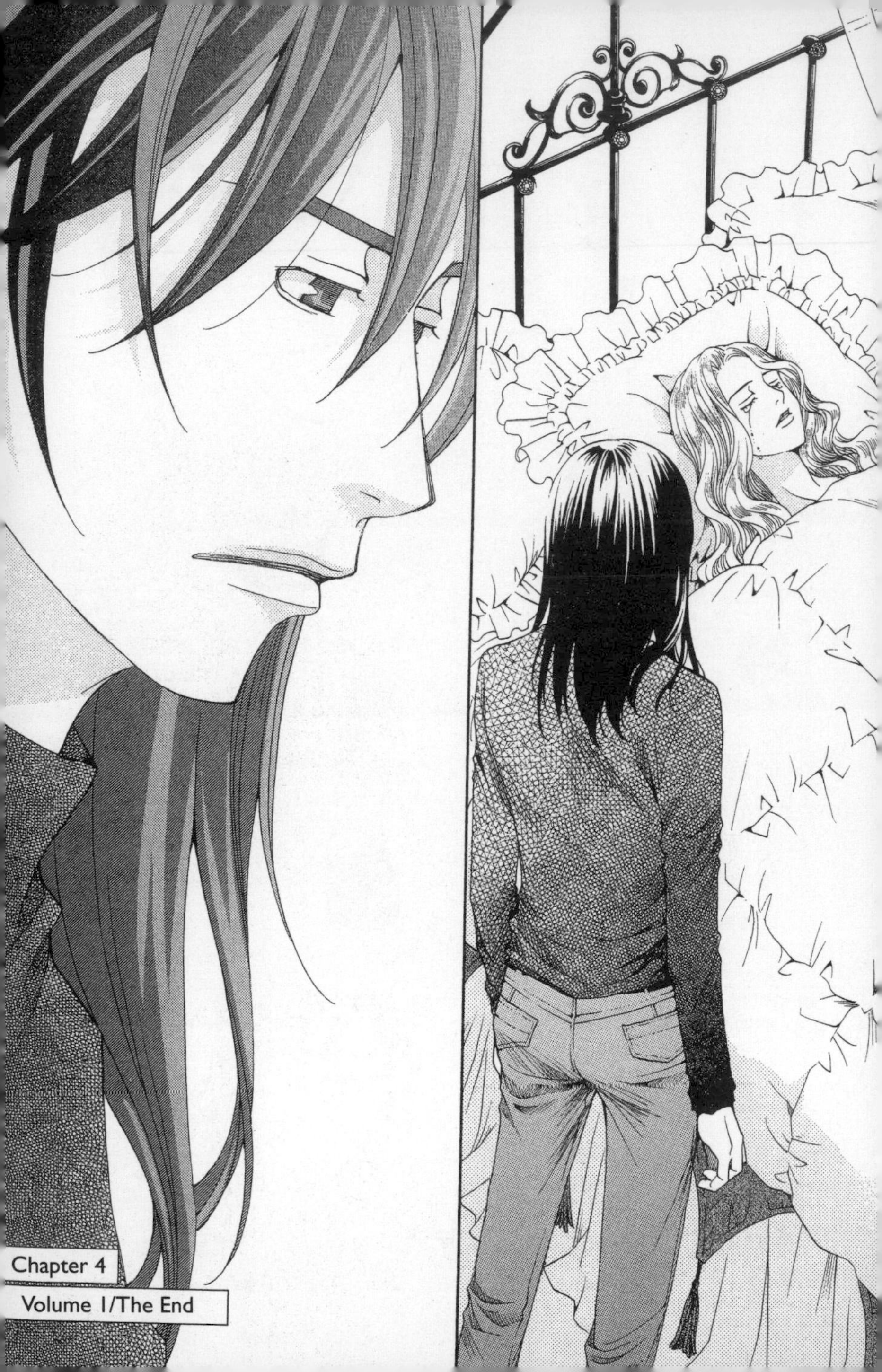
Chapter 4
Volume 1/The End

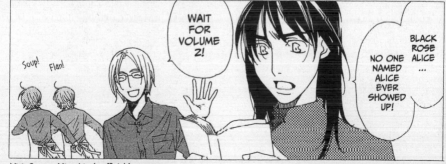

BLACK ROSE ALICE ...
NO ONE NAMED ALICE EVER SHOWED UP!
WAIT FOR VOLUME 2!
Flan!
Soup!

Visit Setona Mizushiro's official homepage:
http://www.page.sannet.ne.jp/setona

I thought about love and reproduction. A male with beautiful wings, a male who sings with a great voice, a strong male who fought and won...and the female who chooses among them. In the natural world, it's basically simple, but it's complicated for human beings.

Sometimes we cling to an unrequited love forever, or we spurn a fine person who has his or her act together in favor of a dangerous no-gooder, or we try to save face instead of simply proclaiming love. When I asked myself why, I only came up with cynical answers. That's no good. I should be dreamier!

I intend to write this story so that sometimes it's cynical and sometimes it's romantic... But I'll go heavier on the romantic!

–Setona Mizushiro

Setona Mizushiro's professional debut was *"Fuyu ga Owarou to Shiteita"* (Winter Was Ending), and her series *After School Nightmare* was nominated for an Eisner and recognized by YALSA as a great graphic novel for teens in 2007.

BLACK ROSE ALICE
VOLUME 1
Shojo Beat Edition

STORY AND ART BY
Setona Mizushiro

English Translation & Adaptation/John Werry
Touch-up Art & Lettering/Evan Waldinger
Design/Yukiko Whitley
Editor/Pancha Diaz

Published by VIZ Media, LLC
P.O. Box 77010
San Francisco, CA 94107

10 9 8 7 6 5 4 3 2 1
First printing, August 2014

www.viz.com   www.shojobeat.com

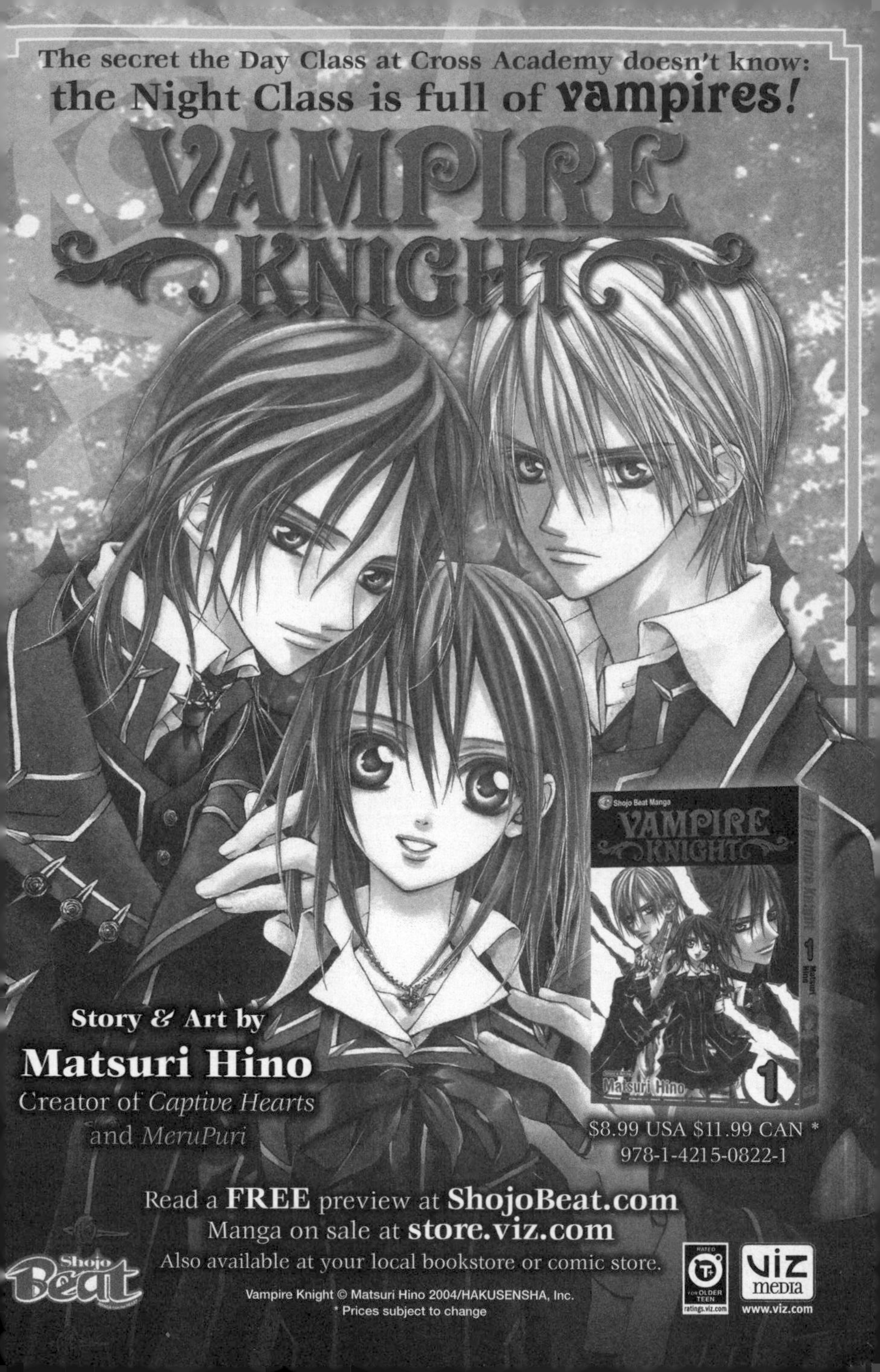
The secret the Day Class at Cross Academy doesn't know:
the Night Class is full of vampires!
VAMPIRE KNIGHT
Story & Art by
Matsuri Hino
Creator of Captive Hearts
and MeruPuri
Shojo Beat Manga
VAMPIRE KNIGHT
Matsuri Hino
1
$8.99 USA $11.99 CAN *
978-1-4215-0822-1
Read a FREE preview at ShojoBeat.com
Manga on sale at store.viz.com
Also available at your local bookstore or comic store.
Shojo Beat
Vampire Knight © Matsuri Hino 2004/HAKUSENSHA, Inc.
* Prices subject to change
RATED T+ FOR OLDER TEEN
ratings.viz.com
viz media
www.viz.com

The Earl & the Fairy
The Earl & the Fairy
1
Ayuko
Original Concept by
Mizue Tani

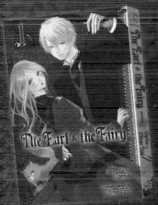

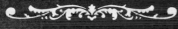

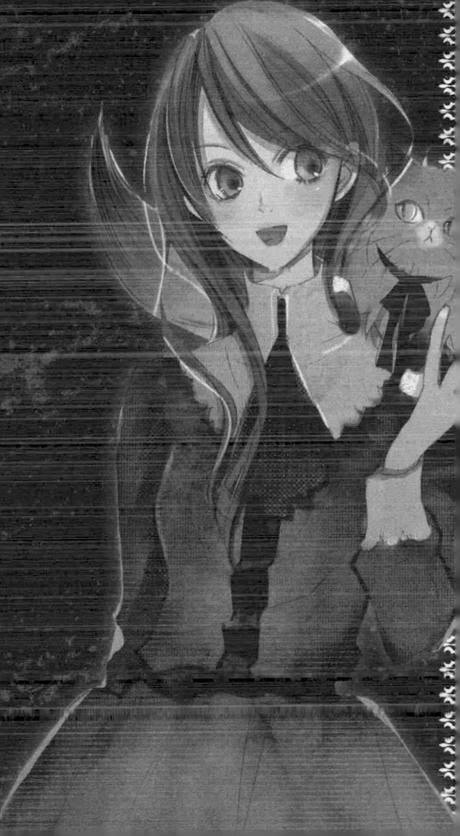